JOSEPHUS
AND THE HISTORY OF
THE GRECO-ROMAN PERIOD

STUDIA POST-BIBLICA

VOLUME 41

JOSEPHUS
AND THE HISTORY OF
THE GRECO-ROMAN PERIOD

Essays in Memory of Morton Smith

EDITED BY

FAUSTO PARENTE

AND

JOSEPH SIEVERS

E.J. BRILL
LEIDEN · NEW YORK · KÖLN
1994

The paper in this book meets the guidelines for permanence and durability of the Committee on Production Guidelines for Book Longevity of the Council on Library Resources.

Library of Congress Cataloging-in-Publication Data

Josephus and the history of the Greco-Roman period: essays in memory of Morton Smith / edited by Fausto Parente and Joseph Sievers.
p. cm.—Studia post-Biblica, ISSN 0169-9717 ; v. 41)
Proceedings of the Josephus Colloquium, held Nov. 2-5, 1992, in San Miniato, Italy.
Includes bibliographical references and indexes.
ISBN 9004101144 (cloth : alk. paper)
1. Josephus, Flavius—Congresses. 2. Jews—History—168 B.C.-135 A.D.—Historiography—Congresses. I. Smith, Morton, 1915-1991. II. Parente, Fausto. III. Sievers, Joseph. IV. Josephus Colloquium (1992 : San Miniato, Italy) V. Series.
DS115.9.J6J65   1994
933'.05'092—dc 20
[B]   94-33782
                                                                        CIP

Die Deutsche Bibliothek – CIP-Einheitsaufnahme

Josephus and the history of the Greco-Roman period: essays in memory of Morton Smith / ed. by Fausto Parente and Joseph Sievers.– Leiden ; New York ; Köln : Brill, 1994
(Studia post-biblica ; Vol. 41)
ISBN 90–04–10114-4
NE: Parente, Fausto [Hrsg.]; GT

ISSN 0169-9717
ISBN 90 04 10114 4

PRINTED IN THE NETHERLANDS

MORTON SMITH

May 28, 1915 – July 11, 1991

CONTENTS

EDITORS' PREFACE AND ACKNOWLEDGMENTS

In the summer of 1990, Professor Morton Smith approached Joseph Sievers with the idea of organizing an international colloquium on Josephus, that should bring together as many specialists in the field as possible, with particular attention to the Hasmonean and Roman periods. Sievers had an opportunity to propose this idea to Professor Parente, who was then President of the Italian Association for Jewish Studies (AISG). In November of that year, a first program proposal was worked out by Parente and Sievers and, with some modification, approved by Smith, who not only promised to participate in the colloquium, but also to underwrite a substantial portion of its cost.

While preparations were well under way, news reached the editors of the sudden death of Professor Smith on July 11, 1991. Grave doubts about the feasibility of the project arose, but within a few days a letter from Professor Robert Somerville, the executor of Smith's estate, indicated that in the will there was a provision for the Josephus Colloquium. At this point the organization of the Colloquium became not only a challenging scholarly enterprize but also a sacred duty. The colloquium took place under the auspices of the Italian Association for Jewish Studies from 2 through 5 November, 1992, at San Miniato near Pisa, Italy. The realization of the Colloquium was made possible through the assistance of the local Savings Bank "Cassa di Risparmio di San Miniato" and through a substantial grant from the Italian National Research Council ("Consiglio Nazionale delle Ricerche").

Since the colloquium was due to the initiative and the support of Professor Morton Smith, it seemed only natural to dedicate it and the publication of the proceedings to his memory. This volume contains revised versions of all the papers prepared for the colloquium with the following two exceptions: Etienne Nodet's paper "About Jews in Galilee" has appeared in a fuller version as "Galilée juive, de Jésus à la Mishna" in F. Blanchetière and M. D. Herr (eds.), *Protochristianisme en Judée*, Paris-Louvain: Peeters, 1993. Professor Applebaum gave a presentation on "Josephus as a Military Commander," but due to health reasons he was unfortunately unable to put it into publishable form.

The style in this volume generally follows that of the *Bulletin of the American Schools of Oriental Research*, which is based on the *Chicago Manual of Style* (13th ed., 1982). We have, however, decided to use footnotes instead of endnotes and adopt some other minor modifications. Internal consistency of each contribution has been deemed more important than an attempt at consistency throughout. Thus different spellings of the same word or name have been allowed to stand. Where they affect items in the subject index, both spellings are referenced. Bibliographical abbreviations have been kept to a minimum, and all except those for classical, patristic and rabbinic literature are included in the bibliography. In rabbinic literature, tractates of the Mishnah, Tosefta, Talmud Yerushalmi and Bavli are identified by *m.*, *t.*, *y.*, *b.*, followed by the (abbreviated) name of the tractate. The writings of Josephus are abbreviated *AgAp*, *Ant*, *JW*, and *Life*, generally without the author's name.

The cumulative bibliography of this volume includes the publications cited in the various contributions. As such it is also an indication of some of the newer directions in Josephus research, without any attempt to be complete. It includes some, but not all the writings of Professor Morton Smith. His complete bibliography may be found in the forthcoming two volumes of his *Scripta minora*, edited by Shaye J. D. Cohen in the Brown Judaic Studies series and titled *Studies in the Cult of Yahweh*.

Beyond the above-mentioned institutions and individuals, the first thanks go obviously to each of the contributors.

Carlo Valentino ably assisted the editors with the technical production of camera-ready copy. Rochelle Losman graciously agreed to go over the entire manuscript and suggested many stylistic improvements. Last not least, we should like to thank Hans van der Meij and the staff at E. J. Brill, Leiden, for accepting this volume for publication and seeing it through the press.

Rome, May 15, 1994

Fausto Parente and Joseph Sievers

IN MEMORIAM MORTON SMITH

MORTON SMITH AND HIS SCHOLARLY ACHIEVEMENT

Shaye J. D. Cohen

Morton Smith (1915-1991) was a great scholar, blessed with extraordinary acuity, mordant wit, and expansive range. He received an A.B. from Harvard College in 1936 and an S.T.B. from the Harvard Divinity School in 1940. At Harvard Smith studied New Testament with Henry Cadbury, Judaism with Harry Wolfson, and Greco-Roman religions with A.D. Nock. Awarded a travel fellowship, Smith spent four years in Jerusalem at the Hebrew University and the American School of Oriental Research, studied Hellenistic Judaism with Moshe Schwabe and Hans Lewy, and Jewish mysticism and magic with Gershom Scholem. Smith returned to the United States in 1944 but continued work on his doctoral dissertation which was accepted by the Hebrew University in 1948. After some post-doctoral work at Harvard and teaching at Brown University and Drew University, Smith joined the History Department of Columbia University in 1957 where he remained until his retirement in 1985.

Smith wrote seven books, some 120 articles, dozens of book reviews, and co-authored two books (one with Moses Hadas, the other with Elias Bickerman). This impressive body of scholarship had four main focal points: Ancient Israel; New Testament and Early Christianity; (Ancient) Judaism; Magic. Of course, many of Smith's works resist monothetic classification, and cross the lines separating these four fields — in fact, one of Smith's major goals was precisely to bridge the gaps between and among these four fields, as I shall discuss below — but this four-fold classification remains useful. It also has the advantage of having been suggested by Smith himself for his Kleine Schriften, a volume to be entitled *Studies in the Cult of Yahweh* that he planned in the mid 1980's and which is now in preparation. I shall briefly assess Smith's contribution to each of these four fields, and then treat some general features of his scholarly achievement.

Ancient Israel

The Hebrew Bible — its text, its history, its background, and its influence — remained one of Smith's central interests from his first publications (Smith 1951b and 1952) to his last (Smith 1984). In this field Smith is probably best known for his *Palestinian Parties and Politics that Shaped the Old Testament* (Smith 1971a). In this book Smith argued that the entire Tanak — indeed virtually all of Israelite and early Jewish history — should be seen as the product of two conflicting schools or "parties." The "Yahweh-alone" party was the party of the prophets and the Deuteronomists, who uncompromisingly railed against the "syncretists." Because the "Yahweh-alone" party ultimately triumphed, it shaped the creation of the Tanak and the historiographical image of the "syncretists" as wicked rebels against God. But, Smith argued, the syncretists were not "sinners" and "apostates" but a genuine and authentic expression of Israelite religion, even older than the monotheists of the "Yahweh-alone" party. Not only in the time of the first temple but even in the second temple period and later as well, syncretistic Judaism was much in evidence; witness the material remains of Judaism in both the homeland (Smith 1975 and 1982) and the diaspora, and, most importantly, the magical texts and rituals of late antiquity. I shall return to this below.

New Testament and Early Christianity

The New Testament, like the Old Testament (if I may use the Christian appellations employed by Smith), was always at the heart of Smith's work and the subject of some of his earliest articles. Smith's doctoral dissertation, originally written in Hebrew but published in English as *Tannaitic Parallels to the Gospels* (1951a), was primarily a contribution to rabbinic studies. Contrary to what the title suggests, this book was not inspired by Lightfoot or Billerbeck; its goal was not the collection of rabbinic passages that illuminate this or that New Testament text. Rather, it was a study of literary form, "the first extensive application, to rabbinic literature, of synoptic criticism and form criticism." This book launched the modern form critical study of rabbinic literature, but its relevance to New Testament studies is obvious as well. In *Heroes and Gods*, published in 1965 and written jointly with Moses Hadas, Smith argued that Jesus should be understood as a "divine man," a type well attested in Greco-Roman antiquity, and that the gospels were akin to an aretalogy, a recitation of the miraculous powers of a god. This book, amplified by some subsequent articles (Smith 1971b, 1977, and 1978b), launched a new approach (or, perhaps better, revived the old *religionsgeschichtlich* approach) to the study of the Jesus traditions.

Smith achieved fame (some would say notoriety) in 1973 with his publication of *Clement of Alexandria and a Secret Gospel of Mark*. While travelling through the Levant looking for manuscripts of the letters of Isidore of Pelusium (Smith 1954 and 1958a), in 1957 at the monastery of Mar Saba (not far from Jerusalem) Smith stumbled on a fragment of an otherwise unknown letter attributed to Clement of Alexandria. In the letter Clement writes to an otherwise unknown Theodore and instructs him how to respond to the Carpocratians, a Christian sect of the second century, who rely on a "secret gospel of Mark" which is similar to, but longer than, the canonical Mark. In his book Smith argued brilliantly that the attribution of the letter to Clement was authentic, a point conceded by most reviewers (except for those who broadly implied that Smith had forged the whole thing), and that the "secret gospel of Mark" was an important source not only for the history of the second gospel but also for the history of earliest Christianity, a point disputed by many if not most reviewers. In Smith's view early Christianity was a Jewish movement which centered on magic, mysticism, healings, heavenly journeys, ecstatic possession, and secret initiations. This portrait was filled in with even greater detail in *Jesus the Magician* (1978a), in which Smith argued that the actions attributed to Jesus by the gospels could best be understood against the backdrop of magic in antiquity. Smith used as evidence not only the gospel accounts but also the traditions about Jesus contained in rabbinic and classical literatures, a perspective also advanced in a wonderful article "Pauline Worship as Seen by Pagans" (Smith 1980). At his death Smith was working on *Paul the Possessed*, whose thesis was to be that Paul is a primary example of "spiritual possession."

Ancient Judaism

All four of Smith's books so far mentioned — *Tannaitic Parallels to Gospels, Palestinian Parties and Politics that Shaped the Old Testament, Clement of Alexandria and a Secret Gospel of Mark*, and *Jesus the Magician* — make direct and important contributions to the study of

ancient Judaism, as I hope my brief summaries above have made clear.
One of his most influential publications was a brief unannotated article
that appeared in a collection of essays of the sort not normally the
expression of innovative and original scholarship. But Smith's essay
was both innovative and original. Entitled "Palestinian Judaism in the
First Century" (Smith 1956), it argued, inter alia, that the Pharisees
were not the dominant religious-political party in Judaean society and
that Pharisaic Judaism was not the dominant or normative variety of
Judaism. But, asked Smith, if this reconstruction is correct, what are
we to make of Josephus' statements explicitly attributing to the Pharisees a predominant influence with the people? Smith answered as
follows (Smith 1956: 75-76):

> Here a comparison of the *War* with the *Antiquities* is extremely informative.
> In the *War*, written shortly after the destruction of Jerusalem, Josephus still
> favors the group of which his family had been representative – the wealthy,
> pro-Roman section of the priesthood . . . . In his account of the Jewish sects
> he gives most space to the Essenes . . . . He says nothing of the Pharisees'
> having any influence with the people, and the only time he represents them
> as attempting to exert any influence (when they ally with the leading priests
> and other citizens of Jerusalem to prevent the outbreak of the war), they fail.
>
> In the *Antiquities*, however, written twenty years later, the picture is quite
> different. Here, whenever Josephus discusses the Jewish sects, the Pharisees
> take first place, and every time he mentions them he emphasizes their
> popularity, which is so great, he says, that they can maintain opposition
> against any government . . . .
>
> It is almost impossible not to see in such a rewriting of history a bid to the
> Roman government. That government must have been faced with the
> problem: Which group of Jews shall we support? . . . . To this question
> Josephus is volunteering an answer: The Pharisees, he says again and again,
> have by far the greatest influence with the people.

The thesis that the Pharisees and their rabbinic continuators did not
dominate the religious life of Judaism was not new, of course. It had
been advanced fifty years earlier by Wilhelm Bousset (1903). But
Bousset's account was flawed in two respects: it ignored rabbinic
material out of ignorance – an ignorance that was seized upon by
Bousset's Jewish critics, notably Felix Perles, and that was remedied
only in the 1926 revision by Hugo Gressman – and it advanced the
very dubious hypothesis that the apocalyptic and pseudepigraphic
works give us a glimpse of real folk piety, of Judaism as lived and
believed. But there is no reason to think that these recondite and

fantastic works represent the mind of the masses any more than the recondite and fantastic works of the rabbis. Smith avoided both of these pitfalls. Unlike Bousset, he knew rabbinic literature first-hand, and his picture of "the people of the land" was far more sophisticated than Bousset's; the apocalyptic and pseudepigraphic works played virtually no role in Smith's reconstruction.

What was entirely novel about Smith's thesis was the historiographical argument. The contrast between the *War* and the *Antiquities* reflects the shift in the fate of the Pharisees and their successors between the pre- and post-70 periods. Smith would later support this thesis in *Jesus the Magician* with the argument that most of the synoptics' references to, and virtually all of the synoptics' polemics against the Pharisees, are found in post-70 CE insertions in earlier material (Smith 1978a: 153-157). Thus in both Josephus and the synoptics the picture of Pharisaic dominance is a projection of post-70 CE conditions upon the pre-70 CE period.

This bipartite thesis — the historical argument that the Pharisees were a small but influential group, and the historiographical argument that Josephus' picture of the Pharisees developed over time — has been enormously influential. It was widely publicized through the voluminous and repetitive publications of Jacob Neusner and has aroused continuing controversy (Schwartz 1990 and Mason 1991). Smith clearly overstated the distinction between the *War* and the *Antiquities*, but put his finger on an important point, and no matter how the Josephan passages are interpreted the problem of the Pharisees and their influence still remains.

The essay "Palestinian Judaism in the First Century" addressed another of his favorite concerns: the Hellenization of Judaism. Smith never ceased railing against the misleading distinction between "Hellenistic Judaism" and "Palestinian Judaism," arguing that Palestinian Judaism was no less Hellenized — albeit in different ways, perhaps — than Judaism of the diaspora. The literary forms, the social types, the scholarly techniques, much of the theology, much of the art, and virtually all of the realia of life, of Judaism in late antiquity were derived from, or at least heavily colored by, the ambient culture (Smith 1958b, 1971a: 57-81, 1987).

Magic

The study of ancient magic was important to Smith for several reasons. First, Smith was always more interested in the narratives about Jesus than in his sayings, and the narratives in large part feature healings and miracles, in other words, magic. Second, magic was the great meeting ground and melting pot of religions in late antiquity. The magical papyri edited in *Papyri Graecae Magicae* are composed of Egyptian, Jewish, and Greek elements, with a generous admixture from other cultures as well. Here, then, was clear proof of cultural and religious mixing, precisely the sort of thing that Smith always found interesting. Third, magic was usually suppressed, and occasionally its practitioners persecuted by the authorities. Magic, then, was the religion of the outsider, the one who did not get to write the canonical books or the authoritative laws. Magic provided clear proof for the one-sidedness of the literary tradition, and for the necessity of reconstructing other traditions alongside those of the "winners." Smith always enjoyed discomfiting "winners" (see below).

Smith planned to write a catalogue of the magical gems of the British Museum and a History of Magic in Greco-Roman Antiquity, but made little progress on either project. Instead, we have extensive discussions of magic in *Clement of Alexandria* (Smith 1973: 220-237), *Jesus the Magician* (passim), and a series of articles on magical gems and magical papyri.

General themes and concerns

Certain themes and concerns unite all of Smith's work. First, a determination to destroy boundaries. Smith was a man who worked comfortably in Greek, Latin, and Hebrew, and had a good working knowledge of Syriac. He read Sophocles, Septuagint, Soferim, and Cyprian with equal ease. He believed that the world of antiquity was a single whole, and that the scholarly conventions of dividing the ancient world into Jewish, Christian, and classical, and subdividing in turn each of these three, were impediments to scholarship. Smith argued that early Christianity was part of Judaism, that Judaism was part of the Hellenistic world, and that neither Christianity nor Judaism nor Hellenistic culture could be understood in isolation from the other. Because of his ability to see the ancient world as a whole, Smith was capable of some remarkable insights. Nehemiah was a tyrant of the sort described by Herodotus (Smith 1971a: 136-144); through their conquests the Maccabees created a league of 'Ιουδαῖοι similar to the Aetolian league and the other leagues of Hellenistic Greece (Smith forthcoming); Jesus was a magician like other ancient magicians (Smith 1978a); as a social type the rabbis of the Mishnah were philosophers (Smith 1956).

Second, a concern for varieties of Judaism and Christianity, especially varieties that would counter the traditional and respectable versions of Judaism and Christianity known to most people. Smith saw his own work as complementing that of Walter Bauer on early Christianity and Erwin Goodenough on early Judaism (Smith 1968: 10-11). In his *Orthodoxy and Heresy in Earliest Christianity*, Bauer argued, against Eusebius, that "Orthodoxy" does not precede "heresy" but the opposite: early Christianity was a variegated phenomenon in which many movements and schools which would later be styled "heretical" were at first not heretical at all but were perfectly valid and (in their own environment) acceptable forms of Christianity. They did not become "heretical " until an emerging "Orthodoxy" would later make them so. In his *Jewish Symbols in the Greco-Roman Period* Goodenough argued that the medieval triumph of rabbinic Judaism should not obscure the fact that in Roman and early Byzantine times rabbinic Judaism was neither dominant nor "Orthodox"; among Greek-speaking Jews and the Jewish masses there thrived a decidedly non-rabbinic, mystical, and Hellenized Judaism. Goodenough found evidence for this non-rabbinic Judaism in various patristic texts, in ancient magic, and especially in Jewish art. Like Bauer, Smith argued that in Judaism, as in Christianity, heresy preceded orthodoxy: the "Yahweh-alone" party was a pietist reaction to the reigning syncretism of the day; the Pharisees were an important, but hardly the dominant group in the Judaism of the first century CE. Like Goodenough, Smith argued that Jewish magic and art provided clear evidence that non-rabbinic Judaism persisted well into "the rabbinic period." In a brilliant review article of Goodenough's work, Smith observed that Goodenough's mystical thesis failed to convince, but that Goodenough, like Columbus, had discovered new worlds in the process of his failure (Smith 1967).

Third, the concern for varieties was abetted by a great concern for terminological precision (Smith 1983b). Smith argued that scholars use words like "Judaism," "Hellenism," "gnostic" (Smith 1981) and "apocalypse" (Smith 1983a) without realizing their ambiguities and without defining them precisely. The exact meaning of "Jew" or 'Ιουδαῖος was a question to which he returned a number of times in

the course of his life. In an influential article Smith argued that Sicarii
were not Zealots, and Zealots were not Sicarii; the terms and the
groups must be kept distinct (Smith 1971c).

Fourth, a concern for the big picture. Smith never allowed himself
to be so blinded by varieties as to deny the fundamental unity of the
phenomena we conventionally call Judaism and Christianity. A current
scholarly fad is the term "Judaisms"; I believe that Smith never used
this awkward word, always preferring instead "varieties of Judaism" or
similar locutions. Smith believed that one could talk meaningfully of
ancient Judaism, its patterns and paradigms (Smith 1960-1961).
Similarly, one could even speak of "The Common Theology of the
Ancient Near East" (Smith 1952).

Fifth, scorn for pseudo-scholarship, that is, pronouncements and
opinions born of religious faith and confessional conviction but
masquerading as "objective scholarship." Smith argued that "the
Bible" is a theological category inherited from Judaism and Christianity and is an obstacle to a proper understanding of ancient Judaism and
Christianity. Smith had only scorn for those who believed that any
truth might somehow be lurking in the New Testament miracle stories
(except insofar as the cures might have been psycho-somatically
induced cures of psycho-somatically induced illnesses). Smith had only
scorn too for those who saw any truth in the prophetic experiences of
either the Old Testament or the New Testament, as if God or any god
would ever or did ever communicate in such a way with humans. For
Smith the ideal of scholarly objectivity could be met only through
atheism or Epicureanism, that is, the assumption that if the gods exist,
they intervene not at all in human affairs. (Whether Smith actually was
an atheist or an Epicurean, I do not know.)

Smith never tired of discomfiting the faithful. An ordained Episco-
palian priest who left the church, Smith knew well that his portrait of
Jesus the Magician, and his picture of a Christianity dominated by
magic, heavenly ascents, and spiritual possession, was far from the
respectable, rational, middle-class Christianity of most of his readers.
Smith knew well that his picture of a syncretistic Judaism living on
from biblical to rabbinic times would discomfit many of his Jewish
readers. Smith reveled in this. But in private life Smith was hardly the
wild-eyed radical or the strident orator. In private life, on the contrary,
he was staid and somewhat stiff, always well-dressed and perfectly
mannered. He was an impeccable gentleman. His memory will endure.[1]

---

[1] On various points I was aided by Calder 1992.

PART I

PHILOLOGICAL QUESTIONS

THE *ΠΟΛΙΤΕΙΑ* OF ISRAEL IN THE GRAECO-ROMAN AGE

Lucio Troiani

I

According to the tenets of certain modern scholarship, the πολιτεία in Jewish-Hellenistic authors such as Philo, and above all Josephus, is often linked to the integration and assimilation of Judaism into Greek civic life, (I am thinking of Tcherikover's 'Prolegomena' to the *Corpus Papyrorum Judaicarum*, for example: *CPJ* 1.61-74). On the other hand, studies such as those of Smallwood (1976: 358ff; 1970: 5ff.) or Kasher highlight the importance of the Jewish institution in Greek civic life. In Kasher's opinion, the Jews of Alexandria were Jewish πολῖται, and were considered πολῖται because they had their own independent πολιτεία. Likewise, the Jews of Sardis would have been πολῖται, not as citizens of the πόλις, but as members of the Jewish πολίτευμα of Sardis, permanent residents of the city, and organized separately from the πόλις (Kasher 1985: 237, 260). As the so-called *Letter of Aristeas* clearly shows Alexandrian Judaism delighted in giving suitable emphasis to its own internal organization (*Ep. Arist.* 310; Jos., *Ant* 12 § 108; cf. Delia 1991). I certainly do not mean to enter here into a technical-juridical debate as to the position of Judaism in the Greco-Roman Age (for this see Juster 1914; Rabello 1980: 662-762), nor to draw any general conclusions, which is always dangerous to do. I wish only to draw attention to some ancient texts which can clarify the notion of πολιτεία in the context of some Greco-Roman Judaism. The evidence of Josephus is naturally fundamental. In *Ant* 4 § 198-302, he lists everything that Moses would have arranged in the matter of πολιτεία. The Greek reader, used to the political language of contemporary treatises,[1] discovered that the form of government was rather low on the list (*Ant* 4 § 223), and that this list indicated the standards of behaviour: from the duty of the three pilgrimage festivals to the forbidding of blasphemy, the rules regarding sacrifices to the prohibition against insulting the city gods, the reading of the laws in the Holy City every

---

[1] Cf. Plutarch's definitions of πολιτεία in *De tribus rei publicae generibus* 2.826C-D.

seven years, prayers and private devotion, the laws on seed-sowing, the
rules on witness, the laws of marriage and the education of children,
the forbidding of usury and legislation on theft, the norms on deposits,
and the laws in time of war. As in Cicero's ideal constitution, religion
is in first place. Furthermore, against the danger of centrifugal forces,
absolute pre-eminence is given to the principle of one temple and One
God (Cic., *De legibus* 2.7-22). The political constitution is part of a
religious system.

Essentially, Josephus seems to mean by "the laws regarding the
πολιτεία," those laws which would permit the Jews, especially those
of the diaspora, to live respecting Mosaic legislation. Supplementing
the Book of Deuteronomy, which seems to be his source, Josephus
states: "those coming from the ends of the earth must meet three
times a year for the principal festivals in the Temple of Jerusalem;" in
fact "it is right, he adds, that they do not ignore each other, being co-
nationals, and sharing the same precepts" (*Ant* 4 § 204).

As the Second Book of Maccabees shows, πολιτεύεσθαι in the laws
of God soon becomes the slogan of Jerusalem's anti-reformists, those
whom we call orthodox. In the New Testament, which seems in large
part to be the echo of the rethinking and the ideology of certain
Hellenistic Judaism, the term often means the militancy in the divine
laws that follows fixed laws and ethical norms (Moulton-Milligan 1930:
s.v.). The *Antiquities* of Josephus, which speak of the relationship
between Judaism and the Hellenistic and Roman authorities, in
general understand the πολιτεία as a kind of honour that the kings or
the Caesars gave in tribute to the Jews in exchange for their expertise
and loyalty; these honours were expressed in concrete fashion, from
what we can understand, in the authorization "to use the ancestral
laws." For example, Greeks from Ionian cities petition Marcus Agrippa, Caesar Augustus' right hand man: the right to take part in the
πολιτεία granted earlier by King Antiochus II can only be given to
them. They add that if the Jews want to participate in the πολιτεία
they will have to worship the city's gods. As has been noted by Stern,
Josephus does not return after explaining the situation, as we would
expect him to, to the question of "citizenship," but contends that the
Jews had the right to follow their own customs (*Ant* 12 §§ 125-127 =
Stern 1976-84: No.86). The ambiguity between the right of citizenship
and Moses' πολιτεία (*Ant* 3 § 322), seems to inspire these apologetic
pages. According to Philo and Josephus, the concession of the πο-

λιτεία on the part of the authorities, the kings or the Caesars and their representatives, to the Jews of Ephesus, Antioch, Alexandria, or Cyrene, equates them to citizens; "those of ours who live in Antioch call themselves Antiochians. In fact, the founder Seleucus gave them the πολιτεία; equally the Jews of Ephesus and from the rest of Ionia have the same name as the indigenous inhabitants (*AgAp* 2 § 39)." Philo fears aggression, in the wake of Flaccus' odious measures, on the part of the inhabitants of Greek towns against "their Jewish fellow citizens (*In Flaccum* 47; 53)." The "struggle for the πολιτεία" with which the diplomatic mission to Caligula was charged, was sustained in order to defend "our πολιτεία" as abrogated by Flaccus. As Philo explicitly shows, "being Alexandrian" did not consist only in the participation of political rights (*Legatio ad Gaium* 349; *In Flaccum* 53). When Josephus touches on the subject, he usually speaks of "equal citizenship," (ἰσοπολιτεία), not of "citizenship." The previous kings had conceded "equality of political rights" (ἰσονομία *Ant* 16 § 160) to the Jews of Asia and of Libya. Alexander the Great allowed the Jews of Alexandria to live in the city "on terms of equality" (ἐξ ἰσομοιρίας) in respect to the Greeks (*JW* 2 § 487). As the edict of Claudius reported by Josephus (*Ant* 19 § 281) clarifies, the Jews have obtained ἰσοπολιτεία, equal citizenship, from the kings (Stern 1976-84, 1.399-403; Kasher, 1985). It was understood from the bronze stele that Julius Caesar erected for the Alexandrian Jews, as Josephus says, that they are πολῖται ᾿Αλεξανδρέων and not simply Alexandrian citizens (*Ant* 14 § 188). As an ancient inscription says, the ἰσοπολιτεία between Milesians and Heracleans will be such that "the Milesians will be fellow citizens of the Heracleans, and the Heracleans of the Milesians" (*SIG* 633,33). By ἰσοπολιτεία the citizens of Keos are fellow citizens (αὐτῶν πολῖται) of the Milesians (Robert 1927: 206-207; 1974; 1977). We observe how the Greek ἰσοπολιτεία can be used to indicate foreign institutions and different levels of citizenship, as is shown by Dionysius of Halicarnassus, who uses the term to designate now *civitas sine suffragio* now *ius Latii* (Lécrivain 1899: 587; Oehler 1916: 2227-2231). In his polemical emphasis against the presumed calumnies of Apion, Josephus stresses that the Alexandrian Jews had "equal honour" with the Macedonians; Alexander made the Jews of Alexandria ἰσοπολῖται with the Macedonians; Seleucus I "declared (the Jews) to have equal privileges" (ἰσοτίμους ἀπέφηνεν) with the Greeks and the Macedonians (*Ant* 12 § 119; cf. *AgAp* 2 § 35; Stern 1976-84,

1.399-403; Kasher, 1985). In the decrees of the Roman authorities in the *Antiquities*, the Jews exempted from military service are equally defined as πολῖται 'Ρωμαίων and not as Roman citizens (*Ant* 14 §§ 228, 232, 234, 237). In the first Pseudo-Clementine Homily Clement is defined in the same way and the report has preserved in all probability a terminology used in diaspora Judaism.[2] Even a superficial reading of Josephus' texts suggests that one can conclude that the acquisition of the title of πολῖται, in the interpretation that he gives to these documents, does not end with the acquisition of political rights: at the solicitation of the Roman authorities, those of Laodicea, Halicarnassus, Sardis and Ephesus, for example, concede privileges in respect of the Jewish πολιτεία, and it is for this reason that in Josephus the title of πολῖται for the Jews of Antioch as for those of Rome seems really to involve the exemption of the citizen from certain duties. Josephus does not speak of Jews as Alexandrian or Roman citizens, but πολῖται 'Αλεξανδρέων or 'Ρωμαίων. They did not have the same citizenship, but equal citizenship. The Jewish πολῖται 'Αλεξανδρέων, "so-called Alexandrians," as the above quoted edict of Claudius illustrates, are established in the city together with the Alexandrians from the very beginning, having obtained "equal citizenship" from the (Ptolemaic) kings (*Ant* 19 § 281). It is legitimate to ask whether the title of "Ephesians," "Alexandrians," "Romans," "Antiochians," or "Sardians," referring to the Jews of the Greco-Roman Age, should not be linked to the institution of ἰσοπολιτεία.[3] As *Ant* 19 § 306 explains, the Jews have obtained the privilege "to enjoy the same civil rights as the Greeks" (συμπολιτεύεσθαι τοῖς "Ελλησιν).

The disorder which broke out in Caesarea between the Jews and the Syrians, did not really concern the πολιτεία, but the ἰσοπολιτεία. The Syrians of the city tried to extort a letter from Nero, that would abrogate the Jewish ἰσοπολιτέια (*Ant* 20 §§ 182-184). One of the explanations of these expressions is that offered by Kasher. His thorough and erudite analysis depicts an autonomously organized urban Judaism, and interprets the Jewish πολιτεία as being really a political entity, separate inside the one πόλις, on an equal basis with the Greeks. As Philo explains, however, participation in political rights

---

[2] Ps Clem, *Homiliae* 1,1,1: ἐγὼ Κλήμης, 'Ρωμαίων πολίτης ὤν.
[3] Robert 1964: 54-55; *Ant* 14 §§ 235, 245, 259; Trebilco 1991; Philo, *In Flaccum* 47: πολίταις αὐτῶν 'Ιουδαίοις.

was one of the components of the πολιτεία (*In Flacc* 53). In his view, urban Judaism feared that the negative judgment of Caligula against the πολιτεία of the Alexandrian Jews would signal the abrogation of the laws of Moses and of the rights the Hebrews had in common with each of the cities (*Legatio* 371). An almost unbreakable bond seems to be established between the right of citizenship, (of Alexandria as of Antioch), and Moses' πολιτεία, as much in the general view as in the use of the terms. If they are not "Antiochians" or "Alexandrians," they cannot observe the Mosaic laws. In the concession of the πολι-τεία on the part of the authorities, as we noted above, Josephus stresses "using the native laws." For this πολιτεία also seems to have pre-eminent ideological value in our texts, and indicates active membership in Judaism. The πολιτεία is, above all, the constitution of Moses. This superimposition can be expressed in the formula of the ἰσοπολιτεία: in point of fact, the expression used by Philo to indicate the juridical situation of the Jews in the Greek cities, ("rights in common with each of πόλεις"), recalls the clauses for those who wanted to exercise the rights of the citizen in the decrees of the ἰσοπολιτεία (cf. Robert 1927: 206-207; 1974; 1977).

II

Philo of Alexandria wrote his *Legatio ad Gaium* at the time of Claudius. Although it deals only incidentally with the vicissitudes of a delegation of Alexandrian Jews in Rome, headed by Philo himself. They had come to plead the case of the Jews of their city after the disorder which broke out in Alexandria in June, 38 CE. The delegates, anxious about the possible outcome of the audience with the eccentric Caesar (Gaius Caligula), were constantly moving around trying to follow the trail of the restless and unpredictable Caesar. Their expectations were abruptly put in proportion by a very upsetting piece of news. Word came that the emperor had expressed his intention to introduce an idol of colossal dimensions into the Holy of Holies of the Jerusalem Temple. The news prompted a train of thought in Philo that can perhaps be useful for our argument. According to him, the threatened desecration of the Temple makes the mission's purpose suddenly futile. He reasons that the efforts "to show that we are Alexandrians," are absolutely pointless, "when the more general πολιτεία of the Jews is in very grave danger" (*Legatio* 194). The

expression would seem to indicate that the "struggle for the πολιτεία"
that the delegation was called upon to sustain in front of Caesar,
regarded, as in the case of the documents handed down by Josephus,
the defence of some practices connected to "the more general πολιτεία of the Jews." The fears of the pious ambassadors were that the
rumored desecration of the Temple would expose the Jews indiscrimi-
nately to a situation of "irreparable illegality" (*Legatio* 190).

Worries about the Alexandrian πολιτεία again enter into the same
context: "How will it be possible to open our mouths in front of
Caligula regarding the profaned synagogues, when he is about to
profane the Holiest?" In Philo's description, the diplomatic mission
presented itself to Caesar to ask for the restoration of those standards
that guaranteed life to the Alexandrian Jews in accordance with the
laws of Moses. The contemplated attack by the emperor against the
more general πολιτεία of the Jews produced in its extreme consequences the same dangers run by the Alexandrian πολιτεία. Philo
seems to see the Alexandrian πολιτεία as part of a "more general"
πολιτεία. Naturally, his writing is apologetic. Judaism for him is
represented by congregations consisting largely of the pious, whose
only concern is not to change even a title of the precepts of the
fathers, which have the age-old approval of the established authority.
To fight for the πολιτεία means to fight "not to abandon everything
to irredeemable illegality." As is natural, the link between the πολιτεία and observant Judaism returns in other apologetic writings of the
Roman Age. We can legitimately ask if Philo's celebrated outburst in
the preamble to the third book of his *De specialibus legibus*, in which
he laments having been distracted from the meditative life by the
solicitudes in the πολιτεία, does not again refer to his activities as
defender of observant Judaism. As we understand immediately afterwards, this activity must have encountered opposition. His exegetical
work rather than his political activity must have been put in question.
Philo has harsh words for those who "have a dislike for the πολιτεία
of the fathers" (*Spec. leg.* 3.3-6; *Conf. ling.* 2-4). According to 3 Macc
3:4, observant Judaism in Alexandria is opposed to the impious who
have abandoned the laws of the fathers; the pious Jews refused to
have anything to do with the pagans "worshipping God and conducting
themselves by His law," (τῷ τούτου νόμῳ πολιτευόμενοι). In the
Fourth Book of Maccabees, a sermon crammed with ideas that are
predominantly identified as stoic, the faithfulness of the heroic martyrs
of the persecution of King Antiochus is expressed in the same way.

The captivating words of the tyrant Antiochus seek to induce the martyrs to "renounce the native statute of your πολιτεία." In the solemn dedication, which the author sees as a fitting epitaph for the fallen heroes, he speaks of "the violence of the tyrant who wanted to wipe out the πολιτεία of the Hebrews" (4 Macc 17:9; 5:16; 8:7). In the apologetic prose of Greco-Roman Judaism, faithful observance of the Mosaic Law is in reality seen as a sort of civil obedience. An inscription from Stobi, presumably belonging to the end of the third century CE, celebrates Claudius Tiberius Polycharmus, also called Achyrius, "the father of the synagogue of Stobi," πολιτευσάμενος πᾶσαν πολειτείαν κατὰ τὸν Ἰουδαισμόν. As Frey's commentary on the inscription explains, the expression means that the donor has conformed his entire conduct during his life to the laws and customs of the fathers, i.e., has been a practicing Jew (*CIJ* 1 No. 694; see also Hengel 1966). In Justin's *Dialogue with Tryphon* we find analogous expressions. As is natural, diaspora Judaism, even of the most observant kind, did not exist in isolation. It assimilated expressions from the outside world. Plutarch shows us that among the various meanings of πολιτεία there is also that of a particularly splendid single action, carried out in the public interest, "such as donations of money, the ending of a war, the introduction of a decree" (*De tribus rei publicae generibus* 2.826C-D). On the other hand, in the language of Imperial inscriptions πολιτεύεσθαι and πολιτεία do not indicate the exercise of rights of citizenship. Such is the case, for example, with the formula πολιτευόμενος δὲ καὶ ἐν ταῖς κατὰ Λυκίαν πόλεσι πάσαις in the Lycian inscriptions. The individuals in the Lycian inscriptions do not have the right of citizenship in all cities, but have performed services in the public interest in all the cities. As Louis Robert explains, πολιτεία in the Imperial Age often has the meaning of "civic activity," "civic duty" (Robert 1968: 325). The Jewish communities were so often in danger of being overwhelmed by the rampant conformism of the so-called outside world that faithful observance of the Mosaic law must have been considered by them a very real civic activity, and in consequence, a title of distinction and an example for the whole community.

III

Observance of the Mosaic law indicated membership in the Jewish nation, persistence in the πολιτεία showed who the real πολῖται were. The Jewish expert in Greek literature who invited his fellow Jews in the cities to return to the law of Moses and not to allow themselves to be seduced by the charms of the Gospel, addressing them, in Greek, with the term "πολῖται," left Origen incredulous (*Contra Celsum* 2:1). In the ordinance of Dolabella to the municipal authorities at Ephesus the envoy of Hyrcanus II, the high priest and ethnarch of the Jews, is defined πολίτης of the Jews of Asia Minor (*Ant* 14 § 226). Similarly, in the decree of the city of Sardis that permits the Jewish community to "live according to the laws," the Jewish πολῖται who live in the city are perhaps subjects of Hyrcanus II, as has been proposed by Elias Bickerman (*Ant* 14 §§ 259-60; Bickerman 1958: 335 n. 39). As Philo explains in the final part of his *Legatio ad Gaium* the Jews observe the "special laws" (of Moses) in their civic context, while enjoying the political rights of their respective cities (*Legatio* 371; cf. *Ant* 14 § 235). Perhaps for this reason the Jews of Alexandria or of Rome are not defined by our sources as being "Alexandrian citizens," or "Roman citizens." The πολιτεία went beyond the rights of citizenship in the single city. It must have also indicated the bond that united the Jews of the Greek diaspora, who were therefore πολῖται. This interpretation which we obtain from reading some ancient texts will naturally have a bearing on the most disparate and unpredictable cases. In Luke's parable the Prodigal Son, having squandered the money inherited from his father in vice and loose living, was able to live by putting himself into the service of one of the πολῖται of the region in an unspecified far-off land.[4] As the concordance to Josephus indicates, one of the central meanings of the term πολίτης in his work, is "conational" (Rengstorff 1973-83: 3.476). Similarly Caesar, the young son of Germanicus, according to Philo rebukes King Agrippa for the arrogance "of your fine and good πολῖται." In an apologetic passage Philo explains that "the Jews welcome foreigners who show respect and consideration for them, no less than their own πολῖται" (*Legatio* 265; 211). Philo has harsh words for those μικροπολῖται who would interpret the profound truth of the Scriptures in a dull way (*De somn.* 1.39). To use a felicitous expression of Martin Goodman, "like the Romans and different from the Greeks, the Jews accepted the notion that their *politeia* was not fixed to any particular locality" (Goodman 1992: 61). Acccording to 2 Macc 9:17-19, after tremendous punishment

---

[4] Luke 15:15; *Ep. Arist.* 3 distinguishes τοῖς σὺν ἑαυτῷ (i.e. Eleazar, the High Priest) from τοῖς κατὰ τοὺς ἄλλους τόπους πολίταις.

inflicted by Heaven, King Antiochus decided to become a Jew. In a letter stating this he turns to the Jewish πολῖται as a consequence, wishing them health and prosperity. We might suspect that the term was already present in the work of Jason of Cyrene, a diaspora Jew. In the symbolic language used by Philo for the exegesis of the Old Testament, full citizenship is made to coincide significantly with the acquisition of suitable title for being members of Israel. Philo also uses the verb πολιτεύομαι frequently to express observance of the Mosaic laws. We see how another diaspora Jew, perhaps a younger contemporary of Philo's, Paul of Tarsus, protests "in all good conscience" his qualifications as an observant Jew, using the same expression in front of the Sanhedrin, arousing the disdain and anger of the high priest.[5] Eph 2:12 reminds its addressees that "once they were deprived of or alienated from the πολιτεία of Israel" (ἀπηλλοτριωμένοι τῆς πολι-τείας τοῦ Ἰσραήλ). The same expression occurs again in Col 1:21. As 3 Macc 1:3 shows, the verb ἀπαλλοτριόω might preferably be used to indicate the abandoning of the precepts of the fathers (Hatch-Redpath 1897: 116). In the first Pseudo-Clementine Homily the preaching of Jesus has the purpose of "readjusting the πολιτεία of the Jews" (1.6.2). Jewish apologetic in Greek language delighted in connecting the πολιτεία to the origins of Greek urban Judaism, preceding the actual founding of the cities. Philo emphasizes the "foresight of Moses," who wanted the Jews "to seek their laws not after having obtained the cleruchies and having lived in the city, laws by which they would have been ruled; instead they had to settle with the rules of the πολιτεία already ready" (*De Decal.* 15). In a book of propaganda attributed to the Greek historian Hecataeus of Abdera, an authority on Greek ethnography at the time of the Diadochi, a Jewish high priest, a certain Ezechias, who is depicted as a valued advisor of King Ptolemy, had the πολιτεία written when on the point of founding another Jewish colony in Egypt (Stern, 1976-84: 1, No. 12 = *AgAp* 1 § 189). In Philo's above-mentioned outburst (*Spec. leg.* 3.3-6) "the great sea of worries in the πολιτεία," seems to refer to exactly this context. The πολιτεία is first of all that of Moses. In fact he protests: "I not only do dare draw near the sacred exegesis of Moses, but also . . . to unfold and reveal what is not known to the multitude." As the

---

[5] Acts 23:1-2; Philo, *Leg. all.* 3.2; *De somn.* 1.48; *Spec. leg.* 4.219; *Virtut.* 161; *Praem.* 4; G. Mayer 1974: *s.v.*

papyrus letter of Claudius to the Alexandrians fortuitously reveals, the diplomatic mission led by our author was only one of two Jewish delegations, "as if the Jews were residents in two cities" (*CPJ* 2, No. 153.90-91).

To sum up, in the Jewish texts of the diaspora, which are for the most part apologetic and edifying, πολιτεία and πολίτης come to mean sometimes a sort of "civic" obedience, almost promoting the cliché that the urban Judaism of the Greco-Roman Age exercised its own particular citizenship, parallel and equal to that of the "native" citizens. Josephus explains that the Jews of Ephesus "have the same name as the indigenous citizens" (*AgAp* 2 § 39). As a rule, ἰσοπολι-τεία would allow the Jewish citizenry to reconcile their dual loyalties, to Moses and to the πόλις. To the Roman tribune who had mistaken him for an Egyptian fomenter of disorder, Paul proudly replies that he is a Jew from Tarsus, πολίτης of a not unimportant city of Cilicia (Acts 21:37-39).

IV

When we read of the πολῖται in the texts of Hellenistic Judaism, we should not forget its basic text, the Septuagint. As the lexicons instruct us (Hatch-Redpath 1897: 1180; Zorell 1904: *s.v.*), the Alexandrian translation often uses the term πολίτης for the Hebrew word "fellow citizen" (רֵעַ). In the Greek translation of the Book of Proverbs the Greek speaking Jew read that "the snare for the πολῖται is in the mouths of the impious" (Prov 11:9 LXX), in accordance with a model constantly proposed by parenetic literature, (e.g., in the Books of Maccabees). Thus it came about that the term "citizen" made its entry into the patriarchal and seminomadic society of Abraham, Isaac, and Jacob (Gen 23:11 LXX). The men instructed by Moses are defined by Josephus as "citizens" (*Ant* 1 § 21). The invective in the Greek version of Jeremiah was hurled against those who committed adultery with the wives of their πολῖται (36[29]:23 LXX). According to his prophecy (Jer 38[31]:34 LXX) as quoted in Heb 8:11, on the day in which Israel will be a people for God, "no-one will instruct his own πολίτης any more." The Greek version of the Book of Proverbs again admonishes not to bear false witness "against one of your own πολῖται" (Prov 24:43[28] LXX). The anonymous author of the Second Book of Maccabees who claims to summarize the five books of a work by a Jew of the Greek diaspora, Jason of Cyrene, speaks of some hostile behaviour toward his fellow Jews, the πολῖται (2 Macc 5:23). It is no wonder then, that in Christian texts which seem largely to derive from the meditations and rethinking of the Jewish diaspora in the Greek language, faithfulness to the Gospel comes to be compared to a sort of civic loyalty. Paul invites the Philippians to πολιτεύεσθαι in a way befitting Christ's Gospel (Phil 1:27). Citizenship of heaven will become one of the most popular slogans of Christian kerygma. Paul already proclaims that "our πολίτευμα is in Heaven" (Phil 3:20). The anonymous rhetorician of the *Letter to Diognetus* declares that the Christians are spending a short time on earth, but that their πολιτεία is elsewhere, they are "citizens of Heaven." He stresses that which he calls "the paradox of Christian life." It consists among other things of the singular contrast between on the one hand the simple and anonymous way of life which on the surface conforms to the different local usages, and on the other hand the marvels of the inner being and the moral revolution announced by them in the secrecy of their conscience: "they show the praiseworthy, but certainly paradoxical nature of the constitution of their πολιτεία" (*Diogn.* 5).

   In the Jewish community, as in the Christian one, the connecting bond is not only the worship of a god; active participation in Judaism or Christianity requires obedience and standards of behaviour imposed by a real and actual 'constitution'. As Josephus shows, the persistence of the πολιτεία ended in exasperating its detractors (*Ant* 3 § 322). One could be active in the Christian αἵρεσις, as in that of the Pharisees, yet be part of the very same πολιτεία. The observance of Judaism is put on the same level as the laws of the city. Socrates is a martyr for Jews and Christians. An adversary like Apion can exclaim "why then, if they are πολῖται, do they not worship the same gods as the Alexandrians?" (*AgAp* 2 § 65).

V

This picture, based primarily on ancient literary texts, naturally reflects the aspirations and ambitions of an elite; we may suspect that not all of diaspora Judaism proved so careful and solicitous for the πολιτεία as a Philo, or the zealous authors of the Books of Maccabees, to whom we owe large part of what we know about so-called Hellenistic Judaism. We can imagine that Josephus' fears for the πολιτεία of the

Jewish communities, above all for the great centers of the ancient Mediterranean, worries that reverberate through the entire structure of his books of Hellenistic and Roman history, were not in reality so common or widespread. The picture of a Judaism on the defensive and besieged by an idolatrous external world, is a cliché created by its proponents. The Maccabaean epics, the four Books of Maccabees, proudly vindicate the πολιτεία and claim a superior obedience against occasional dissident voices inside it. On the other hand, the Jewish-Hellenistic historians, whose works were transmitted by Christians, served to enlighten readers on the protohistory, so to speak, of the Christian movement. They were consulted on ancestral history. As the philosopher Epictetus suggested at the beginning of the second century CE, adherence to Judaism did not prevent frequent compromises. They led to his grave and austere question, "Why do you pass yourselves off as Greek, when you are a Jew?" At times, the most uninhibited and vitriolic intellectuals of the Julio-Claudian age, such as Petronius, could pillory the implacable (and broken) rigour that the Jewish πολιτεία had to impose on its adherents in the Greek city. Certainly, the diffusion of this sort of civil obedience must have seemed to a Seneca or a Tacitus, a very real threat of "superstition" against free civil living. Strabo could speak of the ethnarch of Alexandria as an absolute chief, who didn't depend on an superior power," he commands over an autonomous and sovereign πολιτεία" (Stern 1974-84: 1, Nos. 254, 195, 186, 105; 2, No. 281).

From the times of Cyrus, the πολιτεία was imposed on the Jewish community by the authorities. For this reason, in the passages from Josephus' *Antiquities* on the rights of the Jews to the πολιτεία, the emphasis is always placed on "using the native laws." For this reason again, in Philo, in the troubled and uneasy audience with Caligula, the outcome of the audience on "Alexandrian citizenship" is connected indissolubly with the destiny of all the other cities of the empire: "What other city will remain tranquil? Which will not attack the Jews that live there? Which synagogue will be left intact?" (Philo, *Legatio* 349-373; Bickerman 1935; 1946).

ΊΟΥΔΑΙΟΣ ΤΟ ΓΕΝΟΣ
AND RELATED EXPRESSIONS IN JOSEPHUS

Shaye J. D. Cohen

The goals of this paper are rather modest. In twelve or thirteen passages Josephus describes various persons as Ἰουδαῖος/Ἰουδαῖοι (τὸ) γένος. What exactly does this phrase mean? This modest question impinges directly on two immodest questions, which I cannot avoid entirely here but which await detailed investigation: what exactly does Ἰουδαῖος/Ἰουδαῖοι mean in Josephus? how does Josephus understand Jewish identity and "Jewishness"?[1]

I

Here are the Josephan passages. The translations are drawn from the Loeb Classical Library edition of Josephus.

1. *JW* 2 § 101: "At this time a young man who, though by birth a Jew (Ἰουδαῖος μὲν τὸ γένος), had been brought up at Sidon at the house of a Roman freedman . . . passed himself off as the prince Alexander." Paralleled by text **6** below.

2. *JW* 2 § 119: "The followers . . . of the third [of the three schools of Jewish philosophy] are called Essenes . . . . Of Jewish birth (Ἰουδαῖοι μὲν γένος ὄντες), they show a greater attachment to each other than do the other sects."

3. *JW* 2 § 308: "For Florus ventured that day to do what none had ever done before, namely, to scourge before his tribunal and nail to the cross men of equestrian rank (ἄνδρας ἱππικοῦ), men who, if Jews by birth, were at least invested with that Roman dignity (εἰ καὶ τὸ γένος Ἰουδαῖον ἀλλὰ γοῦν τὸ ἀξίωμα Ῥωμαικὸν ἦν)." The text is somewhat uncertain.[2]

---

[1] On the varied meanings of the word Ἰουδαῖος/οι, see (inter alia) Lowe 1976 and 1981; Solin 1983: 647-651; Tomson 1986; Kraemer 1989; Cohen 1990; Smith (forthcoming). I know of no study of Josephus' conception of Jewish identity and Jewishness.

[2] Instead of Ἰουδαῖον, some manuscripts (followed by Niese) read Ἰουδαίων, others Ἰουδαῖοι. These readings preserve the appositional formula, while the text

4. *Ant* 11 § 207: "Some time afterward Bagathoos and Theodestes plotted against the king, but Barnabazos, the servant of one of these eunuchs, who was a Jew by race (τὸ γένος ὢν Ἰουδαῖος), discovered their plot."

5. *Ant* 17 § 141: "This Acme was a Jewess by birth (Ἰουδαία μὲν τὸ γένος) but a slave of Caesar's wife Julia."

6. *Ant* 17 § 324: "After these matters had been disposed of by Caesar, there appeared a young man, Jewish by birth (Ἰουδαῖος μὲν τὸ γένος) but brought up in the city of Sidon by a Roman freedman, who represented himself as related to Herod." Paralleled by text **1** above.

7. *Ant* 18 § 103: "Artabanus sent as a hostage to Tiberius his son Darius, together with many gifts, among which he included a man seven cubits tall, a Jew by race (Ἰουδαῖον τὸ γένος), named Eleazar, who on account of his size was called the Giant."

8. *Ant* 18 § 196: "[One of Agrippa's fellow prisoners sees Agrippa and inquires as to his identity.] Upon learning that his name was Agrippa, that he was a Jew by race (Ἰουδαῖον δὲ τὸ γένος), and that he was one of the most notable men of Judaea , he asked the soldier . . . to allow him to approach."

9. *Ant* 20 § 173: "There arose also a quarrel between the Jewish and Syrian inhabitants of Caesarea on the subject of equal civic rights. The Jews claimed that they had the precedence because the founder of Caesarea, their king Herod, had been of Jewish descent (Ἡρώδην αὐτῶν βασιλέα γεγονέναι τὸ γένος Ἰουδαῖον)[3]; the Syrians admitted what they said about Herod, but asserted . . . ."

10. *Life* § 16: "Landing safely at Dicaearchia, which the Italians call Puteoli, I formed a friendship with Aliturus, an actor (μιμολόγος) who was a special favourite of Nero and of Jewish origin" (Ἰουδαῖος τὸ γένος).[4]

11. *Life* § 382: "The king [Agrippa] promised to come [to the aid of Tiberias], writing a letter in reply, which he handed to a Jew named Crispus (Κρίσπῳ μὲν τοὔνομα, τὸ δὲ γένος Ἰουδαίῳ), a groom of the bedchamber."

---

printed in the Loeb edition does not. The meaning is unchanged.

[3] The epitome reads Ἰουδαῖον τῷ γένει.

[4] Ἰουδαῖος τὸ γένος is omitted by one testimonium.

12. *Life* § 427: "Afterwards I [Josephus] married a woman of Jewish extraction (τὸ δὲ γένος Ἰουδαίαν) who had settled in Crete. She came of very distinguished parents, indeed the most notable people in that country."

13. *AgAp* 1 §§ 178-179: "'Well,' said Aristotle, 'in accordance with the precepts of rhetoric, let us begin by describing his race (τὸ γένος αὐτοῦ) . . . the man was a Jew of Coele-Syria (τὸ μὲν γένος ἦν Ἰου-δαῖος ἐκ τῆς κοίλης Συρίας). These people are descended from the Indian philosophers. The philosophers, they say, are in India called Calani, in Syria by the territorial name of Jews (παρὰ δὲ Σύροις Ἰουδαῖοι, τοὔνομα λαβόντες ἀπὸ τοῦ τόπου); for the district which they inhabit is known as Judaea.'" This passage, of course, is a quotation from Clearchus of Soli and not by Josephus, but I am including the passage in my corpus for the sake of completeness.

The Loeb translators consistently translate Ἰουδαῖος/α "Jewish" or "Jew/ess," but adopt various translations for τὸ γένος. They take γένος to mean either "birth" ("a Jew by birth," **1,2,3,5,6**), or "race" ("a Jew by race," **4,7,8**), which in this context I assume has the equivalent force of the word "nation" (γένος = ἔθνος and λαός), or "origin" ("of Jewish descent," **9**; "of Jewish origin," **10**; "of Jewish extraction," **12**; I assume that these translations are synonymous). The word γένος has other meanings too, of course, both within and without the Josephan corpus (Feldman 1992a: 7 n. 18), but these other meanings do not enter into consideration here.[5] In the phrase Ἰουδαῖος τὸ γένος, the word γένος means either birth, nation, or origin. In two passages the Loeb translation omits the word altogether (**11,13**), as if the words τὸ γένος add nothing to Ἰουδαῖος.

The Loeb translators ignore the ambiguity of Ἰουδαῖος, an ambiguity even greater than that of τὸ γένος. Ἰουδαῖος can be either an "ethnic-geographic" term or a "religious" term.[6] As an ethnic-geographic term, it designates someone who is a member of the nation (ἔθνος, λαός, sometimes γένος) of Ἰουδαῖοι. The homeland of Ἰουδαῖοι, of course, is Ἰουδαία, so that the ethnic meaning of

---

[5] Feldman shows that γένος does not always mean "nation," but does not clearly distinguish between the meanings that it does have.

[6] Solin 1983: 647 n. 150, correctly notes that Lowe 1976 overemphasizes the geographical aspect, virtually ignores the ethnic aspect, and too cleanly separates the geographical from the religious aspect. But Lowe's discussion is good nonetheless; on Josephus see Lowe 1976: 104-105.

ʼΙουδαῖος is inseparably linked with a geographic meaning, just as the terms Phrygian, Egyptian, Lydian, etc. are both ethnic and geographic. In certain contexts, of course, the ethnic meaning may have primacy over the geographic, while in other contexts the geographic meaning may have primacy over the ethnic, but both meanings are always present.

As an ethnic-geographic term ʼΙουδαῖος is more ambiguous than Phrygia, Egypt, Lydia, etc. because ʼΙουδαία is the name of both a country and a specific part of that country. ʼΙουδαία is the name of the entire land of Israel, including its districts Idumaea, Judaea, Samaria, Galilee, etc.; ʼΙουδαία is also the name of a specific district, Judaea, in contrast with the other districts Idumaea, Galilee, Peraea, Samaria, etc. (for example, *JW* 2 § 95-96, 247; 3 § 35-58; *Ant* 13 § 50; 17 § 318-319). Thus, a ʼΙουδαῖος, that is, an inhabitant of Judaea, can be contrasted with an Idumaean, Galilean, Peraean, Samarian, etc. This usage is attested most clearly in *JW* 2 § 43 (my translation):

> A countless multitude ran together [to Jerusalem] from Galilee and from Idumaea, from Jericho and from Peraea beyond the Jordan, but the genuine nation from Judaea itself (ὁ γνήσιος ἐξ αὐτῆς ʼΙουδαίας λαός) exceeded them in both number and eagerness.

The parallel in *Ant* 17 § 254 runs as follows (my translation):

> Many, many myriads of people gathered together [in Jerusalem], Galileans and Idumaeans, a multitude of Jerichonians and those who dwell across the Jordan. And of the Judaeans themselves (αὐτῶν ʼΙουδαίων) there was a multitude who joined all these and who were much more eager than the others.

I think that these two texts mean the same thing even if the wording of the *War* is much more striking than that of the *Antiquities'*. The nation from Judaea itself is genuine (γνήσιος) in that the name ʼΙουδαῖοι is entirely appropriate to them, while it is only partly appropriate for Galileans, Idumaeans, and Peraeans. Galileans et al. are ʼΙουδαῖοι insofar as they inhabit the land of ʼΙουδαία broadly defined and are members of the ἔθνος of the ʼΙουδαῖοι broadly defined, but insofar as they do not live in ʼΙουδαία narrowly defined and are not members of the ἔθνος of the ʼΙουδαῖοι narrowly defined – Galileans like Idumaeans can be said to constitute an ἔθνος of their own (*JW* 2 § 510; 4 § 105, 243, 272; *Ant* 15 § 257) – they are not

Ἰουδαῖοι. Only the Ἰουδαῖοι of Ἰουδαία narrowly defined are Ἰουδαῖοι in all respects. In several other passages too Josephus explicitly or implicitly distinguishes Ἰουδαῖοι from Galileans and Idumaeans, but in other passages Josephus includes both of these groups among the Ἰουδαῖοι.[7]

Separate from, or in addition to, this ethnic-geographic meaning, Ἰουδαῖος can also have a religious meaning. A Ἰουδαῖος is someone who believes (or is supposed to believe) certain distinctive tenets, and/or follows (or is supposed to follow) certain distinctive practices, and/or is a member (or is supposed to be a member) of certain distinctive religious organizations – in other words, a Ἰουδαῖος is a Jew, someone who follows Judaism, the way of life of the Jews. The clearest Josephan examples of this usage occur in the *Antiquities'* account of the conversion of the royal house of Adiabene: Izates realizes that "to truly be a Ἰουδαῖος" (εἶναι βεβαίως Ἰουδαῖος) is impossible without circumcision (*Ant* 20 § 38), but his mother warns him that his subjects will not tolerate rule by a king who is a Ἰουδαῖος (*Ant* 20 § 39).[8] In these passages, which speak about conversion to Judaism, the ethnic-geographic meaning of Ἰουδαῖος is entirely absent, and only a religious meaning is intended. A gentile can become a Ἰουδαῖος, a Jew.

---

[7] *Idumaeans*: The Idumaean contingent is explicitly grouped among the Ἰουδαῖοι in *JW* 6 § 148. It is Antigonus, not Josephus, who calls Herod "an Idumaean, that is, a half Jew" (*Ant* 14 § 403). Of course before the Hasmonean conquests the Idumaeans are not Ἰουδαῖοι (*Ant* 11 § 61; 12 § 327-328, 353). *Galileans*: Γαλιλαῖοι are Ἰουδαῖοι: *JW* 2 § 232 (but note that the parallel in *Ant* 20 § 118 makes no such implication); 3 § 229 (frequently in this section, beginning with 3 § 110, Josephus alternates between Ἰουδαῖοι and Γαλιλαῖοι); *Ant* 13 § 154 (Demetrius supposes that Jonathan will not let the Galileans be attacked because they are "his"; text somewhat shaky); 18 § 38 (the foundation of Tiberias violates the ancestral usages of the Ἰουδαῖοι); 20 § 43 (a Ἰουδαῖος from Galilee); *Life* § 74 (Ἰουδαῖοι live in Caesarea Philippi – or does Ἰουδαῖοι here mean "Judaeans"?); § 113 (Josephus refers to the Galileans as Ἰουδαῖοι). Γαλιλαῖοι are not Ἰουδαῖοι: *Ant* 20 § 120 (contrast between Γαλιλαῖοι and τὸ πλῆθος τῶν Ἰουδαίων); *Life* § 346 (Sepphoris forbade any of its citizens from serving with the Ἰουδαῖοι); § 349 (no city of Ἰουδαῖοι near Tiberias; cf. § 221 (Ἰουδαῖος probably means Judaean).

[8] Cf. "the king has become a Jew" (Ἰουδαῖος γέγονεν ὁ Βασιλεύς, Bel and the Dragon 28), and the deathbed promise of Antiochus Epiphanes that he would become a Jew (Ἰουδαῖον ἔσεσθαι) and proclaim the power of God (2 Macc 9:17).

The religious meaning is evident too in another passage (*Ant* 20 § 142), "He [Felix] sent to her [Drusilla] one of his friends, a Jew named Atomos, a Cyprian by birth [or: by nation, Κύπριον τὸ γένος]."[9] This is the only Josephan passage in which a person is said to be both a Ἰουδαῖος and a member τὸ γένος of an ethnic-geographic group (in this case, Cyprians). It is possible that Ἰουδαῖος here has a geographic meaning (Atomos is ethnically a Cyprian but is residing in Judaea), but surely it is much simpler to take Ἰουδαῖος as a religious term (Atomos is a Cyprian but a Jew). The passage, then, is analogous to Mark 7:26, "the woman was Greek, a Syro-Phoenician by birth (Ἑλληνίς, Συρο-φοινίκισσα τῷ γένει)." The term "Greek" Ἕλλην - Ἑλληνίς is no less ambiguous than Ἰουδαῖος, but the presence of an unambiguous ethnic-geographic term ("Syro-Phoenician") implies that "Greek" should be construed here as a religious term, meaning "pagan."

In many passages, of course, perhaps most, the religious meaning is present alongside the ethnic-geographic meaning, but the distinction is important nonetheless. In order to highlight the distinction between the ethnic-geographic and the religious uses of the term, I shall translate Ἰουδαῖος "Judaean" when the former meaning is paramount, and "Jew" when the latter is paramount.

To summarize: the Loeb translators give three different translations for the phrase Ἰουδαῖος τὸ γένος, but these three do not take into account the ambiguity of the word Ἰουδαῖος. The phrase might be translated in any of the following five ways:

a Jew by birth
a Jew by origin
a Judaean by birth
a Judaean by origin
a Judaean by nation

The last three of these are in turn rendered somewhat ambiguous because "Judaea" can have either a narrow or a broad meaning. I omit "a Jew by nation" (equivalent to the Loeb's "a Jew by race") because once we have distinguished between "Jews" (a religious term) and "Judaeans" (an ethnic-geographic term), the translation "a Jew by nation" becomes a logical impossibility. Jews did not constitute an ἔθνος, Judaeans did. The distinction between "Judaean by birth" and

---

[9] The text is somewhat uncertain: some testimonia read "one of his Jewish friends" (τῶν ἑαυτοῦ φίλων Ἰουδαίων) rather than "one of his friends, a Jew" (τῶν ἑαυτοῦ φίλων Ἰουδαῖον); some manuscripts read Σίμων instead of Ἄτομος.

"Judaean by nation" will be, in the vast majority of cases, insignificant. A "Judaean by birth" will be, in the vast majority of cases, a member of the Judaean ἔθνος, and a "Judaean by nation" will be, in the vast majority of cases, a Judaean by birth. The expressions are virtually synonymous, differing only in nuance.

II

The phrase Ἰουδαῖος τὸ γένος has many analogues in the Josephan corpus. Josephus regularly uses τὸ γένος (or τῷ γένει or γένει or γένος) in apposition to adjectives or proper nouns denoting origin. The origin being denoted is either (a) a country or ἔθνος, (b) a city or village, or (c) an Israelite tribe or group.

(a) τὸ γένος in apposition to adjectives or proper nouns denoting origin from a country or ἔθνος. This pattern is precisely parallel to Ἰουδαῖος τὸ γένος. Josephus speaks of individuals who τὸ γένος are:

Idumaean (*JW* 1 § 123; *Ant* 8 § 200; 15 § 253)

Spartan (*JW* 1 § 513)

Arab (*JW* 1 § 576)

Egyptian (*JW* 7 § 199; *Ant* 1 §§ 187, 220; 6 §§ 360-361; 7 § 315; *AgAp* 1 § 73; 2 § 138)

Syrian (*Ant* 6 § 244)

Amalekite (*Ant* 7 § 6; 11 §§ 209, 277)

Jebusite (*Ant* 7 § 330, cf. 7 § 61)

Israelite (*Ant* 8 § 76)

Hebrew (*Ant* 9 § 211)[10]

Ethiopian (*Ant* 10 § 122)

Cuthaean (*Ant* 11 § 302, cf. 13 § 255)

Parthian (*Ant* 20 § 81)

Cyprian (*Ant* 20 § 142)

Chaldaean (*AgAp* 1 § 129)

In addition, Josephus in the *Against Apion* refers several times to "Egyptians (plural) τὸ γένος" (1 §§ 252, 275, 298, 317; 2 §§ 8, 28).

(b) τὸ γένος in apposition to adjectives or proper nouns denoting

---

[10] I do not include in this corpus *JW* 1 § 3 which has Josephus describe himself as "a Hebrew by race" (γένει Ἐβραῖος), because the phrase is almost certainly an interpolation (it is unknown to Eusebius *Hist. eccl.* 3.9.1).

origin from a city or village.[11] Josephus speaks of individuals who τὸ γένος are:

Gerasene (*JW* 4 § 503)
Apamean (*Ant* 13 § 131)
Jerusalemite (*Ant* 17 § 78; 20 § 163)
Samarian (*Ant* 18 § 167)[12]
Nehardean (*Ant* 18 § 314)
Clazomenian (*Ant* 20 § 252)
Dabarittan (*Life* § 126)
Heliopolitan (*AgAp* 1 § 250, a quotation from Manetho; also § 265)

(c) τὸ γένος in apposition to adjectives or proper nouns denoting origin from an Israelite tribe or group. Josephus speaks of individuals who τὸ γένος are Benjaminites (*Ant* 7 § 47), Levites (*Ant* 7 § 83), priests (*Ant* 7 § 315; 10 § 80; cf. *JW* 4 § 225 and *AgAp* 1 § 54; see D.R. Schwartz 1981), and Naphtalites (*Ant* 8 § 76). Most striking is Josephus' repeated use of the phrase Ἐσσαῖος τὸ γένος (*JW* 1 § 78; 2 § 113 // *Ant* 17 § 346) or Ἐσσηνός τὸ γένος (*Ant* 13 § 311) to designate individual Essenes. The Essenes (*Ant* 13 § 172; 15 § 371; perhaps *JW* 2 § 160) constitute a γένος — Pliny the Elder calls them a *gens*.[13] What exactly this means is not clear, but is not my concern here.[14]

These passages reveal three important points. First, if Ἰουδαῖος τὸ γένος is indeed parallel τὸ γένος Ἰδουμαῖος and γένος Λακῶν and the other phrases collected above, Ἰουδαῖος must mean "Judaean" rather than "Jewish." Γένος refers to ethnic origin, or ethnic-geographic origin, not "religion." Elsewhere too Josephus uses γένος with ἐκ or ἀπό in an appositional phrase in order to indicate ethnic/geographic origin. For example, Niger was called "the Peraitan" because he was

---

[11] Cf. also πολίτιδος τὸ γένος (*Ant* 9 § 186) and ἀστῆς τὸ γένος (*Ant* 9 § 216, 260).

[12] The text is somewhat uncertain. Σαμαρεύς might mean "Samaritan" rather than "Samarian."

[13] Pliny, *Nat. hist.* 5.73 = Stern 1974-84: no. 204, . . . *Esseni . . . gens sola et in toto orbe praeter ceteras mira*. Stern comments, "Did Pliny or his source think of the Essenes as a special *gens*, separate from the Jewish nation though geographically included in Judaea . . . ? This view is perhaps echoed by Josephus, who finds it necessary to emphasize that the Essenes are Ἰουδαῖοι τὸ γένος (*JW* 2 § 119)." See below.

[14] Josephus also refers to the γένος of the Sadducees (*Ant* 13 § 297) and the γένος of the Zealots (*JW* 7 § 268), but never uses the phrase "a Sadducean τὸ γένος."

"by birth from Peraea beyond the Jordan" (γένος δ'ἦν ἐκ τῆς . . . Πε-
ραίας) (*JW* 2 § 566). In other words, he was Περαιτὴς τὸ γένος.[15]

Second, in virtually all of these passages the translations "by origin,"
"by birth" and "by nation" are equally possible. Although there is no
clear way to decide between them, I think that "by birth" is a somewhat more natural rendering, and in several passages "by birth" seems
preferable.[16] If there are no indications to the contrary I shall hence-
forth, for the sake of convenience and consistency, translate τὸ γένος
"by birth." This rendering is supported by *Ant* 10 § 237 which has
Belshazzar's grandmother tell her grandson that "there is a certain
captive from Judaea, who was born there (ἔστι τις ἀπὸ [or ἐκ]
τῆς Ἰουδαίας αἰχμάλωτος ἐκεῖθεν τὸ γένος) and was brought [to
Babylon] by Nebuchadnezzar when he sacked Jerusalem." Not only is
Daniel "from Judaea," but his γένος also is from there; in other
words, he was born there too. Josephus could have said ἔστι αἰχμά-
λωτός τις Ἰουδαῖος τὸ γένος and the meaning of the passage would
not have changed.[17]

Third, these passages demonstrate that generally the function of the
phrase τὸ γένος is to limit the scope of the identity indicated by the
ethnic noun. Daniel R. Schwartz has argued that Josephus uses the
phrase ἱερεὺς τὸ γένος to designate men who were priests by birth but
not priests by function, that is, men who were of priestly lineage but
who did not actually officiate as priests in the temple of Jerusalem.
Priests functioning in the temple would simply be called ἱερεῖς
(Schwartz 1981). Similarly, someone who is an "Idumaean by birth,"
is, in all likelihood, an Idumaean *only* by birth; by some other criterion
he either is not an Idumaean, or is no longer an Idumaean, or is not
behaving as an Idumaean might be expected to behave. In the *JW* 1 §
123, Josephus says that Antipater was "an Idumaean by birth (γένος
δ'ἦν Ἰδουμαῖος) who was one of the most prominent men of his
people (ἔθνος)." The qualification "by birth" prepares the reader for

---

[15] *JW* 1 § 432 (γένος ἦν ἐξ Ἱεροσολύμων); 5 § 532 (γένος ἐξ Ἀμμαοῦς); 6 § 54
(γένος ἀπὸ Συρίας); *Ant* 19 § 17 (ἐκ Κορδύβης . . . γένος).
[16] "Birth" clearly seems the preferable alternative in *Ant* 17 § 78 (cf. *JW* 1 §
432); 18 § 314; 20 § 163; *Life* § 126; cf. *AgAp* 1 § 250 and 265 (Manetho). In any
case in (b) above the translation "by nation" is unlikely, since cities do not
constitute ἔθνη.
[17] The phrase ἐκεῖθεν τὸ γενος is Josephus' addition to Daniel: 5.10,13; the
phrase is not found either in our Aramaic Daniel or in the Septuagint or in
Theodotion.

the fact that, when we meet him, Antipater is no longer active in Idumaea but is devoting all his time and attention to Judaean politics, specifically the interests of Hyrcanus against Aristobulus.[18] Similarly, Eurycles is called a "Spartan by birth" because when we meet him he is far from Sparta (*JW* 1 § 513). Corinthus was an "Arab by birth" but was brought up not in Arabia but in Herod's kingdom (*JW* 1 § 576). Rufus was "an Egyptian by birth," but is a Roman soldier (*JW* 7 § 199). And so on for the bulk of the passages listed above under (a), (b), and (c). Τὸ γένος indicates that the ethnic-geographic identity denoted by its apposite noun is offset at least to some degree by other considerations. These other considerations might be explicit or implicit. Of the thirteen Josephan passages with Ἰουδαῖος τὸ γένος, all except one (**9**) use τὸ γένος in this manner.

In contrast, in some passages τὸ γένος serves to strengthen the identity indicated by the ethnic noun. If you call someone an "Idumaean by birth," you might be suggesting that that person is a native Idumaean, that is, a *real* Idumaean, perhaps in contrast with others whose Idumaean-ness is questionable or has somehow been compromised. Costobar was "by birth an Idumaean" (*Ant* 15 § 253), a prominent member of his people, a governor of Idumaea (*Ant* 15 § 254), and an Idumaean patriot who resented the imposition of the customs of the Ἰουδαῖοι (*Ant* 15 § 255). In other words, he was a real Idumaean. Haman was an "Amalekite by birth," that is, a real Amalekite, "an alien among those of Persian blood" (*Ant* 11 § 277). The noblemen of Adiabene, tired of the Jewish ways of their king Izates, asked the Parthian king to kill Izates and to appoint in his stead a new ruler, "a Parthian by birth," that is, a real Parthian (*Ant* 20 § 81). Herod the Great removed the high-priesthood from his father-in-law Simon son of Boethus in order to bestow it on Matthias son of Theophilus, a "Jerusalemite by birth" (*Ant* 17 § 78). Matthias was a real Jerusalemite, unlike his predecessor who was a parvenu from Alexandria (*Ant* 15 §§ 319-322). In these cases τὸ γένος strengthens the ethnic-geographic identity denoted by its apposite noun, and that identity is not offset or compromised by other considerations. Of the thirteen Josephan passages with Ἰουδαῖος τὸ γένος, only one (**9**) uses τὸ γένος in this manner.

---

[18] The parallel in the *Ant* 14 § 8 omits τὸ γένος and simply calls Antipater an Idumaean, because that passage is interested in affirming Antipater's Idumaean identity (14 § 9).

III

I return to our thirteen Josephan passages. I shall re-translate each of them, translating Ἰουδαῖος τὸ γένος "Judaean by birth," and comment briefly on each passage.

1. *JW* 2 § 101: "At this time a young man who, though Judaean by birth (Ἰουδαῖος μὲν τὸ γένος), had been brought up at Sidon at the house of a Roman freedman . . . passed himself off as the prince Alexander." Paralleled by text **6** below. Τὸ γένος indicates that the Judaean-ness of the young man is offset by his Sidonian and Roman upbringing.

2. *JW* 2 § 119: "The followers . . . of the third [of the three schools of Jewish philosophy] are called Essenes . . . . They are Judaeans by birth (Ἰουδαῖοι μὲν γένος ὄντες), but they show a greater attachment to each other than do the others." The precise meaning of the phrase here is not entirely clear. Apparently Josephus means the following: although the Essenes are devoted to each other — more devoted to each other than are the followers of any other school[19] — nevertheless, at least by birth, they are Judaeans, that is, members of the ethnic community of Ἰουδαῖοι.[20]

3. *JW* 2 § 308: "For Florus ventured that day to do what none had ever done before, namely, to scourge before his tribunal and nail to the cross men of equestrian status (ἄνδρας ἱππικοῦ τάγματος), men whose birth may have been Judaean but whose dignity nevertheless was Roman (εἰ καὶ τὸ γένος Ἰουδαῖον ἀλλὰ γοῦν τὸ ἀξίωμα Ῥομαικὸν ἦν). The contrast between Ἰουδαῖον and Ῥομαικόν makes certain the rendering of the former as "Judaean." Judaean birth and Roman rank offset each other. Γένος here clearly means birth; γένος meaning "birth," and ἀξίωμα meaning "dignity" or "rank," form a pair also in *JW* 4 § 358 and 4 § 416.[21]

---

[19] Taken by itself the sentence could be translated "they show a greater attachment to each other than the other Ἰουδαῖοι show to each other," but *JW* 2 § 166 implies that "the others" are the Pharisees and the Sadducees.

[20] It is most unlikely that Ἰουδαῖοι here means "Jews," for what sense is there to say that the Essenes are Jews by birth? Beall (1988: 37) thinks that the phrase implies that "the Essenes did not permit any non-Jew to become a member of the sect." This is far from the simple meaning of the text. See note 13 above for Stern's comment on the passage, but Stern too ignores the structure of the sentence.

[21] Feldman (1992a: 7 n. 18) correctly translates γένος in our passage as "birth," but supports that translation with an incorrect argument: γένος cannot mean nation here because "clearly neither Josephus nor Florus would grant that these

4. *Ant* 11 § 207: "Some time afterward Bagathoos and Theodestes plotted against the king, but Barnabazos, the servant of one of these eunuchs, who was a Judaean by birth (τὸ γένος ὢν Ἰουδαῖος), discovered their plot." The Judaean-ness of Barnabazos (an invented character not in the book of Esther) is offset by his Persian name, his residence in Susa, and his status as a slave.

5. *Ant* 17 § 141: "This Acme was Judaean by birth (Ἰουδαία μὲν τὸ γένος) but a slave of Caesar's wife Julia." Acme's Judaean-ness is offset by her Greek name, her residence in Rome, and her status as a slave.

6. *Ant* 17 § 324: "After these matters had been disposed of by Caesar, there appeared a young man, a Judaean by birth (Ἰουδαῖος μὲν τὸ γένος) but brought up in the city of Sidon by a Roman freedman, who represented himself as related to Herod." See text **1** above.

7. *Ant* 18 § 103: "Artabanus sent as a hostage to Tiberius his son Darius, together with many gifts, among which he included a man seven cubits tall, a Judaean by birth (Ἰουδαῖον τὸ γένος), named Eleazar, who on account of his size was called the Giant."[22] Eleazar's Judaean-ness is offset by his geographic setting: he is being sent from Parthia to Rome.

8. *Ant* 18 § 196: "[One of Agrippa's fellow prisoners sees Agrippa and inquires as to his identity.] Upon learning that his name was Agrippa, that he was a Judaean by birth (Ἰουδαῖον δὲ τὸ γένος), and that he was one of the most notable men there, he asked the soldier . . . to allow him to approach." Here Ἰουδαῖος must mean "Judaean," because it provides the antecedent reference for "there" (ἐκείνη); the translator in the Loeb edition, taking Ἰουδαῖος to mean "Jew," had to supply the phrase "of Judaea" to translate "there." Agrippa's Judaean-ness is offset by the fact that at that moment he was a prisoner in Rome.

9. *Ant* 20 § 173: "There arose also a quarrel between the Judaean and Syrian inhabitants of Caesarea on the subject of equal civic rights.

---

equestrians were members of a Jewish nation." This is wrong; they were by birth members of a Jewish (that is, Judaean) nation, the ἔθνος of the Ἰουδαῖοι.

[22] This giant may also be mentioned by Columella 3.8.2 = Stern 1974-84: no. 185, "recently we ourselves might have seen, among the exhibits of the procession at the games of the Circus, a man of the Jewish race (*Iudaeae gentis*) who was of greater stature than the tallest German" (LCL translation). See Solin 1983: 601-602.

The Judaeans claimed that they had the precedence because the founder of Caesarea, their king Herod, had been Judaean by birth ('Ηρώδην αὐτῶν βασιλέα γεγονέναι τὸ γένος Ἰουδαῖον); the Syrians admitted what they said about Herod, but asserted . . . ." The struggle is not between Jews and Syrians but between Judaeans and Syrians. The Judaeans claim Herod as one of their own; he was, they say, a native Judaean, that is, a real Judaean. Not only was Herod "king of the Ἰουδαῖοι" (*Ant* 15 § 409 and elsewhere), he was a Ἰουδαῖος himself.[23] It is somewhat surprising to find Judaeans loudly claiming Herod as one of their own, given the ambiguous relationship of the Ἰουδαῖοι to the Idumaeans in general and Herod in particular, but in order to win their debate they put aside whatever doubts they may still have harbored about the dead king. It is somewhat suprising to find Syrians readily conceding that Herod was a Judaean, given the fact that Herod was of Idumaean origin, but perhaps outsiders were not well informed about the ethnic sub-divisions within the ethnos of the Ἰουδαῖοι.[24]

10. *Life* § 16: "Landing safely at Dicaearchia, which the Italians call Puteoli, I formed a friendship with Aliturus, an actor (μιμολόγος) who was a special favorite of Nero and a Judaean by birth Ἰουδαῖος τὸ γένος)." The Judaean-ness of Aliturus is offset by his residence in Italy and perhaps by his name.

11. *Life* § 382: "The king [Agrippa] promised to come [to the aid of Tiberias], writing a letter in reply, which he handed to a man named Crispus, a Judaean by birth (Κρίσπῳ μὲν τοὔνομα, τὸ δὲ γένος Ἰουδαίῳ), a groom of the bedchamber." The force of the phrase here is not clear. Perhaps Josephus means that Crispus was born in Judaea in the narrow sense, but was now active in Galilee. Other passages too in the *Life* contrast Galileans with Judaeans.[25] Or perhaps — I think this explanation is more likely — Josephus means that the foreign name Crispus should not obscure the fact that he was a Judaean (whether in the narrow sense or the wide sense) by birth. Compare the case of Aliturus, just discussed. Compare too *JW* 6 § 54, a reference to a man "named Sabinus, by birth from Syria" (Σαβῖνος τοὔνομα, γένος ἀπὸ Συρίας). Sabinus is an unlikely name for a Syrian, but, Josephus insists, he was a Syrian ("from Syria") native.

---

[23] The parallel in *JW* 2 § 266 omits τὸ γένος and the emphasis.

[24] Tomson (1986: 124 n. 13) observes that Plutarch too calls Herod ὁ Ἰουδαῖος (*Life of Antony* 61.3 and 71.1 = Stern 1974-84 nos. 267 and 268).

[25] See note 7 above.

12. *Life* § 427: "Afterwards I [Josephus] married a woman, a Judaean by birth (τὸ δὲ γένος Ἰουδαίαν) who had settled in Crete. She came of very distinguished parents, indeed the most notable people in that country." The woman's Judaean-ness is offset by her residence in Crete. Her parents were distinguished Judaeans in Crete.

13. *AgAp* 1 §§ 178-179: "'Well,' said Aristotle, 'in accordance with the precepts of rhetoric, let us begin by describing his nationality (or: his birth, τὸ γένος αὐτοῦ) . . . the man was from Coele-Syria, a Judaean by birth (τὸ μὲν γένος ἦν Ἰουδαῖος ἐκ τῆς κοίλης Συρίας). They are descended from the Indian philosophers. The philosophers, they say, are in India called Calani, in Syria Ἰουδαῖοι, taking this name from the place (παρὰ δὲ Σύροις Ἰουδαῖοι, τοὔνομα λαβόντες ἀπὸ τοῦ τόπου); for the district which they inhabit is known as Judaea.'" The near equation of "birth" and "nation," each called γένος, is clear in this passage. The meaning Judaean for Ἰουδαῖος is also clear. The man who so impressed Aristotle had been born in Judaea but was travelling in Asia Minor.

IV

As promised, my conclusions are rather modest. I have argued that the Josephan phrase Ἰουδαῖος τὸ γένος should always be translated "Judaean by birth." The difficult part of the phrase is not τὸ γένος, for whether it is translated "by birth" or "by nation" its meaning is more or less the same. The difficult part is the word Ἰουδαῖος, usually translated "Jew," but which often has an ethnic-geographic meaning best captured by the word "Judaean." Of course, with few exceptions virtually all "Judaeans" will have been "Jews," and most "Jews" in Judaea will have been "Judaeans," that is, members of the ethnic-geographic polity of Judaeans.[26] Thus, the practical consequences of the distinction between "Judaean" and "Jew" may not have been great, but the exegetical consequences are significant.

When Josephus calls someone "Judaean by birth," he does not mean that the person was "Jewish," that is, a follower of Judaism. Rather he means that the person was born in Judaea. There is no reason to assume that any of the people called Ἰουδαῖος τὸ γένος

---

[26] Whether "Jews" in the diaspora will have been "Judaeans," that is, members of the ethnic communities of people hailing from Judaea, will have varied from place to place, depending on the nature of local communal organization.

were born outside of Judaea (broadly conceived). In nine or ten of our thirteen passages, the location of birth seems to be the main point of the phrase: education or activity outside of Judaea should not obscure Judaean birth (**1,4,5,6,7,8,10,11?,12,13**).[27] Ἰουδαῖος is not (and, as far as I have been able to determine, never was) a purely geographic term (Solin 1983: 647; Cohen 1990), but in these nine (ten?) passages the geographic component of the phrase is paramount. In the remaining three passages the ethnic component of the phrase is paramount: the Essenes (**2**), the men punished by Florus (**3**), and Herod the Great (**9**) were all "Judaeans by birth," that is, members by birth of the ethnic community of the Ἰουδαῖοι. There is no reason to think that any of these ethnic-geographic Judaeans were not also Jews, but their religion is not relevant to Josephus' use of the phrase.[28]

The ethnic-geographic usage of Ἰουδαῖος τὸ γένος is Hellenistic: it is attested in Clearchus c. 300 BCE (**13**) and in two inscriptions from Delphi from the second quarter of the second century BCE.[29] In the Hellenistic period this usage is not surprising since before the Macca- bees Ἰουδαῖος was exclusively an ethnic-geographic term; the citizens of Judaea did not yet conceive of "Judaism" as a religion and Ἰουδαῖος had not yet evolved to the meaning "Jew" (Cohen 1990). But by the Roman period the religious connotations of the word Ἰουδαῖος will have been known to all. By the sixth century CE Ἰουδαῖος became exclusively a religious term, and we find such expressions as "a Jew by religion" and (in contrast) "Hebrew by

---

[27] The meaning and force of the phrase in **11** are obscure. Barnabazos has a Persian name, perhaps suggesting that Josephus imagined him to have been born in Persia (**4**); if this is correct, then Ἰουδαῖος τὸ γένος here must mean "a member of the ἔθνος of Ἰουδαῖοι" (cf. *Ant* 11 § 198). But there is no compelling reason to reject the interpretation "a native of Judaea" even here. Artabanus sent a giant to Tiberius as a gift; I suppose that the most natural assumption is that the giant was a native of Parthia, but the name Eleazar strongly suggests that he was a native of Judaea (**7**). Was the actor Aliturus a native of Italy or Judaea (**10**)? I think the latter is more likely; cf. Acme (**5**), hardly a native of Italy.

[28] Thus among those misled by the translation "Jew by birth" are Beall 1988 (see above) and Williams 1990: 199 (". . . Jews from birth, people whom Josephus regularly calls Ἰουδαῖοι τὸ γένος").

[29] *CIJ* nos. 709 and 710: a woman and a man being sold as slaves are described as τὸ γένος Ἰουδαῖον/Ἰουδαίαν. Here too the translation "Judaean by birth/nation" seems best (contrast Tomson 1986: 125 n. 19). The inscriptions "possibly relate to prisoners of war from the Maccabean period, sold as slaves and taken to Greece"; see Millar apud Schürer 1973-87: 3.1.65.

nation."[30] Josephus too uses the word to mean "Jew," even where no ethnic or geographic component is present (see above). Thus in the first century CE the phrase Ἰουδαῖος τὸ γένος should have meant "a Jew by birth." Josephus' near contemporary, the author of 3 Macca-bees, describes Dositheus son of Drimylus as "a Jew by birth (τὸ γένος Ἰουδαῖος) who later changed his customs (νόμιμα) and became es-tranged from his ancestral doctrines (δόγματα)" (3 Macc 1:3). Here Ἰουδαῖος means "Jew" (perhaps also "Judaean"): Dositheus was a Jew by birth but not by practice or belief. But Josephus does not use the phrase Ἰουδαῖος τὸ γένος to mean "Jew by birth." When he wishes to describe an "apostate," he avoids the phrase τὸ γένος Ἰουδαῖος. "The successor of Fadus was Tiberius Alexander, the son of that Alexander who . . . surpassed all his fellow citizens both in ancestry and in wealth. He was also superior to his son Alexander in his religious devotion, for the latter did not stand by the practices of his people" (*Ant* 20 § 100). In other words, like Dositheus son of Drimylus, Tiberius Alexander was a Jew by birth but not by practice or belief. Josephus might have called Tiberius Alexander Ἰουδαῖος τὸ γένος but did not, because for Josephus the phrase still had its Hellenistic meaning "Judaean by birth" rather than "Jewish by birth." Why Josephus retained this archaic usage, I do not know.

Various Israeli scholars have suggested that Josephus in the *War* conceived of Judaism (or Jewishness) in national political terms, while in the *Antiquities* and his other late works he conceived of it in religious terms (Schwartz 1987: 66). Whether this analysis is correct is not my concern here, but I note that the phrase Ἰουδαῖος τὸ γένος retains its meaning unchanged from Josephus' earliest work (the early books of the *War*) to his latest (late books of the *Antiquities*, *Life*, and *AgAp*). We may be sure that Josephus' views on many subjects changed during the twenty or twenty-five years of his literary career, but regarding the notion of Judaean-ness by birth, his views changed not at all.[31]

---

[30] "A Jew by religion": *CPJ* 3 no. 508 (Ἰουδαῖος τὴν θρησκείαν, 542 CE); Suda, s.v. Καικίλιος = Jacoby, FGrH 183 T 1 (τὴν δὲ δόξαν Ἰουδαῖος). "Hebrew by nation": *CPJ* 3 no. 511 (Ἑβραῖος τῷ ἔθνει, c. 570 CE).

[31] I could not have written this paper without the assistance of *A Complete Concordance to Flavius Josephus* (Rengstorf et al. 1973-1983). All translations of Josephus, unless otherwise indicated, are from the Loeb Classical Library, whose editors and translators are Henry St. J. Thackeray, Ralph Marcus, Allen Wikgren, and Louis H. Feldman.

PART II

THE SOURCES

JOSEPHUS' PORTRAYAL OF THE HASMONEANS COMPARED WITH 1 MACCABEES

Louis H. Feldman

1. *Introduction*

If we wish to study Josephus' historiographical goals and methods we are most likely to achieve satisfactory results when we compare him to his known sources. Unfortunately, for the most recent period of his history, sources such as Nicolaus of Damascus are largely lost. Hence, our best avenue of investigation would seem to be to compare Josephus' paraphrase of the Bible[1], the Letter of Aristeas (Pelletier 1962) and 1 Maccabees, where it is clear what his source is, though, of course, we can never be sure of the exact text that he used. Despite the fact that there have been a number of attempts to compare Josephus' account with that of 1 Maccabees,[2] these have been concerned primarily with determining which text, whether Greek or Hebrew, he employed,[3] or with discussing which sources other than 1

---

[1] See Feldman 1968b, 1988a, 1968a, 1984a, 1984-95, 1988-89, 1992e, 1991-92, 1989b, 1986, 1988b, 1992g, 1982, 1989a, 1976, 1992b, 1992d, 1992a, 1992c, 1992f, 1970, and 1988c.

[2] See, in particular, Grimm 1853, Bloch 1879, von Destinon 1882, Büchler 1896, Drüner 1896, Hölscher 1904, Ettelson 1925, Cadbury 1927, Momigliano 1930, Melamed 1951, Levenson 1966, Goldstein 1976, and Gafni 1980.

[3] Josephus was undoubtedly attracted to using a Greek text for his paraphrase of the Bible inasmuch as he was writing in Greek; but the very fact that Josephus sought assistants (*AgAp* 1 § 50) to help him with his Greek style when he wrote his *War* and that he admits (*Ant* 20 § 263) that despite laboring strenuously to master Greek literature, he had failed to attain precision in the pronunciation of Greek because of his habitual use of his native Aramaic, should lead us to suspect that he felt more at home in Hebrew and in Aramaic than in Greek. Moreover, the fact that he chose to paraphrase the Bible in Greek would seem to indicate that he hoped to improve on the rendering in the Septuagint. For the Pentateuch, at least, there is strong evidence, as I have indicated, that his main source was a Hebrew text and/or a targumic paraphrase in Aramaic, whereas for the other books of the Bible, he is generally aligned with the Septuagint in the proto-Lucianic version. See Feldman 1988c: 460-66. For the account of the Hasmoneans Josephus apparently relied exclusively, or at least almost exclusively, upon the Greek text, despite the attempts of Perles 1921: 179; Schwabe and Melamed 1928:

Maccabees Josephus employed, or with comparing the general outlook of the two works, or citing places where Josephus shows verbal dependence upon 1 Maccabees, or simply listing a selection of passages where Josephus departs from 1 Maccabees, rather than, as in the present essay, comparing the actual portrayals of the Hasmoneans themselves.

There are those who deny any independent value to Josephus' account of the Hasmoneans;[4] but, we may suggest, while it is true that the author of 1 Maccabees was closest to the events and perhaps even participated in some of them, Josephus was a descendant of the Hasmoneans and undoubtedly had oral traditions about the earlier family tradition; moreover, as a non-participant, he was more objective, as we shall see, than the author of 1 Maccabees. In addition, as a priest, he often appears to supplement from personal knowledge, as

---

202-4; Melamed 1951: 122-30; Drüner 1896: 35-50; Ettelson 1925: 340-41; and Zeitlin 1950: 57-58, among others, to indicate that he also used the Hebrew text. As Bar-Kochva 1989: 193, has stressed, the differences between Josephus and the Greek text of 1 Maccabees can be explained by Josephus' tendency to simplify or to adapt the account for the needs of his Greek and Roman readers; indeed, as Thackeray 1905: 464 and Bar-Kochva 1989: 339, have noted, Josephus often has the same corruptions that are found in the Greek text of 1 Maccabees. Another explanation, we may suggest, for coincidences between Josephus and a Hebrew text of 1 Maccabees may be that the Greek text of 1 Maccabees available to Josephus was different from ours, just as, for example, the new fragments from the Dead Sea caves illustrate that their Greek text of Samuel was closer to our Hebrew text.

[4] E.g., Ranovič 1950; German trans. 1958, 114. On the contrary, Josephus' version is sometimes of considerable value. Thus, he sometimes (e.g. *Ant* 12 § 411, cf. 1 Macc 7:46; *Ant* 13 § 21, cf. 1 Macc 9:40; *Ant* 13 § 161, cf. 1 Macc 11:69) gives us numbers not found in 1 Maccabees, or he disagrees (e.g. *Ant* 12 § 408, cf. 1 Macc 7:40; *Ant* 12 § 422, cf. 1 Macc 9:5; *Ant* 13 § 14, cf. 1 Macc 9:49; *Ant* 13 § 163, cf. 1 Macc 11:74) with its numbers. Moreover, he gives us other precise information not found in 1 Maccabees, such as the name of the officer, Apelles, slain by Mattathias (*Ant* 12 § 270, cf. 1 Macc 2:25). Furthermore, if not for Josephus (*Ant* 12 §§ 257-64) we would not know of the Samaritan appeal to Antiochus Epiphanes. Nor, if not for Josephus (*Ant* 12 § 405), would we know that Judah Maccabee was defeated by Nicanor at Kapharsalama, rather than the reverse, as implied in 1 Macc 7:31-32, unless we adopt Dindorf's emendation of Josephus. Josephus' brief summary at the beginning of the *Jewish War* contains a number of errors on essential points, as Hölscher 1904: 4-5 and Goldstein 1976: 60, have noted; and yet, as Bar-Kochva 1989: 186, has remarked, even that summary (*JW* 1 §§ 41-46) is of considerable value for reconstructing the battle of Beth-Zechariah, since it accords very well with the military and topographical possibilities.

well as from family tradition, in matters concerning the priesthood (since the Maccabees were priests) and the Temple. Moreover, as Dancy (1954: 29-31), Abel-Starcky (1961: 9), and Stern (1965: 7-11; repr. 1980: 37-48) among others, have contended, Josephus may also have used as sources the works of Nicolaus of Damascus, and, to a lesser degree, Polybius, Diodorus, Posidonius, Aristeas, Timagenes, and a narrative describing the founding of the temple of Onias. Büchler (1986), von Destinon (1882: 60ff.), and Hölscher (1904: 52) have argued that for the opening chapters of the *War*, at least, Josephus utilized neither 1 nor 2 Maccabees but an unknown source.

As a measure of the importance for Josephus of the material in 1 Maccabees about the Hasmoneans we may note that he devotes 2015 lines (*Ant* 12 §§ 237-256, 265; 13 §§ 61; 80-108, 121-134, 145-170, 174-214) in the Loeb Classical Library text to the material which he parallels in 1 Maccabees (1:1-13:42). This gives a ratio of 1.30 of Josephus to the Greek text of 1 Maccabees. To appreciate the significance which Josephus attached to this account we may note that the ratio of Josephus' account to the Greek text of the LXX for Nehemiah is only .18, .55 for Gideon, .65 for Hezekiah, .68 for Daniel, .72 for Elisha, .72 for Ezra, .89 for Samson, .96 for Elijah, 1.02 for Abraham, 1.14 for Absalom, 1.15 for Josiah, 1.16 for Samuel, 1.22 for Jehu, 1.28 for Ahab, and 1.29 for Jeroboam. It is higher only for David (1.34), for Jehoshaphat (1.36), for Balaam (1.39), for Joseph (1.47), for Jehoram of Israel (1.49), and for Saul (1.71).

2. *The Hasmoneans as Leaders*

In his portrait of the Hasmoneans Josephus places the emphasis upon the importance of leadership. Indeed, throughout the first half of the *Antiquities*, where he parallels the Bible, one of Josephus' major goals is to build up the characters of the major Biblical heroes, perhaps in response to the charge (*AgAp* 2 § 135) that the Jews had failed to produce any geniuses. That one of the major purposes of the *Antiquities* was to build up the Biblical personalities in answer to this canard is clear from Josephus' own statement (*AgAp* 1 § 36) that "our own famous men are deserving of winning no less praise" than the great heroes produced by the Greeks. Consequently, Josephus, in a series of purple passages, proceeds to build up the great Biblical heroes.[5]He here follows Thucydides, Plato, and the Peripatetic tradition[6] (indeed, his chief source after he ceases to employ 1 Maccabees, and, to some extent, perhaps even while he is using 1 Maccabees is Nicolaus of Damascus, a well-known Peripatetic) in stressing the role of great men in history.

2.1 *Mattathias*

In Josephus' narrative each of the Hasmoneans is built up as a personality beyond the account in 1 Maccabees. Thus we see the aggrandizement of Mattathias (*Ant* 12 § 278), who, in a statement that has no parallel in 1 Macc 2:46-48, is described as driving out the officers who had been appointed to prevent the circumcision of Jewish boys. Furthermore, there is no indication in 1 Maccabees as to the length of time that Mattathias led the fight against the Syrian Greeks; Josephus (*Ant* 12 § 279), on the other hand, has him in command for a respectable period of a year.

One of the questions that must have occurred to those conversant with the events was who appointed Mattathias to be the leader of the Jews. From the text of 1 Macc 2:17 we know only that Mattathias is a leader in his town of Modin. Josephus (*Ant* 12 § 275) makes it clear that Mattathias was appointed to be leader by his followers. Indeed, in the *War* (1 § 37) Josephus is even more explicit in stating that Mattathias' expulsion of the foreigners led his countrymen willingly to submit to his rulership.

Mattathias, in turn, exercises leadership (*Ant* 12 § 276) by instructing his men to fight even on the Sabbath; in 1 Macc 2:40-41 the decision is much more vague, being ascribed to Mattathias and his friends. In his long farewell address (245 words) to his sons as he lay dying, Mattathias in 1 Macc 2:49-68 reviews Jewish history from Abraham to Daniel, stressing their faithfulness to the Law in time of trial; Josephus (*Ant* 12 §§ 279-284), in an address almost as long (209 words) spends no time reviewing Jewish history but rather, unabashedly, urges his sons to follow in his own spirit. The scene is clearly reminiscent of that in which Aeneas (Virgil *Aen.* 12.435-440) bids

---

[5] See my essays on Josephus' portraits of Abraham, Jacob, Joseph, Moses, Joshua, Samson, Saul, David, and Solomon (above, n. 1), among others.

[6] See my essay on Saul 1982: 46-48.

farewell to his son Ascanius before going off to his final battle with Turnus; there, too, the father tells the son to learn from and be inspired by the example of him, the father.[7]

2.1.1 *The Goals of the Hasmoneans: Liberty*

Josephus portrays the Hasmoneans as devoted to the very ideals which were most important for the Romans, namely liberty, country, laws, and piety, and the readiness to die for these ideals. That liberty was a key concept for the Romans may be seen in the fact that when the conspirators to assassinate the Emperor Gaius Caligula choose a password (*Ant* 19 § 54), the word they select is "liberty" (ἐλευθερία). Josephus goes out of his way to stress the Jews' devotion to the ideal of liberty, as we see, for example, in the great effort (*Ant* 2 § 290) which Moses devotes to procuring his people's liberty from the oppressive Egyptians. Indeed, when the Israelites angrily complain against him because of their lack of food and water in the desert Moses (*Ant* 3 § 19) answers them by declaring that it was not from negligence that G-d had thus tarried in helping them but rather to test their manhood and their delight in liberty (τῆς περὶ τὴν ἐλευθερίαν ἡδονῆς).

Indeed, almost at the very beginning of his account of the Hasmoneans, Josephus (*Ant* 12 § 267) has the patriarch of the family, Mattathias, declare that it is better for him and his sons to die for their country's laws than to live ingloriously, whereas in 1 Macc 2:13 there is no mention of the cause of the country's laws, and Mattathias and his sons merely put on sackcloth and mourn bitterly. Likewise, when Mattathias issues the call to rebellion, in 1 Macc 2:27 he shouts, "Let everyone who is zealous for the Law and would maintain the covenant follow me." In Josephus (*Ant* 12 § 271) the emphasis is on patriotism when he says, "Whoever is zealous for our country's customs (τῶν πατρίων ἐθῶν) and the worship of G-d let him follow me." Grimm (1853: XXVIII-XXX) perceptively suggests that Josephus is here echoing the kind of patriotic appeal found in Livy (12.53), "Qui rempublicam salvam volunt me sequantur," which would certainly appeal to his Roman readers. Again, in his farewell address to his sons, Mattathias

---

[7] As to whether Josephus might have known the works of Virgil or Latin literature in general, we may note that he does mention Livy on one occasion (*Ant* 14 § 68). As to his knowledge of Latin see Thackeray 1929: 119-20; Nadel 1966: 256-72; and Daube 1977a: 191-4.

in 1 Macc 2:49-68 delivers a history lesson noting, one by one, the patriarchs who had received personal rewards for their zeal for the Law. In Josephus' version Mattathias (*Ant* 12 §§ 281-282), in words that would have been appreciated by patriotic Romans, for whom the highest bliss was to die for one's country, urges his sons to be prepared not merely as in 1 Maccabees to trust in G-d but to die for the laws and declares that G-d will give them not personal rewards but national liberty in admiration for their heroism: ἀρετή (a word which was crucial for the Greek code of behavior but which is missing in 1 Maccabees). The cause (*Ant* 12 § 280), in a passage that would have reminded readers of the preface to Livy's history, is "to restore our ancient form of government" (τὴν ἀρχαίαν πολιτείαν ἀνακτᾶσθαι). The famous words of Ennius come to mind: "Moribus antiquis res stat Romana viresque" (*Annals* 5.156[500]). Moreover, Mattathias' address introduces a philosophical note (*Ant* 12 § 282), which would have appealed particularly to Stoics in his audience, namely that through the memory of one's deeds one can attain the heights of immortality.

Again, whereas in Judah's address to his men at Emmaus, according to 1 Macc 3:58-60 there is mention only of the Temple but not of liberty for which they are fighting, Josephus' version (*Ant* 12 §§ 302-303) speaks of the goal of recovering liberty (ἐλευθερία), "which is loved for its own sake by all men, but to you most of all happens to be desirable because it gives you the right to worship the Deity." Now, says Judah, it is within their power to regain this liberty and consequently to live a happy and blessed life. This is particularly striking because one would have expected Josephus, who is so proud of his priestly status, to emphasize, as does 1 Maccabees, the Temple and, indeed, to be wary of mentioning the goal of liberty, since this would seem to imply, in his own day at least, revolt against the Romans. But for Josephus, liberty, as here defined (*Ant* 12 § 303), is life in accordance with the laws and customs of the fathers; and hence this would be different from the goal of political liberty of the Fourth Philosophy (*Ant* 18 § 23) and would not be regarded as subversive by Romans in his reading audience.

This emphasis on liberty may also be seen in Josephus' version of the battle at Emmaus. According to 1 Macc 4:25, Israel had a great deliverance (σωτηρία μεγάλη) on that day; in Josephus' version the victory "contributed not a little to the regaining of their liberty (πρὸς τὴν ἐλευθερίαν συνεβάλλετο, *Ant* 12 § 312)." Likewise, in the battle at

Beth-Zur, in 1 Macc 4:35, the Syrian general Lysias observes how ready Judah's soldiers are either to live or to die nobly, whereas Josephus (*Ant* 12 § 315) adds the key phrase that they are ready to die if they cannot live as free men (ἐλεύθεροι). When Judah finally falls in battle, 1 Macc 9:21 laments him as "the mighty savior of Israel," but Josephus (*Ant* 12 § 433) eulogizes him as a valiant man and a great warrior who had had the fortitude to do and suffer all things for the liberty of his fellow-citizens. Again, when, after Judah's death, his companions beg his brother Jonathan to assume the mantle of leadership, they recall Judah (*Ant* 13 § 5) as one who, in his concern for his countrymen, had died on behalf of the liberty of them all.

2.1.2 *The Goals of the Hasmoneans: Martyrdom*

In particular, Josephus (*Ant* 12 § 304) advocates martyrdom. Whereas the corresponding passage in Judah's address to his men at Emmaus (1 Macc 3:59) likewise indicates a preference for death in battle rather than to look upon the tragedies of "our nation and our sanctuary," Josephus adds a practical reason for preferring martyrdom, namely that death is the portion even of those who do not fight, as well as a philosophic reason for martyrdom, namely that it will gain eternal glory for the martyr.

When Judah enters his final battle against Bacchides, and his men (*Ant* 12 § 422), dismayed at being so vastly outnumbered, abandon him, he strikes the pose of a martyr (*Ant* 12 § 425) who valiantly endures all things rather than flee. Indeed, in his encomium for Judah, Josephus (*Ant* 12 § 433) says that he suffered all things for the liberty of his fellow-citizens. Finally, when Judah's followers approach his brother Jonathan to succeed him (*Ant* 13 §§ 5-6) they recall that in his concern for his countrymen he had died on behalf of the liberty of them all, whereupon Jonathan assures them that he, too, is ready to die for them.

2.1.3 *Opposition to Zealotry and Disunity*

We may note that the key feature in Josephus' remolding of the character of Elijah is his elimination of the features of a Zealot. Thus, most notably, whereas in the Bible (1 Kgs 18:40) after his victory in the contest with the priests of Baal he tells the Israelites to seize the prophets of Baal, and he himself kills them, in Josephus (*Ant* 8 § 343) it is not Elijah but the Israelites who kill the prophets of Baal.[8] Again, when Elijah, fleeing from Queen Jezebel, takes refuge in a cave and a voice (1 Kgs 19:9) asks him why he has done so, his biblical answer (1 Kgs 19:10) is that he has been very zealous (קַנֹּא קִנֵּאתִי) for the Lord; but in Josephus (*Ant* 8 § 350) he makes no mention of his zealotry. Once again, when, according to the biblical version (1 Kgs 19:14), the still small voice asks Elijah what he is doing, he replies that he has been very zealous (קַנֹּא קִנֵּאתִי) for the L-rd. He then, zealot that he is, bitterly proceeds to indict the people of Israel as having forsaken the covenant, thrown down G-d's altars, and slain the prophets. All this is omitted in Josephus' version (*Ant* 8 § 352). In Josephus the divine voice exhorts the prophet not to be alarmed and assures him that none of his enemies will succeed in getting him within their power.

Similarly, one of the problems that confronted Josephus in dealing with the Hasmoneans was that they seemed to be the ancestors of the revolutionary Zealots of his own day,[9] whom he so hated and despised. Hence, whereas in 1 Macc 2:24 when Mattathias sees a Jew coming forward to sacrifice to the pagan gods, he is filled with zeal (ἐζήλωσεν), in Josephus' version the zeal is changed to rage (θυμωθείς) (*Ant* 12 § 270). Again, whereas in 1 Macc 2:26 Mattathias, by killing this Jew, is said to show his zeal (ἐζήλωσεν) for the Law and is compared to the great prototype of zealotry, Phinehas, and then shouts that everyone who is zealous (ζηλῶν) for the Law should follow him, in Josephus' version (*Ant* 12 §§ 270-271), significantly, the reference to Phinehas is omitted and the word zealous (ζηλωτής) occurs only once (*Ant* 12 § 271), and there with reference to zeal for the ancestral customs (πατρίων ἐθῶν).

Hence, Josephus, as Gafni (1980: 125) has remarked, has been careful to depict the Hasmonean uprising as a "just war" against those who had defiled the name of G-d, in contrast to the unjust war waged

---

[8] There is, to be sure, an inconsistency in Josephus in that when Elijah (*Ant* 8 § 350), upon entering a cave, is asked why he had left the city, replies that he has done so because he has killed the prophets of Baal and is consequently being pursued by Queen Jezebel.

[9] Indeed, Farmer (1956) argues, to be sure unpersuasively, that the Jewish nationalists of his own day were not only counterparts of the Maccabees but that they deliberately modeled themselves upon them. In particular, we may remark that the Hasmoneans sought both religious and political liberty, whereas the all-consuming goal of the Zealots was political independence. Again, the Hasmoneans lacked the eschatological drive of the Zealots.

by the revolutionaries of his own day. A just war, as Josephus (*AgAp* 2 § 272) defines it, is not "for self-aggrandizement but in order to preserve our laws and willingness to die therefor." Likewise, whereas, in Mattathias' dying charge to his sons (1 Macc 2:50), he bids them to be zealous for the Law (ζηλώσατε τῷ νόμῳ) Josephus (*Ant* 12 § 280) avoids mention of zeal and instead tells them "to preserve our country's customs and to restore our ancient form of government." There also (1 Macc 2:54) he cites the example of Phinehas as being zealous in his zeal (ζηλῶσαι ζῆλον); whereas Josephus omits all mention of Phinehas. Likewise, in stating that Judah turned wrath from Israel, 1 Macc 3:8 is clearly recalling the picture of Phinehas (Num 25:11), who "turned back my wrath from the people of Israel"; and here again Josephus (*Ant* 12 § 286) avoids this phraseology and is content to say that Judah made an end of those of his countrymen who had violated their fathers' laws and purified the land of all pollution.

Another problem that confronted Josephus was the fact that a group known as the Hasidim, who are described in 1 Macc 2:42 as an exceedingly forceful (ἰσχυροὶ δυνάμει) group in Israel, who offered themselves willingly in defense of the Law, are clearly separate from the Hasmoneans, whom they originally joined in the war against Antiochus Epiphanes but who were the first to withdraw (1 Macc 7:13) from the struggle once a peace offer had been made by the Syrian Bacchides guaranteeing the right of the Jews to practice their religion. Here Josephus was clearly confronted with a dilemma. On the one hand, as a lackey of the Romans he seemed to identify with the ideological viewpoint of the Hasidim in seeking only religious autonomy rather than an independent state; on the other hand, he was a descendant of the Hasmoneans, who insisted on the latter as well. At first sight, at least, it would seem that the Pharisees, in their opposition to the Hasmoneans and to Herod, had inherited the point of view of the Hasidim, whereas the revolutionaries of Josephus' day had inherited the viewpoint of the Hasmoneans. Josephus' solution is carefully to sidestep the issue by not mentioning the Hasidim at all in his entire narrative, despite the fact that he so closely paraphrases the 1 Maccabees in *Ant* 12–13, and hence to avoid the division between the Hasidim and the Hasmoneans. Instead, he astutely (*Ant* 12 § 284) has the dying Mattathias advise his son Judah to admit to his ranks "the righteous and pious," without specifying the Hasmoneans by name, and thus to increase his power. Indeed, whereas 1 Macc 7:13 specifies that the Hasidim took the lead among the Israelites in accepting the peace offer of the Syrians, Josephus (*Ant* 12 § 395) says merely that "some of the citizens" gave ear to Bacchides' proposals.[10]

Josephus, clearly mindful of the fact that disunity had cost the Jews so heavily in the revolution against Rome, uses every opportunity in his paraphrase of the Bible to stress the importance of unity and the dangers of civil strife, thus appealing to his politically-minded audience so familiar with Thucydides' description (3.82-84) of the disastrous effects of the revolution at Corcyra.[11] Indeed, one of the charges made by the anti-Jewish Apion (*AgAp* 2 § 68) is that of fomenting sedition in Alexandria; and Josephus stresses throughout that the Israelites are conspicuously well aware of the dangers of such strife, and that it is the enemies of the Jews (namely the Egyptians) who are the real promoters of sedition, whereas the Jews are noted for their concord. Hence, it is most effective when Mattathias (*Ant* 12 § 283), in a passage that has no parallel in 1 Macc 2:64-66, urges his sons, in his dying speech, "most of all . . . to be of one mind (ὁμονοεῖν) and to yield to one another in whatever respect one is superior to the other."

2.2 *Judah the Maccabee*

Josephus (*Ant* 12 § 268) shifts early the emphasis from Mattathias to his sons, whereas 1 Maccabees plays down the role of Judah the

---

[10] Efron 1987: 24, argues that there was no split between the Hasmoneans and the Hasidim. He cites the Syriac translation of 1 Macc 7:13, which speaks not of Hasidim but of "a congregation of scribes." But it is clear that this Syriac version is a paraphrase rather than a literal translation; and, indeed, another Syriac version of this passage specifically mentions "the heads of the Hasidim." Efron cites the Vulgate, which likewise speaks of "a congregation of scribes," but he neglects to note that immediately thereafter this version mentions that the Hasidim were the first among the Jews who sought peace from the Syrians.

[11] Thus Josephus (*Ant* 1 § 117) portrays the punishment inflicted by G-d upon the builders of the Tower of Babel as discord (στάσις, a word not found in Gen 11:9 LXX), created by having them speak various languages. Similarly, in his treatment of the rebellion of Korah (Num 16) Josephus (*Ant* 4 § 12) remarks that it was a sedition (στάσις) "for which we know of no parallel, whether among Greeks or barbarians," clearly implying that information about seditions was familiar to his readers. Likewise, in discussing the consequences of the seduction of the Hebrew youth by the Midianite women, Josephus (*Ant* 4 § 140) remarks that the whole army was soon permeated by a sedition far worse than that of Korah.

Maccabee, in particular, to a considerable degree.[12] Indeed, 1 Maccabees associates with Mattathias the events at Modein, as well as the decision to fight on the Sabbath, the alliance with the Hasidim, and the spread of the rebellion in Judaea. Again, whereas in 1 Macc 2:17 the officers of the Syrian king declare that Mattathias is firmly supported by sons and brothers, Josephus remarks that it is especially because of his goodly sons that Mattathias is held in esteem. Moreover, the stature of the Hasmonean family is elevated by Josephus' omission (Ant 12 § 269) of the offer of the king's officers (1 Macc 2:18) to honor them with silver and gold and many gifts, inasmuch as even the very mention of such a bribe would be demeaning. Rather, the matter is placed on a higher plane by Mattathias' statement that even if all the other nations obey the commands of Antiochus whether through fear or desire to please him, they would never be persuaded to abandon their native form of worship.

Judah the Maccabee, in particular, is elevated in stature in Josephus' portrait. Thus, whereas 1 Macc 3:11 declares that in the battle between Judah's men and those of Apollonius many fell wounded and the rest fled, Josephus (Ant 12 § 287) puts the spotlight to a greater degree on Judah by stating that it was he who killed many of the enemy and left more of them wounded. Again, whereas 1 Macc 3:13 states that Judah mustered a company of faithful men, along with others accustomed to going out to war, Josephus (Ant 12 § 288) describes the men whom he attracted in more positive terms as "a force to be reckoned with (ἀξιόλογον) in a contest of war." Likewise, whereas in 1 Macc 3:24 it is Judah's men who pursue Seron down the descent from Beth-Horon and we hear (in the passive voice) that eight hundred of the enemy are slain, Josephus (Ant 12 § 292) transfers the credit to Judah alone for pursuing the enemy and for slaying the eight hundred. Moreover, Josephus adds to the respect for Judah's military ability by adding (Ant 12 § 306) that Judah showed ingenuity by surprising the enemy through leaving many fires in his camp when he

---

[12] In this respect Josephus is closer to the viewpoint of 2 Maccabees (e.g., 8:5, 10:21, 13:15, 14:17), which exalts Judah and obscures the other brothers, even Eleazar, who performed the daring exploit of attacking an elephant. The Talmudic tradition (Mishnah, Middoth 1:6) is in accord with 1 Maccabees in giving credit to all the Hasmoneans for the victory over the Syrian Greeks.

left for Emmaus.[13] Judah's military ability is further highlighted by the fact that at Emmaus, whereas 1 Macc 4:12-14 states merely that the heathen raised their eyes when they saw Judah and his soldiers advancing against them and that they were consequently crushed, Josephus (*Ant* 12 § 308) puts the spotlight upon Judah and dramatically describes him as falling upon the unsuspecting enemy, striking terror into their hearts, and throwing them into confusion, while all who were in the rear fell by the sword, with no indication of the actual role of Judah in all of this; and, furthermore, in place of the passive voice of 1 Maccabees we have the statement that it is Judah who killed many of those who opposed him. Likewise, the purification of the Temple and the reconstitution of its vessels is, in 1 Macc 4:42-51, the work of the priests whom Judah selected, whereas in Josephus (*Ant* 12 § 318) it is Judah who purifies the Temple and brings in new vessels.[14] Again, whereas in 1 Macc 5:16 we read that Judah and the people hear that the Gentiles in Galilee have gathered to destroy the Jews and that a great assembly is called together to decide what to do, in Josephus (*Ant* 12 § 332) it is Judah alone who decides what to do; he has no need of an assembly. Furthermore, 1 Macc 5:43 gives the credit to Judah's army for crushing the Ammonite Timotheus' army, but for Josephus (*Ant* 12 § 343) it is Judah who falls upon them, killing some and striking fear into the others, forcing them to throw away their arms and to flee. Likewise, whereas in 1 Macc 5:43 Timotheus and his men are crushed by Judah's forces, in Josephus (*Ant* 12 § 343) it is Judah who falls upon the enemy; again, whereas in 1 Macc 5:44 it is Judah's army which captures the city of Carnaim, in Josephus (*Ant* 12 § 344) it is Judah who does so. Similarly, Josephus (*Ant* 12 § 401) transfers to Judah alone the charges which, according to 1 Macc 7:25, the wicked high priest Alcimus brings against Judah and his men, and

---

[13] The stratagem of leaving fires burning to deceive the enemy, as Goldstein (1976: 264) notes, was a commonplace of Greek war narratives, as we see, for example, in Herodotus (8.19) and Thucydides (7.80.3). Goldstein adds that Josephus may have inserted this remark to add to the interest of the story without realizing that he was thus impairing the effort to portray Judah's feat as parallel to that of David (2 Sam 5:23-25, 1 Chr 14:14-16); but as we have noted above, Josephus had ambivalent feelings about David.

[14] Whereas Josephus here attributes the candelabrum to Judah, the Talmudic tradition (*b. Rosh Hashanah* 24b, *b. Avodah Zarah* 43b), as Strauss 1960: 122-29 (trans. into German 1962: 43-63), has noted, attributes the golden version of the candelabrum to the later Hasmoneans.

adds that the injuries which he had suffered at his hands would become still greater unless Judah were punished by having a strong force sent against him.

Moreover, whereas in 1 Macc 7:26 the Syrian king Demetrius sends his general Nicanor to get rid of the people (ἐξᾶραι τὸν λαόν), in Josephus (*Ant* 12 § 402) it is Judah's growing strength, which he deems hazardous to his own interests, which prompts him to this action. Likewise, whereas in 1 Macc 7:35 Nicanor directs his anger at Judah and his army, swearing that unless they are delivered into his hands immediately he would burn the Temple, in Josephus (*Ant* 12 § 406) Nicanor's anger is against Judah alone and his threat is that if the people do not give Judah up to him he will destroy the Temple. Furthermore, in the encounter which ensues, 1 Macc 7:43 states that the armies met in battle, whereas Josephus (*Ant* 12 § 409) again shifts the attention to Judah by asserting that Judah led his men out to battle. Moreover, whereas 1 Macc 7:43 declares that in that encounter Nicanor's army was shattered, in Josephus' version (*Ant* 12 § 409) it is Judah who defeats his adversaries after a severe fight and kills many of them. The achievement of Judah is all the greater because he adds that Nicanor fought gloriously. Likewise, 1 Macc 7:45 speaks of Judah's men as pursuing Nicanor's army after the battle, whereas Josephus (*Ant* 12 § 410) speaks only of Judah as pursuing the enemy.

Again, whereas 1 Macc 3:42 states that Judah and his brothers saw that their misfortunes were increasing and that armies were encamping on their borders, in Josephus (*Ant* 12 § 300) it is Judah alone who catches sight of the camp and the great number of the enemy and tries to persuade his men to have courage. Similarly, after the battle of Beth-Zur, Judah and his brothers in 1 Macc 4:36 propose to rededicate the Temple; in Josephus (*Ant* 12 § 316) the initiative is Judah's alone. Likewise, according to 1 Macc 5:10, the Jews who have taken refuge in the fortress of Dathema appeal for help in a letter sent to Judah and his brothers, whereas in Josephus (*Ant* 12 § 330) they write to Judah alone. Moreover, when Joseph the son of Zachariah and Azariah are routed, this is due, according to 1 Macc 5:61 to their failure to obey the orders of Judah and his brothers, whereas in Josephus it is only Judah's instructions which they have neglected to obey; he then pays tribute to Judah's foresight when he adds that "in addition to the other instances of Judah's stratagems (πρός γὰρ τοῖς ἄλλοις αὐτοῦ στρατηγήμασιν, 'tricks,' 'devices') one might well admire him also for having foreseen that such a reverse would come to the men under Joseph and Azariah if they departed in any respect from the instructions given them" (*Ant* 12 § 352). It is significant, in this instance, that despite the fact that Josephus is closely paraphrasing 1 Maccabees he omits, presumably because he regarded it as dogmatic and parochial, the statement (1 Macc 5:62) ascribing their defeat to the fact that they were not of the family, that is the Hasmoneans, "into whose keeping was entrusted the power of saving Israel" — and this despite the fact that he himself was descended from the Hasmoneans.[15] Another example where Josephus (*Ant* 12 § 403) has highlighted Judah alone is where, according to 1 Macc 7:27-28, the Syrian general Nicanor sends a deceitful message to Judah and his brothers inviting them to make peace; indeed, he adds to this deceit by promising that he will give an oath that Judah will suffer no harm at his hands.

Judah's skill as a general is all the greater because Josephus embellishes the power and tactics of the enemy. Thus, whereas 1 Macc 5:2 states very simply that the heathen planned to destroy the Jews who were among them, Josephus (*Ant* 12 § 327) states not that they planned but that they actually destroyed many of the Jews and describes their methods, namely through ambushes and plots, so that Judah had to wage continuous war against them in order to check their inroads and mischief.[16] Furthermore, whereas 1 Macc 5:29

---

[15] Cohen 1979: 46-47, regards this as an instance of Josephus' inconsistency, but we may perhaps better explain it as an example of his putting greater stress on the individual leader and his qualities than on the family. Goldstein (1976: 56, note 9, 73-74, and 304) tries to explain the apparent inconsistency by asserting that Josephus did not want to claim Judah as a member of the Hasmonean family because of the abuses later committed by that family; but, we might argue, inasmuch as Josephus was a member of the Hasmonean family, he might well have wished to claim him in order to counteract the later members who fell short in virtue. Goldstein: 79-80, notes that in 2 Macc 8:22 we are told that Joseph was a brother of Judah and hence was certainly a member of the family of the Hasmoneans. We may consequently be tempted to say that Josephus was here influenced by 2 Maccabees, but the great majority of scholars — and for good reasons — have denied that Josephus knew that work. See Feldman 1984b: 225-26.

[16] Rengstorf 1964: 106-29, commenting on *Ant* 12 § 327-329 and its parallel, 1 Macc 5:1-5, concerning Judah Maccabee's destruction of his enemies, claims that Josephus here employs an old Oriental *topos* which is found in Assyria and Neo-Babylonia, as well as in rabbinic texts, to depict the radical end of a city. But Rengstorf does not consider to what extent Josephus may have been influenced by the occurrence of this *topos* in Greek, especially historical, literature and

indicates merely that Judah left Bosra by night and arrived at Dathema by daybreak, Josephus (*Ant* 12 § 337) increases our admiration for Judah's endurance by noting that not even when night fell did he call a halt to his march. Even the troops of the Ammonite leader Timotheus, in a remark in Josephus (*Ant* 12 § 339) which has no counterpart in 1 Maccabees (cf. 5:34), recognize the courage (ἀνδρεία) and good fortune (εὐτυχία) of Judah in war, the latter quality of which is clearly a key quality of a general, if we may judge from the stress given it by Cicero in urging that Pompey (*De lege Manilia* 16.47) be given the command against Mithridates of Pontus.

In the battle at Beth-Zechariah Judah's bravery is all the greater because, in an addition to the text of 1 Macc 6:42, Josephus (*Ant* 12 § 372) makes a point of remarking that when he saw the size of the forces of the Syrian general Lysias, he was not terrified; and whereas 1 Maccabees speaks of Judah and his army and uses the passive voice in declaring that six hundred of the king's army were slain, Josephus shifts the focus entirely to Judah and asserts that he valiantly met the enemy's charge and slew six hundred of their number. There is, furthermore, increased admiration for Judah because whereas, according to 1 Macc 9:5 he had three thousand chosen men at Arbela when he faced the Syrian general Bacchides, Josephus (*Ant* 12 § 422) has reduced the size of his force to a mere thousand. Moreover, whereas 1 Macc 9:7 describes Judah as troubled in spirit and discouraged when he sees his army dwindling away, Josephus (*Ant* 12 § 423) omits such details and asserts that he was ready to engage Bacchides with the eight hundred men that were left. Indeed, when he exhorts his men, Judah in 1 Macc 9:8 urges them to go against their enemies if they should be able to fight against them; there is no "if" in Judah's vocabulary in Josephus (*Ant* 12 §§ 423-425): there he exhorts them to face danger bravely and urges them to advance to battle and to show contempt for danger.

When the tide of battle turns against him, and his men urge him to retreat, Judah in 1 Macc 9:10 responds with the brief statement that "if our time has come, let us die bravely for our brothers and not

---

military handbooks, by which he was certainly much influenced elsewhere and which his readers would have appreciated. In any case, the idea of destroying the murderers in a city and then burning it is hardly unique in the passage cited by Rengstorf; it is, in fact, a commonplace in military activities of many nations and many eras.

leave an accusation against our honor." Josephus (*Ant* 12 §§ 424-425) has a much more elaborate response, highly reminiscent of the response of Hector (Homer *Il.* 6.440-465) to Andromache when she urges him not to go forth to battle, that if he must inevitably perish in the fight he will stand his ground rather than bring disgrace upon his former achievements. Josephus, furthermore, has a much more elaborate account of Judah's death in battle. 1 Macc 9:17-18 is content merely to state that the battle became desperate and Judah fell, while the rest of his men fled. Josephus (*Ant* 12 § 430-431) describes him as standing firm while surrounded by the enemy, as killing many of his adversaries, and falling while still performing glorious deeds.

Josephus was confronted with a major problem in that not only was Judah defeated at Beth-Zechariah (1 Macc 6:47) but he retreated to some unknown destination, not to reappear until the invasion of Bacchides many months later. Such passivity and inactivity were hardly compatible with a hero of Judah's stature, and so Josephus (*Ant* 12 §§ 375-382) has Judah retreat to Jerusalem, where he signs a peace treaty with King Antiochus V Eupator which the Jews gladly accept. As Goldstein (1976: 322) has remarked, after the defeat at Beth-Zechariah Judah's name is absent from the rest of the account in 1 Macc 6:49-62, whereas in Josephus' version (*Ant* 12 § 382) Judah is among the last defenders of the Temple. Likewise, in the version of 1 Macc 7:9, King Demetrius of Syria sends Bacchides to take revenge on the Israelites, whereas in Josephus' version (*Ant* 12 § 393) the emphasis is again on Judah, as we hear that Demetrius instructed Bacchides specifically to kill Judah and the men with him.

Josephus, however, was careful not to damage his credibility by exaggerating Judah's strength, just as he was careful to avoid the rabbinic exaggeration of the strength of Samson (Feldman 1988b: 183). Thus, Josephus totally omits the comparison in 1 Macc 3:3 of Judah to a giant when he donned his breastplate and to "a lion in his deeds, like a lion's whelp roaring for its prey." Likewise, though the detail (1 Macc 6:37) that upon each of the elephants at Beth-Zechariah there were thirty-two (thirty, according to a variant reading) officers would have added to Judah's bravery since it would have shown how mighty the enemy was, Josephus (*Ant* 12 § 371), apparently realizing that such a detail would render his account less credible, omits it.

A key attribute connected with wisdom, as we may see in Thucydides' (2.60) portrait of the ideal statesman, Pericles, is the ability to persuade. Thus Josephus remarks (*Ant* 1 § 154) that Abraham was persuasive with his hearers, πιθανὸς τοῖς ἀκροωμένοις (a word used especially of students who listen to lectures in the philosophic schools, Feldman 1968a: 151-152) and was not mistaken in his inferences. His power of persuasion is seen particularly in his ability to convince the Egyptians (*Ant* 1 § 167) on any subject which he undertook to teach. As to Moses, it is nothing short of amazing that Josephus is able to praise his extraordinary ability in addressing a crowd (*Ant* 3 § 13, 4 § 328), despite the fact that the Bible (Exod 6:12) declares that he had a speech impediment. Similarly, in the case of Judah, in 1 Macc 3:23 we read that when he encountered the Syrian Seron he addressed his men in an effort to inspire them, but that when he stopped speaking he drove suddenly at the enemy, with no indication in the text that he had actually succeeded in persuading his own men. Josephus (*Ant* 12 § 292), on the other hand, clearly states that Judah succeeded in persuading his men to hold in contempt the great numbers of their adversaries and to encounter Seron.

Finally, in a significant addition to 1 Macc 9:57, Josephus (*Ant* 12 § 414), in a statement twice repeated (*Ant* 12 § 419; 434) and actually contradicted by him at a later point in his history (*Ant* 20 § 237, where he states that after the death of Alcimus there was no high priest in Jerusalem for seven years), declares that when the high priest Alcimus died the people gave the high priesthood to Judah. Here, as Fischer (1975: 46-49) suggests, we have an indirect recognition of the Jewish high priestly state, inasmuch as what immediately follows is an account of the treaty of friendship which Judah, presumably in his role as high priest (inasmuch as the treaty is explicitly [*Ant* 12 § 419] dated, "when Judah was high priest"), negotiated with the Romans.[17] Indeed,

---

[17] Goldstein, 1976: 357, appositely remarks that if Judah took the initiative to negotiate a treaty one would expect him to have held some legal office. And yet, the only title, according to 1 Maccabees, that he had was "commander of the army," and that through the mouth of Mattathias rather than through popular election. Since Mattathias was a guerrilla chieftain he had no legal national authority to convey his office. Whereas the later Hasmoneans are spoken of in 1 Maccabees (11:23; 12:6, 35; 13:36; 14:20, 28) as having legal titles, the silence of 1 Maccabees with regard to Judah would seem to indicate that he had no legal right on behalf of the nation to negotiate the treaty with the Romans. Josephus, on the other hand, because he believed that the high priest had the authority to send embassies (e.g., *Ant* 11 § 111; *AgAp* 2 § 185 and 188), elevates Judah to this position, knowing that the Hasmoneans later held such an office. Josephus' problem, however, was that Alcimus was the high priest at this time (1 Macc

Josephus' final statement in his eulogy of Judah (*Ant* 12 § 424) is that he held the high priesthood for three years.

In view of this increased emphasis on Judah we may wonder why Josephus systematically omits the passages in 1 Maccabees (e.g., 3:25-26, 3:43) in which the language about Judah is clearly reminiscent of David's exhortations and exploits. We may likewise note Josephus' omission (*Ant* 12 § 314) in Judah's prayer at Beth-Zur of the reference in 1 Macc 4:30 to David's defeat of Goliath, which would seem to be a most apt analogy in view of the tremendous odds against Judah at this time.[18] The answer may lie in the fact that Josephus systematically diminishes the importance of David as king both in sheer length of general treatment and in the length of his final encomium (*Ant* 7 §§ 390-391), especially as compared with King Saul and, more important, in terms of qualities of character. This may have been due to the fact that Josephus himself was descended from the Hasmonean kings rather than from the line of David, or because of David's importance as the ancestor of the Messiah – a figure who was clearly anathema for the Romans, inasmuch as the key goal of the Messiah was the establishment of an independent state (for other possible explanations see Feldman 1989a: 172-174).

We may suggest that political considerations were similarly behind Josephus' omission of the reference in 1 Macc 4:46 to a prophet who, in the future, would advise the Jews what to do with the stones of the altar which had been defiled. Similarly, whereas 1 Macc 9:27 declares that the distress that befell Israel after Judah's death was greater than any that had befallen them since prophets had ceased appearing to them, Josephus (*Ant* 13 § 5) avoids mentioning this cessation of prophecy and instead says that it was greater than any that they had experienced since their return from Babylon, presumably because such a mention of prophecy might have conjured up thoughts of a Messianic era, as noted in the prediction cited by Josephus (*JW* 6 § 312), Tacitus (*Hist* 5.13.2), and Suetonius (*Vespasian* 4.5). Elsewhere (*AgAp*

9:54-57), and so he has Alcimus die shortly after the victory over Nicanor, thus making room for Judah's election to the high priesthood. Bauer 1958: 223-24; Jeremias 1962: 197-204; and Lieberman 1955-58: Pt.4, 909 n. 48, all note, however, that the term ἀρχιερεύς may refer to any distinguished member of the priesthood.

[18] Josephus (*Ant* 12 § 312) omits other intimations of David's victories alluded to in the narrative of 1 Maccabees, notably 4:25, which echoes 1 Sam 19:5; 2 Sam 23:10, 12 and 1 Chr 11:14.

1 § 41) Josephus speaks of the failure of the exact succession of the prophets in the reign of Artaxerxes in the fifth century BCE[19] This revival of prophecy, we may assume, would be associated with the Messianic era; and any hint of a messiah would, of course, be anathema to the Romans whom Josephus was trying so hard to please.

2.3 *Jonathan*

Just as Josephus builds up the figures of Mattathias and Judah, so he does with Jonathan, Judah's brother and successor. Thus, whereas 1 Macc 9:60 states that the Syrians were unable to arrest Jonathan and his men because their plot became known, Josephus (*Ant* 13 § 25) gives the credit to Jonathan himself for becoming aware of the plot and for consequently guarding himself closely and gathering a large force (*Ant* 13 § 28). Moreover, Jonathan is painted as a magnanimous leader, who not only proposes to Bacchides that he make peace and release his Jewish prisoners (1 Macc 9:70), but also that he enter into a friendly alliance and that both sides exchange prisoners. Indeed, whereas in 1 Macc 9:71 Bacchides alone swears never to seek evil against Jonathan as long as he lived, the oath is mutual in Josephus (*Ant* 13 § 33). Furthermore, we obtain a picture (*Ant* 13 § 38) of Jonathan's power from the fact that the Syrian King Demetrius writes flattering words to him in fear that he may bear him a grudge for his former enmity. In particular, Josephus stresses Jonathan's courage, for whereas Alexander Balas, the Syrian king, in his quest for allies, asks (1 Macc 10:16) whether it is possible to find another one such as Jonathan, Josephus (*Ant* 13 § 43) spells out that there was no better ally than Jonathan, who was courageous in battle. Again, when King Demetrius of Syria writes (1 Macc 10:25), he addresses the nation of the Jews, but in Josephus (*Ant* 13 § 48) the letter is sent to Jonathan and the Jewish nation. A measure of the increased regard which Demetrius had for Jonathan may be seen in the fact that whereas in 1 Macc 10:40 he promises to given him fifteen thousand shekels (that

---

[19] See Feldman 1990: 400-7, for a discussion of this statement and of the apparent exceptions in Josephus in the instances of Cleodemus and John Hyrcanus. When Josephus (*Ant* 12 § 352) says that Judah foresaw the reverse that would occur to Joseph son of Zachariah and Azariah if they deviated from his instructions, this is not an instance of prophecy but rather of insight based upon knowledge, as we see from the verb which is used, συνῆκεν, which implies understanding or realization.

is, sixty thousand drachmas) of silver annually, in Josephus (*Ant* 13 §
55) this become 150,000 drachmas.

Moreover, Jonathan's military ability is highlighted by the fact (*Ant*
13 § 94), unparalleled in 1 Maccabees (cf. 10:80), that he drew up his
army in a square and thus prepared to fight the enemy on either line
by opposing them whether they attacked his front or his rear. We see
his military genius in his tactics against Apollonius. 1 Macc 10:80
declares that the enemy surrounded Jonathan's camp and shot darts
at his people without indicating Jonathan's tactics in response. Josephus (*Ant* 13 § 95) describes these tactics in detail, that he ordered his
men to make a fence of their shields and thus succeeded in warding
off the javelins thrown by the enemy horsemen. It is Jonathan who
gets credit for the rout of Apollonius: whereas 1 Macc 10:83 reports
that the enemy fled to Ashdod, Josephus (*Ant* 13 § 99) adds that
Jonathan pursued them as far as Azotus, slaying many of them.

There is an increased premium placed upon Jonathan's military
value in Josephus' version (*Ant* 13 § 102 vs. 1 Macc 10:88), where
Alexander Balas, after hearing the news that Jonathan had defeated
Apollonius, gives him rewards and honors; these are all the more
meaningful because of Josephus' addition that Alexander pretended
to be pleased as if it had been against his will that Apollonius had
fought with Jonathan. His military ability is further increased by
Josephus' added remark (*Ant* 13 § 122, cf. 1 Macc 11:21) that the
traitorous Jews who held the citadel in Jerusalem made light of
Jonathan's devices for capturing it, so confident were they in the
strength of the fortress.

Furthermore, Jonathan's value as an ally is clear from the fact that,
in contrast to 1 Macc 11:60, where we read only that Jonathan went
forth when requested by Antiochus VI to fight against Demetrius'
generals, in Josephus (*Ant* 13 § 148) he does so with alacrity, thus
emphasizing for Josephus' readers how reliable the Jews are when it
comes to helping their non-Jewish allies. Moreover, whereas in 1 Macc
11:60 Jonathan receives the help of the entire army of Syria as allies,
in Josephus (*Ant* 13 § 148) we hear that though the cities of Syria and
Phoenicia receive him splendidly they give him no troops, and so he
must fight alone. Josephus (*Ant* 13 § 149) paints a splendid picture of
Jonathan the loyal ally, for whereas 1 Macc 11:60 states simply that he
went to Askalon, Josephus (*Ant* 13 § 149) adds his success in persuading the people of Askalon to ally themselves with Antiochus. Indeed,

when Jonathan defeats King Demetrius II in Galilee, 1 Macc 11:74 merely gives the number of the enemy who were slain; Josephus (*Ant* 13 § 163), on the other hand, terms it a brilliant (λαμπρῶς) victory.

In a note which would have especially appealed to the Stoics in his audience, Josephus (*Ant* 13 § 163), in an addition to 1 Macc 12:1, declares that when Jonathan saw by G-d's providence (πρόνοια) that all his affairs were going according to his liking, he decided to send envoys to Rome. Significantly, however, when Jonathan writes to the Spartans seeking their alliance, in 1 Macc 12:15 he indicates that aid had come to him from Heaven, whereas in Josephus (*Ant* 13 § 169) his superiority is placed on a military plane in his success in overcoming his enemies.

Moreover, as with Judah, the great leader must be skilled in the art of persuading and inspiring his men. Hence, we read, in a passage (*Ant* 13 § 176) that has no counterpart in 1 Maccabees (cf. 12:27), that he succeeded in exhorting his men, during the continuing struggle against Demetrius II, to keep their spirits high and their senses alert and to fight even at night if necessary so that they might not be caught unprepared. Though, to be sure, 1 Macc 12:28 paints an effective picture of Jonathan's opponents being struck with terror and having their courage melted, Josephus (*Ant* 13 § 177) goes even further in describing the effect of Jonathan upon his enemies, namely that they were unable to use sound judgment and were no longer a match for Jonathan's men, inasmuch as their stratagems had failed.

Again, in a comment (*Ant* 13 § 182) unparalleled in 1 Maccabees (cf. 12:37, Jonathan shows military foresight in advising the people to erect fortresses throughout the country that were far stronger than those in their current state. Finally, whereas, after Jonathan has been captured, we read in 1 Macc 13:2 that the people were trembling with fear, Josephus (*Ant* 13 § 195) goes much further in his tribute to Jonathan's courage (ἀνδρεία) and foresight (πρόνοια). The Jews, he adds, were afraid that the surrounding nations would rise up against them since it was only because of Jonathan that they had remained quiet.

Moreover, Josephus highlights the status of Jonathan as high priest by constantly referring to him thus (eg., *Ant* 13 §§ 83, 121, 133, 212), whereas 1 Maccabees usually omits this title (e.g., 1 Macc 10:59; 11:20, 41; 12:23). His role as high priest is emphasized by the fact that whereas in 1 Macc 12:35 Jonathan calls together the elders of the

people, in Josephus (*Ant* 13 § 181) it is specifically in the Temple that
he gathers them and it is the part of the wall around the Temple
which he bids them set up and it is the precincts of the Temple that
he asks them to fortify. Finally, his status is elevated by the fact that
whereas in 1 Macc 10:65 King Alexander Balas inscribes him among
his best friends, in Josephus (*Ant* 13 § 85, so also 13 § 146) he is
inscribed as his First Friend.

2.4 *Simon*

As with Mattathias, Judah, and Jonathan, so with Simon, Josephus
aggrandizes his personality. Thus, whereas 1 Macc 9:68 speaks of the
defeat inflicted upon Bacchides by Simon and his men, in Josephus
(*Ant* 13 § 29) it is Simon alone who is given credit for burning the
siege-engines of the Syrians and slaughtering a considerable number
of their men, thus causing Bacchides to become despondent, disturbed,
and confounded, and not merely enraged, as in 1 Macc 9:69. We see
Simon's military ability in the engagement with Apollonius, where 1
Macc 10:82 says merely that he threw in his army, whereas Josephus
(*Ant* 13 § 97) declares that when Simon perceived that the enemy were
weary, he wisely engaged their main body and succeeded in routing the
enemy through the great ardor which his soldiers showed. In the rout
of the enemy which ensued, 1 Macc 10:82 declares that Simon completely defeated them and they fled, whereas Josephus (*Ant* 13 § 98)
elevates the role of Simon by noting that it was in disorder and
confusion that they fled, with the result that their lines were broken
and they were scattered everywhere in the plain.

We see Simon's military skill in that whereas 1 Macc 11:63 states
simply that he encamped against Beth-Zur, fought against it for a long
time, and blockaded it, Josephus (*Ant* 13 § 156) adds such specific
details, probably derived, to be sure, from military handbooks, as that
he raised earthworks and set up siege-engines, so that the soldiers of
the garrison were afraid that the place might be taken by storm and
they be destroyed. Again, as with Judah, the key concept for which
they are fighting (*Ant* 13 § 198) is liberty (ἐλευθερία), and he, too, like
his brothers, expresses his readiness to die for this principle, whereas
in 1 Macc 13:3 there is no mention of liberty or martyrdom and only
of the devotion to the laws and to the sanctuary.

Again, as with his brothers, the great hero must excel in exhorting
and inspiring his people; hence, whereas 1 Macc 13:7 says simply that

he succeeded in rekindling the spirit of the people, Josephus (*Ant* 13 § 201) elaborates by adding that from having been crushed in spirit through timidity they were now raised to a better spirit and good hope. Josephus (*Ant* 13 §§ 205-206), moreover, magnanimously and democratically, paints a picture of Simon consulting his people before deciding to accept Tryphon's treacherous offer to free his brother Jonathan in return for sending him a hundred talents of silver and Jonathan's two sons as hostages; in 1 Macc 13:17 Simon makes the decision on his own.

As with Judah and Jonathan, Josephus focuses upon Simon's role as high priest; and so, in an addition to 1 Macc 13:2, he indicates that it was in the Temple that he gathered the people and exhorted them to fight against Tryphon. Finally, again with Simon as with Judah and Jonathan, Josephus (*Ant* 13 § 213), in a passage that has no counterpart in 1 Maccabees (cf. 13:33), emphasizes his role as high priest, noting that he was thus chosen by the populace. It is this high priesthood that is the basis of Simon's political power, as we see in Josephus' added remark (*Ant* 13 § 213) that in the first year of his high priesthood he liberated (ἠλευθέρωσεν) the people from servitude to the Macedonians. While it is true that 1 Macc 13:42 does mention that Jews began to date their documents from the first year of Simon "the great High Priest and General and Ruler of the Jews," Josephus (*Ant* 13 § 214) adds that they dated them "from the first year of Simon, the benefactor and ethnarch of the Jews," so great was their respect for him, and that they prospered exceedingly and overcame the foes that surrounded them.

3. *Theological Considerations*

Throughout most of the *Antiquities* Josephus, while focusing on the achievements of his heroes, de-emphasizes the role of G-d. Thus he stresses Abraham's address to Isaac (*Ant* 1 §§ 228-231) when he is preparing to sacrifice him and omits any appeal to G-d, fraught as it is with the problem of theodicy, in contrast to the rabbinic emphasis on Abraham's address to G-d. There is likewise a de-emphasis on the role of G-d in the narrative of Joseph and Potiphar's wife (*Ant* 2 §§ 41-59). Perhaps the most striking example of the diminution of the role of G-d is in the Ruth pericope (*Ant* 5 §§ 318-336), where Josephus nowhere mentions G-d despite the fact that the Biblical account mentions Him seventeen times.

Similarly, whereas in 1 Maccabees Judah places all his trust in G-d, for "strength comes from Heaven" (1 Macc 3:19), in Josephus (*Ant* 12 § 290) the deliverance is transferred from G-d's unconditional benevolence to the piety and righteousness shown by Judah and his men. Even when he cites (*Ant* 12 § 291), in addition to 1 Macc 3:19, the example of the forefathers in inspiring his soldiers, Judah stresses that it was because of their righteousness and their struggles on behalf of their own laws that they gained the mastery over the enemy. Again, at Emmaus Judah closes his exhortation to his men with the statement (1 Macc 3:60) that G-d will do whatever be His will. Josephus (*Ant* 12 §§ 302-304) shifts the focus to the men themselves, and Judah tells them that it lies within their power to recover their liberty and to regain a happy life in accordance with the laws of their fathers or to suffer the most shameful fate. He delineates their cause as liberty (ἐλευθερία), country (πατρίς), laws (νόμοι), and religion (εὐσεβεία) — precisely, as we have noted, the ideals that would mean most to the Romans. Likewise, at Emmaus, whereas in 1 Macc 4:10 Judah tells his men to cry to Heaven to see whether G-d will have mercy upon them and will be mindful of the testament of the fathers, Josephus' Judah (*Ant* 12 § 307) appeals not to G-d's mercy but rather to the admiration which G-d has for the courage of men, and consequently urges them, in an addition to 1 Maccabees, to fight even if with unarmed bodies. Again, at Beth-Zur, where 1 Macc 4:30-33 has a long prayer by Judah to make the enemy cowardly and consequently to let all who know His name praise Him, Josephus (*Ant* 12 § 314) has a single phrase which places G-d's role on a military level, namely to be his ally (σύμμαχος) against the enemy.

Likewise, when they see the desolation of the Temple, Judah and his men cry out to Heaven in 1 Macc 4:39-40, but Josephus (*Ant* 12 § 317) merely has them lament, with no mention of the appeal to G-d. Similarly, in his version of the rededication of the Temple, Josephus (*Ant* 12 § 321) omits mention of the praise to Heaven uttered by all the people (1 Macc 4:55). There is a similar shift of centrality from G-d to the fighters themselves in Josephus' version of Judah's address to his troops before the battle of Adasa. In 1 Macc 7:41-42 Judah prays, reminding his men that when the messengers of the Assyrian king spoke blasphemy (2 Kgs 9:35), G-d's angel struck down 185,000 of the enemy and asks G-d to do likewise with Nicanor's forces. In Josephus (*Ant* 12 §§ 408-409) Judah does not pray but exhorts his men. There is no mention of G-d or G-d's angel or of the previous biblical precedent of a miracle; instead Judah inspires his men not to be overawed by the number of the enemy but rather to take pride in their cause and to face their foes bravely.

4. *Apologetics*

One of the recurrent charges against the Jews is hatred of mankind. Even Hecataeus (*ap*. Diodorus 40.3.4 = Stern 1976-84: 1, No. 11), who is otherwise well disposed toward the Jews, describes the Jewish way of life as "somewhat unsocial" (ἀπάνθρωπόν τινα) and hostile to foreigners (μισόξενον). Throughout his *Antiquities* Josephus is concerned with refuting these charges (Feldman 1988c: 494-96). Thus he notes that Abraham is moved with compassion for his friends and neighbors the Sodomites (*Ant* 1 § 176), that Joseph sells grain to all people and not merely to native Egyptians (*Ant* 2 § 94 and 101), that David, far from being a misanthrope, is described as φιλάνθρωπος, and that Solomon asks that G-d grant the prayers not only of Jews but also of foreigners (*Ant* 8 §§ 116-117). Jews, says Josephus (*Ant* 4 § 207 and *AgAp* 2 § 237), following Exod 22:28 LXX, are forbidden by the Torah to blaspheme the gods of others out of respect for the very word "god."

Inasmuch as Josephus is writing for a primarily non-Jewish audience (Feldman 1988c: 470-71), he could hardly afford to offend these pagan readers. Hence, it is not surprising that he totally omits (*Ant* 12 § 290) the reference in 1 Macc 3:49 to the incident in which the "nations" (ἔθνη) drew the likenesses of their idols upon a scroll of the Law. Again, whereas we read in 1 Macc 3:25 that after Judah crushed Seron the fear and dread of Judah and his brothers began to fall upon the nations (ἔθνη) around them, Josephus (*Ant* 12 § 293) omits mention of the effect upon the nations.

Similarly, at Emmaus, whereas Judah, according to 1 Macc 3:58 exhorts his men to be ready early in the morning to fight the nations (τοῦ πολεμῆσαι ἐν τοῖς ἔθνεσιν) who have gathered against them, Judah in Josephus (*Ant* 12 § 302) once again omits all reference to the nations and instead concentrates on instilling in his men courage and contempt for danger. Likewise, at Emmaus, whereas, in the version of 1 Macc 4:10, Judah tells his men to appeal to G-d so that all the nations (ἔθνη) may know that there is One who will redeem Israel,

Josephus (*Ant* 12 § 307), seeking to avoid a confrontation with non-Jewish readers, again omits the reference to the nations. Furthermore, in describing the battle that ensued, Josephus (*Ant* 12 § 307) refers to the enemy but not to the "nations," as 1 Macc 4:14 does. Again, whereas 1 Maccabees refers several times (4:45, 54, 58, 60) to the desecration of the Temple by the "nations," Josephus (*Ant* 12 § 320) in his paraphrase omits all mention of the "nations."

Indeed, in the one place (*Ant* 12 § 327) where Josephus does refer to the "nations," he is speaking not of the heathens generally but rather of the nations geographically surrounding Judaea. Likewise, the statement in 1 Macc 5:5 that Judah ritually doomed the tribe of Baean to complete destruction might well have seemed utterly cruel to his readers, and so it is not surprising that Josephus (*Ant* 12 § 328) omitted it. Furthermore, in 1 Macc 5:19, Judah instructs Joseph the son of Zechariah and Azariah not to engage the heathen (ἔθνη) in battle until he returns; but Josephus (*Ant* 12 § 333) avoids the slight to the Gentiles by having Judah instruct them not to join battle with anyone (μηδένα) until he returns. Again, whereas 1 Macc 5:43 states that all the heathen (ἔθνη), that is, Timotheus and his men, were crushed by Judah's army, Josephus (*Ant* 12 § 343) once again avoids using the word for heathen and says simply that he fell upon his foes (ἐπιπίπτει τοῖς ἐχθροῖς). Moreover, whereas 1 Macc 5:68 states that Judah turned aside to Azotus (Ashdod) in the land of the Philistines, pulled down their altars, and burned up the carved images of their gods, Josephus (*Ant* 12 § 353), realizing that this would be viewed by his Gentile readers as showing disrespect for the religions of others, omits these incriminating details and is content merely to indicate that he took the city of Azotus and sacked it. Similarly, Josephus is careful to omit other details which would hurt the feelings of his Graeco-Roman readers. Thus, 1 Macc 7:47 has the gruesome details that Judah's army cut off Nicanor's head and right hand and hanged them near Jerusalem, whereas Josephus (*Ant* 12 §§ 410-411) totally omits them.

5. *Summary*

It should not be surprising that Josephus, clearly proud of his descent from the Hasmoneans, devotes as much attention to them as he does. In general, in his paraphrase of the 1 Maccabees, he follows the same pattern that he does in his paraphrase of the Bible, namely aggrandizing the chief personalities in the belief that history is the biography of great men and, following his great model Thucydides, that leadership is the most important ingredient in the success of states. In the speeches, in particular, which he assigns to the Hasmoneans, he stresses those ideals of liberty, country, laws, and piety, and the readiness to die for these ideals, which would have appealed so much to his Graeco-Roman audience.

Josephus had to be careful to avoid unduly stressing the ideal of political liberty, since this would have given the appearance of endorsing the goals of the revolutionaries of his own day. Thus he carefully shuns the references in 1 Maccabees to the zealot Phinehas as the model for the Hasmoneans. Hence, for him liberty means life in accordance with the laws and customs of the fathers; it is almost as if he endorsed Ennius' above-quoted famous line, "Moribus antiquis res stat Romana viresque" (*Annals* 5.156[500]). He likewise avoids mention of the Hasidim, since this would require him to explain the split between them and the Hasmoneans. Indeed, he uses the occasion of Mattathias' dying speech to stress the importance of unity.

The figure of Judah Maccabee, in particular, is elevated in Josephus' portrayal. It is he, rather than his brothers or his men, who is given credit for the tactics that win battles; and it is he, rather than the priests whom he appoints, who is responsible for the purification and rededication of the Temple. And yet, in order not to lose credibility, Josephus does not unduly exaggerate Judah's strength. Furthermore, as a great leader, Judah must be presented as having, like Pericles, great powers of persuasion. Finally, he must be the legitimate head of state, and this Josephus achieves by speaking of him as being chosen to be high priest. It is in this capacity that he negotiates the key treaty of friendship with the Romans.

And yet, Josephus, significantly, avoids the comparisons of Judah with King David such as we find in 1 Maccabees, perhaps because David was the ancestor of the Messiah, who, as a political leader, would reinstitute a politically independent Jewish state, and who consequently was a source of embarrassment to the Roman lackey, Josephus. Likewise, he avoids mention of the cessation or reinstitution of prophecy, since this, too, would be connected with a messianic era.

Judah's successors, his brothers Jonathan and Simon, are likewise painted larger than life. In particular, their courage and their loyalty as allies of the Syrians are stressed — qualities that would serve an important apologetic purpose in Josephus' history. Likewise, their status as high priests, and consequently as heads of state, is similarly stressed.

Josephus, in his portraits, de-emphasizes the role of G-d and instead places the stress on the righteousness, piety, and bravery of his heroes. Their leaders do not so much pray as exhort their people to exemplify these ideals.

Finally, in order to avoid giving the appearance of disrespect for the beliefs of non-Jews, Josephus avoids the references in 1 Maccabees to Gentiles or heathen as the enemies of the Jews.

ONIAS III' DEATH AND THE FOUNDING
OF THE TEMPLE OF LEONTOPOLIS

Fausto Parente

1. In recounting the Maccabean revolt in the *Antiquities*, both in the single episodes and in their order of occurrence, Josephus follows 1 Maccabees relatively faithfully; his account of the immediately preceding events, however, concerning the revolt's antecedents, given in the first chapter of 1 Maccabees and at greater length in 2 Maccabees draws on other sources and gives new data even with respect to 2 Maccabees which he most certainly was not familiar with.[1]

The problem to be examined here is the role of the high priest Onias III in the whole matter, and in particular his part, if any, in founding the temple of Leontopolis in Egypt.

2. The third chapter of 2 Maccabees which opens the narrative proper, begins by praising Onias III: "While the Holy City was administered in complete peace, and the law was observed there most scrupulously, owing to the pious nature of the High Priest Onias and his hatred of evil . . ." (2 Macc 3:1-2). Onias, son of Simon II, with whose praise Ben Sira concludes his book (Sir 50), belonged to the priestly family whose genealogy Josephus traces as follows in *Antiquities* 12-13: Onias I, the successor of Yaddua' ('Ιαδδοῦς; LXX: 'Ιαδού, 'Ιεδδου L, Neh 12:11,22), the high priest who allegedly received Alexander in Jerusalem (*Ant* 11 § 347); his son Simon "who was surnamed the Just" (*Ant* 12 § 43, 157)[2]; Eleazar, brother of Simon "the Just", mentioned in the

---

[1] For Josephus' sources see: Bloch 1879; Destinon 1882; Büchler 1896-1897; 1897a; Albert 1902; Hölscher 1904; Motzo 1924; 1924a; Ettelson 1925; Momigliano 1930; Shutt 1961: 79-109; Feldman 1984: 392-419.

[2] Simon "the Just" (צדיק; δίκαιος) is Simon II father of Onias III and not, as stated by Josephus (*Ant* 13 § 43), Simon I. See: Herzfeld 1863: 1. 368; Derenbourg 1867: 46-47; Willrich 1895: 105-115; Schürer 1901-1911: 1. 181-182; 2. 355ff.; Moore 1927; Marcus 1943: 732-736. See: *m. Abot* 1:2 and Marti-Beer 1927: 6-7; *b. Yoma* 39a-b. Sir 50:1-6 praises his activity after the restauration of the Temple authorised by Antiochus III.

Letter of Aristeas (§§ 33 etc.) (*Ant* 1 § 11; 12 § 44 etc.); Manasseh, uncle of Eleazar (*Ant* 12 § 157); Onias II, son of Simon "the Just" (*Ant* 12 § 44, 157) and Simon II, son of Onias II (*Ant* 12 § 224). In *Ant* 12 § 261, Josephus states that he "had attempted to document the succession of high priests serving throughout the period of two hundred years", which would seem to indicate his reliance upon written documentation. As Feldman has pointed out, given the amount of new material in the list, the summary in *Ant* 20 §§ 224-251 hardly seems a resumé of previous statements (Feldman 1965: 507 n. d).

However, 2 Macc 3:4 continues, one Simon "of the tribe of Bilga," (τις ἐκ τῆς Βαλγέα),³ who held the position of προστάτης τοῦ ἱεροῦ or financial overseer of the Temple, clashed with Onias in his attempt to obtain for himself the position of ἀγορανόμος, at the time a sort of notary public (Abel 1946, 57-58). Thwarted, Simon went to Apollonius "of Tarsus", who was then governor of Coele-Syria and Phoenicia (Polybius 31. 13 [21]. 3), in 2 Macc 4:4 defined "son of Menesteus" (Abel 1949: 300), and drew his attention to the Temple's considerable wealth which, he insinuated, could become the property of the king (2 Macc 4:6). Seemingly this is an invitation to ἱεροσυλία (Xenophon *Apol. Socr.* 25; Dittenberger, *Syll.*, 1017, 17). This was perfectly understandable given the considerable financial problems caused Seleucus IV Philipator by the indemnity demanded by the Romans after the Treaty of Apamea in 188 BCE (Polybius, 31.40-43; Livy 38.38). In 2 Maccabees it is made the beginning of the famous story of Heliodorus' miraculous ejection from the Temple, which takes up the rest of the chapter (2 Macc 3:7-40).⁴

As stated at the beginning of the following chapter, faced with the behaviour of Simon and Apollonius, Onias "benefactor of the city, and protector of his fellow men" (2 Macc 4:3), decided to go to Antioch and expound the problem to the king (2 Macc 4:5-6). On September 3, 175 BCE, however, Seleucus IV was the victim of a conspiracy

---

³ Cf. 1 Chr 24:14; Neh 12:5,18. Βαλγεα: the text has Βενιαμιν, not a priestly family. Herzfeld (1863: 1. 218) proposed to read *Minyamin* (1 Chr 24:9; see De Vaux 1936), but De Bruyne (1932: 117-118) on the ancient Latin translations proposed Βαλγεα (Balgea) and this reading is generally accepted. See Abel 1946: 52-56; 1949: 316-17; Tcherikover 1959: 403-4; Hengel 1969: 508-9; Hanhart 1964: 483-84; Habicht 1976: 210. But see Bickerman 1944: 8, n. 22: the προστάτης τοῦ ἱεροῦ was not of priestly lineage.

⁴ See Bickerman 1944: 10-13 for the possible reasons of Heliodorus' request.

planned against him by Heliodorus (Appian *Syr.* 45). A few months later he was succeeded by his younger brother, Antiochus IV, who took the appellative of Ἐπιφανής (2 Macc 4:7; Appian *Syr.* 45; Polybius 26.1a [Athenaeus 10.439a], although the title appears on coins only in 173/2, (Mørkholm 1963: 34-37; 1966: 48). He adopted Antiochus, Seleucus IV's son, took him as a co-ruler and possibly married the dowager queen.[5]

One of the new king's first actions was to remove Onias from office and replace him with his brother, Jesus-Joshua, who had changed his name to Jason. Jason, 2 Macc 4:8 informs us, had promised the king an increase in the tributes which Judaea paid to the royal treasury with the offer of more money if the king would authorize him "to institute, by his own authority, a gymnasium and an *ephebeia*, and to register the Antiochenes of Jerusalem" (2 Macc 4:9; Parente 1994). 1 Macc 1:13-15, states that "there were those who hastened to the king, seeking authorization to observe pagan practice. They constructed a gymnasium in Jerusalem, according to the custom of the nations, rebuilt their foreskins, and renounced the holy alliance to put themselves under the yoke of the Gentiles".

3. In 172 BCE Antiochus was in Joppa (Jaffa). He had sent Apollonius "son of Menesteus" (2 Macc 4:4) to the coronation (προτοκλησία) of Ptolemy VI Philometor (the latter's mother, Cleopatra I Syra, sister of Seleucus IV and Antiochus IV, her son's regent, had died in 176 BCE). The previous year, 173 BCE, Apollonius had been sent to Rome to ensure the alliance (Livy 42. 6.6ff), and a Roman embassy travelled to Antioch some time later (Livy, 42. 6.7-8). Antiochus was keen to secure Rome's support, Cleopatra's death having reawoken Egypt's slumbering ambitions to reconquer Coele-Syria, lost after the battle of Paneion in 200 BCE, which, according to Egyptian propaganda, had been promised Cleopatra Syra, Antiochus III's daughter, as dowry for her marriage to Ptolemy V Epiphanes in 193 BCE.[6]

This was the reason for Antiochus's journey to Joppa. He then proceeded to Jerusalem, where Jason received him with great ceremo-

---

[5] See *OGIS* 1, no. 252 with Dittenberger's commentary: Bouché-Leclercq 1913-14: 246 and Mørkholm 1966: 49-50.
[6] See Polybius 28. 20. 9; Appian *Syr* 5; Josephus *Ant* 12 § 154; Eusebius *Chr* 136.26-137.2 Helm; Jerome *In Dan* 11:17 (*PL* 25:564A). Holleaux 1899; Bouché-Leclecq 1903-7: 382-387; 1913-14: 185 and 572-576; Cuq 1927.

ny: "he was welcomed with a torchlight procession and shouts of applause" (2 Macc 4:22). In 170 BCE Antiochus sent a further embassy to Rome, lead by Meleager (Polybius 27.19), denouncing Egypt's threatened aggression, but Rome was engaged in the war against Perseus of Macedonia, and the Senate was not able to receive the ambassadors until the beginning of 169 BCE, at which time only evasive answers were forthcoming (Polybius 27.20.9).

By this time the young Ptolemy VI Philometor's two regents, Eulaios and Lenaios (Mørkholm 1961), had set out from Alexandria with troops. The first skirmish, which took place between Pelusium and Mount Casius (Porphyry in Jerome *Comm. in Dan.* 11:21ff; *PL* 25: 566C = *F.Gr.Hist.* 260 fr. 49a) ended in a clear victory for Antiochus, who had moved in good time and thus pre-empted the Egyptians, defeating them on their own ground (November, 170 BCE). The battle of Mount Casius was followed by a truce (Diodorus 30.18.2; Mørkholm 1966: 73-76 with chronological table).

In Jerusalem this situation gave renewed vigour to both the pro-Seleucid party, led by Jason and the Tobiads, and the pro-Ptolemaic one, led by Onias. "Jason sent Menelaus, the brother of Simon, of whom we have spoken [2 Macc 3:4 and 4:1], to the king" (2 Macc 4:23). Menelaus went to deliver tribute, but in return for a considerable sum of money (three hundred silver talents), he managed to obtain for himself the high priesthood and "Jason, who had dispossessed his own brother, was in his turn dispossessed by another, and was forced to seek refuge in the land of Ammanitis" (2 Macc 4:26), probably in the fortress of 'Araq el-Emir, the *Birta* (*CPJ* 1: 116; 119) of Hyrcanus, the last eminent member of the Tobiad family, who had taken his own life when Antiochus came to the throne (*Ant* 12 § 236) (Will and Larché 1991).

Menelaus failed to keep his side of the bargain despite the pressure exercised by Sostratus, the "ἔπαρχος of the Acropolis" (2 Macc 4:28), head of the garrison and responsible for collecting tributes. Both were convened to Antioch; Menelaus put his brother Lysimachus in his place, while Sostratus left Crates the head of the Cyprian mercenaries (2 Macc 4:27-29).

Antiochus in the meantime had been forced to go to Cilicia to quell an uprising (Bouché-Leclercq 1913-14: 250), leaving as his regent a dignitary of the kingdom, Andronicus (2 Macc 4:30-31). Menelaus was quick to take advantage of the situation and plundered the Temple of its gold vessels, thereby gaining the approval of Andronicus, while Onias, in hiding in the famous sanctuary in Daphne near Antioch (hence the name, Ἀντιοχεία ἡ ἐπὶ Δάφνῃ, Strabo 16.2.4 [719]; Pliny the Elder 5.79; Benzinger 1901; Stillwell 1938) sacred to Apollo and Artemis, took Menelaus severely to task for his behaviour. Menelaus convinced Andronicus of the need to eliminate the high priest and Andronicus in turn persuaded Onias to leave his hiding-place and "put him to death instantly, with no thought of justice" (2 Macc 4:32-38).

4. In the foregoing account of the facts, Onias III undoubtedly has a role of some importance, and for the author of 2 Maccabees he is clearly a principal figure. At the conclusion of the book, in the description of the preparations for the battle of Adasa (161 BCE) against Nicanor, the general of Demetrius I Soter (1 Macc 7:26-32), Judah has a vision in which Onias appears beside Jeremiah, "outstanding in age and dignity", comforting him in the moment of danger (2 Macc 15:1-16).

The account is seemingly consistent and cohesive (so, e.g., Niese 1903: 229-30), but a number of doubts arise on closer examination and on comparing it with parallel sources, namely Josephus' versions of the same events in the *Jewish War* and in the *Antiquities*.

In 2 Macc 3:1, Onias is presented as a pious and observant Jew: "the holy city was administered in complete peace, and the law was there observed most scrupulously, owing to the pious nature of the High Priest". According to 2 Macc 3:33, Heliodorus was spared by God on account of Onias' intercession. Simon implies that Onias is the actual cause of Heliodorus' failure (2 Macc 4:1). When Antiochus came to the throne in 175 BCE, the first thing he did was to depose Onias, who was recognised as leading the pro-Ptolemaic party. In the description of the introduction of Hellenism to Jerusalem, in fact, 2 Maccabees never mentions Onias' name. He is not seen upbraiding his brother Jason for his impious act, so he presumably lived at some distance from Jerusalem, hidden in the Temple of Daphne where he had quite plausibly managed to save his own life. A high priest scrupulously observant of the Law such as Onias, however, should have considered his life in serious and imminent danger from the very fact of taking shelter in the τέμενος of a pagan temple, by definition impure, a danger which could come from the king and his courtiers. It is, then, somewhat improbable that he could reproach Menelaus for his sacrilegious plunder (2 Macc 4:33), let alone that he should leave his shelter for a reassuring hand-shake (2 Macc 4:34). That Antiochus, on his return, should be "grieved to the depth of his soul" by his death (2 Macc 4:37), and should have Andronicus put to death on this account (2 Macc 4:38) is unlikely in the extreme.

This last doubt, however, is not the subjective impression of the reader of 2 Maccabees. We know from Diodorus (30. 7.2-3) and John of Antioch (Müller *FGH* 4 [1851], 558b n. 58), both quoted by Constantinus Porphyrogenitus in his *Excerpta de insidiis*, that Andronicus was actually condemned to death by Antiochus IV for having killed the young son of Seleucus IV Philopator and Laodice also called Antiochus. The latter had been accepted — as we have noted — as co-ruler by Antiochus IV at the time of his accession to the throne (Mørkholm 1964; 1966: 38-50 with full bibliography). Antiochus himself had commissioned the crime, but Andronicus was an inconvenient witness, and, as Diodorus puts it, "it is the habit of the dynasts to save themselves from danger by sacrificing their friends". According to Bouché-Leclercq, the killing of Onias offered the perfect pretext for eliminating Andronicus: "Mais ici reviennent les soupçons transformés en affirmation par Jean d'Antioche, et l'on se demande si par hasard Antiochos n'avait pas saisi l'occasion de se défaire d'un complice fort au courant de la façon dont avait disparu le prince royal" (1913-14: 250-251).

There could, however, be a different explanation. Wellhausen maintains that the author of 2 Maccabees simply substituted the killing of Onias for that of the young Antiochus.[7] Abel is sceptical: if this is the case, we should therefore deduce that it was Onias III and not his son who built the temple of Leontopolis in Egypt (Abel 1949: 343-344). This version, however, is given credence by a number of sources, and is not to be rejected *a priori*, as almost always happens today.

5. Josephus knows a tradition in which the builder of the Temple of Leontopolis is unequivocally Onias III. In *JW* 1 §§ 31-33, he states that

---

[7] Wellhausen 1905: 127 "Darnach ist es höchst wahrscheinlich, dass die Ermordung des seleukidischen Prätendenten mit ihren Umständen auf den hohenpriesterlichen Prätendenten Onias übertragen ist. Dieser wird dadurch vorzeitig zum Märtyrer gemacht". It was Willrich who first cast doubt on the account of 2 Maccabees about the death of Onias III. Along the same line which makes Onias III the founder of the Leontopolis temple see: Motzo 1924b: 185-186 note, and Momigliano 1930: 38-39.

"Onias, one of the high priests, once in a position of advantage, then expelled the Tobiads from the city. They thereupon sought refuge with Antiochus, offering to guide him if he should invade Judaea". The king agreed, having for long considered the idea; gathering an army, he stormed the city, killing large numbers of Ptolemy's followers and interrupting the daily sacrifice for three years and six months. "Onias the high priest sought the protection of Ptolemy and having obtained from him land in the νομός of Heliopolis, did there construct a small town, modelled on Jerusalem, and a similar temple [to that in Jerusalem]. We shall return to this in due course".

The "due course" is *JW* 7 §§ 420-436, which recounts how, after the fall of Masada, in 74 CE, one unidentified Lupus (Λοῦπος or Λοῦππος who τότε διῴκει τὴν Ἀλεξάνδρειαν § 420; ὁ τῆς Ἀλεξανδρείας ἡγεμών, § 433), having informed the emperor of Jewish uprisings in Egypt, received orders to "demolish the Jewish temple in the district called of Onias". "This", Josephus continues, "is a colonised region of Egypt which received its name in the following circumstances: Onias, son of Simon [i.e. Onias III], one of the high priests of Jerusalem, fleeing from Antiochus, King of Syria, then at war with the Jews, πολεμοῦντα τοῖς Ἰουδαίοις, having been received by Ptolemy [VI Philometor] ... requested permission to build, in some part of Egypt, a temple for the worship of God according to the customs of the fathers .... Ptolemy granted him land in what is called the νομός of Heliopolis. Here Onias erected a fortress and constructed a temple which is not in the likeness of that in Jerusalem, but is like to a tower ...." The altar and cult objects, however, were like those in Jerusalem, Josephus adds, with the exception of the lampstand. The whole place was surrounded by a brick wall, with a door in stone.[8]

In so doing, however, "Onias was not moved by honest motives" (οὐ μὴν Ὀνίας ἐξ ὑγιοῦς γνώμης ταῦτα ἔπραττεν *JW* 7 § 431), but because of resentment towards such as had enforced his exile, and he hoped to draw crowds away from the temple of Jerusalem. There existed a prophecy of Isaiah [Isa 19:18-19] announcing the erection of a temple in Egypt by a Jew. In 74 CE Lupus closed the temple

---

[8] The many problems posed by the temple itself are not discussed here. See: Frankel 1852; Herzfeld 1863: 2.460-462 and 557-559; Ewald 1864: 462-468; Jastrow 1872; Naville 1890: 20; Schürer 1901-1911: 2.144-148; 3.42-43; Petrie 1906: 19b-27b; Bickerman 1934; Du Mesnis du Boisson 1935; Beek 1943; Baruq 1957; Tcherikover 1959; Steckholl 1967; Delcor 1968; Rappaport 1969; 1972; Hayward 1982; Schürer 1973-87: 3.47-48 and 145-147. See the following note 10.

without, however, destroying it (*JW* 7 §§ 433-436). It is clear that the passage from Book 7 (probably added after the work had been completed) substantially differs from the version given in the summary at the beginning of Book 1: the temple of Leontopolis is simply a tower, while in both passages it was unequivocally Onias III, "son of Simon" (7 § 423), who constructed it. It should be added that this second passage is decidedly derogatory in tone as regards Onias: in *JW* 1 § 32 Onias flees to Egypt when in Jerusalem the perpetual sacrifice is interrupted, obviously to take it up again in Egypt. In the passage in Book 7 it is primarily within the context of the antagonism between Ptolemies and Seleucids that the facts find an adequate explanation, Onias founds the temple out of hatred against those who had condemned him to exile. That Onias had thought of "attracting the Jewish multitudes to Leontopolis" is a clearly tendentious statement, and its source clearly anti-Ptolemaic and anti-Oniadic. Furthermore, the source of the passage in Book 7 would not seem to tally with that of the similar passage in Book 1. One can therefore conjecture that at least two traditions exist, one positive, the other negative, in which Onias III is considered the founder of the temple of Leontopolis.

6. Theodore of Mopsuestia (d. 428 CE), however, knew of a third tradition. In the introduction to his commentary on Psalm 54 (55), he gives a summary of Jewish history, and in the parts concerning Antiochus IV he follows the account in 2 Maccabees. When, however, he gets to the foundation of the gymnasium in Jerusalem by Jason, he adds: "Observing these things, the blessed Onias was grieved, and lamented and protested. Since he saw that evil was increasing, he left the city and departed for Egypt where he raised an altar and constructed a temple." It is impossible to ascertain Theodore's sources; the fact remains, however, that while he seems to have half an eye on 2 Maccabees not only does he not mention the death of Onias but he actually states quite explicitly that when Hellenism was introduced into Jerusalem Onias went into hiding in Egypt and there constructed an altar and temple so that the Jews (all of them, it would seem) could worship the divinity. The source seems decidedly favourable towards Onias.[9]

---

[9] Baethgen (1886: 277-283, esp 277) noted how closely Theodore followed 2 Maccabees up to this point. Stern 1960 (and 1974-84: 1.406) asserts that Theodore depends on Josephus but in his commentary the Heliodorus episode absent in Josephus plays a central role.

7. Rabbinic literature, as we shall also see below, speaks of the temple of Leontopolis, the "House of Onias" (בית חוניו); its cult, with few exceptions, is not considered valid. As regards the priests who worshipped in Leontopolis, *m. Menahot* 13:10 states that: "Those priests who have officiated in the House of Onias may not officiate in the Temple of Jerusalem; this is the more true for [priests who have officiated] in other things [in idolatrous cults] since it is written: 'priests of other places will not approach the altar of the Lord in Jerusalem, but will eat unleavened bread with their brothers' [2 Kgs 23:9]". The *gemarah* (*b. Menahot* 109b) first of all draws the logical conclusion: "Therefore the House of Onias was not a sanctuary of idolatry". It continues by giving a *haggadah* according to which Onias (whose name sometimes appears as נחוניה, and who is here the son of Simon the Just, i.e. Onias III) is designated by his father on his death bed to succeed him over the head of his elder brother Shim'ei (Simon). The latter, under pretext of instructing him in the temple services, tricks him into subjecting himself to ridicule (by wearing women's clothing), until his fellow priests decide to kill him. This was the reason why Onias fled to Alexandria, where he then "built an altar and sacrificed thereon to the idols." Further on, however, it states that he "offered sacrifices in God's honour since it is written: 'In that day shall there be an altar for the Lord in the land of Egypt, and a pillar to the Lord on its borders'" [Isa 19:19]. The passage clearly documents how, for the compilers of the *Babylonian Talmud*, the history of the founding of the Leontopolis temple drew on traditions which gave Onias III as the founder, a figure towards whom their reactions are both positive and negative. A parallel passage in the *Jerusalem Talmud* (*y. Yoma* VI, 3) similarly gives Onias (נחוניה) as the founder of the temple, and expresses a similar ambivalence: Isa 19:19 is quoted in support of the favourable opinion.[10]

8. In the *Antiquities* Josephus gives a totally different version of the death of Onias and of the founding of the temple from that in the *Jewish War*. In *Ant* 12 § 237, after the "tales" of the Tobiads which end with the suicide of Hyrcanus at the time of Antiochus IV's accession, Josephus thus begins his description of the internal struggle which

---

[10] On the temple of Leontopolis in rabbinic literature see Hirsch 1906 and Tchernowitz 1946.

eventually leads to the introduction of Hellenism into Jerusalem: "At about that time, the High Priest Onias died and Antiochus invested his brother [Jason] with the high priesthood, the son of Onias being yet an infant, but I shall give an account of facts relating to this child in due course." Thus in 175 BCE Onias had apparently and plausibly died a natural death, leaving a young son. According to Josephus' source here, Simon II had had three children: Onias (III), Jesus-Joshua, who had changed his name to Jason, and "Onias, who was called Menelaus" (*Ant* 12 § 239).

As we know from 2 Macc 4:23, Menelaus was not the brother of Onias III (in which case two of Simon's sons would have had the same name), but of Simon προστάτης τοῦ ἱεροῦ. Josephus' source therefore can hardly be presumed reliable. It also states that Jason was replaced by Menelaus, and that Menelaus and the Tobiads (and not Jason, as in 2 Maccabees) were responsible for introducing Hellenism into Jerusalem, Onias III having died before any of the above events.

In *Ant* 12 § 382, Josephus paraphrases 1 Macc 6:48ff. and its account of how, after Beth-Zur had been taken, (1 Macc 6:50), Lysias had attacked the Temple hill (1 Macc 6:51-53). Given the scarcity of food, since it was a sabbatical year (163/162 BCE) (1 Macc 6:54), Lysias offered the Jews a revocation of the edict, in the name of the infant king (Antiochus V Eupator). However once the defenders of the fortress of Mount Zion had surrendered, Lysias promptly "gave orders for the destruction of the surrounding walls" (1 Macc 6:62).

At this point Josephus introduces a digression which is absent from 1 Maccabees (*Ant* 12 §§ 383-388). After this last action he states that the king returned to Antioch in the company of the high priest Onias "also named Menelaus" (who, according to *Ant* 12 § 238 was the brother of Onias III and Jesus-Jason). Lysias had advised him to put Onias-Menelaus to death in order to appease the Jews, since he had been responsible for persuading Antiochus IV to "force the Jews to abandon the religion of their fathers" (ἀναγκάσαι τὴν πάτριον θρησκείαν καταλιπεῖν *Ant* 12 § 384); the king had him killed at Aleppo. In 2 Macc 13:3-4 it is God himself (βασιλεὺς τῶν βασιλέων) who provokes Antiochus' anger against Menelaus who, obviously, was not the brother of Onias III and Jason.

Josephus goes on to recount that Menelaus, for ten years high priest (172-162 BCE), had been "iniquitous and ungodly" in forcing the people to violate the law in order to achieve complete control of the situation. His successor was Alcimus, also called Jakeimos, who in 1 Macc 7:9 is confirmed high priest by Demetrius I Soter in 161/160 BCE.

At this point (162 BCE), "Onias, son of the high priest [i.e. Onias the son of Onias III], as stated hitherto [*Ant* 12 § 237], was but a child on his father's death [in 170 BCE]. Seeing that the king [Antiochus V Eupator] had killed his uncle Menelaus [Onias, brother of Onias III] and had granted the high priesthood to Alcimus . . . he fled to Ptolemy [VI Philometor], king of Egypt. He was treated with all honour by the king and his wife Cleopatra [II], receiving land in the νομός of Heliopolis, whereon he built a temple like (ὅμοιος) that in Jerusalem. Of this we shall speak at the opportune moment [*Ant* 13 §§ 62-73]" (*Ant* 12 § 387-388). Josephus' account continues with Demetrius I Soter's flight from Rome, thus taking up again his paraphrase at 1 Macc 7:1.

Josephus then follows Onias' Egyptian episode with some attention, inserting it into the paraphrase of 1 Maccabees and uniting the different parts according to his traditional method. In *Ant* 13 § 62, after speaking of the death of Demetrius I Soter, killed in battle against Alexander Balas (1 Macc 10:48), he breaks off the account of events related in 1 Maccabees and introduces the story of the building of the Temple of Leontopolis (*Ant* 13 §§ 62-73).

In *Ant* 12 § 387 Josephus had stated that Onias had fled into Egypt in 162, i.e. at the beginning of Demetrius I Soter's reign. In *Ant* 13 § 62 he states that "the son of the High Priest Onias who bore the same name as his father", having taken refuge with Ptolemy named Philometor (Ptolemy VI, 181-145 BCE), "lived in Alexandria as we have recounted." He then gives as synchronism for the construction of the temple the death of Demetrius I Soter (*Ant* 13 § 68), who died after reigning for eleven years (*Ant* 13 § 61): 162-151 BCE. Polybius (3.5.3) calculates a reign of twelve years, which puts the construction of the temple at about 150 BCE.

In this version, then, at the moment of his father's death, in 175 BCE (when Antiochus IV ascended the throne), Onias son of Onias III was a young boy of about ten. In 162, at about twenty three years of age, he fled to Egypt; in 150 BCE, at thirty-five, he founded the temple of Leontopolis.

His reason for requesting the king's authorisation to construct the temple was that he "saw that Judaea had been ravaged by the Macedonians and their kings", and that he "craved to acquire for himself eternal fame and glory" (*Ant* 13 §§ 62-63). By 150 the Temple of Jerusalem had been reconsecrated for fifteen years (1 Macc 4:52). Thus it was necessary to justify the erection of a temple of this kind. Deut 12:11 excludes any sacrificial cult other than that practised "in the place where YHWH shall choose to cause his name to dwell," i.e. in Jerusalem. Indeed Josephus states that Onias "was particularly encouraged in his desire by the words of the prophet Isaiah . . . who had prophesied that a temple to the Great God, τῷ μεγίστῳ θεῷ, would be raised in Egypt by a Jew" (*Ant* 13 § 64).

This passage (Isa 19:19) is found in a later gloss (19:16-25) to the "Oracle on Egypt" (19:1-15), which contains a clear allusion to the Jewish colonies known to us above all from the Elephantine papyri. Verse 18 possibly contains a reference to Heliopolis: the Qumran scroll (1Q Isᵃ) reads עיר ההרס, "city of the sun", instead of עיר ההרס, "city of destruction" (on חרס see Job 9:7 and Dhorme 1926:117); Symmacus has ἡλίου (Field 1875: 2.463b); the *Targum* בית שמש. But this does not necessarily imply an *ex eventu* prophecy – something also suggested by the fact that the text of Isaiah speaks, not of a "temple" but only of an "altar" and "pillar." "In that day there will stand an altar (מזבח) consecrated to YHWH in the land of Egypt, and a pillar (מצבה) for YHWH on its borders". Isa 19:19 would then seem to be used to justify the temple, rather than fabricated to justify its construction.

There follows in Josephus (*Ant* 13 §§ 65-71) a correspondence between Onias and Ptolemy VI Philometor and Cleopatra II. "Many and great are the services I have rendered you in the course of the war, with the help of God, when I was in Coele-Syria and Phoenicia and when I arrived with the Jews in Leontopolis in the νομός of Heliopolis" (*Ant* 13 § 65), Onias' letter begins. This seems to be the Onias whom Ptolemy VI Philometor and his wife Cleopatra placed with Dositheus at the head of the whole army (*AgAp* 2 § 49). In *AgAp* 2 §§ 49-51 Josephus mentions an episode which occurred after the death of Ptolemy VI Philometor (thus after 145 BCE) in which Onias was instrumental in saving Cleopatra II's life. The rest of the letter speaks of Jewish settlements, almost all of which possessed a temple (ἔχοντας ἱερά): built without regard to the rules, these had caused contention and division among the faithful. Given that the letter is almost certainly spurious, it is hard to gauge the exact significance of this. A. Vincent maintains that Onias' intention was to build only one ἱερόν for the whole country (Vincent 1937: 334), but this is nowhere stated in the letter. Its tone is decidedly hostile to the Leontopolis temple, since Onias states that he had found a suitable site in the fortress named Ἀγρία Βούβαστις (Naville 1891), with an abundance of trees and sacred animals. Adding his intention to purify it, he invokes the prophecy of Isaiah (*Ant* 13 §§ 62-68).

In their reply the sovereigns ask "whether this temple, built in an impure place and full of animals, can be pleasing in the sight of God" (*Ant* 13 § 70), and give their authorisation, while expressing their desire not to be guilty of violating Jewish law (*Ant* 13 § 71). Josephus' source is thus decidedly hostile to the Temple of Leontopolis, but its identity remains unknown to us.

9. As mentioned above, the *Mishnah* states precisely (and as the temple ceased its functions in 74 CE it can be considered reliable testimony) that the temple of Leontopolis was called the "House of Onias" (בית הוניו), and that it was considered unsuitable in some cases for precepts and vows. "[If one should say] 'I shall work to offer the holocaust,' he must offer it in the Temple [of Jerusalem]. [If one should say] 'I shall offer it in the House of Onias', he must offer it in the Temple [of Jerusalem] . . . [If one should say], 'I wish to become a *nazir*', he must make offer of his hair [*m. Nazir* 2:5] in the Temple [of Jerusalem]; if he makes the offer in the House of Onias, he has not met his obligations. [If one should say], 'I shall make my offer in the House of Onias', he must make it in the Temple [of Jerusalem], but, if he should make the offer at the House of Onias, he will have met his obligations. R. Simeon says: 'This man may not be considered a *nazir*'" (*m. Menahot*, 13.10).

The prevailing opinion, then, although a number of sages demur, is that the temple of Leontopolis had some legitimacy, albeit limited; it was certainly not considered idolatrous, as we have observed. It could therefore be deduced that, at the moment of its construction, it was accorded a legitimacy which was less than that accorded the Temple of Jerusalem, but which was based on the fact that the Egyptian temple acted as a surrogate for the one in Jerusalem. In other words, the *Mishnah* passage in question justifies the hypothesis that the temple of Leontopolis was founded during the period in which the Temple cult of Jerusalem was abolished: between 167 and 164 BCE.

In this period the Isaiah passage could in effect have constituted sufficient justification for a temple in Egypt wherein to practise the sacrificial cult of the Jewish God. The fact that it is mentioned and its legitimacy discussed in the *Mishnah* would indicate that it was different in character from the other minor Jewish sanctuaries, which had probably existed in Egypt for years but had never been mentioned in rabbinic literature.

According to 2 Maccabees, Onias III died around 170 (between 172 and 170), in the prime of life but, as already mentioned, when the author describes his appearing to Judas Maccabaeus before the battle of Adasa (2 Macc 15:13) he depicts him as "outstanding in age and dignity." This is not necessarily significant in itself, of course, but there are other elements which cast doubt on the account of his death in 2 Macc 4:30-38, besides those already given.

As Seeligmann has observed, "there is a definite gap between 2 Macc 4:6 and 7". In 4:1-6, Onias intends to report Simon to the king after realising that it would be futile to do so to Apollonius, governor of Coele-Syria and Phoenicia. In 4:7, however, Seleucus is already dead, Antiochus has already succeeded him, and Onias has been deposed and succeeded by Jason. It is then more than likely that "a great deal of the history of Onias III has been deleted between 2 Macc 4:6 and 7 by the Palestinian elaborator of the book, notably the passage dealing with the manner of his flight to Egypt when Jason usurped the high-priesthood, and the story of his establishment of the sanctuary of Heliopolis" (Seeligmann 1948: 91-92).

Jason of Cyrene, as a man of the diaspora, should have been interested in the building of a temple in Egypt. The epitomator however, probably from Jerusalem, who puts Onias in a highly positive light, must have found it unseemly for him to found a temple, not unlike that in Jerusalem, on Egyptian soil, in open violation of the norms of Deuteronomy.

10. Someone like Onias III could indeed have found credence at the court of Alexandria, anxious as it was to maintain a strong pro-Ptolemaic party in Jerusalem. While Antiochus IV punished the Jews for rebelling against their sovereign at the mere rumour of his death (2 Macc 5:5), depriving them of their traditional privileges and of the chance of worshipping their God in the Temple of Jerusalem (2 Macc 6:1; Parente 1994: 25-29), Ptolemy VI allowed a Jerusalem high priest,

unjustly robbed of his dignity, to recreate in Egypt conditions whereby sacrificial rites to the God of Israel could be duly performed.

All of this has a certain logic. It is considerably less likely, however, that the son of a high priest, with no such official role, and who had lived at the court of Alexandria since fleeing from Jerusalem when little more than a child, should have requested and been granted permission to build a temple like that in Jerusalem when the original one was once again fully functioning.

If, however, the temple had been erected in answer to a specific need, it might have been allowed to continue to function even after the rededication of the Jerusalem Temple, since the legitimate sacerdotal line represented by Onias probably refused to recognise the authority of the Hasmonean line which had established itself in Jerusalem.[11]

11. Besides the occasional references in Josephus, a papyrus and an inscription also refer to family history of the Oniads in Egypt, which I shall now examine more closely. The overall impression from these documents is that the family of the Oniads must have acquired a position of considerable importance, both in the administration and in the army, with excellent contacts at court. It is clearly a case of a number of generations, the succession of which must be precisely established.

Josephus provides sufficient elements to calculate the year of Onias III's birth, which we can take as the departure-point for further chronological calculations. In *Ant* 12 § 224 he states that, at the beginning of the reign of Seleucus IV Philipator (and not "Soter", as he writes), i.e. about 187 BCE, both the Tobiad Hyrcanus and Onias II died, the latter leaving the high priesthood to his son, Simon II, father of Onias III.

Onias II, son of Simon "the Just" (*Ant* 12 §§ 156-159: see above n. 2) was a narrow-minded, mean-spirited man who when Antiochus III and Ptolemy V Epiphanes (204-181 BCE) struck up an alliance, and Antiochus gave his daughter Cleopatra in marriage to Ptolemy (193 BCE), refused to pay the tributes stipulated by the agreement. For this

---

[11] Both Willrich (1895: 128) and Motzo (1924: 186 note) explain the presumed change from Onias III to his son as founder of the Leontopolis temple by an attempt to deligitimate the temple.

reason (*Ant* 12 § 160) the young Tobiad Joseph, son of Onias II's sister, travelled first to Jerusalem to persuade his uncle to accept the conditions and then to Alexandria, where he begged Ptolemy to "pardon his uncle on account of his great age" (*Ant* 12 § 272). Onias II was the son of Simon "the Just" (*Ant* 12 § 44), a contemporary of Ptolemy II Philadelphus (282-245 BCE), and a boy when his uncle Eleazar succeeded Simon during the reign of Ptolemy II (*Ant* 12 § 157). He must have been around seventy in 187 BCE, and must have been born about 260 BCE. His son Simon II would therefore, have been born around 235 BCE, and Onias III, Simon's son, around 215-210 BCE. Consequently in 175 BCE, the date of Antiochus IV's coronation and, approximately, of his own flight into Egypt or of his death, Onias III was around forty, and his son around ten or fifteen.

In 1865 W. Brunet de Presle published in Paris a papyrus discovered some years earlier by J.A. Letronne in the *Sarapieion* near Memphis, which Letronne had already studied (Brunet de Presle 1865: 360-374, esp. 361). It contains three letters from the διοικητής Herod to three different people, the first of whom, according to Letronne's reconstruction, was one Theon ('Ηρώιδης [Θέω]νι χαίρειν). The letter, dated September 21, 164 BCE, is addressed to a member of the court circle, of elevated rank, and gives news of the king and queen. The king is the pro-Jewish Ptolemy VI Philometor.

From his re-examination of the papyrus in 1913, however, U. Wilcken proposed a rather different reconstruction, claiming to read an *omikron* before the letters νι, making the heading: 'Ηρώιδης ['Ο]νί[αι] χαίρειν (Wilcken 1927: 473-496, esp. 487). The tone is very different from that of the other two, mere copies of documents dealing with agricultural questions. Given the place of discovery, Wilcken posits that the addressee might be the στρατηγός of the Heliopolis νομός. If we accept Wilcken's reconstruction, and consider the date, the letter must be addressed to Onias III, then fifty years old, and not his twenty or twenty-five-year-old son, since the recipient is clearly a high-ranking official of considerable influence. In this case the founder of the Temple of Leontopolis is necessarily Onias III and not his son.

In an aforementioned passage from *Against Apion* (2 § 49), Josephus affirms that Ptolemy VI and Cleopatra II "entrusted their entire kingdom to the Jews, and put Onias and Dositheus at the head of the whole army . . . that [Apion] might admire their exploits . . . and be grateful to them for having saved that city of which he had proclaimed himself a citizen". However exaggerated, this must contain an element of truth. The events referred to took place in the years immediately after the death of Ptolemy VI Philometor, (i.e., ca. 145 BCE), when Cleopatra II had proclaimed their son, Ptolemy Neos Philopator, king; Philometor's brother, Ptolemy VII Euergetes II called Physcon, came from Cyrene to Alexandria at the request of the Alexandrians, killed the young king, and seized possession of the kingdom by marrying the queen.

Nothing more is known about Dositheus. T. Reinach identifies the above Onias as the founder of the Leontopolis temple (Reinach 1930: 67 n. 3). This Onias undoubtedly belongs to the generation following Onias III and could therefore be his son, born around 190 BCE. Thus he would have been about forty-five in 145 BCE, a plausible age to lead, if not the whole Egyptian army, as Josephus claims, at least a regiment of Jewish mercenaries.

Josephus informs his readers in *Ant* 13 § 285 that when John Hyrcanus conquered Samaria (107 BCE), Queen Cleopatra was assisted in the war against her son, Ptolemy IX Soter II Lathyrus, by two Jewish generals, Chelkias and Ananias, "sons of the Onias who had built the temple in the νομός of Heliopolis, similar to the one in Jerusalem, as we have stated above [*Ant* 13 §§ 62-73]". If Onias, son of Onias III, really had been born in ca. 190 BCE, he could plausibly have sons born between 160 and 150 BCE, who had reached the highest military grades by the last decade of the century. One observation about this passage, however. Josephus takes his information including the names of the generals from Strabo, (whom he cites specifically): "only those Jews of the district which had taken the name of Onias remained faithful to her, since their fellow citizens Chelkias and Ananias were held in special honour by the queen" (*Ant* 13 § 287). The note that Chelkias and Ananias were sons of the founder of the temple of Leontopolis is surely Josephus'. With his fondness for internal references, he must have introduced it into the text in order to recall the passage about Onias and the founding of the temple (*Ant* 13 §§ 62-73). Strabo stated only that Chelkias and Ananias came from the district "which had taken the name of Onias."

An inscription discovered in Cairo possibly confirms that Chelkias belonged to the second generation after Onias III. The inscription was published by Willrich in the first volume of *APF* (dated 1901) and discussed by T. Reinach (Reinach 1900; Willrich 1901; see *CIJ* 2. no.

1450; Strack 1902-3: 554; Gabba 1958: 36-38). In Reinach's opinion it is an honorary decree from between 108 and 101, or 102 and 99 BCE. In the "premise" Chelkias' name in the genitive is quite clear (line 2). This Chelkias is almost certainly neither the benefactor nor the beneficiary of the decree, the latter being his son, whose name according to Reinach's, reading [Ὀνίας] Χελκίου στ[ρατηγός], was Onias. Chelkias' son, a commander-in-chief, would then have been a low-ranking official, as designated by the term στρατηγός in late second century BCE Egypt.

The name of "Onias" here while pure conjecture, based on the passage from Josephus discussed above, is, however, fairly plausible. If Chelkias was born around 150 BCE, as stated above, he might well have had a son who born around 125 BCE, by the end of the century was holding a reasonably important administrative position. According to Reinach the decree might have been granted by the members of the "people of the τέμενος," i.e., people living in the district of Heliopolis around Onias' temple, according to his reconstruction of line four reading: "ὑπὲρ τοῦ πλή]θους τῶν ἐν τῶι τεμένει κατοικούντων". The stone could be from the Temple of Leontopolis, not far from Cairo.

If we accept Wilcken's reconstruction of the papyrus discovered by Letronne, and T. Reinach's of the Cairo inscription, we then possess relatively precise information about four generations of Oniads in Egypt: 1) Onias III, founder of the temple of Leontopolis; 2) his son, of the same name, a general in the service of Ptolemy VI and Cleopatra II; 3) his two sons, Chelkias and Ananias, generals in the service of Cleopatra III; 4) Onias, son of Chelkias, an official in the Ptolemaic administration. Unfortunately, conjecture however plausible and convincing, is not necessarily fact, but our case for the Oniad family tree must rest on this. What is certain is that the family had soon risen within the Ptolemaic administration and army. This was probably one of the reasons why the Leontopolis temple continued to function until 74 CE.

12. The temple maintained a mostly local relevance, but caused some problems in Jerusalem. It is mentioned significantly in the *Mishnah* but not in Jewish-hellenistic literature (but see Delcor 1968: 201-202).

The passage in *Sibylline Oracles* 5.492-511, often read as a reference to the temple in question, almost certainly has nothing to do with it, as Geffcken noted (1902: 26). The fifth book of the *Sibylline Oracles* is a collection of six oracles against various nations in which the central figure is the born-again Nero returning as an adversary with the Parthians. The book is entirely Jewish apart from a Christian interpolation at 256-59, and was written in Egypt. The passage containing the putative reference to the temple of Leontopolis is in the sixth oracle, which speaks of a temple to the true God and its successive destruction by the Ethiopians. The reference is chronologically plausible, since the book certainly dates from around the end of the first century CE, but the temple in question cannot be that of Onias. In Egypt, the passage states, "there shall be a great, holy temple," (ναὸς μέγας ἔσσεται ἀγνός. Its construction is part of the eschatological process, as is its destruction. The divine wrath falls here when the Ethiopians destroy it as the first of their evil acts "until the last things may come to pass" (Sibyll. Or. 5.501-506).

Josephus reports that the temple was closed, not destroyed. Certainly it is difficult to see how its putative destruction could be considered the prime cause of the eschatological process, or how it could be defined a "great holy temple."

According to Collins (1974: 49-53), the third book of the Sibylline Oracles, written in Egypt in the mid-second century BCE and characterised by the expectation of salvation by a Ptolemaic king who assumes a Messianic character, could be the expression of the Jewish circles dominated by Onias, founder of the Temple of Leontopolis. This is not implausible. Alexandrian Judaism remained essentially extraneous to the eschatological and messianic aspects of Palestinian Judaism in the first centuries BCE and CE, which essentially recognised a royal messiah (of David's line), and a superhuman messiah (the Son of Man). This attribution of messianic characteristics to a king of the Ptolemaic dynasty belongs in part to the conceptual framework in which, according to Deuteroisaiah, Cyrus is YHWH's "anointed". From the evidence examined above, the founder of the Temple of Leontopolis and his descendants do indeed appear to be closely connected with single members of the Ptolemaic dynasty, not least of whom the pro-Jewish Ptolemy VI Philometor. If, however, a Jewish colony of an unequivocally military nature was able to express its politico-religious expectations in elaborate hexameters, it was necessarily much more socially articulate than the evidence we have of them would lead us to suppose.

13. These observations, however, are only marginally relevant to the problem under discussion: whether the founder of the Leontopolis temple was Onias III or his son, or, in other words, whether Onias III was assassinated by Andronicus in 170 BCE at Antioch, as stated by 2 Macc 4:32-35, or whether he fled to Egypt as attested by Josephus in *JW* 1 §§ 31-33.

Most historians still read in Dan 9:26 and 11:22, and *1 Enoch* 90:8 allusions to Onias III's violent death. Should this be so, the balance would hang decidedly in favour of the son of Onias III being the founder of the temple.

The most important passage is the first one: "And after sixty-two weeks, an anointed one shall be cut off (יכרת משיח) and there shall not be for him . . . . As to the city and the sanctuary, the people of a leader who is to come shall destroy them. Its end will come to pass in a flood, and until the end shall there be terrible war and devastation". This occurs in the explanation given Daniel by the angel Gabriel (9:21-22) of the seventy years prophecy in Jer 25:11-14: "In the first year of Darius . . . I, Daniel, did read in books the number of years which, in accordance with the word of YHWH to Jeremiah the prophet, shall pass over the ruins of Jerusalem: seventy years" (Dan 9:1-2). Gabriel's explanation is that "seventy weeks [of years] are fixed for your people and your holy city to cease all iniquity, to put an end to sin, to expiate the offence . . . since the pronunciation of the word on the reconstruction of Jerusalem until the anointed leader, seven weeks. Sixty-two weeks, fortress and moat will be rebuilt, but in a time of misadventure. And after the sixty-two weeks, an anointed one shall be cut off . . . " (9:24-26).

The "anointed leader" (משיח נגיד) of 9:25 is almost unanimously read today as the high priest Joshua (Hag 1:1, 14; Zech 3:1), rather than Cyrus (cf. Isa 45:1), and the "anointed one that shall be cut off" as Onias III, even though the sixty-two weeks, i.e. 434 years, exceed by 64 years the period from the restoration to Antiochus IV.

14. The interpretation of this passage has an interesting history.[12] As seen above, Dan 9:26 has a gap: ואין לו, "and there shall not be for him . . . .". LXX gives an interpretation which presupposes a slightly

---

[12] For the history of interpretation in ancient and medieval times see Fraidl 1883.

different Hebrew text, but with the same gap: ἀποσταθήσεται χρῖσμα καὶ οὐκ ἔσται, "the anointment shall be removed and shall not be . . .": instead of מָשִׁיחַ, "anointed one", LXX has read מִשְׁחָה, "anointment" (e.g. Lev 7:36 P), "the anointment (the priesthood) shall be removed (interrupted)". In the Hebrew text, however, the verb, יִכָּרֵת, is the *nifal* imperfect of כרת, which in H and P is the technical term to indicate the act of "being cut off" from the community due, to some crime carrying the sentence of capital punishment (Gen 17:14; Lev 7:20, 21, 25 and 27; Num 9:13 etc.; Zimmerli 1954 esp. 13ff.; Boecker 1964, 145 note 4; Hasel 1984), i.e. the Hebrew verb presupposes a person as subject. The LXX interpretation is further developed by Theodotion, who completes the gap thus: ἐξολοθρευθήσεται χρῖσμα, καὶ κρῖμα οὐκ ἔστιν ἐν αὐτῷ, "the anointment shall be destroyed (abolished) and there shall no longer remain judgement (משפט Nestle 1884) in it", while Symmachus translates the Hebrew literally: ἐκκοπήσεται χριστός and Aquila gives ἐξολοθρευθέσεται ἠλειμμένος, "the anointed one shall be destroyed", presupposing not simply the Hebrew מָשִׁיחַ but also a Greek χριστός given that Aquila (a revision of previous translations rather than a new one) everywhere substitutes ἠλειμμένος for χριστός, which had become a Christian technical term.

The Vulgate has *occidetur Christus*, filling the gap with an openly Christian gloss: *et non erit eius populus qui eum negaturus est*. *Occidetur Christus* is also certainly a translation that has been aligned to Christian usage since in Tertullian (or pseudo-Tertullian), *Adv. Iudaeos* 8:6 we read: *Et post ebdomadas has LX et II semis exterminabitur unctio, et non erit; et ciuitatem et sanctum exterminabit cum duce adueniente,* (1358, 3-5 Kroymann) with the explanation *expletis his quoque temporibus et debellatis inde Iudaeis postea cessauerunt illic libamina et sacrificia, quae exinde illic celebrari non potuerunt. Nam et unctio illic exterminata est post passionem Christi* (8,17; 1363, 4-8 Kroymann). *Unctio*, then, is the Hebrew priesthood abolished on account of the destruction of the Temple and, previously, of Christ's redemption.

Eusebius takes substantially the same line. "In the Book of Daniel", he writes (*HistEccl* 1.6.11), "having established very clearly the exact number of weeks until the anointed leader, ἕως χριστοῦ ἡγουμένου [Dan 9:24] as we have demonstrated elsewhere [*Ecl.proph.* 3.26, 153,12-165,7 (Gaisford) and *Dem.Evang.* 8.2.55-129] it is shown that, when these weeks have passed, the anointment will disappear from among the Jews (ἐξολοθρευθήσεσθαι τὸ παρὰ Ἰουδαίοις χρῖσμα), and this can clearly be seen to have come to pass at the moment of the birth of Our Saviour Jesus Christ" (1, 52, 14-15 Schwartz). The passage in the *Demonstratio Evangelica* alluded to by Eusebius contains an interesting observation: the succession of legitimate pontiffs was interrupted by Herod's killing of Hyrcanus II (384 Heikel). The idea was taken up by Theodoret in what is for us the first complete commentary on Daniel (*PG* 81: 1480-1481 on Dan 9:26): from Herod onwards the high priests were not consecrated, i.e. anointed, according to the Law, but merely nominated by foreigners like Herod himself, Archelaus, and the Roman procurators.

This was the interpretation given the most credence in late antiquity and the early Middle Ages, well summarised by Isidore of Seville in his *Chronicon* 66 (*PL* 83:1038B): *Octavius Augustus regnat annis LVI . . . sub cujus imperio septuaginta hebdomadae in Daniele scriptae complentur, et cessante regno et sacerdotio Judaeorum, Dominus Jesus Christus in Bethleem Judae ex Virgine nascitur, anno regni eius XLII.*

A calculation of weeks could have given different dates, but the significance of the passage in Daniel was clearly understood: the birth of Christ and subsequent redemption had abolished the priesthood and the Jewish cult. Isidore spoke for the seventh century; in the eleventh, in his *Antilogus contra Judaeos* 4, Peter Damian was to write: *Quid apertius, quid expressius de morte Christi dici potest eo, quod dicitur,* "*occidetur Christus*"? (*PL* 145: 55A). The passage quoted is from the Vulgate, and it is therefore singular that the expression *occidetur Christus* only refers to the death of Jesus after a certain point in time. What had happened between Isidore and Peter Damian?

The answer is to be looked for in the ever-growing importance, from the ninth century onwards, of converted Jews to Western ecclesiastical culture. Indirect testimony (indirect in that the text was known only subsequently) is that of the short *De adventu messiae praeterito liber* by Rabbi Samuel Marochianus, written in Arabic in 1085 and translated into Latin by Alfonso Bonomo in 1339.[13] Rabbi Samuel, a converted Jew from Fez, writes (in the Latin translation):

---

[13] The work was first published in Basle in 1474; republished ten times before 1500 and many times during the 16th century. It was translated into Flemish, German, Italian, and Spanish. The Latin text was republished in the *Bibliotheca Patrum* (1589), in the *Maxima Bibliotheca Patrum* (1677) and eventually in *PL* 149: 335-368.

Certe, domine mi, ego non video evasionem contra prophetiam istam, quia
de facto isto probatur nobis quod postquam a reaedificatione fuerunt
completae septuaginta duae hebdomadae supra annos, qui sunt anni CCCC
et XXXIII, tunc fuit Jesus occisus a patribus nostris, et postea venit dux,
scilicet Titus et populus Romanus, et fecerunt nobis secundum prophetiam
istam, hodie sunt mille anni et ultra, et nihilominus si in ira Dei sumus, et
tamen in ipso speramus (*PL* 149: 344D).

The exegesis of a converted Jew was based on the Hebrew text, a text
which amply justified the interpretation whereby one "anointed one"
had been killed and whereby the prophecy could only refer to the
death of Jesus. This interpretation soon became, as it were, official and
the prophecy of Daniel's seventy weeks of years accordingly became
one of the many christological prophecies of the Old Testament.

15. The calculations could, however, produce quite different results by
taking a different starting point. In 1672 John Marsham, in a seminal
work in the history of chronography, affirmed that the angel announced to Daniel two "reconsecrations" (ἐγκαινισμοί) of the
Temple: *Prior, post captivitatem Babylonicam, à Josuâ & Zerobabele;
posterior, post alteram* Unctionis excisionem *(nunc primum Danieli
revelatam) a Judâ Maccabaeo celebratus est* (Marsham 1672: 572). This
consequently places the destruction of the first Temple as the starting-
point for the calculation, and identifies Antiochus IV's profanation of
the Temple with the *unctionis excisio* of Dan 9:26.

An interpretation based on the LXX whereby ἀποσταθήσεται
χρῖσμα indicates an interruption either of the legitimate priestly line
or of the cult leaves, however, unresolved the problem raised by the
MT where it is a person who is killed; and this person is clearly
referred to as "anointed," i.e., consecrated (and therefore a king or
priest). A solution satisfying both the chronological calculation, placing
the event at the beginning of the Maccabean period, and the precise
semantics of the Hebrew text was found by Jean Hardouin, the
ingenious if eccentric librarian of the Collège de Clermont, in 1677.

Onias, qui summus sacerdos ante annos sex fuerat, *Antiochiae secus
Daphnem*: ubi tuto loco se continebat, interficitur ab Andronico, qui eum
astu *de asylo* retraxerat. 2 Mach. IV,33 . . . Onias summus sacerdos, post
LXII hebdomadas interfectus, ante abominationem desolationis in templum
ab Antiocho inferendam, typus Christi occidendi ante excidium aedis &
Urbis fuit: quemadmodum & quod post Oniae occisionem desertus est a Deo

> populus, qui eum urbe expulit . . . . Discrepat toto genere Josephi narratio
> ab ista. Oniam enim ille ponit aperte ante annos quinque diem supremum
> placide obiisse, priusquam Iason sacerdotium iniret, libro XII. Antiq. cap. VI.
> Exspecto qui se Catholicos dicant, & Josephum anteponant auctori libri
> Machabaeorum; cui tamen sacro scriptori Danielis etiam vaticinium (ut
> inferius videbimus) aperte suffragatur (Hardouin 1699: 182-183)

As he himself points out, Hardouin's interpretation satisfied chronological needs while opting between two contrasting versions of events
for the one given in a canonical, and therefore inspired text. Since,
however, the "anointed one cut off" had for centuries been identified
as Christ and it was impossible to wipe it away with one stroke,
Hardouin felt the need to describe Onias as a *typus Christi*.

His hypothesis, defined *nova et inepta*, found few followers and
aroused violent reactions. Bernard Lamy, an Oratorian who in his
youth had been a friend of Richard Simon's, had gone carefully over
the calculation of the weeks, reaching the conclusion that they ended
exactly in 33 CE, the year of Christ's death. *Sic medium ultimae
hebdomadis; id est media pars septem annorum, incidit in annum aerae
Christianae 33. in quo Jesum Christum passum esse demonstravimus*
(Lamy 1699: 1.181). This obviously excludes any plausible identification
of Daniel's "anointed one" as Onias III, who as Lamy observes, had
no merits to justify the *typus Christi* appellative. *Expende, lector, an viro
qui meritus sit dici Christi typus, conveniat ut reciperet se ad gentes, &
moraretur in fano, hoc est, inter idola, occidereturque extra Judaeam; cum
affirmante Domino, Christus non extra Hierosolyma occidendus esset?*
(Lamy 1699: 182).

Hardouin replied by praising the LXX, the "prophetic text" by
definition, which formulates all the christological prophecies of the OT
with utmost clarity. *Fuere igitur ex eorum numero Septuaginta Interpretes,
qui vel Messiam occidendum esse non crederent, vel ne crederetur,
falsandam esse potius scripturam sacram censerent?* (Hardouin 1709:
898a). If the prophecy in Dan 9:26 really did refer to Christ, the LXX
would certainly not have interpreted it as it did.

Augustin Calmet, while citing diverse and more "orthodox" opin-
ions, seems to have been convinced by both Marsham and Hardouin.
In his commentary he avoids taking any definite stand, but in the
Dissertation sur les Septante semaines de Daniel writes:

> *L'Oint du Seigneur mis à mort à la fin de la soixante deuxième semaine*, est le
> Grand-Prêtre Onias. Trois ans & demi après sa mort, c'est-à-dire au milieu

de la septantième & dernière semaine, les sacrifices cessèrent dans le
Temple, & l'abomination de désolation y fut placée. Elle y demeura trois
ans, jusqu'à la fin de la septantième semaine, que Judas Maccabée nettoya
le Temple, & y rétablit les sacrifices, & le culte du Seigneur. Tout cela est
bien prouvé dans l'Histoire des Maccabées . . . (Calmet 1726: 620).

Battle-lines were now firmly drawn up, and Calmet was violently
attacked. In a note added to the 1745 republication of Robert
Estienne's Latin Bible (on Dan 9:26) we read:

Ac de Scriptoribus *Christianis* Marshamum non moramur, praeter luctuosa
Antiochi Epiphanis tempora nihil in toto *Dan* 9°. cap. cernentem. R^m. P^m.
Calmet miramur, qui postquam in Diss.de 70.Hebd. p.618 & contra Ecclesiae
mentem, & multis praeterea ex partibus peccare Marshami systema ostendit
. . . . Tamen in v. 26 *Christum occidendum* interpretatur Calmet cum
Harduino Oniam pontificem, loco Marshami sacerdotii & c. (Vatable 1745:
640a-b).

16. In the early nineteenth century Hardouin's hypothesis was accepted
by the majority of Protestant historians (but not by the Anglicans such
as Pusey 1876: 167-233 with throughgoing discussion of German literature), though with the occasional important exception. Hofmann (1836:
51ff.); Wiesler (1839: 49-58); Hitzig (in the second edition 1850: 162,
contrary to the first one 1838) were for Onias III; Rösch (1834:294);
von Lengerke (1835: 445) and Ewald (1868:435) maintained that the
"anointed prince", משיח נגיד, of 9:25 was not the high priest Joshua
but Cyrus, who had been given the title in Deuteroisaiah and that the
"anointed one cut off" of 9:26 was Seleucus IV Philopator, brother of
Antiochus IV, killed by Heliodorus (Appian *Syr.* 45) about 176-175
BCE and very clearly alluded to in Dan 11:20. On the other hand in
9:25 the "anointed one" is a משיח נגיד, an "anointed prince", an
expression which hardly covers a high priest, particularly in a period
when he was still far from being "head of the people", and in this case
allied with a Persian governor to boot (Ezra 5:2; Hag 1:1). Furthermore, the clearly incomplete expression ואין לו, "and there shall not
for him", at 9:26 could be reconstructed: "and he had no descendants"
(Bertholdt 1806-8: 663-664 and many others). Antiochus IV did indeed
rush to kill Antiochus, the young son of Seleucus IV whom Heliodorus
had proclaimed king. As Ewald comments, "Nachher, heisst es v.26,
wird *ein Gesalbter* ausgerottet d.i. gewaltsam getödtet oder *umgebracht
werden und niemanden haben*, keinen nächsten nachfolger oder erben

haben, nämlich Seleukos IV. Philopator, welcher im j.176 v.Chr. von Heliodor umgebracht wurde ohne dass ein sohn oder verwandter um ihn war der nach seinem willen ihn beerbte" (Ewald 1868: 3.435).

Wellhausen (1905: 125-127), in casting doubt on the reliability of the news of Onias III's assassination by Andronicus in 2 Macc 4:43-50, is evidently considering his teacher's hypothesis regarding Dan 9:26. For early-twentieth-century commentaries on Daniel (Bevan 1892; Driver 1900; Marti 1901; Montgomery 1927; Charles 1929) the "anointed one cut off" of 9:26 has automatically been taken as Onias III, and the difficulties largely ignored. Recent criticism adopts similar positions. L. F. Hartman in his commentary on Daniel accepts the current hypothesis and adds: "The story of these events is told at length in II Macc. 4:1-38, which is substantially historical" (Hartman and Di Lella 1978: 252).

Dan 11:21 speaks of Antiochus IV's accession to the throne: he will "take possession of power by means of intrigue." The following verse explains how this took place, by killing the "prince of an alliance," נגיד ברית. Here too the use of the term נגיד makes it less probable that it alludes to a high priest rather than the legitimate successor of Seleucus IV. ברית seems here to be given a profane meaning: see 9:27.

1 Enoch 90:8 is part of the *Book of Dreams* (83-90) comprising the account of two of Enoch's dreams. The first (83-84) concerns the Flood, the second (85-90) is a compendium of the history of the world from creation to the messianic era. The first five verses of chap. 90 cover the period from Alexander the Great to the Maccabean revolt. Verses 6-7 refer to the birth of the *hasidim* movement. Having joined forces with Mattathias (1 Macc 1:42), they successively separated from the Maccabees and were reconciled with Alcimus (1 Macc 7:13): "And the sheep no longer bleeted at them, and they took no further heed of their words, but became as deaf, and their eyes were ever more blinded" (*1 Enoch* 90:7). The passage seems to allude to the *hasidim*'s change of attitude (1 Macc 7:12-13), and therefore to 161/160 BCE, more than ten years after Antiochus IV's accession and the presumed death of Onias. *1 Enoch* then adds, for what it is worth given the overtly apocalyptic language: "I saw as in a vision the crows fall on the lambs, grasping one, tearing the rams apart and devouring them" (90:8). But this verse can hardly refer to a murder such as that of Onias described in 2 Macc 4:43-50. The text points to a wholesale slaughter (in battle or other circumstances) and the capturing (but not killing) of an eminent person who is apparently killed later. As Dillmann posited, this corresponds better to the last episodes in Jonathan's life than to Onias: Jonathan was defeated by Tryphon at Ptolemais in 143 BCE, captured, and successively put to death (1 Macc 12:48 and 13:23) (Dillmann 1853: 277-78). Even though the common dating of *Enoch* 85-90 before 160 BCE would militate against this identification, there is in any case no clear reference to Onias.

17. Before drawing some conclusions from the points discussed, let me first list the single documented traditions:

a) 2 Macc 4:31-33. Between 172 and 170 BCE Onias III was assassinated by Andronicus in Daphne, near Antioch, at the suggestion of the high priest Menelaus, brother of Simon, προστάτης of the Temple (2 Macc 4:23), who succeeded Jason (2 Macc 4:26), brother of Onias III. There is no mention in 2 Maccabees of the Temple of Leontopolis or a son of Onias III.

b) Josephus.
   1) *JW* 1 §§ 31-33. On the occasion of the profanation of the Temple by Antiochus IV (end of 167 BCE), Onias III flees to Alexandria and founds the Temple of Leontopolis.
   2) *JW* 7 §§ 420-436. Onias "Son of Simon", i.e. Onias III flees to Alexandria "when Antiochus was at war with the Jews" because he was reluctant to renounce a position of prestige and pre-eminence.
   3) *Ant* 12 §§ 237-239. Onias III dies (a natural death) in 175, before the Hellenisation of Judaea. The Temple of Leontopolis is founded by his son, of the same name.
   4) *Ant* 13 §§ 383-388. In 162 BCE, Antiochus V Eupator has Onias "also named Menelaus" put to death, i.e. (according to *Ant* 12 § 238) the younger brother of Onias III and Joshua-Jason. Another Onias, son of Onias III, flees to Egypt "because Antiochus V had killed his uncle." The news of Menelaus' murder is confirmed by 2 Macc 13:3-4, but Menelaus is the brother of Simon, προστάτης of the Temple (2 Macc 4:23), and not of Onias III.

c) Theodore of Mopsuestia, commentary on Psalm 54. Onias III, on Jason's building the gymnasium (175 BCE), leaves Jerusalem to seek refuge in Egypt where he erects a temple. For all preceding information Theodore seems to rely on 2 Maccabees.

d) Rabbinic literature. The founder of the Temple of Leontopolis is an Onias (חוניו, נחוניו). According to *b. Menahot* 109b, the Onias in question is the son of Simon the Just, i.e. Onias III, and he had an elder brother called Simon.

e) The papyrus discovered by Letronne, published by W. Brunet de Presle and examined by Wilcken. Dating from 164 BCE, with Wilcken's reconstruction ['O]νί[αι] it necessarily refers to Onias III.

The account in 2 Macc 4:31-33 is the most widely accredited and followed by historians and forms the basis for the equally widely accepted interpretation in Dan 9:26. It is, however, totally unreliable: the description of the killing of Onias III contains a number of implausible details. The narrative frame of the murder may be in reality that of the young Antiochus, the son of Seleucus IV Philopator, for which Andronicus was put to death; as Seeligmann has observed, there is an unequivocal gap between 2 Macc 4:6 and 7.

Theodore of Mopsuestia's version, seemingly based on 2 Maccabees since it mentions Heliodorus' abortive attempt to sack the Temple, has it that faced with the introduction of Hellenism into Jerusalem, the then-deposed Onias III hid in Egypt and there built an altar and temple to continue cult worship. This tradition is also documented by Josephus in *JW* 1 §§ 31-33 and 7 §§ 420-436. It should be observed that the first of these two passages refers to the prologue, the second to the epilogue, so that neither is an integral part of the work, both having been added successively. The second is inexact in stating that Menelaus was Onias III's brother; it is also decidedly hostile to Onias.

The fact that both the rabbinic traditions and those drawn on by Josephus present Onias alternatively positively and negatively reflects attitudes towards the temple of Leontopolis itself — now positive (justifying its existence), now negative (denying its legitimacy). Similarly, the *Mishnah* states that the validity of certain sacrificial offerings made there (connected with the completion of nazirate vows) was recognised. This is explicable only by presupposing that in a given period, and in exceptional circumstances, full validity had been granted to sacrifices made in the temple. As stated above, this could only have been when the Temple of Jerusalem had ceased to function, i.e., between 167 and 164 BCE.

If we accept this deduction, the tradition documented by Josephus in *JW* 1 §§ 31-33 and 7 §§ 420-436, by rabbinic literature (*b. Menahot*

109b) and by Theodore of Mopsuestia in his commentary on Psalm 54 emerges as clearly the most plausible, particularly if we consider that Wilcken's proposed reconstruction of Letronne's papyrus is the result of direct inspection, and not mere conjecture.

Onias III, as head of the pro-Ptolemaic party, was deposed by Antiochus IV immediately after his accession to the throne. From his refuge with Ptolemy VI, Onias had no part in the opposition to the introduction of Hellenism into Jerusalem led by his brother Jason, who had replaced him as high priest. Having received from Ptolemy VI an administrative position, most probably as στρατηγός in the Heliopolis νομός, when the Temple of Jerusalem ceased to function, Onias obtained from the king permission to found a temple which might in some way replace it, justifying the procedure on the basis of Isa 19:19. Only an illegally deposed high priest would had the authority to take such a step. In Egypt his descendants were active above all in the army as leaders of Jewish mercenaries. They probably also held more important positions, defending as we have seen above different members of the dynasty. For this reason they were able to keep the temple of Leontopolis functioning, rejecting the Hasmonean sacerdotal line, even after the Jerusalem Temple had been reconsecrated. For the same reason a number of Sages continued to recognise the Egyptian temple as valid.

Successively, Onias III had to appear in a positive light even though the construction of a rival temple constituted a patent violation of the law. The undertaking was, therefore, attributed to a son by the same name — a detail which is far from straightforward. To remove all blame from Onias it was said that he had died previously, without specifying how. This is the version Josephus gives in *Ant* 12 §§ 237-239 and 383-388.

The author of 2 Maccabees, greatly inclined to find tragedy and high drama everywhere, adopted this version but without mentioning the temple of Leontopolis, and transforming the death of Onias into his murder. Wellhausen is probably right in asserting that the same author also simply replaced the murder of Seleucus IV Philipator's young son Antiochus with that of Onias, a hypothesis which is far from "du pur arbitraire", as Abel would have it (Abel 1949: 343-344).

That said, reasons remain for believing that the description of the death of Onias was not part of the original epitome of the work of Jason of Cyrene. The image of the stately, elderly Onias accompanying

Jeremiah in Judas Maccabaee's nocturnal vision (2 Macc 15:12-14) may well derive from Jason, who maintained that Onias had not been assassinated. However, the textual gap perceived by Seeligmann (1948: 91-92) between 2 Macc 4:6 and 7 invites caution. The news of Onias' flight into Egypt seems to have been removed from 2 Maccabees at some stage after the text had been completed, since the gap is still visible. Therefore it follows that the report of his murder was added afterwards.

The traditions which present Onias III in a positive light must have originated from the party hostile to the Hasmonean priestly line. Having Onias killed by Andronicus meant making a martyr of him, thus extolling the legitimacy of the Oniads as against that of the usurping Hasmoneans.

Conversely, affirming that Onias had fled to Egypt at the time when Antiochus was profaning the Temple, moved by resentment at those who were forcing him into exile, and with the idea of attracting the multitudes away from the Temple of Jerusalem, means accusing the line of the Oniads of treachery, thus implicitly extolling the Hasmonean line which had stayed put, faced the Syrians, reconsecrated the Temple, and once again made worship of the God of Israel possible. This contraposition is also echoed in rabbinic literature.

In any case, we do have a tradition that is well-documented in a variety of sources, according to which Onias III was the founder of the Leontopolis temple. Given this fact, the question arises how such a tradition could have originated, if Onias III had really been killed in 170 BCE as 2 Maccabees affirms.

If, however, this reconstruction of the facts is accepted, the ingenious hypothesis of the Collège de Clermont's clever and eccentric librarian (Hardouin 1699: 182-83; 1709: 898a), which now enjoys almost unanimous critical consensus, has to be jettisoned, and the problem of the "anointed one cut off" of Dan 9:26 roundly thrown open once again.[14]

---

[14] The author is grateful to Professor Frederick E. Brenk, S.J., for many suggestions that have considerably improved this paper.

FLAVIUS JOSEPHUS, HISTORIAN OF ROME

Mireille Hadas-Lebel

Flavius Josephus is generally described as a Jewish historian, which he most certainly was, occasionally as a Greek historian because of the language in which his works have reached us, but never as a Roman historian. Yet it is in Rome that Josephus, a Roman citizen since the year 69, spent at least half of his life; it is in Rome that he wrote his entire works; and the shadow of Rome hovers over most of the period he describes.

The time has come, as we shall try to demonstrate here, to render Josephus his dimension as an historian of Rome. The passages in *Ant* 18-20 devoted exclusively to Roman history do not suffer by comparison to parallel passages by Suetonius or Tacitus. How is it that Josephus had information that is often more detailed than that offered by these acknowledged historians of Rome? His credibility regarding the Rome of his time depends on the answer to this question.

1. *Written Sources of* Antiquities *18-20*

The last three books of the *Antiquities* cover a period of 60 years (6 through 66 CE, when the revolt broke out). Josephus, who was born in 37 CE, the first year of Caligula's reign, can be considered a reliable witness from about the year 50 onward. He was able to obtain information on Nero's reign during his trip to Rome in 64/65, but who provided him with such valuable data on the reigns of Caligula and Tiberius to whom relatively long passages are devoted? These passages are so long that they can appear to be tedious digressions, described by Thackeray (1929: 68) as "interesting but strictly *irrelevant* detail(s) concerning Roman court history" (emphasis added). One of the explanations offered by the latter is that while Josephus was busy writing his *Jewish Antiquities*, the Emperor Domitian meditated on the reign of Tiberius: according to Suetonius "Except for the memoirs[1] and deeds of Tiberius he read nothing" (*Domitian* 20). Thackeray says "We can imagine that he (Domitian) would not refuse Josephus access to this source" (1929: 68). This implies that the two were on excellent terms, which is questionable, at a time when Tacitus was in favor at the imperial court.

Furthermore, such an explanation is only valid in the case of the reign of Tiberius. It cannot explain the origin of the extremely detailed account of Caligula's death that is found in *Ant* 19. One must assume that Josephus had the works of a contemporary Latin author translated (it is unlikely that he knew Latin well enough).

Ever since Th. Mommsen suggested it in 1870 (320-22), one name is used with disconcerting unanimity by all of those puzzled by this long digression on Roman history: Marcus Cluvius Rufus. This attribution deserves to be more closely re-examined.

In the modern editions a character by the name of κλουιος or κλουιτος, possible transcriptions of Cluvius, appears once in *Ant* 19 § 91, but Josephus never identified him as an historian or claimed him as a source. He is merely termed a "consular personage" and his presence in the account is justified only by the prudent answer he is said to have given to the Senator Vaticinius who questioned him about the conspiracy against Caligula. He is reported to have said, quoting the Iliad: "Noble friend, hold your tongue for fear that any other Achean hear your words" (14.90-91).

The assumption commonly accepted since Mommsen expressed it is based on the fact that a Roman historian by the name of Cluvius did live at the time of these events but his works have disappeared.[2] Pliny and Tacitus, who mention him, link his works rather to the reign of Nero.[3]

The truth is that while all pertinent Josephus manuscripts contain the name κλουιτος, the name Cluvius is found in none. In fact the entire assumption rests on the corrections made by Hudson in the

---

[1] cf. *Life of Tiberius* 61: "In a memoir in which he rapidly summarized his life, he dared write he punished Sejanus because he had discovered his fierce hatred for the children of his son Germanicus."

[2] Cf. Feldman, *Antiquities* vol.9 LCL pp. 212-13; 582 (bibliography). Feldman and others do however express some doubts.

[3] Pliny *Epist.* 9.19.5; Tacitus *Annals* 13.20 and 14.2. Plutarch mentions Cluvius (*Quaest. Rom.* 107) but in connection with an ancient event dated 361 BCE.

eighteenth century (χλουβιος) and Niese in the nineteenth (χλουιος). The uncertain spelling of a consular personage's name that, once modified, brings to mind that of an historian whose lost works deal with another era is meager evidence to justify such unanimity.

All of the other suggested written sources have already been recorded by L. Feldman (1962). Since all of these works have disappeared any conceivable content can be attributed to them: whether it be the story of Aufidius Bassus, Pliny the Elder, Servilius Nonianus, Seneca the Elder, Fabius Rusticus or of the Emperor Claudius who, according to Suetonius (*Claudius* 41), wrote the account of his youth.

These assumptions provide only names - one may or may not accept them - and leave the true question unanswered: why was Josephus suddenly so interested in Roman events?

Thackeray, who can at least be credited with raising this question, offers a purely formal explanation: Josephus took as a model the history of Dionysius of Halicarnassus in twenty volumes; however, since he probably lacked data, he did not hesitate to add padding, "notwithstanding its irrelevance to his proper subject" (Thackeray 1929: 69). This is an example of the casualness with which contemporary critics treat ancient authors! Thackeray however does not tell us why Josephus chose precisely the episode of the murder of Caligula. He does not consider either that Josephus could have apportioned his material otherwise in order to fill twenty volumes.

Two more plausible explanations were suggested by Feldman (1962: 329) but they are relevant only to Caligula's death. This event saved the Jews from disaster, as the insane emperor had planned to erect a statue of himself in the Temple of Jerusalem; to narrate his punishment would therefore be a fine way to praise Divine Providence. Moreover, as the intervention of Agrippa I had moderating effects on Caligula, Josephus saw an opportunity to flatter his son Agrippa II, another protegé of the Flavian emperors.

All this is not very convincing because in order to demonstrate the action of Divine Providence (as Philo did in the lost part of the *Legatio*), Josephus hardly needed to describe the details of the organization of the conspiracy against Caligula; furthermore, he had other, more direct means of flattering Agrippa II.

In the same article, Feldman suggests that Josephus may have thought this epic description could help to sell his work. But one wonders what Roman would have purchased the twenty volumes of the *Antiquities* for this digression alone.

2. *Oral Sources*

For all these reasons, the oral sources suggested by Feldman seem more promising. Indeed, Josephus knew many witnesses to recent events of Roman history: not only King Agrippa II who had obtained accounts from his father, but also the Jewish actor Aliturus who had helped him during his mission in 65 (*Life* § 16) and, above all, his protector Epaphroditus, Nero's freedman (*Ant* 1 § 8; *AgAp* 1 § 1; 2 §§ 1, 296; *Life* § 430). The latter two could have informed Josephus about political life in Rome under Nero, but hardly about events during previous reigns. And how could Agrippa II possibly remember so many details about events of his childhood? The war of the Jews against Rome, in which he had participated, was the subject of additional information he provided to Josephus by letter[4] and after the completion of the book; even if Josephus had frequent opportunities to meet with the king, it would seem that the latter did not engage in lengthy memory-filled conversations.

There is ample reason to give credit to oral testimonies recorded by Josephus. The events narrated are often anecdotes, and, most important, often contradict or are more complete than the parallel accounts by Tacitus or Suetonius on the reigns of Tiberius and Caligula. For example, Josephus credits Antonia, the mother of Germanicus with a considerable role in the disgrace of Trajan (*Ant* 18 §§ 181-82). He provides a much more prolix account of the scandal of the temple of Isis, which brought about the expulsion of the oriental cults (*Ant* 18 §§ 65-80). His narration of the death of Tiberius and of Caligula's accession to the throne differs greatly from those of Tacitus and Suetonius. The latter calls on at least two written sources concerning this matter, obviously not used by Josephus: Pliny and Seneca.

A discrete witness appears in Josephus' account; he is treated with consideration disproportionate to his rank and political role: Thaumastus, a former slave of Caligula's to whom Agrippa I, while still a prisoner of Tiberius, is said to have promised freedom in exchange for

---

[4] *Life* § 366: "If you will come to meet me, I shall also inform you about matters generally not known."

a drink. "He kept his word and repaid him as he had said; later, having become king, he set Thaumastus free with great ceremony who had been offered to him by Gaius the emperor, and he appointed him administrator of his fortune. When he died he left Thaumastus to serve his son Agrippa and daughter Berenice in the same function. Thus Thaumastus died at an old age with this title but this occured much later" (*Ant* 18 §§ 193-94).

Josephus can hardly be more explicit about having known Thaumastus since the latter "died at an old age." He obviously obtained all the anecdotes concerning the imprisonment and liberation of Agrippa I directly from him, since the young slave then lived within the imperial court. Josephus could easily question a freedman, a Greek as indicated by his name, who had probably learned Aramaic at the court of Agrippa II and to whom he viewed himself as socially superior. Josephus could have obtained his testimony in Rome where they both landed after 70 CE. Being in possession of little-known information of whose value he was aware, he chose to divulge it in his works.

Another indicator seems to corroborate this hypothesis. At various times, when evoking the reigns of Tiberius and Caligula, Josephus mentions the names of slaves unknown elsewhere: Eutychus, Caligula's coachman (*Ant* 18 § 179), Ballas, Antonia's emissary to Tiberius (*Ant* 18 § 182), Marsyas and Stricheus, two of Agrippa's freedmen (*Ant* 18 § 184), Evodus, Tiberius' freedman for whom Josephus had the most esteem (*Ant* 18 § 205), Callistus, Caligula's venal and insolent freedman who claimed he spared Claudius whom he was supposed to poison (*Ant* 19 §§ 64-69). These were all companions of Thaumastus' youth, saved by Josephus from oblivion.

3. *Josephus' Contribution to Roman History*

Josephus not only transcribed the words of the administrator Thaumastus, he also lived during the wars of Judea, a page of Roman history. Whether he be a direct or an indirect witness to the events he described, he indisputably offers historians of Rome additional information, which they too rarely think to seek in his works.

The works of Tacitus, our main source of data on the history of the High Empire, have not come down to us in their entirety. Unfortunately the books of the *Annals* concerning the disgrace of Sejanus (Book 5), the reign and the assassination of Caligula (Books 7-8) and the accession to the throne and reign of Claudius (Books 9-10) have been lost. This is precisely the period covered by Josephus in *Ant* 18-19. Brotier, an almost forgotten eighteenth century French commentator, saw their value and used them as sources of inspiration to reconstitute the lost works of Tacitus. This approach strikes us as exemplary.

Tacitus, whose anti-Judaism is well known, carefully concealed the friendship of Antonia, the mother of Germanicus and Claudius, with Berenice, the mother of Agrippa I; he thoroughly ignored the return of the latter to the throne thanks to Caligula's assistance; and he did not mention the protection Claudius granted to Agrippa II. Independently of their belonging to Jewish history, elements of this type would be useful to anyone wanting to study the relationship between Rome and the various vassals of the Empire.

The death of Tiberius offers an example of a case for which we have Josephus' account as well as that of Roman historians. Josephus offered a considerably more detailed narration of the last moments of Tiberius' life and of his succession than either Tacitus or Suetonius did. Tiberius who, all authors agree, believed only in fate, had left a will designating as equal heirs his grandson Tiberius, the son of Drusus, and Gaius, the son of his adopted son Germanicus. As it had been predicted to him that his successor would be the first one to visit him the following day, he sent the tutor for the young Tiberius. The former, on his way to the palace, met Gaius and let him go in first . . . .

Even more valuable information is found in Josephus' work, for he himself witnessed an event crucial to the future of the Roman Empire: the accession to the throne of Vespasian.

We know the importance of this event in the life of Josephus: he survived only because after the siege of Jotapata in 67 he had predicted to Vespasian that he would become emperor; two years later the prediction came true and Josephus was freed by the new emperor and then became an historian. Suetonius, while evoking the portents that let Vespasian hope to become emperor mentions that "a noble captive by the name of Josephus declared with utmost confidence, when he was imprisoned, that he would soon be delivered by the very same Vespasian, then emperor" (*Vespasian* 5). This substantiates the testimony of Josephus.

We possess three parallel accounts of the election of Vespasian to the throne. In chronological order they are: that of Josephus (*JW* 4 §§

616-20) towards 75, that of Tacitus (*Histories* 2.81) towards 106 and that of Suetonius (*Vespasian* 6) towards 120 CE. According to Tacitus, the choice was made by Tiberius Alexander, prefect of Egypt, on July 1 of the year 69 CE and welcomed with enthusiasm by the army of Judea on July 3.

Suetonius reported that as other armies had done after Nero's suicide the preceding year, the two thousand men of the army of Moesia decided to designate the new emperor themselves. Though they were "both unknown to him and distant from him" their preference went to Vespasian, and they inscribed his name on all of their banners. Tiberius Alexander is said to have made his army swear fidelity to Vespasian on July 1, and the army of Judea is reputed to have followed suit on July 10.

The narration by Josephus was written prior to the other two and published during the lifetime of Vespasian. (Would he have dared to do so had it been incorrect?) It is extremely realistic and abounds in detail: Vespasian, indignant upon learning of the election of Vitellius to the throne, did not sail for Rome despite his impatience; his troops shared his indignation and compared the merits of their leader to those of the newly elected cruel and debauched emperor; they implored Vespasian to save the Empire; he cautiously hesitated and then declined. "But his officers insisted strongly, and the soldiers, who had gathered around him sword in hand, threatened him with death if he refused to live in a manner worthy of him;" he finally accepted. Before leaving for Rome, he wanted to secure the loyalty of Egypt, the bread basket of the Empire; he therefore wrote to Tiberius Alexander, who immediately had his army take the oath of fidelity. The legions of Moesia and Pannonia, hostile to Vitellius welcomed the news with joy.

Not only is Josephus' account superior in literary terms to the two others, it is also more convincing. What could be more natural than Vespasian's troops trying to bring him to power in this "year of the four emperors" during which the Roman army became aware of its political role? Without doubt they revered their commander and hoped to see his merits rewarded; they probably also expected to benefit from being known by the new emperor.

In addition to these reasons that could have motivated the army to designate Vespasian as the new emperor, one more must be added: the whole army knew that a Jewish captive by the name of Josephus, son of Matthias, defeated at Jotapata, had predicted that his vanquisher would become emperor. Predictions sometimes come true because they tend to provoke the event they foretell. Under this hypothesis Josephus could be credited with a much greater role. His account has the merit of explaining the election, which to many historians is still "not fully elucidated,"[5] of a man who apparently was not destined to become emperor.

How is it that Josephus' works are so rarely used as sources by historians of Rome? We believe the main reason to be that for centuries he was the only known historian contemporary of Jesus to have written about him. (We will not discuss the authenticity of the well-known *Testimonium Flavianum* in *Ant* 18). Since the first works on the history of Rome and that of Christianity, historians referred to Josephus as a witness of the "time of Jesus" and reserved pagan sources for purely Roman history. Though the Gospels and the works of Josephus display a few incompatibilities, the latter remains surrounded by a sacred aura that disqualified him in the eyes of secular historians.

The time has come to realize that Josephus' works contain more than what theologians sought therein: secular history prevails over sacred history.

---

[5] Cf. Le Glaz 1991: 260. He adds (262) "It is perhaps because Titus existed and had a brother that Vespasian was chosen to be emperor. His succession was practically certain." When Josephus briefly evokes this reason, it looks like flattery towards Titus. Many other generals throughout the Empire must also have had sons!

PART III

LITERARY AND OTHER MODELS

AMALEK IN THE WRITINGS OF JOSEPHUS

Johann Maier

1. *Introduction*

1.1 *Biblical evidence*

In Gen 36:12, 22 Amalek is one of the grandsons of Esau and in other Biblical texts he appears as a fierce archenemy of Israel. The Amalekites were the first who according to Exod 17:8-16 attacked the Israelites after their exodus from Egypt and together with other groups barred direct access to the Land of Canaan. They also figure among the most threatening neighbours throughout the early history of Israel. King Saul is said to have almost totally annihilated them. It was David, however, to whom the Bible attributes the elimination of this threat from the southern borders. Consequently, Amalek should have been regarded later on as a figure of the past but in traditional Jewish historiography he appears nevertheless as the *typus* of the foremost and irreconcilable enemy of Israel. Already in the Torah (Deut 25:17-19; cf. Exod 17:17-19; 1 Kgs 15:2-3) Israel is commanded a) always to remember what Amalek had done, b) to try to blot out the memory of Amalek, and c) not to forget it. The territory of Amalek is regarded as part of Israel's heritage just like the land of the Canaanites (Num 14:25) or the seven nations which God commanded and promised to expulse or to extirpate. In this respect they were (cf. Deut 2:4-9) in spite of their alleged descendance from Esau clearly distinguished from the Edomites "who live in Seir" and are called brothers of the Israelites and whose territory must not be invaded by the Israelites (cf. Deut 2:19 concerning the sons of Lot).

In the literature of early Judaism we find only a few references to Amalek outside the materials dealing with Biblical traditions. Some of them indicate an increasing interest in Amalek as a *typus*, a fact which is corroborated by the addition of the name Amalek on certain occasions by some translators or scribes of the Greek Bible.[1] The Biblical and early Jewish picture of Esau/Edom and Amalek is already a complex product of historical experiences and metahistorical evaluations (Dicou 1990; Hartberger 1986).

It is evident that Amalek represented an actual enemy for the early Jewish authors and not only one of the past. This image was possible by assuming that the Amalekites were still a living ethnic group trying to harm Israel and they were often identified with some dangerous contemporary tribes in the area. On the basis of the Book of Esther (see below) even Agagites, descendants of the Amalekite king Agag, were said to have survived. In other instances the designation "Amalek" had no genealogical implication at all but served as a mere code name for the most dangerous contemporary enemy (Nöldeke 1864). This metahistorical application remained in use throughout the centuries; even today it may be found in connection with Nazi-Germany and with Palestinians.[2] Both methods of application, the genealogical and the symbolical intertwined regularly. For Amalek remained in Jewish historiographic-political consciousness a figure in intimate relationship to "Esau/Edom" even when reduced to a mere *typus* without any stated genealogical links. One reason for this was that Esau/Edom himself constituted a metahistorical code name for the Roman empire in its quality as the most threatening political and eschatological power in the sense of Daniel's fourth kingdom.

It is the function as *typus* in this sense which is the subject of this paper. Not the historical relationship between the Edomites (Weippert 1982 with bibliography; Bartlett 1989; Axelsson 1987) and the Amalekites on the southeastern borders of Israel/Judah,[3] nor the real history of these ethnic groups but the use of their name as a symbol or a code name is what we are treating.[4]

The origins of the symbolic application of "Esau/Edom" to the Roman empire is difficult to trace. It is obvious that historical experi-

---

[1] 2 Kgdms 10:6 (B) for MT מעכה; Judg 7:1 (A); 1 Kgdms 15:13; 31:13 /2 Kgdms 1:1. On the other hand, the name Amalek has been eliminated in Judg 5:14 (A); perhaps due to an alternative reading, e.g., as a result of a correction as in Judg 12:15 in connection with a mountain called הר העמלקי in the land of Ephraim. See Thomas 1895: 426-28.

[2] Paganoni (1986) used "Amalek" for representatives of the anti-Zionist left.

[3] See esp. Bartlett 1989; Sawyer and Clines 1987; Bienkowski 1992; Finkelstein 1992.

[4] Daube (1977: 13) referred only to *Mekhilta R. Jishmael* on Ex 8-12.

ences during the late period of the kingdom of Judah, at the time of its fall from the 7th to the 6th century BCE and during the Persian period,[5] shaped the image of Esau/Edom as the menacing rival "brother" and neighbour of Israel. The geographical basis of this threat was the Negev, south of Judah, and it was this specific confrontation which overshadowed also the Biblical items which point to an original location of Amalek on the eastern side of the Arabah (Simons 1959: 1-2; Thomas 1895: 427-32). According to Exod 17:8-16 and Num 13:28-29 it is evident that the Amalekites lived in the Negev, blocking the highways from the south and from the desert of Sin to the Land of Canaan. This is corroborated by (see below) Num 14:40-45 and Deut 1:44. According to Judg 1:16 the Amalekites were neighbours of the Kenites, and in 1 Sam 15:4-6 they are connected with the locality of Telaim/Telem which is in the Negev (Simons 1959: 317, 143). This is also mentioned in 1 Sam 27:8, a text which defines the regions of the Amalekites, Geshurites and Girzites as extending from Telaim to Shur near Egypt. The proximity to Egypt is also expressed in 1 Sam 15:7 ("from Havilah to Shur"). It seems therefore that during a certain period in Israel's history a group of tribes not only east of the Arabah but especially west of it, on the Sinai Peninsula was regarded as Amalekites or their allies. It is this situation which led to the description of Amalek as the ראשית (the best, the elite; LXX: ἀρχή) of the nations" in Num 24:20.

It was particularly the location on the western side that embarrassed some Jewish authors during the late Second Commonwealth. They tried to displace Amalek, locating them exclusively in the east again and thus excluding any claims from foreign tribes on the southern territories in question.

There is, however, another aspect which needs to be considered. 1 Chr 4 contains traditions (not attested elsewhere) about some southern clans of Judah. Beginning with v 24 there appear some strange remarks about the Simeonites and 4:41-43 report about a campaign of the Simeonites against Hamites[6] in the days of King Hezekiah of Judah. In vv 42-43 we read: "And five hundred men of these Si-

---

[5] Recent archaeological finds contributed much to the understanding of the historical relationship between Israel/Judaea and Edom. It was evidently the role of Edom after its expansion into the Negev and into the southern parts of Judaea which provoked the rivalry reflected in the Biblical texts. See Beit-Arieh 1989.

[6] See below on *Testament of Simeon* 6:3.

meonites, led by Pelatiah, Neariah, Rephaiah and Uzziel, the sons of Ishi, invaded the hill country of Seir. (43) They killed the remaining Amalekites who had escaped (cf. 1 Sam 30 in *Ant* 6 §§ 356-67), and they have lived there to this day." According to this tradition, Seir is evidently south of Judah and the remnant of the Amalekites from the days of David had found refuge here. There is no other historical evidence for this statement. The polemics in the Biblical prophetic books against hostile foreign nations do not include Amalek as a target while polemical sayings against Edom are quite common (Kaufmann 1977: 431-33; Cresson 1972). Thus the real enemy was "Edom" or tribes in the south which in certain traditions were characterized as descendants of Esau "the brother." The reason for the new rivalry was the fact that the Persian province of Edom developed tendencies to expand its territories (de Gens 1979/80). Consequently, the establishment of the new province of Judah with its increasing influence on former Israelite as well as Judaean populations in the south concurred with Edomite aspirations. An even more critical confrontation emerged during the Hellenistic period (Bartlett 1982). At the northern boundaries of Judah (Schreiner 1979: 224-25) the Samarians were playing a similar role and not by accident both groups met a comparable fate under the Hasmonean John Hyrcanus. The historiographical introduction of the Amalekites into the region of Seir/Edom in the south of Judah served perhaps as a basis for an excuse for campaigns into the territory of Edom. In addition, it may be have been done in order to avoid the impression violating the negative command not to attack the descendants of Esau or to invade the land of Edom/Esau (Deut 2:22-25). A hint of such conditions may be found in 1 Kgs 16:6, where the Hebrew textual tradition provides two readings. After his victory over Ahaz of Judah, King Rezin of Syria conquered Elat on the shore of the Red Sea and expelled all יְהוּדִים. He returned this area to אֲרָם, originally evidently אֱדֹם for Aram/Damascus has never been in possession of Elat. Consequently, אֲרָמִים/אֲדֹמִים came to Elat and settled there. The Hebrew Bible editions preferred the reading אֲרָמִים/"Aramaeans," whereas the Greek Bible translated - in a historical sense - "Idumaeans." This was done notwithstanding the accepted reading אֲרָם (and not אֱדֹם) in the first half of the verse, rendered as "Syria." But the authors of 2 Chr 28:4-5 simply skipped the passage in question, while Josephus in *Ant* 9 § 245 preferred in this case "Syrians." He thus followed the reading of the later MT but translated it according to the Greek of the first half of the verse.

By locating the Amalekites in the realm of Edom all military actions in Edomite territories appeared not only permitted but even as fulfillment of a positive command: to extirpate the memory of Amalek and to conquer their land. In later times we find this kind of argumentation in certain Rabbinic traditions (Maier 1993).

1.2 *Josephus' general attitude to "Edom"*

The Edomites ceased to represent an independent ethnic group after their defeat and forced conversion to Judaism under the Hasmonean John Hyrcanus (*Ant* 13 §§ 257-58).[7] The symbolic genealogical position of Esau was now free for a reinterpretation and a new application. This seems to have been a well known concept already at the end of the first century CE: Esau/Edom became a code name for the Roman empire.

Josephus tried to avoid any hint of the disastrous rival attitude toward Rome. Pleading for coexistence, he did not explicitly renounce the traditional eschatological expectations so far as they concerned a remote future. While reworking and interpreting the contents of the Book of Genesis his endeavours met a serious obstacle. The Jacob - Esau stories were at that time already conceived as indicating the relationship between Esau/Edom and Jacob/Israel. Consequently, Josephus had to eliminate any possible interpretion of the rivalry between the Biblical twins Jacob and Esau which represented typologically the rivalry between Israel and Rome. This fact has recently been pointed out again by L. H. Feldman (1987-8: 202-4; 1988-89) and M. Hadas-Lebel (1986; 1987; 1991; cf. Stern 1987). In some respects Josephus anticipated the attitude of some later Rabbis who also tried to avoid a direct confrontation with "Edom" by accentuating Amalek's character as the archenemy of Israel.

2. *Early non-Biblical Jewish evidence*

2.1 In the function as *typus* Amalek was not only conceived as a figure of the past or present but also as an eschatological enemy of Israel. At

---

[7] It is difficult to believe that some OT texts still reflect this new state of affairs, a hypothesis expressed by Diebner and Schult 1975.

the beginning of the "War Scroll" from Qumran we read in 1QM
1.1-2, that the "sons of light" will be waging their final wars ". . .
against the lot of the sons of darkness, against the army of Belial, the
host of Edom and Moab and the sons of Ammon, (2) and the ar[my
(or: the sons) of Amalek and the sons] of Philistaea and against the
hosts of the Kittim of Assur and with them to their help are the
trespassers of (the) covenant."

It is true that in this source the name Amalek has to be restored in
a lacuna. This has led to several alternative suggestions[8]. The given
restoration is rather plausible (Carmignac and Guilbert 1961: 91)
because of Ps 83:7-9 which is evidently the background of the passage.

2.2 In the Pseudepigrapha of the OT there is only one passage dealing
with Amalek, and it occurs again in an eschatological context, in the
Testament of Simeon 6:3, a prophetic oracle (similar to Num 24:17-19
and *Jubilees* 24:27-32):

> "Then the seed of Canaan will be destroyed
> and there will be no posterity to Amalek.
> All the Cappadocians shall be destroyed
> and all the Hittites shall be wholly obliterated.
> (4) The land of Ham[9] shall be wanting
> and all that people shall perish,
> and the whole earth shall be at rest from trouble
> and everything under heaven shall be free from war.
> Then Shem shall be glorified . . . etc" (trans. H. C. Kee in Charlesworth
> 1983: 787).

The traditional names "Canaan" and "Amalek" represent the non-
Jewish population of the Land of Israel and its surroundings (of
"Syria") during the Hellenistic era. The Cappadocians for example,
had a certain reputation as fierce soldiers. They appear in the Aramaic
Genesis Apocryphon from Qumran (1QapGen 21.23), where they
replace "Ellasar" in the MT of Gen 14:9 (LXX Ἑλλασάρ), and "the
land of Ham" points towards Ptolemaic Egypt. It seems that during
the Ptolemaic-Seleucid wars certain indigenous elements in the vicinity
of Judaea tried to gain ground at the expense of the Jews.

---

[8] Vermes (1987: 105): "and [against the army of the sons of the east]."
[9] Cf. above on 1 Chr 4:41-43.

2.3 *Philo Alexandrinus*

In the works of Philo of Alexandria Amalek represents most of all a certain type of immorality. The behaviour of the Amalekites illustrates the disastrous effects of πάθη (*De congregatione* 45-62 on Gen 36; *Legum allegoriae* 3.186-87).

3. *Flavius Josephus and the Biblical traditions on Amalek*[10]

3.1 *Gen 14:5-7 in Ant 1 § 174*

The Masoretic Text reads: ". . . and they defeated the Rephaites in Ashteroth Karnaim, the Zusaites in Ham, the Emites in Shaveh Kiriathaim, (6) and the Horites in the hill country of Seir, as far as El Paran near the desert. (7) Then they turned back and went to En-mishpat, that is, Kadesh, and they conquered the whole territory of the Amalekites, as well as of the Amorites who were living in Chazazon-Thamar."

In the geographical context of this passage, the Amalekites have to be located in the region of Kadesh in the western part of the Arabah. The Greek translators placed on the western side of the Arabah only the leaders of the Amalekites (the ἄρχοντες, reading שׂרי in place of שׂדה), and this only temporarily, during the war.

In *Jubilees* 13 we find a remarkably different but unfortunately not complete résumé of the story. The Aramaic *Genesis Apocryphon* from Qumran (1QapGen 21-22), however, provides a more elaborate version. In 21.28-29 (concerning Gen 14:6) it offers a peculiar reading:

> They defeated the Rephaites of Ashterot Karnaim, the Zumzamites of Ammon, die Emites of Shaveh-Kirioth and the Horites in the mountains of Gebal (replacing Seir!), arriving at El (30) Paran which is situated in the desert. And they turned back [. . .] . . . [. . .] in Hazazon-Thamar.

Unfortunately, the passage regarding the Amalekites is not preserved, but it may be that the announced new critical edition will provide a more complete text. The replacement of "Seir" by "Gebal" is, however, sufficiently suggestive because it places the action unequivocally on the eastern side of the Arabah. Gebal, usually the Hebrew name for Byblos (Ezek 27:9, cf. LXX), refers also in Ps 83:8 (in the LXX

---

[10] Citations from the works of Josephus follow the LCL.

transcribed as Γεβάλ/Ναιβάλ) to a region on the eastern side of the Arabah. Eusebius in his *Onomasticon* (see index in Klostermann 1904) identified it more or less with Arabia Petraea (Simons 1959: 512). Seir, on the contrary, was also connected with areas on the western side, so it seems that certain traditions tried to locate the Amalekites unequivocally and exclusively on the eastern side. In this case Josephus could have used this tradition for the specific purpose of removing the Amalekites from the western side of the Arabah and placing them anyway in a region outside the Roman realm. This tendency is evident in his treatment of more than one Biblical passage, the first being Genesis 14 itself.

In *Ant* 1 § 174 Josephus omitted the passage "En-mishpat - that is, Kadesh - and the whole territory of the Amalekites and Amorites, as well as of the Amorites who were living at Hazor-Tamar" from Gen 14:7(-9). His version reads: "They ravaged the whole of Syria and subdued the descendants of the giants; then, on reaching the region of Sodom, they encamped in the valley called Bitumen pits." Josephus continues immediately with Gen 14:10: "for at that time there were pits." This procedure is almost certainly not an incidental shift but rather a deliberate omission with the aim of excluding any relationship between the region south of Judaea and the territory of the Amalekites.

3.2 *Genesis 36 in* Ant 2 §§ 5-6

a) Genesis 36 contains three lists of the descendants of Esau: (1) Gen 36:11-14 a list of his sons, (2) Gen 36:15-19 a list of rulers (the clans), and (3) Gen 36:40-43 a short list of the chiefs, clans and the regions involved. The list in Gen 36:12 concludes with Timna, calling her a concubine of Eliphaz who bore him Amalek. Gen 36:40-41, instead, as a list according to regions, begins with תמנע.

b) The author of a fragment from Qumran, 4Q252, frg. 1 col. iv, which recently has been published in a preliminary form (Wacholder and Abegg 1992: 214-15), added to the genealogical statement of Gen 36:12 a remark about King Saul and the Amalekites. It is followed by a citation from Deut 25:19 replacing the first part of the verse with באחרית הימים as in Num 24:14: "(1) Timna was a concubine of Eliphaz the son of Esau, and she bore him Amalek. It was he, who had been defea[ted by king] (2) Saul [(lacuna) . . . ,] as He had said to Moses (cf. Deut 25:19): *In the end of days you shall blot out the memory of Amalek (3) from under heaven*."

c) The Biblical designation of Amalek as the son of a concubine was certainly a polemical point and Josephus stressed this by speaking *expressis verbis* of a "bastard."

d) In his *Antiquities*, Josephus began Book 2 (§§ 1-3) with the juridic statement that after the death of Isaac his sons agreed to divide the territorial heritage according to their new changed status. Consequently, Esau left Hebron to Jacob, as told in Gen 36:6-8, and went to "Saeira" where he had lived before (see *Ant* 1 § 336). Immediately after this passage Josephus listed in accordance with Gen 36:9-14 the children of Esau by his three wives adding the sons of Eliphaz and concluding the passage Gen 36:9-14 with "the bastard (νόθος) Amalek" (*Ant* 2 §§ 4-5). Here (after Gen 36:14) he added a significant remark:

> These occupied the region of Idumaea termed Gobolitis and that called, after Amalek, Amalekitis; for Idumaea, formerly extensive, has kept that name for the whole country and in its several provinces preserved the names that were derived from their founders.

It is characteristic of Josephus[11] that after omitting the Amalekites in Gen 14 he tried to give the impression, that the Gobolites and Amalekites occupied a certain (eastern!) part of a territory once called in its entirety Idumaea. Also in *Ant* 3 § 40 and in 9 § 188 he designates this eastern part as the land of the Amalekites which is unequivocally identical with Arabia Petraea. This was at that time actually the realm of the Nabataeans and of other Arab tribes, but still outside the Roman empire. The region was a source of continual trouble until the establishment of the province "Arabia" under Trajan in 105/106 CE and the construction of the Limes (Sartre 1991; Parker 1987).

Thus we may conclude that Josephus deliberately placed the Amalekites in the eastern parts of an allegedly greater Idumaea of the past. This was done not only in order to remove them from the territory of a later Idumaea but also to identify the archenemy of Israel — Amalek — as an actual enemy of Rome. At the same time he tried to transfer the emotional aspects of the hostility between Israel and Amalek to the relationship between Romans and Arabs. This impression may be confirmed by the following passage.

---

[11] Franxman (1979: 218-20) missed the problem connected with the symbolism of the parting of Esau and Jacob in Gen 36. Additionally, he did not realize the significance of the omission of the Amalekites of Gen 14 in *Ant* 1 §§ 171-175.

3.3 *Exod 17:8-16 in* Ant *3 §§ 39-62*

In his *Antiquities* Josephus devoted no less than 24 paragraphs to the short story (of only nine Biblical verses) about the first battle against the Amalekites. This story was, therefore, of special significance for him and for the expression of his intentions.

In *Ant* 3 §§ 39-40 Josephus described the Amalekites as the leading and instigating group among a number of tribes which worried about the approaching Israelites. They argued for a preventive attack on the Israelites in order to avoid a future situation under less favorable conditions. Josephus classified these clever instigators in § 40 *expressis verbis* as "inhabitants of Gobolitis and Petra who are called Amalekites and were the most warlike of the peoples in those parts. It was their king who sent messages exhorting one another and the neighbouring peoples to make war on the Hebrews." The lengthy description of the preparations for the battle by Moses, the admonition before the war, the appointing of Joshua as commander in chief, the admonition before the battle, the description of the victorious battle itself, of the spoils and of the celebration of the victory are together a kind of anticipation of Deuteronomistic warfare laws and war ideology. It is as well a skillful celebration of Jewish heroism in a Hellenistic manner,[12] combined with the religious device that trust in God counterbalances disproportionate military equipment and experience.

God is called νικαῖος ("Giver of victory," for MT יהוה נסי) and the paragraph concludes with the words: "and he predicted [Exod 17:14] that the Amalekites were to be utterly exterminated and not one of them should survive to after ages, because they had set upon the Hebrews at a time when they were in desert country and in sore distress" (*Ant* 3 § 60). This recalls Deut 25:17-19 (cf. *Ant* 4 § 304).

Heroism is a characteristic which Josephus knew how to utilize in various respects. Apart from the wars treated in this paper, heroism plays a prominent role in Josephus' picture of King David (Feldman 1989a). In such contexts he always pursued the same aim. By stressing the aspect of heroism he managed to conceal from non-Jewish readers the militant, eschatological-messianic implications of the traditions in question. The same is true of his treatment of the wars of the Macca-bees and last but not least regarding the Zealotic trends during the

---

[12] In modern research the description of the battle itself is usually regarded as the work of the so-called "Thucydidean assistant."

first century CE. In spite of his generally negative picture of the Zealots, Josephus managed in his formulations of the speeches of Eleazar at the end of the *War* to moderate the negative Zealot image. This was done by stressing the aspects of heroism and of total personal commitment to an allegedly higher religious and national vocation.

3.4 *Num 13:28-29 in Ant 3 §§ 304-5.*

Josephus omitted the Amalekites in Num 13:29, where they appear together with Hittites, Jebusites, and Amorites as inhabitants of the southern part of the land of Canaan. However, he did mention the descendants of the giants at Hebron.

3.5 *Num 14:25 in Ant 3 §§ 311-14*

Josephus omitted the passage about the Amalekites and Canaanites.

3.6 *Num 14:43-45 in Ant 4 §§ 1-8*

Josephus described an unsuccessful campaign against the Canaanites only, omitting the Amalekites.

3.7 *Num 21:1 in Ant 4 §§ 83-89*

Josephus skipped Num 21:1-9, speaking in this context only of Amorites.

3.8 *Num 24:7, 20-21 in Ant 4 §§ 102-24*

Josephus omitted in Balaam's prophecy the passages which deal with Amalek.

3.9 *Deut 25:17-19*

The Biblical passage reads:

> I. Remember what Amalek did to you along the way when you came out of Egypt (18) when they met you on the way and cut off <from you all> (LXX: "the rearguard") those (who were) lagging behind (you) while you were faint and weary, and he did not fear God.
> II. (19) When the Lord your God gives you rest from all the enemies around you in the land which he is giving you to possess as an inheritance, your shall blot out the memory (LXX: τὸ ὄνομα) of Amalek from under heaven.
> III. Do not forget it.

This passage concerning Amalek which plays such a prominent role in
Jewish metahistorical consciousness and which later on was counted as
three (I-III) commandments (two positive and one negative) of the 613
precepts in the Written Torah, appears in *Ant* 4 § 304 only in a
shortened form. At first sight it does not seem to be congruent with
the halakhic tradition:

> He also exhorted (!) the people, once they had conquered the country and
> were established therein, not to forget that insolence of the Amalekites, but
> to take the field against them and exact vengeance for the wrong which they
> had done them when they were in the desert (cf. *Ant* 3 §§ 39ff.).

But in fact Josephus knew very well the significance of this passage, for
he refers to it explicitly as a commandment in the sense of the Biblical
text proper (*Ant* 6 §§ 133, 138-39; 7 § 6).

3.10 *Judg 3:13 in* Ant *5 § 186.*

Josephus omitted the Ammonites and Amalekites as allies of Eglon.

3.11 *Judg 5:14*

Josephus did not reproduce the Song of Deborah.

3.12 *Judges 6-7 in* Ant *5 §§ 210-29*

Judg 6:3, 33 and 7:12 lists the invaders as "the Midianite, Amalekite,
and eastern (tribes)." Josephus added two accentuations: "Barak and
Deborah having died simultaneously, the Madianites, calling the
Amalekites and Arabians to their aid, marched against the Israelites"
(*Ant* 5 § 210).

3.13 *Judg 10:11-12 in* Ant *5 §§ 255-56.*

Josephus skipped the relevant passage.

3.14 *Judg 12:15 in* Ant *5 § 274*

LXX B (not A) reproduced the MT with ἐν ὄρει τοῦ ἀμαληκ (A:
Λανάκ), Josephus gives only the name Pharathon.

3.15 *1 Sam 14:47-48 in* Ant *6 § 129*

When Saul had assumed rule over Israel, he fought against their enemies on every side: (against) Moab, against the Ammonites, against Edom (LXX adds "and against Baitheor"), against the king of Zoba and against the Philistines. ... (48) He fought valiantly and defeated Amalek and delivered Israel from the hands of those who plundered them.

Josephus reproduced the passage thus: "He then reigned happily and, having made war on the neighbouring nations, subdued those of the Ammanites and Moabites, besides the Philistines, Idumaeans, Amalekites and the King of Soba."

3.16 *1 Samuel 15 in* Ant *6 §§ 131-55*

As in the case of Exod 17:8-16 Josephus elaborated the description of the battle against Amalek also in the present chapter, thus indicating a special interest. Reproducing in §§ 132-33 more or less literally the request of God as formulated in 1 Sam 15:2-3 Josephus added in § 133 a reference to Moses (the commandments in Deut 25:17-19). In § 134 Josephus followed the Greek textual tradition which read Gilgal/Galgala in place of Telaim. Galgala was more likely to serve as a starting point for a campaign in territories east of the Dead Sea and the Araba while Telaim (cf. 1 Sam 27:8 below) in the south of Judah was better suited for a campaign in the Negev. To avoid any connection with the Negev, Josephus transposed the passage concerning the Kenites, and in this way gave the impression that Saul invaded the land of the Amalekites immediately after leaving Galgala. On the other hand, according to § 140, Saul conquered "the whole region extending from Pelusium in Egypt to the Erythraean Sea," sparing only the "Sikimites" (according to the context the Kenites transposed from above). According to Josephus, they lived among the more remote Midianites, and not, as in the Biblical text, among the Amalekites of the Negev.

Josephus underlined the religious importance of the commandment to annihilate Amalek by contrasting it with the motivation for Saul's compassion with King Agag: Saul admired Agag's beauty and stature, a noble but human sentiment (*Ant* 6 §§ 136-39). This motif contributed an additional trait to the tragic-heroic character of Saul[13] which

---

[13] Pseudo-Philo's *Liber Antiquitatum Biblicarum* introduced, on the contrary, a negative trait.

certainly fitted the Hellenistic-Roman mentality. In addition, Josephus
stressed that it was Israel's army which had really sinned by looting the
best of the banned goods. Finally, according to § 155 Samuel ordered
Agag to be put to death while according to 1 Sam 15:33 it was he
himself who cut him to pieces.

3.17 *1 Sam 27:8-9 and 28:18 in* Ant 6 §§ 323, 336

> Now David and his men went up and raided the Geshurite (missing in LXX,
> which adds "all"), the Girzite and the Amalekite, for there were the
> populations of the land from ancient times beginning from Telam (cf. 1 Sam
> 15:4, 7 and LXX variants) on your way to Shur and until the Land of Egypt
> (כי הנה ישבות הארץ אשר מעולם בואך שורה ועד ארץ מצרים).

This Biblical text implies in v. 9 that David in turn invaded the
territories of the hostile tribes and that he executed the ban on their
cities (cf. Deut 20:16-18), completely extinguishing their population in
performance of the precepts of Deut 25:17-19 which Saul had neglected. In 1 Sam 28:18 it is stated as a reproach against Saul, and this is
also reproduced by Josephus in *Ant* 6 § 336. But Josephus avoided to
specify the peoples "south of Judah" as in 1 Sam 27:10 (mentioning
the Kenites). It seems that he interpreted the *gentilicia* in 1 Sam 27:8
as covering the whole range from the west to areas east of the Arabah.

3.18 *1 Samuel 30 in* Ant 6 §§ 356-67

As the Biblical text speaks about an invasion of the Amalekites there
was no reason to change the place of action of David's campaign
against the Amalekites.

3.19 *1 Samuel 31* Ant 6 § 371 and 7 §§ 1-6

In the story about Saul's death in 1 Samuel 31 Josephus inserted the
account of the Amalekite in 2 Sam 1:6-10. In *Ant* 7 § 6 he introduced
a special issue, where according to Josephus, David ordered the man
to be put to death because of his Amalekite extraction, thus performing the commandment in Deut 25:17-19. It is noteworthy that, on the
contrary, the authors of 1 Chr 10 in their version of Saul's death have
omitted this Amalekite.

3.20 *2 Sam 8:12 in* Ant 7 §§ 108-9.

Josephus omitted the passage on the dedicated spoils while in 1 Chr
18:11 it is attested.

3.21 *2 Chr 25 in* Ant *9 §§ 188-98*

a) While 2 Chr 25:5-6 does not mention any destination of the preparatory military measures, Josephus adds in *Ant* 9 § 188: "for he had decided to undertake a campaign against the nations of the Amalekites and Edomites and Gabalites." In § 198 he substituted "Edom" of the MT in 25:18 by "Amalekites." There is no question about his intention to localize the campaign on the eastern side of the Arabah, as explicitly attested by the following passage.

b) 1 Chr 25:11-12: "Amaziah then marshalled his force and led his army to the Valley of Salt, where he smote ten thousand of the sons of Seir [2 Kgs 14:7: And he smote Edom]. (12) The army of Judah also captured ten thousand men alive, took them to the top of a cliff and threw them down so that all were smashed." In *Ant* 9 § 191 Josephus identified the cliffs of 2 Chr 25:12 as "the great rock which is over against Arabia."

c) 2 Chr 25:14: "When Amaziah returned from smiting אדמים (LXX: 'Ἰδουμαία), he brought with him the gods of the sons of Seir. He set them up as his own gods, bowed down to them and burned sacrifices to them." Josephus in *Ant* 9 § 198 formulated: "But Amaziah . . . began to neglect God . . . and persisted in worshipping the gods which he brought from the country of the Amalekites."

4. *Haman the Agagite*

The Book of Esther contributed a very special aspect to the development of Amalek as a metahistorical *typus*. In three instances the MT calls the wicked Haman a "son of Hamedatha, the Agagite," a formulation which caused this name to be related to the Amalekite king whom king Saul had taken prisoner. On this basis, Haman received the quality of an Amalekite in the genealogical in addition to the symbolical sense.

In Esth 3:1 the Greek versions have Βουγαῖος[14] as do the *Additions to Esther* (Bardtke 1973: 35-36), the latter with such variants as Γωγαῖος and Μακεδόνα, results of specific actualizations. The same appellations appear in MT Esth 3:10 where the Greek versions only have "Haman." In 8:3 the MT has "Haman the Agagite," and in 8:5 we find again the tripartite appellation , but in the Greek versions we

---

[14] According to Levy (1939) derived from Bagian, a follower of the Mithras cult.

read again only "Haman." The tripartite appellation is found also in the MT of Esth 9:24, where the Greek version replaced "the Agagite" by "the Macedonian."

It is clear that "Agagite" served for different polemical purposes. Josephus made it unequivocally clear that "Agagite" indicates "Amalekite," as in *Ant* 11 § 209: ". . . Haman, the son of Amadathos, who was of Amalekite descent . . . ." And in *Ant* 11 § 211 he explained (as later the Targum) the hatred of Haman against Mordechai and the Jews in general as a consequence of his descent. He "decided to exterminate this whole nation, for he naturally hated the Jews because his own race, the Amalekites, had been destroyed by them." Also in *Ant* 11 § 277 Josephus adds to the content of Esth 9:24 the characteristic remark: "Haman, the son of Amadathos, of the Amalekite race, an alien among those of Persian blood."

5. *Conclusions*

To avoid the impression of an existing linkage between Esau's grandson Amalek and Rome, Josephus emphasized the difference between Edomites/Idumaeans and Amalekites in a geographical as well as in an ethnographical respect and located the Amalekites outside the Roman empire. In most cases, he did this by identifying these enemies of Israel with the inhabitants of the later province "Arabia" and the regions east of it who at that time caused continual trouble at the Roman borders (Kasher 1988). By identifying the archenemy of Israel with those tribes, Josephus achieved three aims: (a) Amalek appears as an enemy common to Rome and Israel; (b) as an enemy outside the Roman empire the archenemy of Israel did not represent any more the non-Jewish inhabitants of Palestine/Syria who had been involved in the riots and quarrels which finally culminated in the Roman-Judaean war of 66-70 CE; (c) very likely Josephus labelled the Arabs as "Amalekites" because of the role Arab soldiers played during that war (cf. *JW* 3 §§ 168, 211, 262; 5 §§ 290, 551-58).[15]

By identifying Haman in the Esther story as an Amalekite Josephus stressed the militant character of the Book of Esther. At the same time he gave the impression that the foremost enemy of the Jewish

---

[15] This convincing argument was introduced by Daniel Schwartz during the discussion of this paper at San Miniato.

people is not to be found within the realm of the Roman empire but in that of its oriental rival power: the Persian/Parthian empire. In later Jewish traditions, we find the opposite tendency, Amalek's character as grandson of Esau was underlined, and thus Israel's archenemy Amalek characterized as the point of Esau's sword.

Modern readers may be astonished by the fact that Josephus wrote without any apologetic considerations about the ban as a kind of "genocide" to have been executed on the "seven nations" of the Land of Canaan and in the case of Amalekites, to be executed also in the future. But in the case of irreconcilable and dangerous enemies the Hellenistic-Roman reader scarcely felt the sentiments which we find already expressed in Rabbinic literature and in mediaeval commentaries. There it was stressed that the Amalekites as well as the seven nations had also been asked to submit peacefully (as commanded in Deut 20:10) and were thus given the chance to escape their sinister fate. The Roman attitude against pertinacious and rebellious tribes was more or less the same. The question[16] of why Josephus did not skip such Biblical passages but even expanded some of them in his account is nevertheless an interesting one. One answer may be derived from the positive effects of heroism and brave commitment to self-defence and defence of their own land in the eyes of the Romans. In addition we have to take into account an apologetical device of Josephus. He underlined repeatedly that the Israelites fought so bravely because they knew that they were fighting not only a "just war" but essentially in the name of God. Still in other cases they were defeated because of their disobedience to God. Josephus described the war of 66-70 CE as the consequence of a wrong Judaean policy which misled the people to believe that the war was something like a "war of the Lord." Josephus could depict the determined commitment to fight in spite of everything as a noble and religious motive.

The effects of such procedures were clear-cut for Roman readers. But Josephus' accounts also included a very clear message to prospective contemporary and future Jewish readers, especially considering the background of increasing Jewish radicalism in the western diaspora: Amalek is to be found outside the Roman empire. But a Jewish reader who knew the Bible and therefore was able to grasp the differences between the Biblical accounts and the formulations of Josephus might

---

[16] Raised by Prof. L. H. Feldman in the discussion at S. Miniato.

well have arrived at opposite conclusions. He could very well attribute the deviations from the Bible in Josephus to tactics. So the first address seems to be the Roman audience. Furthermore, as in the case of "Edom" and the "fourth empire" of Daniel, for Jewish readers there remained a (deliberately conceived?) ambiguity including at least the promise of an eschatological turning point in history. Although this was not intended for the near future because the "iron empire" had to be regarded as the most enduring one of the four. In summary, his treatment of "Amalek" confirms the assumption that Josephus was very well aware of the significance of the metahistorical symbolism connected with "Edom" and its political implications.

JOHN HYRCANUS I AS SEEN BY JOSEPHUS
AND OTHER EARLY JEWISH SOURCES

Clemens Thoma

In *JW* 1 §§ 68-69 and *Ant* 13 §§ 299-300 Flavius Josephus has extraordinary praise for the social and private personality of the Hasmonean high priest and prince John Hyrcanus I (134-104 BCE). Hyrcanus had been all in one: high priest, prince, prophet, and God had a unique relationship of trust with him. Therefore Hyrcanus held three dignities (latin: *tria munera*), which were made possible and were protected through an exceptionally intimate relation between God and him. Josephus does not grant such an overall attestation of perfection to any other personality. The influence of that eulogium spread out to later generations. Since the time of the early Church, traditional Christology attributed the same 'offices' (*munera*) to Jesus as internal union: He is high priest, king and prophet. Moreover Jesus is so distinguished by such an intimate relation to God that the complete being of the Deity dwells embodied in him (Col 2:9). That 'Three Offices Christology' is for instance unfolded in the Church History (1:3) of Eusebius of Caesarea (about 264-340 CE) (Kraft 1981: 90-93). In some cases the 'Three Offices' have been ascribed to the Roman Popes, to the bishops and even to every believing Christian as well. Thus Josephus has become the father of many allegoric adaptations of the three offices of Hyrcanus. Are we to understand the words of Josephus as merely a hyperbolical eulogy of this wise Jewish ruler, or might they have historical roots and imply a Messianic meaning? In order to approach a possibly unambiguous answer to these questions, the relevant texts shall be reviewed below for their historical and exegetical message. A further section deals with the interpretation of John Hyrcanus' life, activities and epoch. The last section will treat the subject of the Messianic hopes, which had arisen so powerfully in various Jewish groups, and their possible connections with John Hyrcanus.

1. *Provisional Exegesis of* JW *1 §§ 68-69 and* Ant *13 §§ 299-300*

There are only slight stylistic differences between the two texts; in their meaning they are in agreement. Therefore, a synthesized text can be elaborated which does justice to both, the *War* and the *Antiquities*. Presumably, Josephus intended his great eulogium to form the keystone in his portrayal of Hyrcanus.

The following synthesized text can be established from *JW* 1 §§ 68-69 and *Ant* 13 §§ 299-300: "Hyrcanus lived happily thereafter; and when he died, after administering the government excellently for thirty-one years, he left five sons. Truly he was a blessed individual and one who left no ground for complaint against fortune (ἡ τύχη) as regards himself. He was the only man to unite in his person three of the highest privileges: the supreme command of the nation, the high priesthood, and the gift of prophecy. For so closely was he in touch with the Deity (*JW* 1 § 69: ὡμίλει αὐτῷ τὸ δαιμόνιον; *Ant* 13 § 300: συνῆν αὐτῷ τὸ θεῖον) that he was never ignorant of the future; thus he foresaw and predicted that his two elder sons would not remain at the head of affairs. The story of their downfall is worth relating, and will show, how great was the decline from their father's good fortune".

This eulogium, as mentioned by Peter Kuhn (1989:192-98), is to be read together with *Ant* 13 §§ 282-83 and the somewhat shorter parallel in *JW* 1 §§ 64-65. There the prophetic quality of Hyrcanus is referred to. While his two sons, Aristobulus and Antigonus, made war against Antiochus IX Cyzicenus in the region of Samaria in the years 108/107 BCE, Hyrcanus is said to have been confronted with a paradox: "The Deity (τὸ θεῖον) communicated with him", which had been quoted in the tradition as follows: "On the very day on which his sons fought with Cyzicenus, Hyrcanus, who was alone in the temple, burning incense as high priest, heard a voice saying that his sons had just defeated Antiochus. And on coming out of the temple he revealed this to the entire multitude, and so it actually happened" (*Ant* 13 §§ 282-88).

The parallel to *Ant* 13 §§ 282-83, in *t. Sota* 13:5-6; *y. Sota* 9/24b and *b. Sota* 33a, is surely not dependant on Josephus or his source. There must have been various early Jewish traditions about the prophetical charisma of John Hyrcanus. The version in *t. Sota* 13:5-6, which is obviously the earliest Rabbinic interpretation of older traditions, reads as follows: "The high priest Jochanan heard a voice in the Holy of

Holies: 'Victorious are the young men who marched to wage war in Antiochia!' That hour and day had been written. And later it was found out that it was right at that hour when their victory occurred." In the *Tosefta* we do not have an historical narration but rather an example of how the Bat Qôl has given a revelation to the high priest Hyrcanus. However, one essential point is made clear by *Ant* 13 §§ 282-83 as well as in the Rabbinic parallels: *Ant* 13 §§ 282-83 par. is not concerned solely with an equivalent series of three offices, charisms, qualities or dignities. The essential point of Josephus is that in the case of John Hyrcanus the questionable double-office of high priest and ruler of the people was not directed against God's will. On the contrary, God has confirmed this double-office by bestowing the gift of prophecy on Hyrcanus. Neither the Pharisees (*Ant* 13 §§ 291 par) nor any Apocalyptics can therefore find any confirmation for their assumption that it should not be permitted to combine the high priestly office with that of ruler in the same person. This is why Josephus probably felt it proper to emphasize the prophetic and charismatic gifts of Hyrcanus so strongly, because Hyrcanus had not yet declared himself king. That was only done by his successors. Hyrcanus looked at the high priesthood as his highest office (cfr. *Ant* 14 § 41).

Several times Hyrcanus heard God's voice. This voice whispered the future into his ear. The truth of these prognoses could be ascertained and verified. The prognoses also had consequences for the Jewish people. Hyrcanus did not only foresee the victory of his sons in Samaria. He also foresaw that both his sons, Aristobulus and Antigonus, would not be able to keep the reign for a long time. According to *Ant* 13 § 322 God appeared to Hyrcanus once in a dream and revealed to him that his son Alexander Jannaeus would be his heir and successor. Foreknowledge given by God, public proclamation of this knowledge and its verifying by the Jewish public – these three points are, according to Josephus, the surest sign that Hyrcanus was chosen to rule and save the Jewish people.

John Hyrcanus has – in Josephus' view – held a high post in the history of revelation. In *Ant* 3 §§ 214-18 he does not name Hyrcanus explicitly, but it is clear that it is him whom he means. Josephus says, that, until the time of Hyrcanus, God had insinuated his special presence at the offerings in the temple by the shining of the precious stones on the high priest's shoulders in a mild glow (αὐγή). In a similar way the precious stones on the high priest's breast-plate lighted up, when God wanted to predict the victory to the Hebrews: "So brilliant a light (αὐγή) radiated from them, ere the army was yet in motion, that it was evident to the whole host that God had come to their aid" (*Ant* 3 § 217). Josephus adds: "Although the αὐγή ceased to shine two hundred years before I composed this work, because of God's displeasure at the transgression of the laws" (*Ant* 3 § 218). Hyrcanus lived about 200 years before Josephus. So he was a high priest living in postbiblical times, but biblical miracles still happened during his lifetime. Therefore the Jewish people lived during his reign happily and secure, and Josephus could rely on him as an important figure of the history of salvation.

For Josephus, Hyrcanus was not only a figure of the past. He looked at Hyrcanus as one of his religious and personal prototypes. In his exemplariness Hyrcanus was presumably comparable to the prophet Jeremiah (cf. *JW* 5 §§ 392-93). Hyrcanus was personally nearer to Josephus than Jeremiah, because he was his forebear. Menahem Stern pointed to a strange discrepancy: On the one side Josephus was a very proud patriot and a very proud descendant of the royal Hasmoneans. On the other side he described particularly the most important Hasmoneans very dryly. Josephus "presents us with a rather cold picture of the three main figures of the Hasmonean monarchy, namely Aristobulus I, Alexander Jannaeus and Salome Alexandra (Stern 1974-84: 1. 230). Stern ascribes this detached attitude of Josephus to his informant, Nicolaus of Damascus. This Hellenistic historiographer is the main source of Josephus for the period between Antiochus Epiphanes (175-164 BCE) and the accession of Archelaos (6 CE). The descriptions of John Hyrcanus' deeds seem to contain far more spiritual-theological infiltrations of Josephus himself than the descriptions of the rest of Josephus' Hasmonean forebears. In the same way as he describes Hyrcanus as high priest, who has received the knowledge about the future by God, and who has proclaimed this knowledge, he also describes his own part during the first Jewish uprising against Rome. Josephus "was an interpreter of dreams and skilled in divining the meaning of ambiguous utterances of the Deity; a priest himself and of priestly descent, he was not ignorant of the prophecies in the sacred books" (*JW* 3 § 352). Because of his foreknowledge he had changed sides from the Zealots to the Romans privileged by God (*JW* 3 § 354). He predicted the office of emperor to Vespasian (*JW* 3

§§ 400-8). This prediction proved true (*JW* 4 §§ 622-28). Thus Josephus gained his reputation anew, and "he became trustworthy in the highest degree whenever the future was at stake" (*JW* 4 §§ 629).

2. *Life and work of John Hyrcanus I*

We can only give limited answers regarding the sources of Josephus for Hyrcanus. With some probability he had, besides oral sources, especially the following works at his disposal: 1. The chronicle of the high priesthood of Hyrcanus, mentioned in 1 Macc 16:24. Probably it was a kind of sequel to 1 Maccabees. Unfortunately this chronicle was lost very early. The report of its existence in the *Bibliotheca Sancta* of Sixtus Senensis (1566: 62; see Schürer 1901-11: 1.201) is too doubtful for drawing any valid conclusions. 2. The work of the Jewish historian Eupolemus (middle of the 2nd century BCE) on the kings of Juda. He may be mentioned in 1 Macc 8:17 and in 2 Macc 4:11. 3. The above-mentioned historian Nicolaus of Damascus, who had been in the service of Herod I. 4. Several Roman historians like Polybius of Megalopolis (middle of the 2nd century BCE), Curtius Rufus (1st cent. BCE), Strabo of Amaseia (1st cent. BCE), Diodorus (1st cent. BCE) (Schürer 1973-87 1. 200-215; 3. 184-187; Schäfer 1977: 539-604; Lebram 1974). The harvest that Josephus could glean from his sources about Hyrcanus is rather meager. Particularly, he could hardly gain any insights into the *motives* which moved Hyrcanus to his deeds and to his decisions. Thus there is a strong discrepancy with the eulogies in *JW* 1 §§ 68f and *Ant* 13 §§ 299f.

As may be gathered from his work, Josephus was at least able to draw out this much from his sources, that the official life of Hyrcanus consisted of three phases. 1. The period of acute danger: from 134 to 129 BCE. 2. The period of successful warfare, diplomacy, inner-Jewish struggles and reforms: 129-108/107 BCE. 3. The sunny period of his old age: 108-104 BCE (Egger 1986:158-59).

(1) The period of acute danger begins with his father Simon's murder by his son-in-law Ptolemy near Jericho (134 BCE). The murderer took Hyrcanus' mother hostage and killed both her elder sons. Hyrcanus managed to avoid this fate by a quick adventurous flight to Jerusalem (1 Macc 16:11-24; *JW* 1 §§ 54-55; *Ant* 13 §§ 228-29). He immediately took on the offices of high priest and prince (ἡγεμών) and undertook to pursue the murderer who had hidden in a fortress near Jericho (*Ant*

13 § 230). Since Ptolemy held Hyrcanus' mother hostage, and what is more, a Sabbatical year (134/133 BCE) had begun, the conquest of the fortress was delayed. When Ptolemy finally realized that his cause was lost, he killed Hyrcanus' mother and then managed to escape (*Ant* 13 §§ 230-35). Soon thereafter the Syrian king Antiochus VII Sidetes invaded Judea. He devastated it and besieged Jerusalem. The plight of the defenders became grim: a famine broke out, and the cause of Hyrcanus and of Jerusalem became hopeless (*Ant* 13 §§ 236-41). Finally on the Feast of Tabernacles Antiochus Sidetes could impose the conditions of peace after diplomatic mediations. Although Hyrcanus was defeated, he did not accept a Seleucid garrison in Jerusalem, but agreed to pay for conquered cities (e.g Joppe), to settle most of the costs of war, to surrender hostages and to provide soldiers for Seleucid war services (*Ant* 13 §§ 242-48). Antiochus VII undertook in 130 BCE a campaign against the Parthians, and Hyrcanus had to take part in it.

(2) The period of successful warfare, diplomacy, inner-Jewish struggles and reforms: The death of Antiochus VII Sidetes in this campaign in 129 BCE (*Ant* 13 §§ 251-59) was "providential" for Hyrcanus (Schürer 1973-87: 1. 207). Antiochus VII's successors proved weak. After Antiochus VII's death John Hyrcanus used every occasion to increase his power and renown. He tried to reach three aims: (1) Enlargement of the Jewish territory. (2) Intensification of diplomatic relations with the Romans with the ulterior motive to use the battles of rivalry between the Ptolemies and Seleucids to spread Jewish influence. (3) Strengthening of the unity in the inner-Jewish domain. About 127 BCE he undertook a campaign against Shekhem, the North of Galilee and Trans-Jordan. During this campaign he conquered Medaba, and brought the temple on Mount Garizim under his control. He also conquered Idumea. The destruction of the Garizim temple (in 127 BCE it may have been only a partial destruction) and the conquest of the small state of Idumea have frequently attracted scholars' interest. The text in *Ant* 13 § 256 lets us understand this interest:

> Hyrcanus captured . . . Shekhem and Garizim and the Cuthaean nation, which lives near the temple built after the model of the sanctuary in Jerusalem, which Alexander permitted their governor Sanballetes to build in honour of his son-in-law Manasses, the brother of the high priest Jaddus.... Now it was two hundred years later that this temple was laid waste. Hyrcanus also captured the Idumaean cities of Adora and Marisa and after subduing

all the Idumaeans, permitted them to remain in their country so long as they had themselves circumcised and consented to observe the laws of the Jews. And so, out of attachment to the land of their fathers, they submitted to circumcision and to adapting their mode of life in all other respects to that of the Jews. And from that time on they have continued to be Jews. (*Ant* 13 §§ 255-58).

Later in 108/107 BCE Hyrcanus undertook another campaign against the city of Samaria. Presumably the Garizim temple was completely destroyed only in 107 together with the city of Samaria. The destruction of the Garizim temple seems to have been directed against a sanctuary, in which a syncretistic cult had taken place, and which, besides, was occupied by foreign Sidonians (Egger 1986:287-300). By these deeds Hyrcanus could gain status as a zealot for the true divine worship and for the national independence of Judaea and Samaria. That goes similarly for the successful forced conversion of the Idumeans. All these conquests gave new encouragement to the national-religious identity in the Hasmonean state. A decree of the Roman Senate shows the successful diplomatic activities of Hyrcanus (*Ant* 13 §§ 260-66). In this decree the conquests of Hyrcanus, made since 129 BCE, are acknowledged and the alliance (φιλία καὶ συμμαχία) concluded between the Romans and the Hasmonean predecessor of Hyrcanus is renewed. Also the coins, which John Hyrcanus had minted with the inscription which probably means: "Jehochanan the high priest and the counsel of elders of the Jews" might have consolidated his position, nationally and internationally.[1]

In this glorious period of conquests and international diplomacy Hyrcanus is also very active in the inner-Jewish religious and political domain. The Mishnah gives some hints of his reforms in the fields of cult and halakhah, which were viewed favorably later on. The traditions of these reforms are not quite clear in every respect (Lieberman 1950: 139-43). According to *m. MSh* 5:15, Hyrcanus regulated the institution of tithing in the temple. He cancelled the obligation that in handing over the tithe one had to say the Short Creed of Deut 26:3-10. He also attended to a better overall view of tributes to the temple. In an explanation to *m. MSh* 5:15 in *b. Sota* 48a it is said that Hyrcanus ordered that the donor of the fruit tithe has no longer to

---

[1]   יהוחנן הכהן הגדול וחבר היהדים. These coins are partly unrightfully attributed to Hyrcanus II; cf. Magen 1986.

ascertain whether the seller of this fruit tithe has already done something which could have defiled these fruits. It only depends on his own ritually pure action. This is the meaning of the sentence in *m. MSh* 5:15, according to which "in the days of the high priest Jochanan (Hyranus) nobody needed to inquire into the doubtfulness any longer". Hyrcanus further forbade the liturgical custom of the "awakeners" (המעוררים). According to *b. Sota* 48a the Levites used to awaken God allegorically every morning from sleep until the time of Hyrcanus, singing among other things Ps 44:24: "Wake up, Adonai, why do you sleep?" Hyrcanus founded his prohibition on Ps 121:4, according to which God knows no sleep.

According to *b. Sota* 48a Hyrcanus introduced changes even in the Jewish butchering of the sacrificial animals. Until then the priests used to wound the sacrificial calves between the horns, so that blood ran into the eyes of the animals, which made it easier to butcher them. Another method was to make them malleable to butchering by flogging. Hyrcanus forbade these practices so as not to give the impression that a physical defect was inflicted upon the animal and therefore it would be unsuitable (according to Lev 22:19-24): During the intermediate non-festive days of the eight-day Passover the workmen, especially smiths, worked in the temple precinct and caused a disturbing noise of hammering (*t. Sota* 13:10; *b. MQ* 11a). John Hyrcanus' prohibition of hammering on these days heightened the feast's dignity. Thus, according to the Mishnah, Hyrcanus was a great and efficient cult reformer and restorer. This image is in agreement with the Festal Letter, recorded in 2 Macc 1:1-9, which was sent from Jerusalem to the Jews of Egypt in 124 BCE. to encourage them to celebrate the Feast of Tabernacles (Bickerman 1933; Habicht 1976: 177-185; 199-201). In 124 Hyrcanus was in the best years of his rule. The question for Hyrcanus was to emphasize Jerusalem, its Temple and the dynasty of the Hasmoneans also in the western diaspora. The composition of 1 Maccabees took place at the time of Hyrcanus too (cf. 1 Macc 16:22-23). Early Jewish and Rabbinic sources present Hyrcanus as a highly gifted high priest, conqueror, zealot against idolatry, advocate of Jewish national interests and a pious mystic with a view for future developments.

Hyrcanus' turning away from the Pharisees to the Sadducees described in *Ant* 13 §§ 288-300 was not an emotional step, as may be inferred from Josephus. Josephus makes Eleazar say to Hyrcanus that he should give up the position of high priest, "because we heard from our elders that your mother was a captive in the reign of Antiochus Epiphanes" (*Ant* 13 § 292). It is to be presumed that his mother had been violated by the soldiers of Antiochus and so would have been unsuitable to become the mother of a high priest (according to Lev 21:12-15). This attack must have made Hyrcanus furious, because it was known that his mother had lost her life as a hostage of his father's murderer (*Ant* 13 §§ 231-235). With a certain probability we can assume that Eleazar was a hidden adherent of the Pharisees. But in *b. Qid* 66a the event does not take place in Hyrcanus' time, but under the reign of Alexander Janneus, and the opponent is not Eleazar but Jehudah ben Gedidyah. According to the Talmud, Jehudah said to Alexander Janneus: "King Jannai, be content with the king's crown and leave the priest's crown to the descendants of Aharon". The Talmud may be inaccurate in its formulation, but in the matter it is exact: The criticism against the Hasmoneans developed fully only after they crowned themselves as kings (D.R. Schwartz 1992: 57-80). Hyrcanus' change to the Sadducees was essentially an act of political cleverness in order to keep his power. In the beginning of the revolution under Mattathias and Judas the Pharisees probably were useful allies of the Hasmoneans (1Macc 2:39-41). Hyrcanus, in his best period, when reforms in the domain of cult and law were at stake, depended on the Pharisees, because they were susceptible to changes. "Hyrcanus also probably tried to settle disputes in Jewish Law through his claim to prophetic inspiration. He may have used his prophetic authority to enforce Pharisaic interpretations and also to justify his own abolition of ancient rites prescribed in the Torah (*m. MSh* 5:15)" (Goldstein 1989: 331). In later years of rule, when abolitions, renewals and reforms were no longer at stake but only the consolidation of the achievement, a change to the traditional priestly authority was a political necessity (Schäfer 1991).

3. *John Hyrcanus' lifework in the Jewish interpretation of the 2nd and 1st centuries BCE*

Josephus saw an especially fortunate Jewish leader and hierarch in Hyrcanus, because in his youth Hyrcanus had escaped his pursuers, because he had come through the initial crises in his reign, because he had proved a clever conqueror, diplomat and ruler, because as high priest he was an active reformer of cult and law and, above all, because in his activity as high priest and prince he was guided in an exceptional way by God and so could foresee and plan ahead things to come. Presumably Hyrcanus inspired Josephus for a theory, as to who of all the Jews was to be considered the greatest and most fortunate: He who holds the three highest positions of high priest, king and prophet and does so with prudence and vigour; who, besides, has especially intimate contacts with heaven and therefore knows about the future.

Whether for Josephus the advantages ascribed to Hyrcanus carry *messianic* implications as well must be denied. He does not make even the slightest allusion in connection with *JW* 1 §§ 68-69 and *Ant* 13 §§ 299-300, that might be understood as messianic. Josephus exercises the utmost restraint in his opus concerning Jewish messianic hopes. He had to do that, among other reasons, because of his Roman addressees and patrons. That he himself accepted messianic beliefs in a restricted way may be gathered from *Ant* 10 §§ 203-15 (if the *Testimonium Flavianum* is left out of consideration). In these paragraphs Josephus interprets the second chapter of the Book of Daniel. In connection with the "stone" mentioned in Dan 2:34,44-45, which would come loose from a mountain by itself without human help and which symbolizes God's final reign, Josephus says in *Ant* 10 § 210: "And Daniel also revealed to the king the meaning of the stone, but I have not thought it proper to relate this, since I am expected to write of what is past and done and not of what is to be; if, however, there is anyone who has so keen a desire for exact information that he will not stop short of inquiring more closely but wishes to learn about the hidden things that are to come, let him take the trouble to read the Book of Daniel, which he will find among the sacred writings".[2] Josephus knew also of messianic speculations and was in agreement with them, at least in part, though he did not connect them with Hyrcanus.

It is not unlikely that Asidean circles in connection with the life and deeds of Hyrcanus were animated to have ideas, still in his lifetime, which can be called messianic in a broader sense of the word. The *Testament of Levi* may be an indication of an interpretation (de Jonge

---

[2] Louis H. Feldman points to the fact that *Ant* 10 § 210 shows Josephus having messianic hopes (Feldman and Hata 1989: 37). Cf. Mason in this volume.

1978:24-50)[3] of John Hyrcanus, that comes close to being messianic. Some passages give the impression that they may be geared to the deeds and prerogatives of Hyrcanus. In the Greek *TestLev* 6:1-7:3, Levi, the Son of Jacob and ancestor of the temple priests, tells the following story given in Gen 34, about Shekhem the ancestor of the Samaritans, respectively the Shekhemites, who had violated his sister Dinah. Together with his brother Simeon, Levi had taken bloody revenge on the Shekhemites out of zealotry. But in doing so he was not sure of himself, as his father was opposed to this blood vengeance. Eventually he recognised, however, that his own and his brother's proceedings against the Shekhemites had been decreed by God himself (ἀπόφασις θεοῦ: 6:8), because the Shekhemites had opposed Israel since Abraham's time: "And they behaved like this to all foreigners: They took their wives from them by force, and then sent them away. But retribution from the Lord overtook them at last (6:10-11)". Certainly this description is motivated by Gen 34. But it was very much topical at the time of John Hyrcanus, who waged war twice against the Samaritans and the temple on Mount Garizim. The author of the *Testament of Levi* may have formulated his theological emphasis of the story in Gen 34 to support ideologically the cultic operations of Hyrcanus against the temple on Mount Garizim and his political actions against the Samaritans. *TestLev* 6:11 could allude to it. In *TestLev* 8 the inthronisation of a high priest takes place, which is recreated in part based on Zech 3-4. The essential point in *TestLev* 8 in comparison with all biblical texts is that the high priest receives, or already possesses, the princely, prophetic and high priestly prerogatives. The text in its most important parts is highly allegorical and goes as follows:

> (1) And after we had been there seventy days, I had another vision just as I had before. (2) I saw seven men clothed in white, saying to me: Get up, put on the crown of righteousness, the breast-piece of understanding, the mantle of truth, the rosette of faith, the turban of the sign and the ephod of prophecy. (3) And one by one they brought these things and put them on me and said: From now on be priest of the Lord, you and your descendants for ever. And the first anointed me with holy oil and gave me a staff of judgement (ῥάβδον κρίσεως). (5) The second washed me with pure water and fed me with bread and wine (the holiest of the holy things) and arrayed me in a holy

---

[3] The translation follows in the main lines that of de Jonge in Sparks 1984: 505-600.

and glorious robe. (6) The third clothed me with a linen vestment like an ephod. (7) The fourth put round me a purple girdle. (8) The fifth gave me a branch of rich olive. (9) The sixth put a crown on my head. (10) The seventh put on my head a diadem of priesthood, and they filled my hands with incense, so that I might serve as a priest to the Lord. (11) And they said to me: Levi, by three functions (ἀρχὰς) will your descendants be distinguished, as a sign of the glory of the Lord who is to come. (12) And he who believed will be the first, and no office shall be greater than his. (13) The second will be the priesthood. (14) The third will be called by a new name, for a king shall arise out of Judah and establish a new priesthood, after the fashion of the Gentiles and for all the Gentiles. (15) And his coming will be marvellous, as that of a mighty prophet of the stock of Abraham our father. (16) Everything that is so desirable in Israel shall be yours and your descendants'; and you shall eat of everything that delights the eye, and from the Lord's table shall your descendants assign themselves a portion. (17) And some of them shall be high priests, judges and scribes; for by their testimony shall what is holy be preserved.

R.H. Charles in his edition (1908) ascribes the *Testament of Levi* to the epoch of John Hyrcanus. He says *TestLev* is the oldest of all testaments of the twelve patriarchs "written in the later years of John Hyrcanus (in all probability between 109 and 106 BCE). The author was a Pharisee, who combined boundless admiration for Hyrcanus, in whom the Pharisaic party had come to recognize the actual Messiah".[4] In these sentences of Charles several theories are contained, which are to be unravelled. First of all, *TestLev* 8:17 speaks in favor of a scribe (not necessarily a Pharisee) as author. This scribe accepts the Hasmonean high priest-prince-ideology. The thus inthroned high priest has not only priestly functions but also princely ones (staff of judgement: v 4; crown: v 9; purple girdle: v 7). Elements of prophecy and wisdom shimmer through: The crown of righteousness, the breast-piece of understanding, the mantle of truth, the rosette of faith, the turban of the sign and the ephod of prophecy: v 2. But the high priest is distinguished from the Messiah named in vv 11 and 14-15.

In the fragments of an older *Testament of Levi*, found in the first and fourth caves of Qumran, the question of a priestly-princely double-function establishes the connection with Levi. It is said in L 32:1: "The office of priestly dignity is more elevated than the function of the sword (מלכות כהנתה רבה מן מלכות חרבה)." This sentence corresponds with the ideology of those Hasmoneans not yet crowned kings;

Hyrcanus was the last of them. The motive of the two מלכיות appears on several Qumran fragments[5]. Prophetic elements are hardly to be perceived directly (in the hitherto published fragments). Spiritual elements stand more in the foreground instead. The high priest and prince being an image of Jacob's son Levi stands in a distinctly intimate relation with God. He says long prayers. And heaven answers him. In L 32:7 celestial characters say to him: "Look! We have made you greater than all! Look how He (sc. God) will prepare for you the perfect fullness of eternity."[6] In L 43-45 Levi - and probably also Hyrcanus as his representative — is called יחיד אל (God's uniquely beloved) (Beyer 1984:207). This expression may be interpreted as a prophetic or charismatic explanation of Levi's or Hyrcanus' identity. The findings of Qumran again speak for the great age of *TestLev*. One manuscript (4Q 213,214) dates from the second half of the 2nd century BCE. Therefore Klaus Beyer dares draw (among others) the inference that "this work was written at the latest for John Hyrcanus I, most certainly in Jerusalem" (Beyer 1984: 189). It is characteristic for all versions of *TestLev* that Levi represents the model of a Hasmonean high priest-prince who has an intimate connection with God. This mythological-historic double-figure is a character for the future, therefore a teleological figure. He is the scion, the root, the father of the future stemming from the past, the type of the coming New Age. He gives the decisive impulse for the future through his sacerdotal and political deeds. He is on his way becoming a Messiah. But he is not an ultimate figure. The final Messiah is shrouded in *TestLev* in the sphere of secrecy. Moreover it is suggested in the Greek *TestLev* 8:14 that the Messiah will create a new priesthood, which will be appropriate for all peoples. This idea may have been created under Hellenistic influence. For the authors of *TestLev* Hyrcanus was not "the Messiah" himself but a precursor of the Messiah and a sign of the dawning of the messianic era. But this interpretation was soon surpassed by other Jewish authors. In the Book of the dream-visions (*1 Enoch* 90:8-12) either Judas Maccabee or his nephew John Hyrcanus is designated as "the big horn", which cannot be conquered by the eschatological enemies. That such a Messianisation was, however, not uncontested,

---

[5] E.g.: in 1Q 21/3: Part of a *TestLev* aram.: Barthélemy and Milik 1955: 88.
[6] Several fragments of the aramaic TestLev from Qumran are to be found in Beyer 1984:188-209. L 32:7 is on p. 195-196.

the Qumran scrolls show. In 1QH 4:16 bitter complaints are made about "Liar-Prophets, enticed by errors." It is also possible that by the repeatedly denounced "wicked Priest" (הכוהן הרשע; 1QpHab 8:8, 9:9, 11:4 etc.) Hyrcanus was meant.

Thus a selection of texts and thoughts ends which, beginning from Josephus Flavius, closes with the Asideans and Qumran-Literature. These pre-Josephan texts suggest a certain reliability of Josephus' reports on John Hyrcanus and his time, including the praises of his priestly, princely, prophetic and charismatic personality. On the other hand we can take from it that John Hyrcanus was, already in his lifetime, subject to different interpretations and that these interpretations are connected with messianic hopes surging in many places in the 2nd century BCE.

CIÒ CHE FLAVIO GIUSEPPE VIDE:
JOSEPHUS AND THE ESSENES

Tessa Rajak

Josephus' descriptions of one of the Jewish sects will, I hope, be an appropriate subject for a memorial tribute to Morton Smith. Smith's brilliant and provocative reading of the historian's statements about the Pharisees in the *Jewish Antiquities* (1956), which he saw as a retrojection to the pre-war period of the religio-political needs of the 90's, has had a major impact on scholarship. As we all know, it was developed in various ways, especially by Jacob Neusner (1972) and by Shaye Cohen (1979). It became almost an orthodoxy. Now Steve Mason (1991) has moved sideways, with his own theory that Josephus never claimed to be a Pharisee. I myself have never been comfortable with Morton Smith's reading, for a variety of reasons (in brief, Rajak 1983: 33-4), but its fruitfulness is not in doubt.

Even more to our purpose, as I was reading for this paper, I recalled that it was Morton Smith (1958) who first queried the precise connection between the notice on the Essenes in Hippolytus of Rome (Smith preferred to refer simply to the anonymous *Philosophoumena*) and Josephus' remarks on the subject. I shall have occasion to consider this study later. There, Smith produced a summary of Josephus' early career which perhaps says all that needs to be said on the subject: "he was able . . . to spend three years with a hermit (evidently, therefore, not an Essene, in spite of the fact that he bathed every day) and returned to Jerusalem by the age of 19, no doubt tired of asceticism and ready for the pleasures of Rome, where he moved in the circle of the Empress Poppaea (who also bathed every day, but was probably not an Essene)" (Smith 1958: 277-8).

The Essenes have another claim to our attention here. We are, hopefully, mapping the present and the future state of Josephus — studies, and it seems to me that one of the most important challenges that lie ahead is to redefine the writer's Judaism, in the light of transformed perspectives in Jewish studies. First and foremost, no one has yet brought the full wealth of the material from Qumran and with it our new view of the spectrum of Second Temple thought, to bear systematically and on a broad front on the study of Josephus' religious ideas. I should, however, like to signal the recent book by Rebecca Gray, based on an Oxford doctoral dissertation, as a large step in the right direction (Gray 1992). Her study demonstrates that Josephus shared fully in the mental world of contemporary Judaism, whatever he made of it for his own purposes. Today's paper is no more than a skirmish on the margins of those concerns.

1. *The problem*

Some extraordinary claims have been made about Josephus' two excursuses on the Essenes. Before the Dead Sea Scrolls were known, it was possible to argue, as no less a scholar than W. Bauer did in the long entry on the Essenes in Pauly's *Realencyclopädie* (1924), that all of Josephus' data on the subject in the *Jewish War* excursus was an idealizing invention of Greek-Jewish writing, an ethnographic fantasy derived – one need hardly say – from some "source" or other, probably Philo (On the persistance of such thinking see Petit 1992: 142, n.9). Well after 1947, Del Medico could still maintain that, while the name Essene originated with Philo, the references and descriptions in our text of Josephus were interpolations by a precursor of the Slavonic translator (Del Medico 1952).

Also quieted today are those vigorous debates about the relation of the literary Essenes to the Dead Sea sect, which marked the first Qumran research, even if "the establishment Essene theory" is a target for occasional snipers (Eisenman and Wise 1992: 5,11,273,275). In Beall's comparative study (1988), the identity of the two groups is taken as a working hypothesis. Beall's commentary serves, among other purposes, to highlight the high level of congruence in points of detail between the Essenes of Josephus and the sect of the sectarian scrolls.

Here, too, it will be supposed that Josephus was describing Jewish ascetics who were, at the very least, part of the same tradition as those who, over the generations, wrote the sectarian scrolls from Qumran, even if the correlation is not exact; and that the portrait is based upon those who occupied, in one fashion or another, at one stage or another, the installations at Qumran. Josephus, as is well known, does not mention the Dead Sea area in connection with his description. The Essenes of Josephus are, however, linked with that area through the mention in Pliny the Elder's short notice on the "Esseni", of the striking, if not one hundred percent correct geographical specification "infra hos Engada oppidum fuit . . . inde Masada castellum in rupe, et ipsum haut procul Asphaltite" (*Natural History* 5.17.4).

To proceed cautiously, we can see from Beall that Josephus had a decent knowledge of a sect which shared practice and doctrine with the people of Qumran. We certainly cannot deny that he supplies genuine information. E.P. Sanders' recent conclusions sum up this position succinctly: "The scrolls allow us to comment on Josephus and also on the relationship between primary sources and secondary description. Josephus was quite a good historian; that is, he had good sources plus some personal knowledge, and he got a remarkable number of things right . . . . When it comes to theology, we find him a little less trustworthy. Certainly, his description does not convey adequately the flavour of the scrolls" (Sanders 1992: 379). Sanders' last point will require further comment.

Josephus' excursuses on the Essenes are, then, due for a fresh investigation in the light of recent scholarly concerns. The complexity of the Qumran material should not deter us. Josephus' remarks are still intermittently important to scrolls research. Issues such as the sectaries' commitment to celibacy and their attitude to sacrifice are discussed by scholars in relation to what Josephus says: those are the terms in which the problems are often posed. Moreover, we are again confronted with radical re-interpretations of the Qumran site, by which even its monastic character is being called into question; from this point of view too it will be important to know how we should view Josephus' remarks about the Essene lifestyle.

Apart from any agenda dictated by Qumran scholarship, with which I cannot deal directly in this paper, there is also the challenge simply of understanding Josephus on his own terms; and nobody here at San Miniato needs persuading of the value of that. In this context, too, the Essenes are an important test case: to find that Josephus knows more or less what he is talking about is certainly not the end of the matter.

A collection of new translations (Vermes and Goodman 1989) brings the texts from different authors together, conveniently reminding scholar and student alike that the texts are more than just repositories of disparate observations (cf. Adam 1972; Dupont-Sommer 1961). Brief footnotes offer Qumran parallels; these, and, more especially Beall's book (mentioned above), which sets out the parallels in detail, invite us to look at the relationship between Josephus' statements and the Qumran texts more closely. It becomes necessary to take these convergences seriously and to think afresh about Josephus' knowledge and its origins.

For all our acceptance of Josephus as a witness, there are limitations in his account, which spring from his *modus operandi* as a historian and from the formal aspects of his text. Josephus' expositions display, as has often been noted, many features typical of the moralizing ethnographical digressions favoured by ancient writers (Trüdinger 1918: esp. 133-45; Müller 1972, 1980). Yet they are also unusual. Writing ancient ethnography usually presupposed knowing rather little about what you were talking about, because, apparently, it was not felt that there was any decipherment to be done (Momigliano 1975; J. Z. Smith 1985: 20-1). Here, by contrast, we have as we presume an author who both had seen for himself and had the capacity to decipher.

It is reasonable to presume, as Sanders does, and as many early commentators did, that Josephus' information has a connection with his personal experience: his statement in the *Life* (§ 11), that he had taken a lot of trouble to try out the practices of all three Jewish sects, can be given some credence even in the case of the Essenes. I have shown that the story is not chronologically impossible, and I would stress again the observation that for the description of the three sects to be an established *topos* is not incompatible with veracity (Rajak 1983: 34-9; for a different defence see Feldman 1984: 81-2). However, those who remain uncomfortable with Josephus' autobiographical assertions have still to give some weight to the consideration that the Jerusalem priestly establishment could hardly have afforded to be wholly ignorant of what radical Jewish sectaries a stone's throw from Jerusalem were thinking and doing. There was no language barrier to stop them from finding out.

The significance of this paper's title should now be clear: the eyewitness element in the descriptions of the Essenes is in my view a very important feature of them. It will not have escaped you that I have inverted a famous title of Arnaldo Momigliano's. In fact, my position is not far removed from the one he took in the essay entitled "Ciò che Flavio Giuseppe non vide" (Momigliano 1980; 1987): for there the focus lay precisely in aspects of Judaism which, in Momigliano's view, Josephus must have been quite aware of, but which somehow he chose not to register — the synagogue, on the one hand, and apocalyptic currents on the other. Here, too, we are thinking about how and why a particular picture of a species of Judaism has been fashioned by an author who could have said so much more. At the same time, Momigliano's interpretation of Josephus' silences was, I think, implicitly psychological and personal — like so much of what is written about Josephus — while mine operates on a literary level and has the aim of explaining how the nature of the narrative limits what is or can be stated.

The position may be summed up by saying that we are dealing not with an *either/or* as tends to be supposed (*either* ethnographic fiction *or* a realistic account), but with a *both/and*. Josephus' digressions on the Essenes are texts which *both* conform to historiographical canons *and* draw upon the author's experience.[1] There is nothing impossible in that. The difficulty lies in understanding how the two elements interact.

The distinctive feature of Josephus' descriptions of the Essenes, especially the longest version, in Book 2 of the *Jewish War*, is precisely this mix of real information with quite considerable modelling and idealization. For both of Josephus' excursuses do, after all, form part of that well known, stylized reading in which he analyses Judaism in terms of three "philosophical schools," with differing views on fate, and in structure and attitude these excursuses are far from representing unmediated information. Some would describe them as "Hellenized" (Moore 1929; Wächter 1969). In a different context, where he introduces Menaham's prophecy of Herod's kingship, Josephus claims that the Essenes followed the Pythagorean way of life (*Ant* 15 § 371).

The Essene digressions are thus very much part of a "text" (in today's sense of that term). But in connection with this sect, in contrast to the other two, our knowledge of the Qumran literature serves as a control on the process, albeit one which needs careful handling. If we can understand what Josephus is up to here, we may obtain some leverage on what he is doing in more opaque areas of his writing. This is a chance to watch Josephus at work. The enterprise becomes even more promising when we take into account the fact that Josephus left us not one excursus on the subject in question, but two; and, again, when we remember that his great precursor Philo had also (in all

---

[1] For Feldman (1984: 416-7), the assumption that personal experience was the "chief source" excludes any use of Philo.

probability) written at least twice about the Essenes, whom he calls
'Εσσαῖοι (while Josephus uses equally the form 'Εσσηνοί and in *Ant*
15 §§ 371-9 even combines the two in one passage). The first Philonic
account, in intricate Greek, is in the Stoically-influenced discussion
Quod omnis probus liber sit (75-91) contained in Eusebius (*Praep. ev.*
8.12) and ascribed by him to Philo, and the other in the *Hypothetica*,
also preserved, in fragmentary form, in the same book of Eusebius
(*Praep. ev.* 8.6,11). Both Philonic accounts must have been known by
Josephus.

2. *Contrasts between the* War *and the* Antiquities

In *JW* 2 §§ 119-61, Josephus describes the Essenes at far greater length
than he does the Pharisaic and Sadducean "philosophies", and he also
puts them before the others. There is undoubtedly some imbalance in
this design, even if Sanders (who locates "common Judaism" around
the Temple) is misleading in speaking of "a tiny and fairly marginal
sect" (Sanders 1992: 341): the urban and village Essenes may quite
well have made a significant impact on Jewish society, especially those
living in Jerusalem, of whom Sanders himself has a fair amount to say.
His undervaluing of the Essenes may, perhaps, be influenced by their
absence from New Testament literature. Furthermore, there is no
reason to think that thoroughgoing Pharisees, still less Sadducees, were
more than a minority in the population as a whole: many "common
Jews" will probably not have been affiliates of any grouping.

The Essenes, then, may have had quite a high visibility. For all that,
the manner in which Josephus parades them shows that he was well
aware of the appeal of the most "philosophical" of the sects to a
Greco-Roman readership. Paul (1992: 131) suggests that Josephus
wished to depict the Essenes to Romans as the quintessential Jews.
Philo had acclimatized the subject to Greek literature and Pliny the
Elder had alerted a Roman readership. Pliny, it would seem, was not
unaware of the Jewish revolt and its consequences for the region, since
elsewhere he mentioned Vespasian's post-war colonization, and noticed Gamala (*Natural History* 5.69). Nor is it out of the question that
Tacitus, in the lost part of *Histories* book 5, had included the grim fate
of the Essenes which Josephus details towards the end of his excursus:
"the war against the Romans fully revealed their souls. During it their
limbs were twisted and broken, burned and shattered . . . ." (2 § 152,

Vermes and Goodman's translation). So the Essenes were undoubtedly a suitable case for treatment, and especially so in the 70's.

When it comes to the *Antiquities* (11 §§ 11-22), the order in which the sects are handled is reversed, and the balance between them is regularized. What is now in need of explanation is the new dependence on Philo, especially on the extended *Quod omnis probus* account. This is associated with the loss of much that was specific and immediate in Josephus' earlier version. The Philonic account is highly philosophical, to the extent where it views Judaism from the outside, and its focus is on extolling a virtuous and free life, lived in community, as designed in accordance with divine inspiration. Distinctly Philonic in Josephus is the attribution to the Essenes of opposition to slavery (*Ant* 18 § 21), a characteristic which Hellenistic writers had fathered on various little known peoples (for example, Megasthenes on the Indians), and on which the Qumran literature seems to be silent either way (Beall: 129);[2] the high valuation on agriculture, which goes together with reservations about all or some crafts (*Ant* 18 § 19); and a degree of detachment about the normal sacrificial ritual (*Ant* 18 § 19).[3] Josephus' celebrated analysis of the sects in terms of their views of divine providence connects with his making Essene determinism his first defining characteristic here, and this may be anticipated in Philo's "the Deity is the cause of all good but of no evil" (*Quod omnis* 84).

These themes in themselves might not seem to be treated sufficiently similarly by the respective authors to assure us of a connection, especially given the textual problems in the Josephus passage. But the total figure of 4,000 for the Essenes which appears in both places clinches the dependance (*Ant* 18 § 20 and *Quod omnis* 75). When one considers Josephus' acceptance of Philo in the *Antiquities*, one cannot help wondering what the historian could have made of the confident assertion in the *Hypothetica* (in Eusebius *Praep. evang.* 8.11.3) that the Essenes allowed no adolescents or young men near them, when he himself had, so he tells us, sampled life in the sect when he was at most seventeen.

Equally, it is reasonable to say that there is remarkably little information unique to the *Antiquities* account. The statement about

---

[2] Slavery appears explicitly only in the CD 11.12; 12.10.

[3] For this purpose, it is unnecessary to discuss the exact statements of either author. There are textual difficulties in both cases, and in Josephus the presence of a negative in the Latin text makes it unclear if Essenes are alleged to have sent sacrifices to the Jerusalem Temple: Vermes and Goodman: 36-7; 55.

Essene sacrifices is garbled, whatever its meaning, and textual problems apart. Then there is the observation that priests have a special
role in the community, and that they are engaged in the preparation
of food (*Ant* 18 § 22). And here we recall that the attribution of a high
position to religious leaders is a familiar element in the Greek portrayal of various strange peoples, as for example the Celtic Druids in the
sketch in Diodorus which is ascribed to Posidonius (Diodorus 5.31;
Momigliano 1975: 69-70). Whatever were the actual functions of
priests at Qumran, and whatever the commitment there to preparing
food in purity, Josephus' culinary priests are plainly bizarre.

Had Josephus, assuming that he was writing from memory, forgotten what he had known perfectly well all those years ago? Was he just
less interested, because the subject was now rather stale to outside
readers? Or, was it that Pharisees were by then claiming the attention
of the Jewish world? Or, perhaps, was Josephus at this stage reserving
material for the projected, but never written work *On Customs and
Causes*? Or, again, had our author just found that a previously unfamiliar section of Philo was wonderfully to his purpose, just as he was
to make good use of the *Hypothetica* when it came to writing the
Against Apion? (Philo, LCL, 9 ed. Colson 1941: 409 n. a). This last
explanation perhaps seems the least likely, since a limited influence of
the *Quod omnis probus* may already be suspected in the *War* version,
especially on the theme of the sectarians' resilience in the face of
torments inflicted by tyrants (*Quod omnis* 89-91; *JW* 2 § 152), where
Josephus seems to offer an update. Beyond this, I cannot see any
sensible basis for choice between these hypotheses.

Morton Smith identified the problem of the gap in content and
quality between the two Josephan accounts, and grappled with it. He
allowed that the *War* version shows "considerable knowledge of the
Essenes" (1958c: 276-8). But his conclusion was that Josephus could
not have written either account: "for had Josephus himself written the
account in the *War* he would probably not, when he came to write the
Antiquities, have replaced his work with a copy or condensation of
somebody else's. Therefore the account in the *War* must also have
been a copy or condensation of some outside source." This reasoning,
perhaps compelling in the case of a modern author, takes insufficient
account of the demand for sheer variety and of the high valuation put
on form by ancient authors.

In any case, the consequence of Josephus' decision is that the earlier version is the important one for us, and not just by virtue of its length. It is the more interesting, and, I would argue, it is the more Josephan — which does not mean that it is the less stylized. If I am right, then it becomes unnecessary to struggle to reconcile the two accounts in terms of real changes over time or of variations in practice in the Qumran community, as some observant investigators have suggested (Vermes 1981).[4]

3. *The framework of the* JW *2 §§ 120-161*

Returning to *Jewish War* 2, it is instructive to consider the overall structure before looking at individual features in the portrayal of the Essenes there. Individual "Hellenizations" tend to catch the eye of commentators, but this structural element is generally overlooked. That is hardly surprising, for at first sight there is a puzzling lack of order. But the key is, I suggest, that the themes are those favoured in descriptions of ideal states in Greek political thought, and that the organization corresponds to a progression appropriate in studying a polity. Greek ethnographic writing, with its large component of idealization and eulogy, was heavily influenced by the philosophers, and Josephus' Essene communities are depicted, like those of other writers on the subject, as a form of ideal society.

The themes may be listed as follows in the order in which they appear. Since the context is inappropriate for geography or topography, first comes the family: the distaste for marriage (but we should note the qualification in Josephus' afterthought, discussed below), the securing of increase through the adoption of children, and a general misogynistic observation on the unfaithfulness of women, which is regrettably quite in keeping with Josephus' own thinking on the subject (Brown 1992). The destructive charms of women are also a feature in Philo, where they are given greater scope (*Hypothet.* in Eusebius *Praep. ev.* 8.11.14), but his problem does not seem to lie with their promiscuity.

Next we learn about the household, where the economy in its literal sense belongs: wealth is despised, while assets are held communally

---

[4] Of course, some discrepancies between sources on the Essenes do invite explanation in terms of variation or change in practice, in the terms indicated by Vermes.

and thus equalized. Dress follows from this, as part of the basic fabric of domestic life: not only the white clothing but also the abhorrence of oil on the skin. The city is the next level up: we are told that Essenes live in various towns offering hospitality to one another. The subject of cities leads to exchange and trade; but here a negative is recorded, since the Essenes of course permit no buying and selling among themselves, and they even avoid buying clothes until their old ones are in tatters.

Cultic habits come in only after all these matters: while not neglected, religious practices rarely have pride of place in Greek writing: we learn about the daily regime of the sect in relation to purity and holiness, starting from the early morning prayers and culminating in the quietness of the cultic meal with the accompanying blessings from the priests. The social hierarchy follows, when the great powers of the overseers are described, with charitable deeds being mentioned as the only area where the individual's freedom of action is preserved. Here, the authority of the traditional texts is also stressed. Education is then represented by the stages of Essene initiation; within this topic comes quite a detailed description of the attitudes and conduct expected of a fully qualified member, as enunciated in his initiation oath. The political and legal system of the Essenes involves total obedience to authority, and the formidable disciplinary requirements, with relentless accompanying punishments, are expanded upon with a rhetorical flourish.

Character — ἔθος — is the beginning and end of any civic organization according to both Plato and Aristotle. Later Greek philosophers thought no differently. Here, the essential virtues required and enhanced by the system are described as courage and wisdom, the latter especially in relation to the good of the soul. Firm convictions about the afterlife are the underpinning, and so a pleasing doctrine of the immortality of the soul is sketched.

The headings which I have teased out are naturally not explicit in Josephus. But what looks at first sight like a random collection falls into place under this ordering. We can understand, too, the otherwise baffling placing of some of the details in Josephus, such as the Essene presence in cities or the hostility to olive oil. Expansion of individual topics is possible up to a point, and Josephus dwells especially on the cultic meals and the content of the initiation oaths. Eating habits, it is worth remembering, are a topic favoured by Greek ethnographers, and

Posidonius appears to have written with particular gusto about the feasts of the Celts (Momigliano 1975: 69). Philo's account of the ascetic Egyptian θεραπευταί in *De vita contemplativa* (64-89) centres on the sect's banquets, in what is an ironic reversal of the familiar, at which he expects his audience to scoff: those banquets are non-banquets, where satisfaction comes from the decorous and joyful singing of the Divinity's praises, and from drinking water, rather than from consumption and carousing.

Yet it is arguable that other important matters, especially in the area of Essene religious practices and beliefs – even the all-important sectarian solar calendar – are given very short shrift or omitted by Josephus, for the simple reason that the scheme does not readily accommodate them.

Where does this analysis originate? The various themes under which the model city is discussed in Plato's *Republic* and in his *Laws*, together with the analysis of the elements of the city in Aristotle's *Politics* (from couple to household to city and so on), probably lie behind all such designs, although the philosophers operate, of course, on a much bigger scale than any ethnographic work seems to have done. Much ethnography appeared in digressions comparable in length to Josephus' miniature composition. The constructions of the philosophers influenced the historians.

To talk of a Platonic lineage in the case of Josephus is by no means fanciful. For if we turn our attention for a moment from structure to content, it is hard to avoid detecting Platonic echoes in Josephus' concluding depiction of the liberation of the souls of the blessed from the bodies in which they have been entangled: we scarcely need the Jewish historian to tell us that the "sons of the Greeks" would be in agreement with the Essenes on the subject, because we already know.

4. *A source for the* War *account?*

But how and why should Josephus hit upon this kind of analysis? No one is going to entertain the idea that he was busily reading the *Republic* at the stage in his life when he was composing the *War*. One solution is to postulate a source for Josephus, and in particular to look to the Platonist Philo.

Such ideas used to be much in favour in Josephus scholarship, and this one is not new. It is therefore worth dispelling at the outset the notion that any external data demands the assumption. A description of the Essenes close in substance to that of Josephus is to be found in the *Refutation of All the Heresies* (9.18-29) ascribed to the third century Roman Christian writer Hippolytus, and the obvious possibility that these similarities are to be explained in terms of a common source, used by both Josephus and Hippolytus, is the main support for the claim that Josephus lifted much of what he says from an earlier writer.

Hippolytus contains strikingly Josephan details, such as his statement that expelled Essenes often starve to death. But why should Hippolytus' account not derive directly from Josephus himself? The acid test is whether there is significant information, coherently structured, that is present in Hippolytus but absent from Josephus: should there be reason to think that this information cannot have been added by either Hippolytus or any other late writer upon whom he depended, and, further, to assume that Hippolytus is likely to have used one source alone, then it follows that there was a common source from which Hippolytus took certain details which Josephus chose to omit.

It was Morton Smith who saw the value of making a detailed comparison of Hippolytus and Josephus, and the key divergences in content are now briefly indicated in Vermes and Goodman. Smith sought to establish the case for a common (he believed Semitic) source − a case, it should be noted, of which his judgment on the Josephus passages had already independently (and in my view mistakenly) persuaded him. Yet, for all his endeavours, nothing of substance emerges. The disparities are entirely explanatory comment, until chapter 26, whose pronouncements can be simply described as a mixture of nonsense and anti-Judaism. The additional details are characteristic of Jews generally, especially the strict Sabbath observance which even forbids carrying coins − a point hardly appropriate to people without private possessions. Zealots are wrongly identified with sicarii; and Hippolytus goes so far as to assert that the sectaries will kill any uncircumcised person caught discussing God or his laws. The vocabulary of the additions is in keeping with Hippolytus generally (Burchard 1977). In chapter 27, the resurrection of the body has replaced some of Josephus' Platonizing account of immortality as the soul's survival. This change is part of a tendency in Hippolytus to "vary", as Smith puts it, "in the direction of Jewish piety." But, at points, some Christianization is also detectable (Burchard 1977).

For those who doubt that Hippolytus himself altered Josephus — in general he does not seem to have reshaped his sources — the hypothesis that he used an earlier Christian rewrite serves to explain all the changes. Baumgarten has claimed (1984) that in describing the Pharisees, Hippolytus must have had a favourable Jewish source apart from Josephus; but this intended "test case" has no relevance to the visibly unfavourable Essene excursus.

5. *Philo and Josephus*

While the arguments from Hippolytus have to be dismissed, it cannot be denied that Josephus had some familiarity with what predecessors wrote about the Essenes. He undoubtedly had parts of Philo at his disposal, and we have detected the earlier author's influence on the *Antiquities* notice.

So it would in theory be not inconceivable for Philo to have originated the framework in the *War*. Moralistic themes comparable to those in Josephus figure in the two Philonic accounts of the Essenes. Yet the thrust in Philo is quite distinct. In both of his descriptions of the Essenes, we find a greater emphasis on the ethical virtues and less on social organization. Community of property and of living looms particularly large in Philo, and this feature of life is linked with a highly moral stance on avarice (*Hypothet.* in Eusebius *Praep. ev.* 8.11.8) and on the corrupting influence of cities (*Quod omnis* 12;75-6, in contradiction to what Josephus writes and also, seemingly, to Philo's own statement, *Hypothet.* 11). It can hardly escape notice that avarice, as πλεονεξία, is one of Plato's *bêtes noires*, and it is in Plato, too (*Laws* 743e etc.) that the agricultural society is labelled the best. So Philo's judgment of the Essenes, not unexpectedly, carries marked Platonic echoes.

I do not wish to claim that these specific Philonic themes are entirely absent from the *War*. They are not. Josephus does not overlook the standard moral topics, — the rejection of pleasure in favour of moderation (*JW* 2 § 120), sobriety and self-control as an escape from the passions (2 § 161). But Josephus' Essenes are by no means Philo's "athletes of virtue" (*Quod omnis* 89; cf. *Hypothet.* in Eusebius *Praep. ev.* 8.11.6). They are not seekers of freedom. Josephus' moral assessments are not presented in the same way as Philo's. What is more, on a general level, such assessments find a place even in the scrolls: not only the *Damascus Document* but *hodayot* and the *pesharim* contain ringing denunciations of riches and of their acquisition, if not precisely of greed (Beall: 43-4). Disapproval of wine is also a feature of the *Damascus Document* (Beall: 62).

The supposition that Josephus got his *Jewish War* framework from a different account of the Essenes by Philo, one that was part of a work which is now lost, is thus a possible but not an attractive solution. The loss of a third and longer Philonic account, perhaps an entire treatise which preceded the surviving *De vita contemplativa*, where there is mention of a passage on the Essenes, was argued by Bauer and has often been taken as fact (Petit 1992: 141). But there are other difficulties in turning this conjectural treatise into Josephus' source. I believe that it makes little sense to ascribe the immediate detail of the *Jewish War* account to Philo, above Josephus himself, whose knowledge should have been considerably more direct and more extensive.

The nature and derivation of Philo's information on the Essenes is, if anything, an even more vexed question than that of Josephus'. That the Alexandrian is the first in the line of surviving writers to find the sect important enough to dwell on is certainly a fact worthy of comment. And unlike Josephus, Philo never incorporates his discussions of the Essenes into any account of the three Jewish groupings: the Essenes stand alone, and they are entirely *sui generis*, as Petit has pointed out (1992: 139). Both Philonic accounts centre on the welfare of the soul. But whether Philo, for his basic information, drew on oral tradition, on what he learnt on his pilgrimage to Jerusalem, or in his own turn, on a written source, Jewish or non-Jewish, is not a question which we have any means of resolving, and Petit's investigation remains wholly inconclusive. The difficulty is, it seems to me, compounded by the impression given in the *De vita contemplativa* (Vermes and Goodman: 75-9) that Philo, for all his stylization (van der Horst 1984: 56), did have a firsthand acquaintance with the ascetic θεραπευ-ταί of Lake Maraeotis, who are distinctly similar in many respects to the Qumran sect. But the identity of the θεραπευταί is a separate problem.

Here, I would suggest that the contribution of Philo to Josephus did not lie in what the Alexandrian knew about the Essenes, but in his literary presentation and in some concepts. Furthermore, while Philo's philosophy was occasionally echoed by the historian, even much of that was unsuitable. Philo could be of only limited use to the writer of the *War* account.

An observation may now be drawn from the relation of framework to content: if much of the substantive information offered by Josephus, especially in the relatively long *JW* 2 passage is taken to reflect the author's own experience, then it is preferable to lay the organization and shaping of the whole at his door as well. It is, quite simply, difficult to conceive of Josephus taking over a structure from an earlier author and then packing this with his own content.

If it is not to be a source, then we have to think of Josephus himself. For him to have supplied a structure, we must suppose that by the time of the writing of Book 2 of the *War*, he had read and absorbed something of that literature in Greek which included portraits of foreign peoples: he could have gone back to the great Posidonius, or he might have been content with reading more recent writing, by Strabo perhaps or by Nicolaus of Damascus. It is interesting that by way of conclusion to the *Antiquities* account, an explicit comparison is drawn between the Essenes and the Dacians, which suggests that by then, at any rate, Josephus had a familiarity with such literature (*Ant* 18 § 22).[5]

For the *War* account, Josephus did not need a source, but he did need sources of ideas and techniques. When so much of Greek historiography is lost, the temptation to speculate on the identity of Josephus' models should be resisted. The important point is that there is no difficulty in principle. After all, what the preparation for writing the *War* necessitated was precisely immersion in the historians.

In an investigation of the tale of Moses' military expedition against the Ethiopians in *Ant* 2 §§ 238-53 (Rajak 1978), a dependance upon Greek ethnographical traditions became apparent from the topography and from other small details of the Josephan narrative. There I posited an Alexandrian source for Josephus. Here, the impact lies in the method more than in the detail. And in this case, although we are concerned not with the *Antiquities*, but with the *War*, written so much earlier, it seems to me appropriate for the reasons I have given to envisage Josephus himself as the author.

---

[5] Note, however, that the Greek text in all MSS is unacceptable as it stands, and, among the emendations proposed, some eliminate the Dacians: Beall: 121-2.

6. *The information in Josephus*

The constraints of structure do not prevent Josephus from giving revealing – even if consciously picturesque – information about Essene practices. Details of customs are the other element in all the best ethnographic writing: again we may point to the Celtic descriptions. In the *Jewish War* excursus, the details are numerous and they regularly echo Qumran literature. Included are observations on the early morning prayer[6], purifications, the strictness of Sabbath observance, the distinctive meal-times in which the dining room is seen as a shrine, the cultivation of silence, the respect for God's name and for that of Moses, the abhorrence of oaths and the formidable initiation oaths (though not the contents of these) together with the stages of initiation – in fact, we have a fair summary of many of the basic elements of sectarian living. Overseers are mentioned (*JW* 2 § 123), a reflection, presumably, of the important figure of the guardian (מבקר) in Qumran literature, even if the obedience of the sectaries to them is interestingly compared, in a nice literary touch, to that of children to their παιδαγωγοί (*JW* 2 § 126). What would seem to be the council of the community also figures, for a council of more than one hundred members acts as the stern administrator of justice.

The three-year phased initiation procedure in the *Jewish War*, as is well known, does not correspond exactly with the arrangements described either in the *Damascus Document* or in the *Community Rule*. The stages specified by Josephus show clear parallels to both provisions, and especially to the latter; but the oaths there appear to come at the end of the initiation process and not at its beginning (Beall: 74-8; Vermes 1982: 129). There is no reason why all three versions could not have represented sectarian practice at some stage of its development.

Especially powerful is Josephus' formidable story of those who are punished by expulsion and then all but starve to death out of continued devotion to the purity laws to which they had sworn allegiance; here he goes somewhat further than the *Community Rule*, which talks of deprivation of the pure food (1*QS* 5.15-16; Beall: 90). At these points, the portrayal of an ideal community gives way to a different

---

[6] The implication of sun-worship which has been read into these words is a red-herring; the Mishnaic benediction of the light which precedes the morning Shema is a convincing parallel: Beall: 52, with n.89, citing the revised Schürer.

kind of rhetorical representation, apparently based in reality, but highlighted for effect.

Contemporary life appears also to obtrude, momentarily at least, in the reference to the torments inflicted during the war with Rome, which Tacitus, perhaps dependant on Josephus, also mentions. This is generally taken to refer to events surrounding the Roman seizure of the site at Qumran. Philo (*Quod omnis* 89-91) has an obscure passage about oppressive kings who had torn Essenes limb from limb, but had eventually had their come-uppance. But what Josephus volunteers in this line, is specific and up-to-date.

Again, we find what is effectively a correction concerning a different group of married Essenes, tagged on to the end of the *War* excursus, as if Josephus wants to get the record straight. This is an interesting case where the evidence wins out in a struggle against the stereotype. It is still not agreed, after much discussion, whether marriage was ever permitted at Qumran itself, though the *Damascus Document* refers to it repeatedly and other texts do not wholly ignore the subject (Beall: 38-42). Josephus offers us a very important modification to the impression of Essene celibacy given earlier. He also gives us here unique and valuable indications of a negative attitude to sexuality within marriage in a Jewish sect, for, we are told, "they observe their women for three years. When they have purified themselves three times . . . then they marry them. And when they are pregnant, they have no intercourse with them, thereby showing that they do not marry for pleasure but because it is necessary to have children" (*JW* 2 § 161). The position of this qualification as a special afterthought, and its factual importance suggest that it should not be read merely as further exploitation of that theme of asceticism that so fascinated Greek readers of philosophical bent.

7. *Josephus' omissions*

But there are significant features of the sect which are not in Josephus and which may be deemed a casualty of the interplay between Josephus the eyewitness and Josephus the Greek theorist. What is missing adds up to what Sanders rightly identified as the "flavour" of the scrolls. It scarcely needs saying that many fundamental features of the Qumran thought-world are absent from Josephus, even if our author does take care to assure us of the Essenes' strong concern for the inherited texts (*JW* 2 §§ 136). And it is hardly to be credited that Josephus simply could not grasp Essene thought, even if this ultimate outsider may have been kept away from some of the sectarian texts — an experience not unfamiliar to the modern scholar. It is somewhat more probable that Josephus perceived what was involved in Essene theology as wholly tainted by dangerously apocalyptic notions. But I hope I have shown that there are other issues involved.

The world of belief was less readily accommodated to the Greek model than the world of social organization and practice. And it is only fair to add that the former was not readily transferred from one language to another. We are, as I have said, told in a sentence about Essene respect for the secret names of the angels (*JW* 2 § 142), a small but clear allusion to the complex world of Qumran angelology (see Hengel 1974: 1.231-4). We learn that Essenes made predictions about the future. We are also made aware of the ferocity of Essene sabbath observance. And the intensity of their conviction makes an appearance in the curious phrase πίστεως πρόστατι (*JW* 2 § 135).

But what we seek in vain is any notion of the Qumran sectaries' dualism, of their powerful awareness of evil, of their concentration on the future, or of their joy in praising God: this last, it should be said, is beautifully captured in Philo's account of the θεραπευταί (*De vita contemplativa* 80-90). We miss, too, in Josephus, much of a sense of the distinctiveness of Judaism: among Josephus' Essenes, there is no covenant, there is no sequence of the festivals, there are no tribes, there are priests but no Levites.[7] We learn nothing of any Essene stance towards the rest of Jewry, even though the sectaries are defined by Josephus as being Jews by birth (*JW* 2 § 119), in contrast to Pliny's description of them as a *gens* in themselves, or, again, to Philo's partial explanation that they live in Judaea, but are not a γένος, just volunteers.

"What Josephus did not see" should therefore perhaps best be reformulated as "what Josephus did see but could not write about." For there were strong constraints upon him, the constraints not (as is so often suggested) of patronage or of dishonesty, not even just those of his own temperament, but something equally pervasive — the constraints of literary form, the tyranny of text.

---

[7] However, some take the four groups of *JW* 2 § 150, to refer to the divisions of priests, levites, laity and novices: Beall: 99.

I do not wish to seem to espouse the naive position that realistic reportage, even if squeezed, can survive such onslaughts intact and be extracted in nuggets from a narrative. The relationship between the two elements is necessarily more complex, for they influence one another continuously. That is why it has not been profitable to subject each Josephan claim in either *War* or *Antiquities* to a test of truth or falsehood, even if there are moments when scholars need to do this over particular claims. For our purposes, it is sufficient to grasp how an eye-witness description can also be a highly literary artefact, and then what impact this has upon content. Some kind of negotiation between the two pure types is, after all, what writing history is about.

In the case of Josephus, it is arguable that the demands of literary form are, all things considered, the largest single determinant in his presentation of Jewish history.

8. *Conclusion*

My starting point was two statements that cannot reasonably be denied: on the one hand, Josephus knew a fair amount about the Essenes while, on the other, he drew on Greek models. My aim has then been to pursue a closer definition of the Greek literary component in the *War* account. I see it as a structural, and therefore a pervasive and also a limiting feature. Such an analysis offers at least some explanation of what Josephus reveals and of what he overlooks in explaining the Qumran sect to his readers. It also points the way to an approach to Josephus' historiography generally, where we often find that literary form controls content to a surprising extent.

I have argued that the long *War* excursus is substantially the author's own, rather than a predecessor's. This is not a matter susceptible to proof, but there is much to support such a conclusion. It does not mean that Josephus had not seen other accounts. The conclusion entails a degree of competence in manipulating Greek forms on the part of the Josephus of the *War* period, beyond what was directly required by the composition of a military history. The underlying structure of the Essene notice is quite sophisticated, conceived in terms of certain categories taken from Greek political thought into ethnographic analysis.

A marked disparity in quality has emerged between the two Josephan accounts, *JW* 2 and *Ant* 18, even allowing for the difference in scale. Whether or not my explanation of it is to be accepted, this phenomenon should, I think, be taken into account by Qumran scholars, who have perhaps been unduly perplexed by various difficulties in the *Antiquities* account – notably, the troublesome assertion that (on the more usual reading) the community sent sacrifices to Jerusalem. These difficult statements cannot, of course, be wholly ignored, but their context must be kept in mind. For students of Josephus, the contrast between the two accounts is surely a fascinating one.

Perhaps I may be permitted to end on a speculative note. To judge by the case in hand, the Josephus of the *Antiquities* lacked the communicative passion of the aspiring younger man. His Palestinian roots had been dislodged; what he had seen counted for less and less, and the Essenes, our present topic, had certainly ceased to matter very much. It was still *de rigueur* to write about them – traditional themes die hard in Greek historiography – but he had little that was new to offer: he shortened the account considerably; but also, for most of his later description he drew, somewhat lazily it may be thought, on a few stereotypes, and he fell back on Philo.

So, finally, I have not managed entirely to escape an analysis in personal terms. And thus we come round again to Momigliano. For we may recall the essay of which I have already spoken, and the seductive portrayal conjured up there of a Josephus who, in his declining years in exile, appears caught between times and places, culturally isolated, somehow out of touch. The immediacy of the *War* was long gone. And so were the realities of Palestine.

JOSEPHUS, DANIEL, AND THE FLAVIAN HOUSE

Steve Mason

As soon as it was written, the book of Daniel became the definitive expression of Jewish apocalyptic hope. It was read by groups of widely different social status and education, including the Hasmonean court, the authors of the Dead Sea Scrolls, the rural and urban followers of Jesus, visionaries, high priests, and rabbis. In his *Jewish Antiquities*, the Jerusalem aristocrat Josephus also confesses an absorbing interest in Daniel. This paper seeks to answer the question: to what degree was Josephus' outlook, especially his view of the Flavian regime, influenced by his interpretation of Daniel? I contend that a particular reading of Daniel was an essential ingredient of his world view by the time that he wrote the *Jewish War*.

Dealing with the problem before us will illuminate some perennial issues of Josephan studie, such as: his degree of biblical knowledge; his self-understanding as a Jew; the nature of his service to the Romans; his motives in paraphrasing the Bible; his use of sources; the relationship between the *War* and the *Antiquities*; and the consistency of his thought.

Our procedure will take us from the known to the unknown. We begin with a summary of Daniel's main themes and the ways in which these were adapted by Josephus' contemporaries. Second, we shall consider the function of Daniel in the *Antiquities*, where he is discussed at length. Finally, we shall ask whether the *War*, though it fails to mention Daniel, is already indebted to the biblical seer.

1. *Background and Context*

To establish an appropriate grid for understanding Josephus, we need first to recall some salient themes of Daniel and to consider their significance for other Jews of the period.

1.1 *The Message of Daniel*

Three features of the book merit special attention here.

1.1.1 First, the Masoretic text is only one incarnation of a considerable tradition concerning the exilic wise man. That this tradition
antedated the canonical book (ca. 165 BCE) by centuries is clear from
the appearance of Daniel's name in earlier documents (Collins 1977:
1-3).[1] And independent Danielic traditions continued to flourish long
after the canonical book was written.[2] The biblical book itself shows
signs of revision (Collins 1977: 8-19; Hartman and Di Lella 1978: 13-
20) and its earliest translation into Greek created a substantially new
work. The OG was such a free rendering (van der Kooij 1986: 72-80)
that later Christians, apparently under Origen's influence, took the
unparalleled step of substituting Theodotion's translation — yet another
incarnation — for the "real" LXX text (Farris 1990: 78-83). Thus we
ought not to imagine the influence of Daniel as emanating from a
single document of the Maccabean period.

1.1.2 Nevertheless, the canonical books of Daniel, Semitic and Greek,
became the chief repositories of several potent Near-Eastern images.
For example, Daniel's expectation of divine intervention to save Israel
from its foreign oppressors has solid parallels in older Egyptian and
Persian documents (Griffiths 1989: 273-93). Daniel's periodization of
history and its metaphor of four metals, representing deteriorating
epochs, have Mediterranean precedents (Collins 1977: 40-41; Gladigow
1989: 263-65). And the four-kingdom scheme, in which a kingdom of
righteousness replaces increasingly unjust regimes, took shape in
Mesopotamia, whence it began a distinguished career in Roman,
Persian, Jewish, and Christian political discourse (Swain 1940; Rowley
1959; Flusser 1972; Lucas 1989). Older still is the figure of the wise
courtier (cf. Dan 3:6), unjustly accused but finally vindicated (Wills
1990). The ubiquitous Ahikar tradition is an example of this *topos*,
which also underlies the biblical stories of Joseph and Esther (Collins
1977: 30; Wills 1990: 39-44, 75-144). In proof of Hegel's claim that the
great person of an era is one who encapsulates its ideals, the book of
Daniel seems to have owed its literary power to the archetypes of
Near-Eastern consciousness that it embodied.

---

[1] Cf. Ezek 14:14; 28:3; the Aqhat legend from Ugarit (*dnil*), and *Jub* 4.20; also
perhaps Ezra 8:2; Neh 8:4.7; 10:6.23. Moreover, the "Prayer of Nabonidus" from
Qumran seems to be an earlier version of the story presented in Daniel 4.
[2] Witness the "apocryphal additions" and the Danielic apocalypse from
Qumran (4QpsDan).

1.1.3 Yet Daniel is much more than an amalgam of folk tale and eschatological vision. Even those who stress the original autonomy of its discrete elements concede that the final form of the book has an overriding unity (Collins 1977: 19). Its message, repeated in five of the six court tales and illustrated in the subsequent visions (chaps. 7 to 12), is that the apparently indomitable kingdoms of earth are in fact *transient* and subject to divine pleasure. It is God who "removes kings and installs kings" (2:21), and only *his* kingdom is everlasting.

The keynote comes in Daniel's interpretation of the statue: "The God of Heaven will establish a kingdom that shall never be destroyed, a kingdom that shall not be transferred to another people. It will crush and wipe out all these kingdoms, but shall itself last forever" (2:44; JPS trans.). Nebuchadnezzar suffers humiliating punishment until he learns:

> That the Most High is sovereign over the realm of man,
> And He gives it to whom He wishes
> And He may set over it even the lowest of men. (4:14; cf. 4:22, 29).

Belshazzar must be scared incontinent by the writing on the wall (5:6) before he accepts the same lesson (5:21). Darius "the Mede", pursued so relentlessly by scholars, is quite possibly a literary invention to stress the nonchalance with which God transfers kingships from one nation to another. He too concludes his act with the now familiar chorus: "He is the living God who endures forever; His kingdom is indestructible, and His dominion is to the end of time" (עַד סוֹפָא; 6:27). In spite of the ostensible mystery of Daniel, therefore, its central message is clear: no matter how indomitable the gentile kings may appear, they rule by divine pleasure and can be removed in an instant. This theme also binds together the two formally distinct halves of the book: parallel chronologies of the court tales and visions — under Babylonian (1:1/7:1), Median (6:1/9:1), and Persian (6:29/10:1) kings — underscore the instability of all earthly rule (Collins 1977: 191).

For our purposes, three ancillary themes are also noteworthy.

(a) Daniel refers often to the "wise" (מַשְׂכִּילִים) and wisdom. This is not the gnomic wisdom of Ben Sira, but rather an occult insight into the meaning of dreams and visions, hence an understanding of the transience of earthly rule. In both the court tales and the visions, revelation is a two-stage process requiring an initial mystery (רָז) — a dream or the writing on the wall — and then the inspired interpretation

(פשׁר). Daniel is a משׂכיל (1:17, 20; 2:30, 47; 5:11–12), who can offer
such interpretations, and the visions look ahead to a time when there
will be true successors to the seer (11:33–35); they will participate in
the eternal kingdom (12:3; Collins 1977: 28-29, 207-12). Daniel distinguishes the few "wise" from the "many" (הרבים), who are open to
persuasion for good or ill (8:25; 11:33).

   (b) Because the wise understand the imminence of God's kingdom,
they do not try to engineer change, which is God's prerogative. Thus
Daniel takes a pronounced *pacifistic* stance. This point has usually
been supported with reference to the "little help" of 11:14, which
Porphyry already understood as a slight of the Maccabees. Although
that interpretation is dubious (Lebram 1989: 182) the book's opposition to armed resistance is clear enough elsewhere. In chapters 2 and
8, the author stresses that the new and eternal kingdom is "not made
with hands" (2:34, 45; 8:25). Describing the conflicts between Antiochus II and Ptolemy IV, Daniel writes that "the lawless sons of your
people will assert themselves to confirm the vision, but they will fail"
(8:14). These historically uncertain opponents of the Ptolemies incur
the author's wrath for their attempt to remove a gentile power by
force (Lebram 1989: 182-184).

   (c) A practical corollary of this pacifistic outlook is Daniel's implied
agenda of *cooperation* with gentile kingdoms. This is the lesson of the
court tales at least: like Daniel and his colleagues, while awaiting
God's perfect kingdom a Jew may participate fully in the apparatus of
foreign government *without* becoming tainted by the association. The
young Hebrew men adhere rigorously to a lawful diet (1:5–16), refuse
to acknowledge foreign gods (3:12), and maintain a regimen of prayer
(6:11). Far from excluding them from positions of power, their behaviour earns them promotion and prosperity (1:20; 2:48; 3:30; 6:29).
Whenever a ruler becomes arrogant and objects to these practices,
God intervenes to save the righteous. The same hope is held out for
those who suffer under Antiochus IV (11:40-12:3).

   All of these themes are harnessed in the service of Daniel's eschatological timetable, which is articulated in three different ways. Chapters
2, 7, and 8 contain visions in which successive gentile kingdoms are
represented by the various parts of a statue (2) or an assortment of
horned beasts (7, 8). The point is that God's kingdom will erase and
supplant the Seleucid regime (2:44; 7:13; 8:25). In chapters 10 and 11,
the angel speaks plainly about the intricate political dealings of the

period before the end. And chapter 9 offers the most tantalizing prediction: there will be a period of "seventy weeks [of years = 490]" between the "word to restore and rebuild Jerusalem" and the arrival of God's kingdom (9:24-27). For the original author, all three schemes converged on the period following the demise of Antiochus IV.

The author of Daniel has woven a patchwork of traditions, distinct in form, provenance, and even language, into a remarkably unified whole. In a time of desperate straits, he reassures the reader that the imposing nations of the world are really pawns in the hands of God. God will soon intervene to end the unbearable oppression of the current ruler. But in the meantime, the wise will maintain their quiet fidelity to the covenant.

1.2 *The Appropriation of Daniel*

As soon as it was written, Daniel found a receptive audience among widely divergent groups. We cannot undertake here a survey of the book's *Wirkungsgeschichte* (cf. Goldingay 1989 xxi-xl), yet it is necessary for our reading of Josephus to have the main interpretive possibilities in view.

1.2.1 Some ancient authors were primarily interested in the *exemplary* value of the conflict stories in Daniel — the fiery furnace and the lion's den (4 Macc 16:21; 3 Macc 6:7; Heb 11:33-34). This use of Daniel completely sidesteps the problem of his unfulfilled expectation of God's kingdom after the death of Antiochus IV. His faith becomes a model for all times and places.

1.2.2 In the centuries following the writing of Daniel, however, most readers valued the book primarily for its apocalyptic agenda. Since the everlasting kingdom had not arrived with Antiochus' death, the timetable required repristination. In the period of our interest, the fourth beast, who would devour the whole earth with his great iron teeth (7:7, 23), could only be Rome, and so the book was unanimously reinterpreted by our sources. Such reinterpretation is anticipated by the author himself, for whom Jeremiah's 70 *years* of desolation should be understood as 70 *weeks* of years (= 490; Dan 9:2, 24; Jer 25:11-12; 29:10). And the end of the book witnesses to editorial revisions of Daniel's 1150 days of desecration (8:14) to 1290 and then 1335 (12:11). Those who wanted to extend further Daniel's 70 weeks had various options. They could reinterpret the starting point, "the going forth of

the word to restore and rebuild Jerusalem", from Jeremiah's prediction of about 594 BCE to the beginning of the exile, or the putative
date of Daniel's vision, or the end of the exile, or Cyrus' decree, or
Zerubbabel, or even Nehemiah in the mid-fifth century. Daniel's
division of the 70 weeks into 7 + 62 + 1 facilitated further recalcula-
tion (Beckwith 1979-81: 528). Later Christians would outsmart Daniel
himself by making each of the 490 years a decade, or each of the 1290
days (12:11) a year (Farris: 180-304)!

The wide-ranging influence of Daniel on subsequent apocalyptic
literature is illustrated by the fourth dream vision of 4 Ezra (chaps. 11-
12). The Most High interprets the dream for Ezra, making Rome the
fourth kingdom: "The eagle that you saw coming up out of the sea is
the fourth kingdom that appeared in a vision to your brother Daniel.
But it was not explained to him as I now explain it to you" (12:11–12;
NRSV, emphasis added). So far, eight fragments of Daniel have been
identified among the Dead Sea Scrolls (Stegemann 1989: 510). Several
studies have shown that Daniel exercised a pervasive influence on the
language and outlook of the Qumraners (Mertens 1971: 51-171; Bruce
1969: 221-235; 1959: 59-65; Beale 1984; Hartman and Di Lella 1978:
72-74). At least one scholar has placed the biblical seer in candidacy
for the long contested role of Teacher of Righteousness (Trever 1985).
Among early Christians, too, the rejuvenation of Daniel's eschatology
continued until about the end of the second century. One need only
think of such NT images as the imminent kingdom of God (Mark
1:15), the "son of man" coming on the clouds (Mark 13:26; 14:62), the
"abomination of desolation" (Mark 13:14), the "man of lawlessness"
(2 Thess 2:3–4), and the ten-horned beast from the sea (Rev 13:1), to
appreciate the depth and breadth of Daniel's contribution to the
young church's eschatological fervour (Gaston 1970: 8-64, 374-428). It
is surely no coincidence that the first biblical commentary written by
a Christian, as far as we know, was Hippolytus' commentary on Daniel.

1.2.3   Another way of appropriating Daniel's eschatological programme was to suppose that God's kingdom was being established
through the agency of divinely chosen leaders, whether the Hasmonean brothers or those who led the rebellion against Rome. Writing
soon after the death of John Hyrcanus (104 BCE; cf. 16:23-24) —
about 490 years after Jeremiah's prophecy — the author of 1 Maccabees seeks to show that the Hasmonean family was chosen by God to
bring salvation to Israel. The author certainly knows Danielic traditions

(cf. 1 Macc 1:41-54/Dan 9:27; 2:59-60) and I would argue that he means to appropriate the influential seer for his agenda (qualifying Goldstein 1976: 42-48). This is clearest in the patriarch Mattathias' deathbed speech, which first adduces a Danielic moral — that faithfulness to the Law is the way to endure against evil (2:61-64) — but then quickly transforms the lesson into a call to arms (2:65-68). It is through the Hasmoneans that "the yoke of the Gentiles was removed from Israel" (13:41; cf. 4:58). If this analysis is correct, then 1 Maccabees effects a double inversion of Daniel's purpose: it dissolves the apocalyptic timetable into a "realized eschatology," and it replaces quietistic pacifism with divinely authorized militancy. This inversion may have provided a precedent for later rebels against Rome, who saw themselves both as heirs of the Hasmonean cause and as fulfilling the vision of Daniel (Farmer 1956: 108; Hengel 1989: 238; Gaston 1970: 458-463).

This brief sketch has shown that the book of Daniel was widely read throughout our period; it was valued mainly as an eschatological programme. In keeping with the diversity of its audience, however, there was no orthodox interpretation.

2. *Daniel in the* Jewish Antiquities

By the mid-nineties, when he wrote the *Jewish Antiquities,* Josephus had developed a sustained interest in Daniel. He knew at least two Greek versions (OG and Theodotion) as well as the Hebrew/Aramaic text and some extrabiblical traditions. He found valuable support in the ancient seer for the main arguments of his magnum opus.

2.1 *Daniel and the Purpose of the* Antiquities

The aims of the *Antiquities* are set out in their preface (1 §§ 1-26). Contemporary Greek and Latin literature indicates that various slanders about Jewish origins and customs were current in first-century Rome (e.g. Tacitus, *Hist* 5.1-13; Whittaker 1984: 35-84). The popular derision may not have had much practical effect on its own, but it can only have been exacerbated by anti-Jewish sentiments arising from the war. Josephus, for his part, considers it urgent to "refute those who in their writings were doing outrage to the truth" (*Ant* 1 § 4, speaking of the *War*). He invites the Greek-speaking reader to judge, on the basis of his narrative, whether the Jewish lawgiver did not impart a worthy conception of God (*Ant* 1 §§ 15, 24). His account of biblical history means to show that Jews have a noble history, embrace the highest ideals of εὐσέβεια and δικαιοσύνη, and are therefore exemplary citizens.

In making this general point, Josephus introduces a number of specific themes that will govern the shape of his subsequent narrative: (a) the Jewish view of God holds that he supervises everything (πάντα ἐπιβλέπων; *Ant* 1 § 20), exercising watchful care over human affairs (cf. πρόνοια; *Ant* 1 §§ 45, 226); (b) Moses has trained the Jews in virtue (ἀρετή; *Ant* 1 §§ 6, 20); and (c) Jewish history demonstrates that God invariably rewards those who practice virtue and live in accord with the laws, while punishing those who transgress. This is the lesson of Jewish scripture (*Ant* 1 §§ 14, 21). Harold Attridge (1976) has shown that these themes emerge repeatedly throughout Josephus' paraphrase of the Bible in *Ant* 1–11.

Other commentators have noted that the preface to the *Antiquities* is laced with the language of contemporary philosophy (Weiss 1979: 421-33). Apparently Josephus wishes to enter Judaism as an option in the philosophical market-place. The Jewish view of God's nature is sophisticated and philosophical, Josephus says, which is why Jewish law accords so perfectly with natural law (φυσιολογία; *Ant* 1 §§ 18–20/ τῇ τῶν φύσει; *Ant* 1 § 24). Moses' teaching will be found "highly philosophical" (λίαν φολόσοφος) by those who care to investigate it (*Ant* 1 § 25). Just as the Greco-Roman schools have their own prescriptions for εὐδαιμονία, Judaism offers this as a reward to those who obey the laws (*Ant* 1 §§ 14, 20). Throughout the following story, Abraham, Moses, and Solomon all appear as wise philosophers, and the Jewish sects are schools (φιλοσοφίαι or αἱρέσεις) of the national philosophy (*Ant* 13 §§ 171–173; 18 §§ 11-25).

This brief sketch will suffice to show that Josephus' substantial paraphrase of Daniel (*Ant* 10 §§ 185–281) is written so as to enhance the overall impact of the *Antiquities*. Most striking is Josephus' concluding statement. Having shown that the exilic figure predicted the persecution under Antiochus IV (*Ant* 10 § 275) and even the Roman destruction of Jerusalem (*Ant* 10 § 276), he points out the folly of the Epicureans, who exclude providence (πρόνοιαν ἐκβάλλουσι) and deny that God supervises human affairs. Daniel proves the *Antiquities'* thesis that God does exercise watchful care over human affairs (*Ant* 10 §§ 277-280). This attack on the impious Epicureans both sustains his argument and makes Josephus a conversation partner with his gentile contemporaries (cf. Plutarch, *Pyth. Or.* 9).

In keeping with this philosophizing tendency is Josephus' interpretation of the diet maintained by Daniel and his friends in Babylon. Whereas the biblical story had clearly stated that the "seeds" (or: vegetables) eaten by the youths were to prevent *defilement* through consumption of potentially unclean food (Dan 1:8, 12), Josephus makes the diet into a philosophical issue: they abstained from animal (ἔμψυχος) food out of a desire to live ascetically (σκληραγωγεῖν), because they were unattracted to it (*Ant* 10 § 190; Satran 1980: 33-48)). Josephus even introduces dates, a Pythagorean favourite, into the menu (*Ant* 10 § 190). David Satran aptly observes (1980: 37), "*amixia* has given way to *enkrateia*". Jewish dietary habits were a target of ridicule, contributing to the charge of misanthropy (Whittaker 1984: 73-80). Josephus makes the Jews' diet a virtue, comparable to that of the Pythagoreans (cf. *Ant* 15 § 371). He observes that the young men's souls were thereby "kept pure and fresh for learning" *Ant* (10 § 194). So Daniel joins the ranks of illustrious Jewish philosophers. His wisdom, both mundane and occult, far surpasses that of the famous Chaldeans and magi.

It is also typical of the *Antiquities* to reflect on the rewards and punishments meted out to appropriate parties. The young men were untouched by the fiery furnace "in consideration of their being thrown into it without having done any wrong"; they were saved by divine providence (θεία πρόνοια; *Ant* 10 §§ 214–215). When Daniel is delivered from the lions' den, his accusers deny that it is due to πρόνοια, charging rather that the animals had been fed beforehand. Thereupon, in Josephus' embellishment, Darius feeds the lions before offering them Daniel's accusers, who are nonetheless torn to pieces and consumed. Josephus attributes this to the wickedness of the men, which was apparent even to irrational animals; God arranged this punishment (*Ant* 10 § 262). Such moralizing reflections are common in this work.[3]

Although the *Antiquities* is no literary masterpiece, Josephus is careful to choose key terms that will produce the desired resonance

---

[3] Cf. *Ant* 1 §§ 46-51, 65-66, 72, 194-95; 4 §§ 45-53, 154-55, 312-314; 5 §§ 107-9; 6 §§ 3-7, 147-151; 8 §§ 190-98, 265, 284, 313-14; 9 §§ 103-4; 10 §§ 37-39; 17 §§ 168-71; 19 §§ 201-11.

with his audience. Whereas, for example, the LXX and Theodotion-Daniel had exclusively used τὸ ἐνύπνιον for "dream", Josephus favours τὸ ὄναρ and ὁ ὄνειρος. He retains the LXX usage five times, but opts for one of these alternatives thirteen times in his Daniel paraphrase. Outside of the Daniel story, he consistently abandons the LXX term except in pejorative usage — of uninspired dreams (*AgAp* 1 §§ 207, 211, 294, 298, 312). Josephus already seems sensitive to Artemidorus' distinction of ἐνύπνιον from ὄνειρος on the criterion that the former refers to an insignificant dream, whereas the latter signifies an event susceptible of interpretation (Oepke 1967: 5.221).

Other characteristic features of Josephus' biblical paraphrase that appear in his treatment of Daniel may be summarily listed. (a) To place Jewish history on the world stage, he must show how it intersects with the records of non-Jewish writers. Therefore he cites a variety of sources that mention the Babylonian and Persian kings under whom Daniel served (*Ant* 10 §§ 219-231). By identifying Belshazzar with [his father] Nabonidus (*Ant* 10 § 231), Josephus quietly solves the problem that Daniel's Belshazzar was not in fact king of Babylon (contra Dan 5:1,5). (b) He attempts to solve obvious difficulties within the biblical narrative, such as the identity of the mysterious "Darius the Mede", whom Daniel makes successor to the Babylonians in contradiction of other biblical texts which assign that role to Cyrus the Persian. Josephus makes the two conquerors relatives and comrades (*Ant* 10 §§ 232, 248). He even tacitly corrects Daniel by noting that several kings came between Nebuchadnezzar and Belshazzar (whom Daniel 5 had made father and son). (c) Josephus introduces all sorts of "novelistic elements" into his paraphrase (Moehring 1957), most notably terms that describe the emotions of the characters: envy and jealousy (*Ant* 10 § 212), grief and unhappiness (*Ant* 10 § 246), hope, courage, and anxiety (*Ant* 10 §§ 257-258).

Although modern scholars often lose the drift of the unwieldy the *Antiquities* Josephus himself maintains a sense of unity. In 10 § 218 he reminds the reader of his goals as defined in the preface.

2.2 *The Message of Daniel in the* Antiquities

Josephus' interest in Daniel goes far beyond supporting the general argument of the *Antiquities*. For him, Daniel was "one of the greatest prophets" (*Ant* 10 § 266), with a distinctive message: he predicted in detail the whole course of subsequent history and so offers the key to understanding the times. We are used to looking for the central panel of ancient text to find the heart of an author's concerns. It is probably no coincidence that Josephus' discussion of Daniel falls in the exact centre of his work.

As is well known, Josephus understands "prophecy" as essentially predictive, minimizing its ethical aspects, and so expresses the greatest interest in those prophets who left written records of the future (Paret 1856: 836-37; van Unnik 1978: 52-54; Blenkinsopp 1974: 244-45; Feldman 1990: 396-97). Moses is called a prophet in part because he foretold Israel's punishments and repeated loss of the temple (*Ant* 4 §§ 303, 313). The whole value of prophecy is that it reveals future events, though Josephus is characteristically ambiguous about the possibility of avoiding what is determined (*Ant* 8 §§ 418–20); his dominant line is that fate is unavoidable. Speaking of the prophets he says that "whatever happens to us whether for good or ill comes about in accord with their prophecies" (*Ant* 10 § 35; Marcus, LCL).

With this background, we are in a position to understand Josephus' special interest in Daniel. For what distinguishes this prophet from the others, Josephus says, is that: "he was not only given to predicting the things to come, just as the other prophets, but he specified a time at which these things will come to pass" (*Ant* 10 § 267). He goes on to note that Daniel alone predicted good things, whereas the others had foreseen catastrophes (*Ant* 10 § 268). If the essence of prophecy is prediction, and if Daniel alone predicted the future in concrete terms, then we can understand why Josephus counts him among the great.

Given this predilection for prophecy, it is remarkable that Josephus' paraphrase of Daniel is mainly devoted to the court tales of chapters 1 to 6, though Nebuchadnezzar's statue dream of Daniel 2 is included. His most significant adjustments to this dream are as follows. (a) The Babylonian kingdom will be ended by "two kings," represented by the two shoulders of the statue, rather than the biblical "kingdom inferior to you" (*Ant* 10 § 208); thus the Bible's allusion to the Median kingdom is altered to a Medo-Persian coalition, in keeping with Josephus' identification of Darius the Mede as a contemporary of Cyrus. (b) This adjustment leaves the third kingdom up for grabs, and Josephus interprets it as "another king, from the west" (*Ant* 10 § 209), which indicates Alexander the Great. (c) This shift, in turn, leaves the fourth kingdom, which biblical Daniel had composed of mixed iron and clay — plainly indicating the Macedonian empires — now to be identified with the Roman empire. Josephus does not make the referent explicit here, but he omits Daniel's mention of clay, emphasizing only the superior "iron nature" of this kingdom, by which it will rule "completely" (εἰς ἄπαντα — not "forever", as Marcus has it; cf. Lindner, 1972: 44). In accord with learned interpretation of his day (cf. *4 Ezra* above), Josephus is able to read Daniel's prediction as referring to his own time.

Yet the fourth kingdom will not last forever, according to the dream, and here we come upon one of the most intriguing passages in Josephus' writings. He vividly describes the stone of Nebuchadnezzar's dream:

> Then you saw a stone break off from a mountain and fall upon the image, breaking it to pieces and leaving not one part of it whole, so that the gold and silver and bronze and iron were made finer than flour, and when the wind blew strongly, they were caught up by its force and scattered abroad; but the stone grew so much larger that the whole earth seemed to be filled with it. (*Ant* 10 § 207)

In the interpretation of the dream, Josephus notes that Daniel revealed its meaning to Nebuchadnezzar, but "I have not thought it proper to relate this (ἱστορεῖν), since I am supposed to write of what is past and done and not of what is to be". Curious readers may consult the book of Daniel itself (*Ant* 10 § 210).

Commentators have almost universally dismissed Josephus' stated motive as a thin disguise of his unwillingness to offend Roman readers by discussing the end of the empire (Bruce 1965: 160; Bilde 1988: 188). I too have supported this reading in the past. But consider the following. (a) Josephus was not compelled to say anything about the stone. In other respects, his biblical paraphrase omits or alters much that is unsuited to his purpose. Yet not only does he choose to mention the stone; he dwells on the thoroughness of its dominion. (b) His description of the stone's actions does not require inspired interpretation. It plainly envisions the ultimate demise of Roman hegemony, and only an obtuse reader could have missed the point. (c) Josephus will go on to say explicitly that Daniel predicted the Roman empire (*Ant* 10 § 276), thus placing the identity of the fourth kingdom, to be demolished by the stone, beyond any doubt. (d) He has already declared, in his account of Balaam's prophecy, that greatness still awaits Israel (*Ant* 4 § 125). If he is concerned about offending Roman readers with such talk, he has already said far too much.

But it is not clear that such language would have offended them, for he removes all traces of Daniel's apocalyptic urgency. The stone is not expected immediately. Long before Josephus' time, Scipio had reflected that Rome would one day fall as Carthage had done (Polybius 38.22.3). And in the *JW* 3 § 396, Titus himself ponders the general instability of human affairs. Josephus' remarks seem likewise to fall into the category of harmless philosophical reflection, not revolutionary aspiration.

Why then does he mysteriously invite his readers to consult Daniel for further information about the stone? His stated reason is that he is writing history, and cannot therefore discuss future events. We are obliged to concede that elsewhere he deliberately neglects large sections of the Jewish scriptures in the pursuit of a single historical thread, excluding all of the wisdom literature and most of the minor prophets; even from his beloved Jeremiah he excerpts the historical material alone (Franxman 1979: 7). The visionary material of Daniel itself (7–12) is reduced to a single composite vision (mainly drawn from Daniel 8); yet this example too pertains to events already past, and is offered as proof of Daniel's veracity (*Ant* 10 §§ 269–76). So Josephus is aware of his task as a historian, and this accounts for his omission of elaborate eschatological scenarios.

Yet his invitation to consult the book of Daniel also serves a rhetorical purpose. We know that Daniel does *not* materially clarify the meaning of the stone beyond what Josephus has said. It is therefore likely that Josephus does not expect his readers to consult the prophet (in Hebrew?) any more than he expects them to look up the "philosophical discussion" of fate and free will in Jewish law (*Ant* 16 § 398) or the public registers of Jerusalem that contain his genealogy (*Life* 6). He wants to leave the impression that the Jewish scriptures contain all sorts of oriental mysteries beyond what he as a historian can presently discuss.

In addition to recounting Nebuchadnezzar's dream, Josephus cites Daniel's predictions of world affairs at three significant junctures. First, in the passage just mentioned, he recounts the vision of the ram and the goat (Daniel 8), while combining some features of the other visions (Goldstein 1976: 561). The goat comes from the West, sprouting first a single great horn and then four smaller horns. A subsequent smaller horn makes war on the Jewish nation and disrupts the temple service for 1290 days (*Ant* 10 §§ 269–71). Since Daniel itself plainly interprets the vision as the Macedonian conquest of Persia and Antiochus' persecution of the Jews, Josephus can only marvel that things happened just as Daniel had predicted "many years before" (*Ant* 10 § 276).

Second, when he is later narrating Alexander the Great's conquest of the East, Josephus has the legendary king visit Jerusalem. On encountering the high priest, the young conqueror prostrates himself in awe, because this was the figure he had seen in a dream back in Macedonia. It was this dream, in which God assured him that "he himself would lead my army and give over to me the empire of the Persians", that motivated Alexander in his eastward march (*Ant* 11 § 334). When the Macedonian goes up to the temple, he is overwhelmed to discover that the book of Daniel had long ago predicted that "one of the Greeks would destroy the rule of the Persians" (*Ant* 11 § 337). Josephus is not merely engaging in the current veneration of Alexander (cf. Plutarch, *Alexander*), although that certainly plays into his hands when he connects Alexander so closely with Judaism.[4] Earlier in the narrative, he had Cyrus the Persian reading Isaiah (44:28) and concluding that "the Most High God has appointed me king of the inhabited earth" (*Ant* 11 §§ 3-5). And Josephus believes with equal conviction that the current Roman regime, which will one day meet its end, was also installed by God. So the Alexander story is not a specific embellishment of his narrative; it evinces his *ongoing* concern to show that the prophets in general and Daniel in particular provide the key to understanding world history.

Finally, Josephus cites the fulfilment of Daniel when he describes the persecution under Antiochus IV. He reminds the reader: "Now the desolation (ἐρήμωσις) of the temple came about in accordance with the prophecy of Daniel, which occurred four hundred and eight years beforehand" (*Ant* 12 § 322). This further reference indicates the consistency with which Josephus wants to present Daniel as an inspired guide to future events. Goldstein has argued, on the whole plausibly (1976: 560), that some of Josephus' adjustments of 1 Maccabees 1:20-64 stem from his "belief in the veracity of Daniel 7-12". Where 1 Maccabees had corrected Daniel, Josephus tried to rehabilitate the

---

[4] Cf. the earlier Alexander romance by Ps-Callisthenes, which makes Alexander the son of the Egyptian Pharaoh Nectanebus II (Griffiths 1989: 273-74).

prophet, while still following the main lines of 1 Maccabees.[5]

Daniel's theme of the rise and fall of world empires performs a critical function in the narrative of the *Antiquities*. On the one hand, it explains why the Jewish nation, if it has such noble traditions, has so long been subject to foreign rule. Josephus is able to use this subservience as proof of Judaism's truth, for the scriptures themselves predicted these developments. He deftly connects the rise of kingdoms with his main thesis, that God inevitably punishes evil. The arch-prophet Moses articulates the programme at the outset:

> Moses predicted, as the Deity revealed to him, that when they strayed from devotion to Him they would suffer ill: the land would be filled with enemy armaments; their cities would be demolished; their temple would be burned down; they would be sold into slavery to men who would take no pity on their misfortunes; and that repentance would be of no use in these sufferings. (*Ant* 4 § 313)

When the first temple is destroyed, accordingly, it is an inevitable response to the Jews' waywardness, and Nebuchadnezzar is God's chosen means of punishment (*Ant* 10 §§ 33, 40, 60, 89, 139). Thus Josephus effects a neat synthesis of Deuteronomy's two ways and Daniel's determinism. Indeed, Daniel had already achieved such a synthesis with the incorporation of a "deuteronomistic prayer" in chapter 9. The resulting theological tension does not bother Josephus as it bothers modern scholars, who isolate Daniel's prayer as an alien tradition. For his part, Josephus innocently declares that the law juxtaposes fate and free will (*Ant* 16 §§ 395–98). The combination of abused freedom and inexorable punishment is a deep current flowing through the *Antiquities*.

On the other hand, Josephus' firm belief in the rise and fall of empires results, as it did for Daniel, in a pacifistic political outlook. One can only accept the divine punishment, as Jeremiah and Ezekiel warned; it is futile to resist. This view is restated with increasing force toward the end of the *Antiquities*, as Josephus describes events leading up to the revolt against Rome. Recapitulating Moses' prediction, he cites an array of transgressions (*Ant* 20 §§ 181, 207, 214, 218) as the grounds of imminent divine punishment:

---

[5] For example, Josephus connects Antiochus's attack on Jerusalem in 169 BCE with his withdrawal from Egypt under Roman pressure (cf. Dan 11:30), maintains two expeditions against Jerusalem (cf. Dan 11:28, 31), and creates a single persecution effort out of distinct episodes in 1 Maccabees.

> This is the reason why, in my opinion, even God Himself, for loathing of
> their impiety, turned away from our city and, because He deemed the temple
> no longer to be a clean dwelling place for Him, brought the Romans upon
> us and purification by fire upon the city, while He inflicted slavery upon us...;
> for he wished to chasten us by these calamities. (20 § 166; Feldman, LCL)

Those who refuse to accept the punishment and so oppose the
Romans — Josephus' "fourth philosophy" — are accused of introducing
an "innovation in the ancestral customs" out of a desire for personal
gain (*Ant* 18 §§ 7–9). Josephus seems to hope for a rebuilding of the
temple more than once (*Ant* 4 § 314), but that must await the cessation of punishment.

In Josephus' wide-ranging advocacy of Judaism, then, Daniel plays
a featured role. The exilic seer provides the basis for his conception of
history as the rise and fall of kingdoms under God's watchful care, an
integration point for determinism and deuteronomistic theology, a
pacifistic political platform, and specific prophecies that have been
strikingly confirmed. These observations support Per Bilde's proposal
that the structure of the *Antiquities* is intended to stress the parallels
between the first and second temple periods (1988: 89-90). Coming at
the end of book 10, Daniel provides a fitting transition: written
immediately after the fall of the first temple, it looks ahead to the fall
of the second, and grounds the whole story in a serviceable theory of
history. For all of its literary fluctuations, detours, and assorted loose
ends, the *Antiquities* have a remarkably tight thematic unity.

2.3 *Daniel and Josephus' Self-Understanding*

Before we proceed to the *War*, we might consider the degree to which
the Josephus of the *Antiquities* found echoes of Daniel's career in his
own. His account of Jeremiah suggests many such parallels (*Ant* 10 §§
80, 89–90, 114, 119, 139). If Jeremiah's life so clearly anticipated Josephus', did he also see himself as a latter-day Daniel?

Two observations confirm that he did. First, in the court tales that
constitute the substance of the paraphrase, young Jewish men "of
noblest birth" (εὐγενής) happily join the court of a conquering king.
Naturally gifted learners (cf. *Life* §§ 8-10), they soon master the foreign (Chaldean and native Babylonian) traditions as well as their own
(*Ant* 10 § 194). Although they operate easily and effectively in gentile
circles, they by no means abandon their own "ancestral laws" (*Ant* 10
§ 214). On the contrary, they win universal respect for their traditions,

which indeed deserve respect because they accord with natural and moral law (*Ant* 10 § 215). Daniel and his colleagues put into practice the pragmatic directives of Jeremiah: "Seek the welfare of the city into which I have exiled you and pray to the Lord on its behalf; for in its prosperity you shall prosper" (Jer 29:7; JPS). Still, the Jewish youths attract jealousy and envy because of their success (10 § 212, 250), but God preserves them. Since Josephus writes all of this as a Jew who is prospering in the Flavian court, having learned a good deal of Greek and Latin literature, who is now defending his ancestral traditions before the literary world, yet who runs into persistent accusations from those who "envy" his success, we can hardly avoid the conclusion that his paraphrase of Daniel 1-6 reflects his own image.

What confirms the association between Daniel and Josephus is the theme of dream interpretation, κρίσις ὀνείρων. In all of Josephus' writings, only four parties are said to be adept at the interpretation of dreams: his biblical namesake Joseph/us ('Ιώσηπος), Daniel, the Essenes, whom he consistently praises, and Josephus himself. This is a select group. Parallels with the biblical Joseph(us) are obvious, and Josephus also closely identifies with the Essenes (*JW* 2 § 158; *Ant* 13 §§ 311-312; 15 §§ 373, 379; 18 § 20), so it is not surprising that the figure of Daniel too was especially significant for him. According to Josephus, Daniel acquired wisdom like his Jewish colleagues, but more than that "he occupied himself with interpretations of dreams (περὶ κρίσεις ὀνείρων), and the Deity used to become clear to him" (*Ant* 10 § 194). Now the *Antiquities* do not mention any of Josephus' interpretations, but the *War* does. The only other occurrence in Josephus of the phrase περὶ κρίσεις ὀνείρων comes when he describes his own credentials while narrating the surrender scene at Jotapata (*JW* 3 § 352). By the time that he writes the *Antiquities*, this ability has made him famous.

In the *Antiquities*, then, Danielic currents run deep. Daniel offered Josephus a *programme*, according to which the consecutive world empires had risen and fallen in keeping with God's providence. Rome too had been promoted by God, though it would likewise fall some day. Josephus saw himself as a pacifistic prophetic figure, trying to convey this message to others.

3. *Daniel in the* Jewish War

Josephus' *Jewish War*, written in the seventies, does not expressly mention Daniel (S. Schwartz 1990: 24-35, 24 n. 3) This is not surprising, since the topic of Josephus' first effort in Greek was the recent conflict, not biblical history. Nevertheless, it has become customary to regard the *War* as an opportunistic tract in defence of Josephus' new patrons (Laqueur 1920: 126; Smith 1956: 67-81), which would mean that he only became seriously interested in Jewish tradition while preparing the *Antiquities* (S. Schwartz 1990: 15-57). Our question therefore is: did Josephus' fascination with Daniel arise only after the *War*, as part of a late interest in his national traditions, or did Daniel's programme shape his thinking from an early date?

We might expect, *a priori*, that Josephus had considered Daniel in his younger years because the book was so widely read among his contemporaries. Josephus himself will exhibit a strong interest in Daniel when he writes the *Antiquities*. And much of the later work's interpretation of history is already apparent in the *War*. For example, Josephus' identification with Jeremiah, which we saw in the *Antiquities* is quite developed in the *War* (Lindner 1972: 32-33):

> For, though Jeremiah loudly proclaimed that they were hateful to God for their transgressions against Him, . . . neither the king nor the people put him to death. But you . . ., you, I say, assail with abuse and missiles me who exhort you to save yourselves, exasperated at being reminded of your sins. (*JW* 5 § 393; Thackeray, LCL).

Like Jeremiah, Josephus is a priestly prophet (*JW* 3 § 352). Both cite their contemporaries' theft, murder, adultery, and temple pollution as causes of the temple's destruction (*JW* 5 § 402; cf. Jer 7:9). Both call for compliance with the foreign regime. Most telling, Josephus consciously adopts the forms and language of "lamentation" (ὀλοφυρμός) and so evokes the book traditionally attributed to Jeremiah (Lindner 1972: 132-141). The *War*'s parallels between the destructions of the first and second temples (cf. *JW* 5 § 411) anticipate the main structural criterion of the *Antiquities*. These examples encourage our suspicion that Josephus had also given some thought to the book of Daniel by the time that he wrote the *War*.

The question of Daniel's influence on the *War* has been taken up most thoroughly by F. F. Bruce (1965). He identifies a "succession of 'abominations'" cited by Josephus in the *War*: the rebels pollute the sanctuary (*JW* 4 §§ 150, 201), appoint an unworthy high priest (*JW* 4 § 157 — a "monstrous sacrilege" for Josephus), and assassinate the former high priest Ananus. Josephus claims that the fall of the city began with this last event (*JW* 4 § 318), so Bruce thinks that Josephus saw Ananus as "the anointed one" who would be "cut off" after 69 weeks, before the cessation of sacrifice (Dan 9:26; Hebrew only). Bruce argues further that "the particularity with which Josephus records the cessation of the daily sacrifice" in 70 (*JW* 6 § 94) indicates that this event fulfilled an important prophecy, and that Josephus saw the crowning "abomination" as the Roman soldiers' sacrifice to their standards in the temple court (*JW* 6 § 316). Finally, Bruce contends that the mysterious ancient oracles cited by Josephus as predicting the city's ruin could all plausibly come from Daniel: the reduction of the Temple to a "square" (*JW* 6 § 311; רחוב in Dan 9:25); the prediction of internal strife as a sign of the end (*JW* 4 § 388; 6 § 109/Dan 11:30/32). The popular expectation of a world ruler from Judea "at that time," whom Josephus identifies as Vespasian (*JW* 6 § 312), is likely based on the prediction of a "coming prince" in Daniel 9:26, because this is the only scriptural passage that provides a dated chronology.

If Bruce is right, then Daniel played a decisive role in Josephus' thinking as he composed the *War*. I hope to show that Bruce's conclusion is correct, but not for the reasons that he gives. Others have noted that his description of the temple calamities as "abominations" skews the evidence, since Josephus nowhere uses Daniel's βδέλυγμα (Farris 1990: 96 n. 27). That unusual term would have drawn immediate attention to Daniel's famous prophecy (cf. the gospels' "let the reader understand"; Mark 13:14), if Josephus had so intended. But he does not use a consistent term corresponding to Bruce's "abominations." Moreover, his sayings about temple catastrophes are part of a much larger priestly-cultic theme in the *War* that is not dependent on Daniel (Lindner 1972: 31-32, 142-43). Finally, Josephus gives numerous causes of the city's destruction; Ananus' death is part of a larger story of rebel atrocities that, once again, is not grounded in Daniel. Nevertheless, our analysis of the *Antiquities* enables us to see that some central themes of the *War* probably do derive from Josephus' "Danielic" outlook. After considering these, we shall return to the "oracles" discussed by Bruce.

3.1 *The Outlook of the* War

In keeping with the conventions of hellenistic historiography, Josephus uses two devices to convey his major themes to the reader: an elaborate preface at the outset, followed by speeches throughout the narrative. Three speeches are definitive: those of Agrippa II (*JW* 2 §§ 345-404), Josephus (*JW* 5 §§ 362-419), and the Masada leader Eleazar (*JW* 7 §§ 323-88).

From the preface we learn that Josephus writes against a background of anti-Jewish sentiment following the revolt (*JW* 1 §§ 1-2, 7-8). An unabashed representative of the conquered nation, who had full access to both sides of the conflict (*JW* 1 §§ 3, 12, 16), he will set the record straight (*JW* 1 §§ 3, 6, 9). His strategy is clear: he wants to isolate entirely the rebel leaders as a handful of murderous τύραννοι, who forced the unwilling δῆμος (*JW* 1 § 10-11) to join them. The people themselves were on the side of the Romans all along, but the rebels' atrocities brought divine punishment on the whole nation (*JW* 1 § 10). This formulation achieves several things at once: while trying to salvage the reputation of surviving Jews around the world, it still affirms the Roman right to rule. Implied (and later stated) is that Jewish tradition accepts foreign rule without demur; those who rebel are innovators (*JW* 2 §§ 118, 414; Mason 1991: 285 n. 22). Yet Josephus does not adopt either a Roman or a Flavian world view (Yavetz 1971: 411-432; Lindner 1972: 64; Rajak 1983: 185-222; Stern 1987). He maintains throughout that it is the Jewish God who uses the Romans to punish his own people (cf. *JW* 6 § 411). As in the *Antiquities*, he seeks to find a place for Jews in the empire by portraying them as good citizens, who typically live in peace and harmony with foreign rulers. The *War*'s insistence that foreign rule is divinely ordained, and the consequences of pacifism and opposition to revolt, anticipate the *Antiquities*, where these themes are grounded in Jeremiah and Daniel.

The three main speeches further develop the preface and also stress that nations rise and fall under God's/Fate's direction. Agrippa, for example, observes that "the purest and sincerest of the δῆμος are determined to maintain peace" (*JW* 2 § 345); he does not want the good to suffer for the bad decisions of a few (ἐνίων). The bulk of his speech (*JW* 2 §§ 358-87) is a catalogue of once powerful nations who now accept Roman rule. Chief among these are Greece and Macedon, who notwithstanding their former glories now "submit to endure such a reversal of Fate and bow before those to whom Fortune has transferred her favours" (*JW* 2 § 360; Thackeray, LCL). The mighty Gauls too acquiesce before the Fortune of Rome, "which brings her more triumphs even than her arms" (*JW* 2 § 373). Josephus' characteristic use of "Fate" and "Fortune" as euphemisms for God (Moore 1929) is clear also here, for Agrippa concludes that divine collaboration, to which the rebels look for help, is on the side of the Romans: "without God's aid, so vast an empire could never have been built up" (*JW* 2 § 390; Thackeray, LCL).

Josephus' speech before the walls of Jerusalem similarly reflects his assumptions about the rise and fall of empires and the obligation of pacifism. The tyrants know that the power of the Romans is irresistible, yet they obstinately persist in rebellion: "For Fortune had passed over (μεταβῆναι) to them from everywhere, and God, *who brings around the rule from one nation to another*, was *now* over Italy" (*JW* 5 § 367). The Jews' ancestors would not have yielded to the Romans if they had not realized that "God was on the Roman side" (*JW* 3 § 368; Thackeray, LCL). Josephus does not view Roman hegemony as the goal and apex of human history; the Romans are merely the current recipients of Fate's pleasure. This presentation intersects neatly with that of the *Antiquities*, though the four-kingdom scheme is not adduced. In both works, Josephus asserts that the Roman regime, which is obviously irresistible, is part of God's established plan. Here too the corollary of Jewish pacifism is pointed. Josephus provides a rhetorical *tour de force,* showing (a) that Jews have always conquered their enemies without resort to arms (*JW* 5 §§ 379–89) and (b) that "if they fought they were invariably defeated" (*JW* 5 § 390; Thackeray, LCL).

Particularly interesting in Josephus' speech advocating pacifism is his reference to the persecution under Antiochus IV. There, if anywhere, Jews could claim success in rebellion, and it seems likely that the rebels of Josephus' day cited the Maccabean revolt as a precedent (Farmer 1956). Indeed, Josephus himself has already praised the Hasmoneans for their courageous and just war (*JW* 1 §§ 34-69). But notice how he bends the story to his current rhetorical purpose. Without mentioning the Hasmoneans at all, he says.

> Or again, when our ancestors went forth in arms against Antiochus, surnamed Epiphanes, who was blockading this city and had grossly outraged the Deity, they were cut to pieces in the battle, the town was plundered by the enemy, and the sanctuary lay desolate (ἠρημώθη) for three years and six months (*JW* 5 § 394).

This passage at last breaks through to the Danielic substratum of Josephus' outlook in the *War*, for only Daniel specifies the period of the temple's desolation as three and a half years. This is one point on which 1 Maccabees corrects the seer (1 Macc 1:54; 4:52). Not only has Josephus adopted Daniel's date; he has taken over that work's repudiation of those who tried to bring in God's kingdom with force.

It is left to the last rebel leader, Eleazar, to articulate Josephus' outlook from the side of the conquered. He comes to realize that he has not been fighting the Romans, hated as they are, for: "by God himself, evidently, we have been deprived of hope for rescue" (*JW* 7 § 331). The Romans are merely instruments in God's hands; a "more powerful cause" has used them to accomplish his own purposes and punish transgression among the Jews (*JW* 7 § 360). Eleazar's synthesis of determinism ("God long ago passed the verdict" — 7 § 359) and free will (our "many unjust acts" — 7 § 332) is characteristic of the *War* and, as we have seen, of the *Antiquities* and Daniel itself.

The *War* does not claim that the Romans have governed Judea well. Josephus freely recounts the governors' and soldiers' many crimes. Still, he asserts that, no matter how unjustly they governed, the central power of Rome is currently ruling according to God's plan and must therefore be endured (*JW* 2 § 352). All of this — the rise and fall of nations under God's supervision, pacifism, and disavowal of rebellion — recalls Josephus' interpretation of Daniel in the *Antiquities* (Lindner 1972: 43). It appears therefore that Daniel, along with Jeremiah, had profoundly influenced his outlook by the time that he wrote the *War*.

3.2 *Literary Allusions to Daniel*

If that is true, then we should expect to find further allusions to Daniel throughout the carefully crafted narrative. The following are enough to suggest that Josephus included the ancient seer in his reservoir of exempla.

3.2.1 In *JW* 2 §§ 111-13, Josephus tells the story of Archelaus' fall from power. He includes an episode in which the ethnarch, before his removal, dreamed of nine ears of corn being eaten by oxen. So, "he sent for the soothsayers and some of the Chaldeans and asked what they thought that it signified" (μεταπεμψάμενος δὲ τοὺς μάντεις καὶ τῶν Χαλδαίων τινὰς ἐπυνθάνετο, τί σημαίνειν δοκοῖεν). When their interpretations disagreed, an Essene named Simon offered his interpretation, which was immediately verified. Thackeray directs the reader to Pharaoh's dream in Genesis as a model for the story, presumably in view of the corn and oxen (cf. Gen 41:2-4). Without denying that parallel, we may note that this passage contains the only occurrence of "Chaldean" in the *War*, and that it seems peculiar (though not impossible) within the context of Archelaus' court. Nor were there Chaldeans in Pharaoh's court according to either Genesis or the *Antiquities*.

The only other passage in Josephus that has μάντεις alongside Χαλδαῖοι is his account of Nebuchadnezzar's first dream (*Ant* 10 § 195). Having forgotten his dream, the Babylonian king "sent for the Chaldeans and the Magi and the soothsayers" (μεταπεμψάμενος δὲ τοὺς Χαλδαίους καὶ τοὺς μάγους καὶ τοὺς μάντεις); he asked them what the dream was and "what was the significance" (τί τὸ σημεῖον). When they were unable to tell him, Daniel provided him with a compelling interpretation (*Ant* 10 § 211). The verbal and formal correspondence is too striking to be coincidental. The *Antiquities* do not match either the OG or Theodotion-Daniel. We are left with the unexpected possibility that Josephus already had the Daniel story of the *Antiquities* in mind when he portrayed Archelaus' removal in the *War*. It may well be, as Josephus suggests in a couple of places, that he had begun to write the *Antiquities* before he wrote the *War* (*Ant* 1 §§ 6-7; 20 § 259).

3.2.2 Worth noting also is Josephus' charged use of the term ληστής (Rengstorf 1973-83: 4. 258)· Martin Hengel (1989: 24-46) has convincingly argued that Josephus uses ληστής (normally "robber" or "pirate") of the Jewish rebels "to brand the Zealots as lawless rebels and criminals in the Roman sense." The unsavoury connotations of this word preclude any serious discussion of the rebels' religious motives; they are merely out for personal gain (*JW* 7 § 256). In view of Josephus' strong emphasis on the rebels' cultic impiety and violent behaviour, it seems plausible that his usage is further influenced by LXX Jer 7:11. Accused of heinous transgressions by Jeremiah, the prophet's interlocutors say, "We have refrained from practising all of these abominations" (βδελύγματα 7:10). Jeremiah responds on behalf of God, "Is my house, where my name is called upon, a den of robbers (σπήλαιον ληστῶν) in your view?" Here ληστής is linked with much more than robbery, and Josephus accuses the rebels of the same list of crimes (Jer 7:9/*JW* 5 § 402). So this passage may be an interpretive key to Josephus' usage of ληστής. But in LXX Jer 7:11, ληστής translates פָּרִיץ, which also appears at Dan 11:14 to describe the "violent ones" (בְּנֵי פָרִיץ) who try to force God's kingdom without waiting for the fulfilment of the divine schedule. Although the OG removes all reference to these persons and Theodotion renders οἱ υἱοὶ τῶν λοιμῶν, it seems plausible that Josephus associated these two pointed uses of פָּרִיץ, by his favourite prophets, when he characterized the rebels as λῃσταί. The word association would have been facilitated by the proximity of βδέλυγμα in Jer 7:10.[6]

3.3 Oracles, Dreams, and the Prediction to Vespasian

Of greatest importance for understanding Josephus' motives is the episode of his surrender to Vespasian, which lies very near the centre of the *War*. The fateful moment was triggered by Josephus' sudden ability to interpret a series of nightly dreams indicating that Vespasian would become emperor.

We had best begin not with the surrender story itself, but with the mysterious oracle mentioned later. Detailing the various omens that God provided to warn the people of coming disaster, Josephus remarks:

> But what especially moved them to war was an ambiguous oracle (χρησμὸς ἀμφίβολος), likewise found in the sacred writings (ἐν τοῖς ἱεροῖς γράμμασιν), that at that time (κατὰ τὸν καιρὸν ἐκεῖνον) someone from their region would come to rule the world. This man they understood to be one of their own (ὡς οἰκεῖον), and many of the wise (πολλοὶ τῶν σοφῶν) were misled with respect to the interpretation (περὶ τὴν κρίσιν); but actually the oracle indicated the rule of Vespasian, who was proclaimed αὐτοκράτωρ in Judea. . . . Of these signs, then, some they interpreted to please themselves (πρὸς ἡδονήν), some they disregarded, until with the capture of their homeland and their own ruin, they were convicted of their foolishness (*JW* 6 §§ 312–315).

Did the oracle come from Daniel? Bruce argued that Josephus must have identified Vespasian as the "coming prince" of Daniel 9:26 because only Daniel specifies a timetable such as Josephus assumes. The problem with this theory is that the coming leader of 9:26 MT is

---

[6] Hengel (1989) suggests that Josephus either took the derogatory word over from Nicolaus of Damascus (p. 41, "probable") or that it is his own contribution (p. 43, "possible").

evidently not favoured by God: his army "will destroy the city and the sanctuary and his (or its) end will be in a flood". The OG does away with the coming prince, and Theodotion seems to have him destroyed along with the city. In spite of these difficulties, Bruce's proposal that Josephus found the oracle somewhere in Daniel seems likely. Josephus' remark that "many of the wise" were deluded in their interpretation of it (*JW* 6 § 313) is noteworthy, since Josephus does not elsewhere use οἱ σοφοί in this absolute way, except in his paraphrase of Daniel (*Ant* 10 § 198). We have seen that this is a significant term in Daniel itself and, moreover, that some of the wise in Daniel also go astray by becoming involved in war (Dan 11:33–35). When we combine this clue with the observation that, for Josephus, Daniel is the prophet who specified the καιρόν of future events (*Ant* 10 § 267) we have good reason for agreeing that this book was Josephus' most likely source.

Taking into account the problems with Bruce's proposal, Roger Beckwith (1979-1981: 532-535) has revived an older suggestion that Josephus identified Vespasian as the "son of man" figure of Dan 7:13. This figure does come from the among the Jews and is given world dominion — forever (7:14). But the eternal character of the rule is a problem: everything we have seen so far, in the *Antiquities* and the *War*, indicates that Josephus did not see Roman rule as eternal.

Nevertheless, Daniel 7 offers other interesting possibilities. Knowing how Josephus will interpret the four-kingdom scheme of Daniel 2, we have strong clues about how he must have read the beast vision of chapter 7:

> Four mighty beasts different from each other emerged from the sea. (7) After that, as I looked on in the night vision, there was a fourth beast — fearsome, dreadful, powerful, with great iron teeth — that devoured and crushed, and stamped the remains with its feet. It was different from all the other beasts which had gone before it; and it had ten horns. (8) While I was gazing upon these horns, a new little horn sprouted up among them; three of the older horns were uprooted to make room for it. There were eyes in this horn like those of a man, and a mouth that spoke arrogantly. (Dan 7:3–8; JPS)

When Josephus read this vision *after 70*, it must have impressed him as a prediction of his own time. He would have seen the fourth beast as the Roman empire, as he had the fourth beast of Daniel 2. Indeed, conflation of the two visions probably explains his claim that the fourth beast of Nebuchadnezzar's dream was made solely of iron. Now

in Daniel 7, the fourth beast has ten horns. And we know that at least
one popular way of counting emperors in Josephus' day was from the
first dictator, Julius Caesar. (Suetonius, *Lives of the Twelve Caesars*;
Sib. Or. 5.12–15; Rev 13:1). The author of 4 Ezra 11–12 uses just such
a scheme to reinterpret this vision — counting *twelve* emperors to
Domitian. In this scenario, the tenth horn/emperor is Vespasian. The
three horns that were "uprooted to make room for" the tenth could
only be Galba, Otho, and Vitellius. Then who would be the "little
horn" that sprang up in addition, before whom the three fell? Obvious
candidates are Titus, who was somehow involved in the short reign of
Galba and subsequently ruled alongside his father, and Domitian, who
was in Rome throughout the year of the four emperors and governed
until his father's arrival; he would later be remembered for remarkable
arrogance during his father's reign (Suetonius, *Domitian* 1-2; Cassius
Dio 65.2.3, 9.3-5).

It is hard to imagine how a Jew living after 70 could have read this
prophecy and *not* identified Vespasian as the tenth horn of the vision.
Still, the tenth horn is not a world ruler from Judea, and Josephus
cannot fairly have criticized his compatriots for failing to see that
Vespasian was the promised ruler "from their region." Perhaps, as
some have suggested, he was conflating a "messianic" prophecy like
Num 24:17 with Daniel — "a sceptre comes forth from Israel; it
smashes the bow of Moab." More likely, however, Josephus is engaging once again in rhetorical sleight of hand. In the preceding sentence
he castigates the rebels for having made the temple "a square" by
destroying the fortress Antonia, even though their scriptures had
declared that the city would be taken when it became square! Wher-
ever Josephus got this from, he is making an *ad hoc* interpretation; of
course the rebels had heard of no such oracle. Similarly in our
passage, he wants to demonstrate the impiety of the rebels by claiming
that they failed to understand Jewish scripture itself. Again, he does
not expect his Roman readers to look up the scripture.

If Daniel 7:3-8 was where Josephus found Vespasian's reign predicted, then presumably he also had this passage in mind when he wrote
the surrender story. While he was trying to surrender without facing
the wrath of his companions:

> suddenly there came back into his mind those nightly dreams, in which God
> had foretold to him the impending fate of the Jews and the destinies of the
> Roman sovereigns. He was an interpreter of dreams (ἦν περὶ κρίσεις ὀνείρων

ἱκανός) and skilled in divining the meaning of ambiguous utterances (τὰ ἀμφιβόλως λεγόμενα) of the Deity; a priest himself and of priestly descent, he was not ignorant of the prophecies in the sacred books (τῶν ἱερῶν βίβλων τὰς προφητείας). At that hour he was inspired to read their meaning . . . (*JW* 3 §§ 351–353; Thackeray, LCL).

The verbal parallels with *JW* 6 § 312 are strong: "ambiguous" utterances found in "sacred writings" concerning the Roman leader(s). Connections with Daniel are equally clear: a Jewish interpreter of dreams prepares to speak to a foreign world leader about his fate, and the revelation comes in two phases — initial mystery and subsequent interpretation. With a play on ἱερεύς/ἱερός, Josephus characteristically claims special competence to interpret the sacred texts (cf. *AgAp* 1 § 54).

We do not learn the content of Josephus' revelation until he has surrendered and is about to be sent by Vespasian to Nero. He objects and, having been granted an audience with the general, remarks:

> To Nero do you send me? Why, then? Will those who succeed Nero before you endure? You are Caesar, Vespasian, and αὐτοκράτωρ, you and this son of yours . . . . You are master not only of me, Caesar, but of earth and sea and of the whole human race. (*JW* 3 §§ 401–402)

There is nothing in the substance of this prediction that could not have come from reflection on Daniel 7, *once Josephus knew* that Vespasian was the tenth "Caesar" and so could identify him as the tenth horn — though he is more sanguine than Daniel about the fate of the fourth beast! That too may be attributed to political and rhetorical constraint.

We are left with the old historical question: when did Josephus know that Vespasian would accede to imperial power — before or after the event? In support of his predictive ability, some have noted the fame that followed him on its account (van Unnik 1978: 42; Lindner 1972: 71). His claim to prognosis was probably known by Tacitus (*infra*), and was cited by Suetonius (*Vespasian* 5.6.4) and Cassius Dio (65.4). Further, Josephus continues to regard himself as a seer, which might be best explained by the premise that one important prediction had been realized. If he did predict the future, we must reckon with good luck, intuition, or divine inspiration.

But the prediction can be more easily explained. First, if the Roman historians took their information ultimately from Josephus himself, then the argument from multiple attestation (van Unnik 1978: 42) should be retired.[7] Space does not permit a full defence of this unfashionable view (Lindner 1972: 71-72; Rajak 1983: 193 n. 18; but Whiston 1987 [1737]: 827 [dissertation 3]) here, but Tacitus reads like a précis of Josephus. The Jewish historian offers a series of six prodigies, followed by the story of Jesus son of Ananias, followed by two oracles. Tacitus, in his much briefer version, mentions four of the prodigies and the oracle that we are discussing. Thus:

JW 6 §§ 288–300	Tacitus *Histories* 5.13
1. Comet over the city for one year.	"Contending armies were seen in the sky,
2. Midnight light at Passover.	arms flashed (5), and suddenly the temple
3. Cow gives birth to lamb.	was illumined with fire from the clouds
4. Temple gates open spontaneously.	(2). Of a sudden the doors of the shrine
5. Armies with chariots fight in the sky.	opened (4) and a superhuman voice cried: 'The gods are departing': at the
6. Voice in temple "as of a host: 'We are departing hence'".	same moment the mighty stir of their going was heard" (6).

Compare also Tacitus' remarks on the oracle with those of Josephus:

> Few interpreted these omens as fearful; the majority firmly believed that their ancient priestly writings (*antiquis sacerdotum litteris*) contained the prophecy that this was the very time when the East should grow strong and that men starting from Judea should possess the world. This mysterious prophecy (*Quae ambages ... praedixerat*) had in reality pointed to Vespasian and Titus, but the common people, as is the way of human ambition, interpreted these great destinies in their own favour, and could not be turned to the truth even by adversity (*ibid.*, LCL).

Notwithstanding Tacitus' adjustment of the oracle to include Titus, his presentation is so similar to Josephus' — the deluded common people; the ancient priestly/sacred writings; "at that time"; "ambiguous" oracle; the real meaning of the oracle; interpreting for one's "pleasure" [strong word in both cases] — that some sort of dependence is indicated. Since Tacitus wrote in the generation following Josephus, the simplest explanation is that he had some knowledge of Josephus' writings.   To be sure, Tacitus' antagonistic account of Jewish history

---

[7] Rajak (1983) distinguishes between the story of the prediction, which the Roman historians did not get from Josephus (191), and the oracles and prodigies, which they did get from Josephus (193 and n. 18). I find the distinction implausible.

shows no evidence of his knowledge of Josephus. But it was the practice of hellenistic historians to rework their sources: critics have long believed that Josephus himself used non- and even anti-Jewish sources (Hölscher 1916). Tacitus could borrow Josephus' prodigy list without accepting his interpretation of history. Perhaps Tacitus even leaves a clue about the origin of his material when he remarks that "the common people" (*vulgus*) interpreted the oracle in their favour. This qualification implies that he knew of another interpretation among the nobility — the few (*pauci*). He must have known who Josephus was, as Suetonius did (*Vespasian* 5.6.4), since Roman aristocratic circles were not large. We conclude that Tacitus knew Josephus' work but did not buy the Jewish historian's attempt to isolate the rebels. Suetonius' account, in turn, was likely taken from Tacitus.

Second, the conditions for the fabrication and spread of such a prediction were all in place. Vespasian was not of noble birth and had no natural link to the Julio-Claudian house. On his accession he proceeded to engage in projects that look like efforts at legitimization with the aristocracy (Suetonius *Vespasian* 1.1; 9.1). A catalogue of favourable omens was an indispensable condition of legitimacy.

Into this situation came Josephus, who had been a reluctant combatant all along because he and his circles espoused a "Danielic" view of foreign rule. Once Vespasian had been acclaimed by his legionaries, Josephus saw him as the tenth horn of Daniel 7 (who followed the rapid displacement of three others) and was eager to tell him that his sovereignty was foreseen in Jewish scripture. Once this gem had been shared, it was in everyone's interest to antedate and publicize it. Josephus could use it as much needed justification of his surrender. Vespasian could use the testimony of this Eastern nobleman as rare and exotic proof of his legitimacy. Since Josephus had been Vespasian's prisoner for two years before the latter's accession, few others would have been in a position to date the prophecy exactly. Interestingly, even Josephus does not claim that he told Vespasian about the prediction immediately upon surrender; it was only Titus' fondness for him that saved his life during his early imprisonment (3 § 397)! Perhaps Josephus had impressed his captors from the first with the general claim that *Rome's* rule was foreseen in Daniel as the fourth kingdom, and then later he was able to "clarify" Vespasian's role.

Although we cannot take Josephus' account of this controversial period in his life at face value, and we must make due allowance for apologetic and rhetorical artifice, it seems more likely than not that he had Daniel in mind when he composed these sections of the *War*. Danielic themes of the rise and fall of nations under divine supervision, Jewish pacifism, and opposition to rebellion run deep throughout his earliest work. It seems, therefore, that this outlook sprang from his youth and education.

4. *Summary and Conclusion*

By the time he wrote the *Antiquities*, near the end of Domitian's reign, Josephus had decided to use Daniel as a basis for his interpretation of world history. He wished to show that Jews held the rise and fall of kingdoms to be under God's providence, and that the secrets of the future were already revealed in Jewish scripture, with the consequence that Jews accepted gentile rule and disavowed rebellion. He even saw himself as a latter-day Daniel, ensconced in the courts of foreign power and advising potentates while faithfully maintaining his native traditions.

Although Daniel is not mentioned in the *War*, it seems that Josephus had already thought much about the ancient seer by the mid-seventies. For the subordinate themes of the *Antiquities*, which explicitly link them to Daniel, are among the dominant themes of the *War*: world empires come and go; God currently supports the Romans and uses their power to punish the Jewish nation for transgression; acceptance of foreign rule is the traditional Jewish position; and rebels are unfaithful to the tradition. Anticipating the *Antiquities*, Josephus appears in the *War* as a Jewish nobleman and interpreter of dreams in the court of the foreign king. He does not consider Roman power eternal. He seems to have Dan 7:3-8 in mind when he "predicts" Vespasian's rise to power.

Identifying this consistent matrix of thought does not require us to force all of Josephus' statements into a systematic whole. We can still make due allowance for his rhetorical exhibition.

We may now fill out our picture of Daniel's influence in the second-temple period. The book had a wide readership among all sorts of groups. Some were mainly interested in its exemplary stories; others rejuvenated its apocalyptic hope for their own day; still others transposed its quietistic programme into an agenda for military action against foreign oppressors. Josephus shows us yet another interpretation. He borrows Daniel's conception of the rise and fall of nations, and also its pacifism, but jettisons any hope of imminent salvation. If we can make the minimal assumption that Josephus' views were not idiosyncratic, then we have discovered an appropriation of Daniel that was favoured by a certain sector of the priestly aristocracy.

PART IV

HISTORY AND TOPOGRAPHY

JERUSALEM, THE AKRA, AND JOSEPHUS

Joseph Sievers

One of the most vexing problems in the history of Jerusalem in the Second Temple period is that of the so-called Seleucid Akra. Generally, in recent studies the Akra's presence is acknowledged whenever 1 Maccabees makes reference to it, but in between these moments, its existence seems to be almost forgotten. It was Morton Smith who first drew my attention to this deficiency. Thus it is with a special sense of gratitude that I dedicate this essay on the history of the Akra to his memory.

1. *The Long-Term Influence of the Akra*

During much of the second century BCE Jerusalem was controlled or influenced by the so-called Akra. The Seleucid takeover in 200 consisted in driving the Egyptian garrison out of the ἄκρα (*Ant* 12 §§ 133,138). Menelaus was able to weather Jason's attack (probably in 168 BCE) by taking refuge in the ἀκρόπολις (2 Macc 5:5). In 168 or 167 BCE Apollonius established what is commonly referred to as the Seleucid Akra. From then until 164, intermittently until 161, and from 161 to 152 the Akra was in control of all of Jerusalem (Sievers 1990: 62-63). After 152, it continued to exist for another eleven years while at the same time the Hasmonean high priests Jonathan and Simon held political, military, and religious leadership functions in Jerusalem.

Apparently only shortly before Jonathan's demise was the Akra seriously attacked and cut off from communication with the rest of the city and the countryside (1 Macc 12:36; *Ant* 13 § 182). Several prior attempts to besiege it had failed because of intervention or threat of intervention by the Seleucid government (1 Macc 6:18-21; 11:20; *Ant* 12 §§ 362-65; 13 § 121). Even after its fall in 141 BCE, Antiochus VII demanded compensation for it (1 Macc 15:28-31), and may eventually have received it (cf. *Ant* 13 § 247).

The Akra should therefore not be seen as an occasional nuisance, but as a constant feature to be reckoned with in the history of Jerusalem in the second century.

2. *Location Is Not Everything*

In the first article of the first issue of the *Revue Biblique*, over one hundred years ago, Lagrange dealt with the topography of Jerusalem. In his discussion of Josephus' description of the city he remarked that "Toute la difficulté est de trouver la colline basse et courbe qui portait l'Acra ou ville basse" (1892: 22). On an accompanying map he indicated with a question mark the two possible locations of the Akra; one to the northwest, the other to the southeast of the temple area (1892: 19).

Before then and since then much ink has been spilled on the problem of the Seleucid Akra. Numerous attempts have been made to pinpoint the location of such a structure. Tsafrir (1975: 504) lists just nine among the many suggested locations, to the north, west, and south of the Temple. At present, a location immediately south of the Temple area seems to be preferred (Tsafrir 1975, 1980; Ben-Dov 1980; Schwartz 1985; Wightman 1989-90), although other proposals have not been abandoned (Luria 1981; Dequeker 1985; Decoster 1989; Bar-Kochva 1989: 460-62; Strange 1991). It appears unlikely that the question can definitively be settled on archaeological or topographical grounds. One reason for this is the fact that it is not even clear how one would recognize the site of the Akra if one found it: should one consider Hellenistic fortification walls, Rhodian wine jars, or traces of extensive levelling activity as referred to by Josephus, the best evidence for the location of the Akra? Over one thousand stamped handles of mostly Rhodian amphorae have been found in excavations on the southeastern hill of Jerusalem, compared with only several dozen specimens from other areas of the city. The vast majority of the datable stamps come from the years 260-150 BCE, and have been taken as indication that a non-Jewish or at least non-observant population such as that of the Akra used these jars (Dequeker 1985: 210). Yet the archaeologist who published these items (Ariel 1990: 18-28) suggests extreme caution in drawing conclusions about the immediate provenance and contents of the amphorae.

For these reasons I will not address the questions of the location of the Akra and whether the Ptolemaic *akra* of Josephus, the early Seleucid *akropolis* (2 Macc 4:12, 28; 5:5) and the later Akra occupied the same location. Instead, I would like to concentrate attention on the problems of the population and functions of the Akra, which up to now have been discussed by only a few scholars (Bickerman 1937: 71-89; Bar-Kochva 1989: 438-444; 1973: 32-47; Dequeker 1985: 196-7). In order to advance the study of this point, a closer look at comparative material from different areas of the hellenistic world might be helpful.

It was normal for a hellenistic city to have a fortified citadel, called *akra* or *akropolis,* at or near the highest point of its walled area. The available evidence suggests that Seleucid citadels were usually built at the edge of town, so that there would be direct access to and from the countryside (Grainger 1990: 86-87; maps 6A-F). This general pattern is best explained by positing that such citadels were meant to control as well as to defend the city (Grainger 1990: 62). In the hellenistic age citadels were regularly occupied by foreign troops (Launey 1949-50: 2.633-34). Such was the case in Jerusalem at the time of the Fifth Syrian War (200 BCE), when Antiochus III conquered the city and expelled the Ptolemaic garrison from the *akra* with the help of the local population (*Ant* 12 §§ 133,138). Apparently this *akra* was not entirely destroyed during the war and was taken over by the Seleucid administration. In fact, 2 Macc 4:28 mentions a certain Sostratos, who in 172 BCE as commander of the *akropolis* (τῆς ἀκροπόλεως ἐπάρχου) had responsibilities connected with the collection of revenue. The meaning of τὼν διαφόρων here is not entirely clear. It may signify "cash," "interest," or "arrears." In any event, both Menelaus and Sostratos were summoned by the central administration for non-payment, viz. non-collection of revenue.

When necessary, the citadel served of course as a defensive structure, as in the case of Menelaus who took refuge in the *akropolis* during Jason's attempted comeback.[1] But it should also be seen in its fiscal and economic function and not only as a military installation.

With the coming of Apollonius in 168 or 167 BCE begins what is commonly referred to as the Seleucid Akra. The account in 1 Macc 1:33 is often taken to mean that an entirely new building complex was created. The verse καὶ ᾠκοδόμησαν τὴν πόλιν Δαυιδ τείχει μεγάλῳ καὶ ὀχυρῷ, πύργοις ὀχυροῖς, καὶ ἐγένετο αὐτοῖς εἰς ἄκραν ("and they *built* the City of David with a great and strong wall, with strong towers,

---

[1] 2 Macc 5:5. Fortresses were often designed to accommodate (part of) the local civilian population in times of danger. See Welles 1934: no. 11.22-25; cf. Briant 1982: 193.

and it became for them a citadel") presents several problems of interpretation. A literal translation is unrealistic, because the City of David by definition existed beforehand. Therefore Goldstein and the NRSV translate ᾠκοδόμησαν as "they fortified." Here and elsewhere in 1 Maccabees the Akra is presented as coextensive with the City of David, or at least the inhabitants of the Akra control the entire City of David (cf. 1 Macc 7:32; 14:36). What was then the relation of the Akra to the City of David? Was the Akra only a citadel or was it a city quarter with a civilian population in addition to a garrison?

3. *The Occupants of the Akra in 1 Maccabees and the* Antiquities

In 1 Macc 1:34 the occupants of the Akra are not identified as a garrison of soldiers, but only as ἔθνος ἁμαρτωλόν, ἄνδρας παρανόμους ("a sinful people, lawless men").[2] The adjectives are rough translations of Hebrew terms such as רשע and בליעל. Especially the latter expression is frequently used in the LXX in general and in 1 Maccabees in particular to designate Jewish adversaries.[3] As has been noted by Grimm (1853: 23), however, grammatically ἄνδρας παρανόμους can here only be read in apposition to or, as he puts it, as "rhetorische Variation" of ἔθνος ἁμαρτωλόν, which is generally understood as a reference to non-Jews (*pace* Goldstein 1976: 124). Similarly, in the War Scroll of Qumran even the *Kittim*, just as other "sons of darkness," belong to the "army of Beli'al."[4]

Therefore it cannot be presumed that the expression ἄνδρας παρανόμους refers exclusively to transgressors of the Torah and that the ancient reader or hearer would have clearly understood that Jewish renegades were intended. Instead, the author of 1 Maccabees emphasizes the foreign character of the Akra's occupants in a poetic lament, perhaps composed by himself (1 Macc 3:45):

> Jerusalem was uninhabited like a wilderness, not one of her children went in or out. The sanctuary was trampled down, and aliens held the citadel, (καὶ υἱοὶ ἀλλογενῶν ἐν τῇ ἄκρᾳ); it was a lodging place for the Gentiles, (κατά-λυμα τοῖς ἔθνεσι) (trans. M. Callaway, *NRSV*).

---

[2] Codex Sinaiticus has παρανους, perhaps a simple scribal error, perhaps an indication of a perceived difficulty.

[3] 1 Macc 1:11 (variant readings!); 10:61 (variant readings!); 11:21; cf. Deut 13:14 (13); 2 Chr 13:7. Cf. Sievers 1990: 18 n. 71.

[4] 1QM 1.1-2; 15.2-3; 18.1-2. Whether the term *Kittim* here refers to the Romans or to other enemies is immaterial. They certainly are Gentiles.

Jewish supporters of the Akra are criticized at 1 Macc 6:21 and 11:21, but they are clearly distinguished from the people in the Akra. Also, the occupants of the Akra are contrasted with the ἄνδρας Ἰουδαίους who replaced them after Simon's conquest (1 Macc 14:37). Nevertheless, even 1 Macc 4:2 offers strong indications of Jewish inhabitants of the Akra. According to this passage, "the sons of the Akra" were chosen to serve Gorgias as guides in the countryside. Thus they were well acquainted with the area, more than a recently installed garrison would be expected to be. 1 Maccabees comes closest perhaps to acknowledging that the Akra included Jews when it accuses "those from the Akra" of providing "support to the Gentiles" (6:18). Even this statement, however, is ambiguous since in the same sentence the people of the Akra are set in opposition to "Israel." Thus it appears that 1 Maccabees is reticent about the presence of Jews in the Akra.

A very different impression is conveyed by Josephus. In the *War* he refers only twice to the Seleucid Akra, and each time in the context of military operations.[5] In the *Antiquities* instead he mentions it on numerous occasions, generally following the outline of 1 Maccabees. He emphasizes quite consistently, however, that not only a foreign garrison lived in the Akra. Time and again he adds that it had Jewish inhabitants as well, as is evident from the synopsis below.

In addition to a "Macedonian"[6] garrison, as Josephus calls it, "there remained nontheless in the Akra the impious of the people and those of evil character" (*Ant* 12 § 252). On about ten occasions he makes specific reference to Jewish residents of the Akra. They are always referred to in unflattering terms, the two most common being φυγάδες ("fugitives," or "exiles," or "deserters" or "renegades") and ἀσεβεῖς ("ungodly"). Sometimes the emphasis on their presence may even be responsible for grammatical or logical inconsistencies in Josephus' account.[7] Clearly he is not only rendering explicit what is

---

[5] *JW* 1 §§ 39, 50. At *JW* 5 § 139, in the famous description of Jerusalem, there is a reference to the levelling of the Akra Hill by the Hasmoneans (without closer identification).

[6] Bar-Kochva (1989: 506) emphasizes that in hellenistic Jewish literature this term frequently refers to the Seleucid army in general.

[7] *Ant* 12 § 362 states that the garrison and the Jewish renegades did much harm to *the Jews* (οἱ ἐν τῇ ἄκρᾳ τῶν Ἱεροσολύμων φρουροὶ καὶ φυγάδες τῶν Ἰουδαίων πολλὰ τοὺς Ἰουδαίους εἰργάσαντο). This reminds one of statements like John 9:22 where Jews are afraid of "the Jews." *Ant* 13 § 133 expands 1 Macc 11:41, but leaves the location of the renegades grammatically unclear.

implicit in 1 Maccabees, but adds to and corrects his source, and this with extraordinary consistency. Indeed in no other case he seems equally consistent in adding factual information to 1 Maccabees. This becomes particularly evident in a synoptic presentation as the one below. Josephus' additions and deliberate changes that emphasize a Jewish presence in the Akra are highlighted.

1 Macc	*Ant*
1:34 καὶ ἔθηκαν ἐκεῖ ἔθνος ἁμαρτωλόν, ἄνδρας παρανόμους	12 § 252 ἔμενον . . . ἐν τῇ ἄκρᾳ καὶ τοῦ πλήθους οἱ ἀσεβεῖς καὶ πονηροὶ τὸν τρόπον
4:2 καὶ οἱ υἱοὶ τῆς ἄκρας ἦσαν αὐτῷ ὁδηγοί	12 § 305 ὁδηγοὺς ἔχοντος αὐτοῦ τινας τῶν πεφευγότων Ἰουδαίων
6:18 Καὶ οἱ ἐκ τῆς ἄκρας ἦσαν	12 § 362 οἱ ἐν τῇ ἄκρᾳ τῶν Ἱεροσο-λύμων φρουροὶ καὶ φυγάδες τῶν Ἰουδαίων πολλὰ τοὺς Ἰουδαίους εἰργάσαντο
συγκλείοντες τὸν Ισραηλ 6:21 καὶ ἐξῆλθον ἐξ αὐτῶν ἐκ τοῦ συγκλεισμοῦ	12 § 364 πολλοὶ δὲ τῶν ἐν αὐτῇ (scil. ἐν τῇ ἄκρᾳ) φυγάδων νύκτωρ ἐξελ-θόντες εἰς τὴν χώραν καί τινας τῶν ὁμοίων καὶ ἀσεβῶν συναγαγόντες
καὶ ἐκολλήθησαν αὐτοῖς τινες τῶν ἀσεβῶν ἐξ Ισραηλ 10:7 τῶν ἐκ τῆς ἄκρας	13 § 40 οἱ ἀσεβεῖς καὶ φυγάδες οἱ ἐκ τῆς ἀκροπόλεως
10:14 πλὴν ἐν Βαιθσούροις	13 § 42 πάρεξ τῶν ἐν Βεθσούρα πόλει καὶ τῶν ἐν τῇ ἄκρᾳ τῶν Ἱεροσολύμων· οὗτοι γὰρ ἡ πλείων μοῖρα τῶν ἀσεβῶν Ἰουδαίων καὶ πεφευγότων ἦσαν
ὑπελείφθησάν τινες τῶν καταλιπόντων τὸν νόμον καὶ τὰ προστάγματα 11:20 συνήγαγεν Ιωναθαν τοὺς ἐκ τῆς Ἰουδαίας τοῦ ἐκπολεμῆσαι τὴν ἄκραν τὴν ἐν Ιερουσαλημ, καὶ ἐποίησαν ἐπ' αὐτὴν μηχανὰς πολλάς.	13 § 121 Ἰωνάθης δὲ ὁ ἀρχιερεὺς ἐξ ἁπάσης τῆς Ἰουδαίας στρατιὰν συναγαγών, προσβαλὼν ἐπολιόρκει τὴν ἐν τοῖς Ἱεροσολύμοις ἄκραν

ἔχουσαν Μακεδονικὴν φρουρὰν καὶ τῶν ἀσεβῶν τινας καὶ πεφευγότων τὴν πάτριον συνήθειαν. |
| 11:21 καὶ ἐπορεύθησάν τινες μισοῦντες τὸ ἔθνος αὐτῶν ἄνδρες παράνομοι πρὸς τὸν βασιλέα 11:41 καὶ ἀπέστειλεν Ιωναθαν πρὸς Δημήτριον τὸν βασιλέα, ἵνα ἐκβάλῃ τοὺς ἐκ τῆς ἄκρας ἐξ Ιερουσαλμ | 13 § 122 ... νυκτὸς δέ τινες τῶν ἐν αὐτῷ πονηρῶν ἐξελθόντες ἧκον πρὸς Δημήτριον 13 § 133 Ὁ δ' ἀρχιερεὺς Ἰωνάθης ἐξελθεῖν βουλόμενος τοὺς ἐν τῇ ἄκρᾳ τῶν Ἱεροσολύμων καὶ τοὺς Ἰουδαίων φυγάδας καὶ ἀσεβεῖς καὶ τοὺς ἐν ἁπάσῃ τῇ χώρᾳ φρουρούς |
| καὶ τοὺς ἐν τοῖς ὀχυρώμασιν· ἦσαν γὰρ πολεμοῦντες τὸν Ισραηλ. | |

13:51 συνετρίβη ἐχθρὸς μέγας ἐξ
Ισραηλ

13 § 216 ἔπαθον ὑπὸ τῶν φρουρῶν
<u>καὶ τῶν φυγάδων Ἰουδαίων</u>

While there are no serious grounds to doubt that Josephus used 1 Maccabees directly (Gafni 1989: 117), he evidently knew about the Akra not only from this work. This becomes particularly clear where his paraphrase of 1 Maccabees breaks off, just before the description of Simon's conquest of the Akra. Josephus at that point recounts, in stark contrast to 1 Macc 14:37, the decision to level not only the Akra itself, but also the hill on which it stood. He ends this story with a concluding remark "Such was the nature of the things accomplished in the time of Simon" (*Ant* 13 § 217). Elsewhere he employs formulas of this kind to indicate not merely the end of a reign, but also the end of a source he used.[8] Thus the concluding formula, the shift from local to Seleucid history, and the reintroduction of "Simon, the high priest of the Jews,"[9] strongly suggest a change from one source to another. It would be unwise and outside the purview of this study to attempt a detailed source-critical analysis. Nevertheless it seems reasonable to suppose that Josephus had at his disposal at least one other source beside 1 Maccabees and Nicolaus of Damascus. This (written or oral) source contradicted 1 Maccabees regarding the disposal of the Akra. Josephus probably stopped using it after its account of the levelling of the Akra. The inconsistency of the concluding formula with what follows and the strong hostility against the population of the Akra suggest that this source was different from Nicolaus of Damascus. Josephus may have learned of the presence of Jewish occupants in the Akra through this source because the "renegades" are mentioned in it (*Ant* 13 § 216). Other channels are of course possible, but it seems unlikely that he was merely interpreting 1 Maccabees or that Nicolaus of Damascus was his main source concerning the Akra.[10]

---

[8] See *Ant* 11 § 296 (end of Esther); cf. 11 § 183 (end of Nehemia), 12 § 118 (end of Letter of Aristeas).

[9] *Ant* 13 § 223. This phrase would normally indicate a non-Judean source – but it is parallel to 1 Macc 15:1 where it serves to introduce Antiochus' letter to Simon. In fact, Josephus continues to relate events described in 1 Macc 15-16, but not coming as close to it as to 1 Macc 1-13.

[10] Hölscher (1904: 11) thought that the account of the levelling of the Akra was derived from folk legend. Bar-Kochva (1989: 452) instead strongly argues that Nicolaus of Damascus was Josephus' source for this story. He attributes the differences between *JW* 1 § 50 and *Ant* 13 §§ 215-217 entirely to the abbreviating

Josephus' accounts of the levelling of the Akra have generally been considered historically indefensible and archaeologically impossible, and rightly so.[11] On the other hand, the presence of Jewish inhabitants in the Akra has been accepted, on the word of Josephus (and of Professor Bickerman and others), so much so that it has influenced the translations of 1 Maccabees.[12] In this case there seem to be good reasons for following Josephus against 1 Maccabees, but it is important to be aware of the fact. Perhaps there are some consequences to be drawn concerning the relative reliability of both 1 Maccabees and Josephus.[13]

4. *The Akra and the Gymnasium*

If the population of the Akra was mixed, consisting of Jewish and non-Jewish inhabitants, what was its status? 2 Macc 4:9 is generally taken to mean that Jason acquired for Jerusalem the status of *polis* or at least moved the city in that direction (Stern 1992a: 239-43). Usually the gymnasium built by him ὑπ᾽ αὐτὴν τὴν ἀκρόπολιν ("right under the Akropolis")[14] is thought of primarily as the symbol of Jerusalem's new civic status or of Jason's hellenistic reform of Judaism and of Jewish education (Doran 1990). Little thought has been given to the gymnasium's relation to the *akropolis* and to the soldiers stationed there. Probably they were at first at least in part Cypriot mercenaries.[15] They would certainly have claimed access to the nearby athletic

---

style of *JW*. However, he does not seem to pay sufficient attention to the discontinuity after *Ant* 13 § 217, pointed out above.

[11] See, e.g., Bar-Kochva 1989: 456-58; Schürer and Vermes 1973-87: 1.192 n. 10.

[12] This fact is noted by Dequeker (1985: 196 n. 13). Dequeker himself, however, seems to read Josephan terminology into 1 Maccabees (1985: 196 n. 15).

[13] Applebaum's interpretation of a fragmentary inscription from Jerusalem would indicate pagan occupants of the Akra (1980: 58), without excluding Jewish inhabitants. Unfortunately the reading and restoration of the inscription is quite uncertain at crucial points. See *Supplementum Epigraphicum Graecum* 30, 1980, no. 1695.

[14] 2 Macc 4:12; 4 Macc 4:20 locates the gymnasium ἐπ᾽ αὐτῇ τῇ ἄκρᾳ.

[15] Cf. 2 Macc 4:29. This verse refers to the time of Menelaus (c. 172 BCE) whereas the gymnasium was built about three years earlier. Although the presence of a Cypriot contingent or of any garrison in the *akropolis* is not attested for the time of Jason, nothing leads us to suspect that there had been a drastic change in the intervening period. On Cypriot and, later, Mysian garrison troops in Jerusalem see Bar-Kochva 1989: 116-19.

facilities and may even have been among the promoters of the construction project. The Jerusalem gymnasium is never mentioned again after the time of Jason, but since we do not hear of its destruction, there is a strong likelihood that it remained in use throughout (most of) the Akra's history.[16] The decision of Antiochus V (i.e., his guardian Lysias) to let Judeans "conduct their affairs in accordance with their ancestral customs" (2 Macc 11:25) basically returned Jerusalem to the status it had been granted by Antiochus III in 200 BCE (Habicht 1976: 258). Tcherikover (1959: 227) claims that as a consequence "As a town and center of the *polis* of Antioch the Akra came to an end in 162; but the Akra as fortress continued to be very important in the view of the Syrian government." This seems to be a neat solution, but does not square with the later history of the Akra. Even though perhaps less than a *polis* (but see Bickerman 1937: 73, 89), the Akra remained more than a military installation. It had a fiscal, economic, and perhaps cultural function and was probably also perceived as a threat to Jerusalem's civic status (cf. *Ant* 13 § 245).

5. *Fiscal, Economic, and Social Functions of the Akra*

We have already mentioned the fact that the Seleucid commander of the *akropolis* was also responsible for collecting revenue and forwarding it to the central administration (2 Macc 4:28). There is no reason to believe that this function was changed either by the decree of Antiochus IV or by its revocation. Responsibility for collecting taxes was most often quite distinct from military positions, but coercive power, also for revenue collection, resided with the military forces, as the Tobiad romance illustrates (*Ant* 12 §§ 169, 175-85). Although military and fiscal administration were generally distinct, they were more closely connected than is often acknowledged (cf. Briant 1982: 210-11).

Before its fall, the Akra was not subjected to a military siege, but to an economic blockade: its inhabitants were prevented from going out to buy and sell (1 Macc 12:36; 13:49). Buying and especially selling

---

[16] Whether or not the old *akropolis* and the Akra of Apollonius the Mysarch were in the same location is in this context less important than the fact that hellenistic garrisons generally required access to a gymnasium. For the importance of the gymnasium to hellenistic troops see G. M. Cohen 1978: 36; Launey 1949-50: 2.847-8.

is of course not the primary activity of an exclusively military establishment. We do not know what the people of the Akra could have sold, but apparently they controlled a section of the countryside. It is no accident that the Akra was captured shortly after Gezer and that the surrender and purification of both places is described in similar terms (1 Macc 13:45-48, 50). Probably there had been close similarities and connections not only militarily, but also economically and perhaps culturally and religiously.

Both 1 Maccabees and Josephus offer indications of how valuable the Akra was to the Seleucid administration. According to 1 Macc 15:28, Antiochus VII claimed the restitution of Joppa, Gezer, and the Akra in Jerusalem: "You hold control of Joppa and Gazara and the Akra in Jerusalem; they are cities (πόλεις) of my kingdom." As an alternative to returning them, Antiochus VII demanded monetary compensation: "Now then, hand over the cities that you have seized, and the tribute (τοὺς φόρους) of the places that you have conquered outside the borders of Judea; or else pay five hundred talents of silver for them and for the destruction that you have caused and for the tribute of the cities another five hundred talents."[17]

It is impossible to be sure whether *polis* with reference to the Akra is intended in its technical meaning (cf. Grainger 1990: 63-65), although Bickerman (1937: 73) thought that the Akra had the constitution of a *polis*. It is equally impossible to extrapolate the exact value assigned to the Akra here, but it constituted a major portion of the expected revenue. This was not general tribute or taxes of Judea, but revenue specifically to be generated by the Akra as by the other "royal" cities. According to Josephus, the same figure of five hundred talents (plus several hostages) was agreed upon later on between Antiochus VII and John Hyrcanus in lieu of a garrison in Jerusalem.[18] Compensation for lost revenue seems to have been a major portion of this sum. Apparently only a minor portion of this revenue, perhaps less than two talents a year, came from the Temple.[19]

---

[17] 1 Macc 15:30-31. It is not clear whether compensation for the destruction is to be included in the first or in the second 500 talents. See the different translations in NRSV and Goldstein (1976).

[18] *Ant* 13 § 247; cf. *JW* 1 § 61; *Ant* 7 § 393; Diodorus 34/35.1.5 (Stern 1974-84, No. 63); Ps.-Plutarch, *Regum et Imperatorum Apophthegmata* p. 184E-F (Stern 1974-84, No. 260).

[19] 1 Macc 10:42 indicates an annual sum of 5000 silver shekels as revenue from the Temple; cf. *Ant* 13 § 55. Usually, 3000 shekels are considered the equivalent

6. *The Akra, Jerusalem, and the Countryside*

If the Akra was supposed to generate revenue, it must have had control over substantial territories and perhaps commercial activities of its own. This should be obvious to any attentive reader of 1 Maccabees and Josephus. But too often one finds reference to the rule of Judas Maccabee, or of Jonathan, in periods in which their situation was rather precarious (e.g. Kasher 1990: 87, 98). Even after the rededication of the Temple, Judas did not control Jerusalem for extended periods of time, much less did Jonathan before 152 BCE. As long as the Akra existed unhampered, even after 152, it is problematic to state that "Jerusalem was ruled exclusively by the Hasmonaean brothers" (Bar-Kochva 1989: 458). In this context, the role of the high priests Menelaus and Alcimus and their relations with the regional commanders and the Akra would need further clarification.

7. *The Akra's Loyalties*

The persistence of the Akra for over 25 years is not explained in any of our sources. Dan 11:39 states that "he (i.e. Antiochus IV) will distribute land as a prize".[20] This statement is often taken to mean that he awarded tracts of land to the garrison of the Akra or to his Jewish supporters.[21] In the Seleucid empire local government presence was frequently maintained through *katoikiai*, in which men with military training were settled, together with their families. They were given allotments of land, often confiscated from the local population. Thus through the acquisition of land also foreign mercenaries might have developed local ties in Judea that would have induced them to

---

of one talent, but there were several different weight standards (cf. *ABD* 6.907-908). At times, substantially higher revenues were expected from the Temple, as 2 Macc 11:3 shows (cf. 2 Macc 4:7-8, 24). According to Josephus, in the Persian period for every lamb offered in the Jerusalem Temple a tax of 50 drachms (12.5 or 25 shekels?) was imposed (*Ant* 11 §§ 297, 301). It is impossible to annualize this figure, which in any case is not representative since it is based on a temporary punitive measure. Cf. Bickerman 1938: 114.

[20] *Or* "for a price"; AB: "as their wages". Koehler-Baumgartner (1967-90: 539) sub voce מחיר I.3: "Lohn, als Belohnung."

[21] So Di Lella, AB; Bar-Kochva (1989: 438-44) thinks that the land was sold "for a price" to hellenized Jews. Not only from Daniel but also from other sources we learn that land was taken away from its original owners, and given to new ones (1 Macc 1:38; 6:24; 7:6; 4:61 with 10:14; cf.3:36; *Ant* 12 §§ 251, 392).

stay on in the Akra beyond their tour of duty. Certainly there were times when the Hasmoneans were able to prevent access to rural landholdings from the Akra, but these periods were quite limited and the communications between the Akra and the countryside seem to have been for the most part undisturbed.[22]

1 Macc 10:14 however distinguishes between foreigners, who fled when Jonathan was authorized to recruit troops, and (pro-Seleucid, hellenized, or simply anti-Hasmonean) Jews who remained in Beth-Zur. Josephus states and the further course of events shows that not only in Beth-Zur but also in the Akra the inhabitants held out. According to Josephus this was because "these consisted of the greater part of the godless and renegade Jews, and for that reason they did not abandon the garrisons" (*Ant* 13 § 42). Clearly it was not primarily military discipline that kept them in the Akra. Also, before the Akra finally surrendered to Simon, according to 1 Macc 13:49, many of its occupants starved to death. It is hardly conceivable that a garrison of mercenaries would show that kind of tenacity, if less dangerous alternatives were available.

Even though the Akra's population did not consist only of a military contingent, it certainly included some form of a garrison. For any such military body to function efficiently, it needs a clear command structure. This was very difficult to maintain in the stormy years of the decline of the Seleucid dynasty. Power struggles led to easily shifting alliances, one of the major questions being who was able to pay the largely mercenary armies, either in cash or through other benefits.

The military or paramilitary personnel of the Akra however, as that of other garrisons, was not directly paid by the royal treasury, but out of local revenue. As we have seen, the Akra was even supposed to generate substantial revenues for the treasury. Therefore it had a certain self-sufficiency.

Generally it seems to have been fairly clear, to which ruler the Akra owed loyalty, but as the struggles between various Seleucid contenders intensified, there must have been problems. When Demetrius permitted Jonathan to raise an army and to retrieve the hostages from the Akra, Alexander Balas outdid him and offered Jonathan the high priesthood (1 Macc 10:6, 18-21). As Jonathan assumed that office, he

---

[22] 1 Macc 13:49; cf. 1 Macc 7:24, where Alcimus and his followers are hindered in their movements.

also collected troops and arms. From that time in 152 BCE, or at least from the time of the death of Demetrius I (winter 151/150) until the arrival of Demetrius II in 147, Alexander Balas, who assigned a prominent role to Jonathan, had no apparent rivals for the sovereignty over Judea.[23] It is not unknown that different military or police forces can work at cross-purposes in the same jurisdiction, sometimes according to the principle *divide et impera*. The complex command structure in the Seleucid empire allowed for such duplication: Pto- lemaios, the *strategos* (military commander) and high priest of Coele-Syria and Phoenicia, apparently did not have direct authority over the garrison commanders (φρούραρχοι) in his territory, as the Hefzibah inscription shows.[24] Similarly, in an earlier period, the more important fortresses in the Persian empire were not under the control of the satrap, but their commanders reported directly to the king.[25] Such a practice was continued also later (cf. Polybius 5.48.14; Diod. 20.107.5). Thus it is conceivable that the Akra was loyal to Alexander Balas without being under the control of Jonathan, his local governor. One indication in that direction is the fact that Jonathan tried for the first time to take the Akra immediately after the death of Alexander Balas (1 Macc 11:20). Yet, it appears problematic that Jonathan would be appointed a member of the circle of "first friends," *strategos*, and *meridarches* (1 Macc 10:65), with the right and the duty to maintain an army, without at least some measure of control over the Akra so close to his own residence.[26]

---

[23] Allegedly, Demetrius I offered to turn over the Akra to the high priest (1 Macc 10:32), but it appears that he probably lacked the power to carry this out. In any event, the provisions of his letter were not put into effect.
[24] Landau 1966, esp. lines 15-16 of the inscription, with comments on pp. 66-67; see emendations by J. and L. Robert 1970; commentary by Taylor 1980; Fischer 1980: 1-3.
[25] Xenophon, *Cyr.* 8.6.9; Briant 1982: 211.
[26] Bengtson (1937-52: 2.151-153) follows Josephus (*Ant* 13 §§ 88, 102) in positing that Apollonius was appointed governor of Coelesyria by Alexander Balas, and not, as 1 Macc 10:69 indicates, by Demetrius II. Bengtson (1937-52: 2.180) also concludes that Apollonius, Jonathan's sworn enemy, must have been in charge of the Akra and the other garrisons in Judea. Most scholars prefer the account in 1 Macc 10:69 as much more plausible (Abel 1949: 197; Goldstein 1976: 420).

8. *An Agreement between Jonathan and the Akra?*

During the seven years (152-145 BCE) in which Jonathan was an appointee of Alexander Balas, with authority to raise an army, the Akra could not have survived without some tacit or probably even explicit agreement with him. It is possible that Alexander Balas permitted the continued existence of the Akra, and perhaps made it a condition of his grant of offices to Jonathan. Still, this would mean that the Akra had lost much of its function as a Seleucid stronghold in Jerusalem.

A direct agreement with Jonathan cannot be proven, but is likely to have been in effect during the reign of Alexander Balas. During that period Jonathan made no attempt to curtail the activities of the Akra. His relations with the Akra as well as with the Seleucid rulers may be the main reason why he is given far less favorable treatment in 1 Maccabees than either Judas or Simon (Sievers 1990: 82, 103).

In conclusion, there remain many open questions about the history of the Akra, its changes in population and function. In some respects it was similar to a military colony so common in the Hellenistic period. In other respects it was a unique entity, even giving Jerusalem at times the character of a divided city. The division however could not last. The 23rd of Iyyar 141 BCE was a day to celebrate, to celebrate the purification of the Akra and the reunification of Jerusalem.[27]

9. *Summary*

We might sum up our tentative findings in the following points:

1. To understand the history of Jerusalem in the years 200 to 130 BCE it is necessary to understand the role of the Akra.

2. The question of the location and possible moves of the Jerusalem *akra/akropolis* is of importance, but should not exclusively dominate the discussion. The problems of history and function or functions should equally be addressed.

3. Josephus and 1 Maccabees offer fundamentally different views of the Akra's population. Scholars usually follow Josephus' view, sometimes without being conscious of it.

4. The Akra cannot simply be identified with the presumed *polis* of Antioch in Jerusalem.

---

[27] 1 Macc 13:51; *Megillat Ta'anit* ad 23 Iyyar.

5. Besides its military function, the Akra had fiscal, economic, and social functions. It was supposed to be a revenue-generating operation.

6. For much of its existence, the Akra was in unchallenged control of Jerusalem and the surrounding countryside.

7. Its inhabitants had reasons to remain there, beyond military orders and even without Seleucid support.

8. The Akra could not have survived for as long as it did without some tacit or explicit agreement with the high priest Jonathan.[28]

---

[28] I would like to thank the colloquium participants, especially Daniel R. Schwartz, for helpful suggestions that have improved the final shape of this paper. All remaining deficiencies are, of course, solely my own responsibility.

JOSEPHUS ON HYRCANUS II

Daniel R. Schwartz

*If you can't stand the heat,
get out of the kitchen.*
(Harry S. Truman)[1]

1. *Introduction*

Hyrcanus II, whose career began by taking him from being the legitimate heir to the Judaean throne to collaboration in the Roman takeover of Judaea, and ended with his return from Parthian captivity to execution by the Idumaean who usurped the Judaean throne, is known to us virtually only from the pages of Josephus. And his image there is far from the best: twice in *War* (1 §§ 109, 203) and numerous times in *Antiquities* (13 §§ 407, 424; 14 §§ 13, 44, 158, 179; 15 §§ 165, 177, 182), we are told that he was by nature unsuited for politics. Moreover, even apart from this summary of Hyrcanus' life, numerous episodes reported by Josephus apparently confirm the same impression.

Sixty-five years ago, Bacchisio Motzo published a little-noticed piece on "Ircano II nella tradizione storica," which remains, to my knowledge, the only study ever devoted to the image of Hyrcanus II; Fausto Parente wisely added that essay to his 1977 collection of Motzo's papers.[2] What moved Motzo to write his study was, it seems, the 1924 publication in the central reference work for classical antiquity of Erich Obst's highly uncomplimentary piece on Hyrcanus II. Obst, following Josephus, had opened his account of Hyrcanus as follows (Obst 1924: 788, cited on Motzo's first page):

> Er war so recht geeignet, das Recht der Erstgeburt in Mißkredit zu bringen, ein schwacher, geistig ziemlich beschränkter, untätiger Charakter ohne allen Ehrgeiz, eine Puppe in der Hand seiner Ratgeber, feig, ohne Ehrgefühl und vielleicht sogar mit Mördern unter einer Decke steckend.

---

[1] Truman 1960: 229.

[2] Motzo 1927. For an idea of how unnoticed this study remained, see Marcus 1943: 514, n. b.

Motzo, in contrast, building primarily on the contrast between Josephus' frequent denigration of Hyrcanus and Julius Caesar's praise for him (*Ant* 14 § 192), and upon the contrast between the prominence of Antipater in the narrative as opposed to that of Hyrcanus in the documents of *Ant* 14 (see, inter alia, § 156 vs. §§ 144,200!), deduced that Josephus' accounts in both *Ant* 14 and *JW* 1 were based upon Nicolaus of Damascus, who had striven to give Antipater all the credit for Hyrcanus' accomplishments. This not only glorified Herod's father; Nicolaus' characterization of Hyrcanus as incapable also served to justify Herod, who took over for him. In fact, however, Motzo concludes, the historian who examines Hyrcanus' life and accomplishments, following not the partisan version supplied by Nicolaus but, rather, the documents and the facts, will conclude that Hyrcanus, in difficult times, was indeed a worthy man to close the Hasmonean line, valorous in war, prudent and capable in negotiations, tenacious in the pursuit of the interests of his family and his people (Motzo 1927: 17-18). Thus, Motzo attempted to set aside the familiar Josephan image of Hyrcanus, summarized so well by Obst, by contrasting Josephus' account with documents preserved by Josephus.

A similar procedure had been followed at the beginning of the century by Karl Albert, whose dissertation on Josephus' use of Strabo emphasized that the picture of Hyrcanus which emerges from Josephus' quotations from Strabo is one of a much more active and successful politician than that supplied by Nicolaus.[3] Albert notes, especially, the contrast between *JW* 1 §§ 187,193-94 and *Ant* 14 § 127,137: while *War* has Antipater throwing his support to Caesar and heroically fighting for him in Egypt, Caesar correspondingly rewarding Antipater and confirming Hyrcanus as high priest *in order to please Antipater*, the *Antiquities* account has Antipater aiding Caesar due to Hyrcanus' orders, and Caesar's rewards for Hyrcanus are mentioned before those for Antipater and are not made dependent upon Anti-

---

[3] Albert 1902: 39-41. It is noteworthy, given a widespread conception about the prejudices of German scholarship, that Albert assumed that Josephus was so honest that he would not correct Nicolaus' account without another one: "Josephus war so ehrlich, seine Quelle nicht willkürlich zu fälschen oder abzuändern; sie zu korrigieren, sah er sich [in *War*] infolge der Unkenntnis anderer Überlieferungen ausser stande. Ganz anders in der Archäologie! Hier hatte Josephus die Bekanntschaft des Strabo gemacht . . ." (p. 40).

pater's merits. This improvement of Hyrcanus' role resulted directly, Albert argued, from the two passages from Strabo which Josephus cites *verbatim* in *Ant* 14 §§ 138-39. While Nicolaus had made it seem that Antipater had done all the work, and that was reflected in the *War* account, in writing the *Antiquities* Josephus had the benefit of new input from Strabo, and he corrected his narrative accordingly.

Thus, where Motzo used Caesar to correct Nicolaus, Albert used Strabo. A major difference between the two scholars was, however, that for Motzo, Caesar's evidence appeared only in isolated sections of *Antiquities* and did not influence the rest of the narrative, so both *Antiquities* and *War* could basically be considered to be dependent upon Nicolaus. For Albert, in contrast, *War* remained roughly equivalent to Nicolaus, but, as we saw in the above example, *Antiquities* had not only been interpolated with material from Strabo, but also rewritten to some extent under the impact of the new material.

Strabo, however, as the briefness of Albert's discussion shows, cannot explain very many differences between the pictures of Hyrcanus and his period in *War* and *Antiquities*.[4] The approach followed by Albert, which understands these differences as a result of Josephus' rewriting of Nicolaus in *Antiquities*, could be applied on a broad front only if the new input was found in a broader source. This is where Richard Laqueur enters. The fifth chapter of Laqueur's 1920 monograph, almost a hundred pages long, constitutes the most ambitious attempt anywhere to analyze the import of parallel narratives in Josephus, and is devoted entirely to *Ant* 14 and its parallels in *JW* 1. Laqueur's main point in this chapter is that in composing *Ant* 14 Josephus had one main Vorlage, viz., his own *War* account, and one new source which — contrary to the localized influence of Albert's Strabo — covered the entire scope of the narrative. That new source, however, was not a literary one, but, rather, Josephus' own mind and emotions: for Laqueur, the *Antiquities* narrative represents Josephus' rewriting of his *War* narrative, which is basically identified as Nicolaus', under the impact of his own newfound, or newly expressible, nationalism. This nationalism took especially the form of anti-Antipatridism: in passage after passage, Laqueur argues, the changes between *War*

---

[4] Although it is of course possible that Strabo's account influenced *Antiquities* in places where no named fragments indicate his influence; see Stern 1991: 424; 454-55.

and *Antiquities* reflect a tendentious effort on Josephus' part to make Antipater and Herod look worse.

Laqueur's efforts achieved an ambiguous result. On the one hand, his call to interpret Josephus in *Antiquities* as a writer motivated by his own values and ideals, not a mere creature of his sources, basically swept the field (see D.R. Schwartz 1992: 262-264). On the other hand, however, his claim that *Ant* 14 had rewritten *War* from an anti-Antipatrid point of view was subjected to much criticism; and rightly so.[5] Although there is some anti-Antipatrid material in *Ant* 14, beginning from the nasty introduction of Antipater where Josephus even troubles to argue with Nicolaus about Antipater's birth (*Ant* 14 §§ 8-9), there is also pro-Antipatrid material – such as the eulogy at *Ant* 14 § 283, where Antipater is termed "a man distinguished for piety, justice and devotion to his country." Why should we depend on the introduction and not on the eulogy? Moreover, there are many changes in *Ant* 14, in comparison to *War*, which do not contribute one way or the other to the anti-Herodian theme, although Laqueur often tries to force their significance. Thus, for example, in the very first section of his discussion Laqueur argues that the notion, found in *Ant* 14 § 7 but not in the parallel at *JW* 1 § 122, that an oath sealed the compromise between Aristobulus and Hyrcanus, was concocted by Josephus in order to increase the guilt involved in Hyrcanus' subsequent opposition to Aristobulus. This guilt, Laqueur further asserts, is really to be understood as that of Antipater's, who was to be responsible for Hyrcanus' renewed opposition: "So wendet sich in letzter Linie die Umarbeitung gegen diesen, den Stammvater der Herodeer" (Laqueur 1920: 136). But before accepting this interpretation we would wish that Josephus at least once pointed to the oath and its breaking in the context of Hyrcanus' opposition to his brother. "Eidbruch" figures prominently in Laqueur's text here, but never in Josephus'.

Similarly, the third section of Laqueur's discussion (1920: 142-145) deals with the parallel narratives of the siege of Jerusalem by Aretas and Hyrcanus, brought to an end by the intervention of Pompey's general, Scaurus (*JW* 1 §§ 126b-130; *Ant* 14 §§ 19-33). Laqueur quite

---

[5] For criticism of this chapter of Laqueur's work, see esp. Helm 1921: 507-513, also the running skirmishing by Marcus in LCL. According to Stern (1991: 454), "In general one may note that in *Ant* 14 Josephus made only minor changes in the panegyric tone [concerning Antipater and Herod] which derives from Nicolaus and is reflected in *War* – despite Laqueur's efforts to prove the opposite."

rightly points out two major differences. First, *Antiquities*, but not *War*, states that the populace (δῆμος) of Jerusalem sided with Hyrcanus, "only the priests" siding with Aristobulus. This, however, Laqueur explains away as being only an implication of the Onias story which Josephus received from Jewish tradition (cf. n. 16) – but Laqueur gives no reason for Josephus' decision to include this story and makes no attempt to interpret its relevance to his theme. As for the other major difference between the two narratives, while *War* reports only that Aristobulus gave Scaurus a bribe, and denounces it as a perversion of justice, *Antiquities* reports that both brothers gave bribes, denounces Hyrcanus as niggardly, and states that Scaurus' decision was based on his appreciation of Aristobulus' superior qualities. Here, again, we have a good example of the forced nature of Laqueur's overall thesis. Laqueur writes as follows:

> Aber die damit [in *War*] gegebene Auffassung, als habe Aristobul seine Anerkennung bei Scaurus nur *durch Bestechung* erwirken können, kann dem zum Gegner des Antipatros gewordenen Josephus nicht mehr genügen. Scaurus musste sich aus *sachlichen* Gründen für Aristobul und gegen Antipater entscheiden (1920: 143 – original emphasis).

This, according to Laqueur, is the reason Josephus composed and inserted *Ant* 14 § 31, which points up Aristobulus' greater wealth, magnanimousness (μεγαλόψυχος) and the greater ease with which his goals could be reached (*ibid.*). But in this entire section, in both narratives (*JW* 1 §§ 126b-130; *Ant* 14 § 19-33), *Antipater is never mentioned*, apart from the very last line where the death of his brother happens to be recorded.

In other words, quite apart from the pro-Antipatrid material in *Ant* 14 which Laqueur was forced to ignore or to explain away, there is also simply a lot of rewriting in *Antiquities* which seems not to have to do with the evaluation of the Antipatrids.

Does this mean, however, that we must simply accept the conclusion that Josephus' *Antiquities* narrative has undergone a tendentious rewriting? Hardly; even Laqueur's most trenchant critic agreed with him that *Antiquities* shows, in general, a "gesteigertes jüdisches Nationalgefühl," and the same point is widely recognized.[6] But Jewish

---

[6] See Helm 1921: 513. Helm's critique focuses mainly on Laqueur's argument that the *Ant* 14 narrative was based on that in *War*, rather than on the latter's source; for this question, see the survey in Cohen 1979: 50-51, also D.R. Schwartz

nationalism could express itself in this case as pro-Hasmoneanism, not only as anti-Antipatridism,[7] and, given Laqueur's attempt one suspects that the analysis should focus on the Hasmoneans themselves, rather than on the Antipatrids.

That is the approach followed, most recently, by Gideon Fuks in a study devoted to "Josephus and the Hasmoneans" (Fuks 1990). Beginning with the second generation of Hasmoneans, where 1 Maccabees left off and Josephus is our major source, Fuks compared Josephus' parallel narratives in some detail and concluded, as Laqueur, that Josephus' presentation of them in *Antiquities* is in general significantly more positive than that in *War*.[8] We note, however, that in making his argument Fuks examines only John Hyrcanus I, Alexander Jannaeus and Mattathias Antigonus — skipping not only the shortlived reign of Aristobulus I but also Salome Alexandra (76-67 BCE) and of particular interest here, Hyrcanus II, who ruled, or was supposed to, during the last quarter-century of Hasmonean statehood (67-40 BCE). That Fuks skipped Salome Alexandra is readily understandable, for Josephus — in *Antiquities* — pours venomous condemnation upon her. Perhaps this is only because she was a woman. But the characterization of Hyrcanus II is not so readily explained away, and should not be ignored.

Moreover, even regarding the monarchs he does discuss, Fuks must conclude that the *Antiquities* picture is at times only marginally more

---

1989-90: 120-29. Our conclusion there about Josephus' failure to depart in *Ant* 14 from the dramatic quality of Nicolaus is not affected by the argument, below, about the changed evaluations of characters. For Josephus' dependence upon Nicolaus in *War* in contrast with the more nationalist standpoint advocated by Josephus in *Antiquities*, and its anti-Herodian implications, see also Stern 1991: 453-459, and, posthumously, Stern 1992: 22-23. On *Ant* 14, however, cf. above, n. 5.

[7] In the introduction to his comparison of *Ant* 14 and *War* 1, Laqueur (1920: 131-132) points to *Ant* 16 § 187 and concludes, "Da sich nun aber Josephus hier ausdrücklich in Gegensatz stellt zu der Herodeer-freundlichen Darstellung des Nicolaus von Damaskus . . . aus seiner persönlichen Stellung zu den Herodeern einer-, den Hasmoneern andererseits, so folgt, daß Josephus durch sein eigenes persönliches Urteil dazu veranlaßt wurde, seiner Archäologie eine anti-Herodische Richtung zu geben . . ." The double-edged protasis should have engendered a double-edged apodosis.

[8] Fuks (1990: 176) explains this in a way only marginally different from Laqueur: whereas Laqueur thought that the change was due to Josephus becoming more independent of his Roman patrons, Fuks thought the recession of the rebellion of 66-70 into the past allowed for the subsiding of Roman feelings which had prevented Josephus from praising a line — his ancestral line — which had fought Rome.

positive than the one in *War*. All of Josephus' extenuations, assembled
by Fuks (1990: 169-70), hardly soften, for example, the terrible picture
of Jannaeus enjoying himself with his concubines while eight hundred
of his enemies were crucified before his eyes and those of their
relations (*Ant* 13 §§ 379-83), behavior which earned him — according
to *Antiquities* in an addition to *War*! — the damning nickname "Thraki-
das" (which Marcus aptly compares to "Cossack"; cf. Stern 1991:
125-127).

Finally, and apart from the incompleteness of the revision (any
narrative based ultimately on one of an opposite point of view will
necessarily retain inconsistencies), there is another problem: by
treating only what changed between *War* and *Antiquities*, Fuks left
untouched some salient elements of the former which remained in the
latter. Presumably, his guiding principle was that Josephus was not
always consistent, so while changes may be ascribed to the nationalist
motive, the retention of *War* (Nicolaus) materials is to be chalked up
to Josephus' sloppiness. However, this should be a last resort. Our
point of departure will be one such item: the fact that in *Antiquities*
(13 § 323), no less than in *War* (1 § 85), Alexander Jannaeus begins his
career by killing one of his brothers — an incident Fuks does not
discuss, and which, presumably, he would view as an inconsistent carry-
over from the hostile *War* narrative. However, Josephus does not
condemn the act. Moreover, it is notable that Jannaeus' brother and
predecessor Aristobulus I is similarly said to have begun his career by
killing his mother, who was supposed to have inherited the throne (*JW*
1 § 71; *Ant* 13 § 302); and Jannaeus' widow and successor, Salome
Alexandra, is also said, in both narratives (*JW* 1 § 109; *Ant* 13 §§
407-8), to have begun her reign by neutralizing the son who should
have reigned (see below) — just as Herod was later to kill Aristobulus
III. Such practice, as Joseph Sievers has recently reminded us in his
study of Hasmonean women, was indeed standard in the Hellenistic
world, and adjudged normal by a contemporary colleague of Josephus.[9] And it seems to provide a starting point, better than simple
anti-Antipatridism or pro-Hasmoneanism, for the understanding of
Josephus' picture of Hyrcanus II.

---

[9] See Sievers 1989: 135, referring to Plutarch, *Demetrius* 3.4, who terms the
murder of brothers "a common and recognized postulate in the plans of princes
to secure their own safety" (trans. B. Perrin in LCL).

In the present study, therefore, we will attempt to combine a number of observations. First, we will assume, as is usual, that Josephus' narrative for this period in *JW* 1 is based upon Nicolaus and reflects his Herodian point of view. Second, we shall assume, as is equally usual, that Josephus' parallel narrative in *Antiquities* is based upon that same source, used directly and/or through the mediation of *War*. Third, however, we will also accept the widespread conclusion that Josephus' increased nationalism comes to expression in *Antiquities*; this resulted in some rewriting, whether or not supported by new material (such as Motzo's documents and Albert's Strabo). The problem will be how to understand Josephus' picture of Hyrcanus II, so pithily summarized by Obst, and so often worse in *Antiquities* than in *War*, in light of these assumptions.

2. *Josephus on Hyrcanus II*

Let us first turn to a passage in *Ant* 14 where, I believe, we can be virtually certain as to where Josephus is following Nicolaus and where he is freely composing. In *Ant* 14 §§ 74-76, Josephus reports Pompey's reorganization of Coele-Syria in 63 BCE: Pompey imposed a tribute upon Jerusalem, confined the Jewish people ("which had raised itself so high") to its own borders and restored cities − previously conquered and in part demolished by the Hasmoneans − to their own inhabitants. The passage is quite detailed, but also quite positive about these Syrian cities, giving the names of the cities "set free" and even pointing out that Gadara was treated favorably due to Pompey's grace to his freedman, Demetrius the Gadarene; the passage also troubles to point out that Herod later refounded Strato's Tower as Caesarea. That is, this passage is full of details about Syrian cities and approves of Pompey's restoration of the natural balance by forcing the Jews back into their own borders and restoring the cities to their inhabitants.

This passage is immediately followed, however, by a passage (*Ant* 14 §§ 77-78) which bewails this misfortune, blaming it on the στάσις of Hyrcanus and Aristobulus; the result is summarized as "our" subjugation to Rome, loss of territories, tribute, and, eventually, the replacement of high-priestly rule by rule by commoners. These comments end with "But of these things we shall speak at the (proper) place."

Here, then, a passage which speaks in details about the Syrians, refers to the Jews in the third person and praises Pompey's measures on behalf of the former at the expense of the latter, is followed by a passage with no new content but which, taking a first-person Jewish point of view, reflects on who was to blame for this misfortune (πάθος) and what its short- and long-term consequences were. Then the writer reveals himself to be the book's author: he promises to return to the latter topic at the appropriate place. It seems obvious that the first passage, *Ant* 14 §§ 74-76, gives us Nicolaus' account, full of details which Nicolaus knew and Josephus wanted to supply; then, in §§ 77-78, Josephus reflects upon the developments. This assessment is bolstered, moreover, by the fact that *JW* 1 §§ 154-57 supplies close verbal and contentual parallels to *Ant* 14 §§ 74-76 and 79. That is, Josephus followed Nicolaus' account closely in both *War* and *Antiquities*, but in the latter he interrupted it with some comments of his own.

Now if we analyze Josephus' comments in *Ant* 14 § 77-78, we find two points which are, to my mind, quite remarkable. The first is that Josephus blames both Hyrcanus and Aristobulus, for their στάσις brought about the catastrophe. This is remarkable, first of all, in that Josephus does not blame only one for contesting the legitimate rights of the other; rights and legitimacy have nothing to do with the matter. Moreover, Josephus' statement here is remarkable because from the very beginning of *Ant* 14 Josephus has made it clear that it was not Hyrcanus, but, rather, Antipater, who was responsible for the στάσις (or for Hyrcanus' part in it). Thus, in the very first passage where he is introduced, *Ant* 14 § 8, Antipater is portrayed as δραστήριος δὲ τὴν φύσιν ὢν καὶ στασιαστής, and it was he who persuaded Hyrcanus to pursue the struggle against Aristobulus despite his agreement, reported in the preceding lines (*Ant* 14 § 7), to retire to private life. Why, then, when summarizing in §§ 77-78 the process which led to Pompey's takeover, does Josephus blame Hyrcanus and Aristobulus?

The other remarkable point in *Ant* 14 §§ 77-78, in my reading – and while I readily admit that the Israeli setting in which I live and work has sensitized me to such matters, I do not believe, in this case at least, that it has led me to see what isn't there – is that Josephus makes no attempt to assess the rights or wrongs of Pompey's territorial arrangements. The regions removed from Jewish control and given to Syrians – were they Jewish territories? Syrian territories? Were

Pompey's arrangements just? Nicolaus evidently viewed them as just; for Nicolaus (*Ant* 14 §§ 74-76), the Jews have their natural borders and the Syrians have their cities, and it is wrong to upset this order and right and praiseworthy to restore it. Josephus, in contrast, while bewailing Pompey's arrangements, did not consider them unjust. He simply bemoans the fact that "the land, which by our arms we had gained possession of from the Syrians, we were forced to return to the Syrians." That is, what matters in affairs of state is who is successful and who is not.[10] Just as with regard to the στάσις of Hyrcanus and Aristobulus Josephus saw no point in inquiring who was in the right and who in the wrong, so too with regard to territory: territory belongs to who can hold it, and a Jew may bemoan as unfortunate, but not as unfair, the loss of territory which his side had previously taken fair and square in war.

That this is indeed Josephus' point of view is shown by the fact that *Ant* 14 is veritably bracketed by similar statements by Josephus. Namely, on the one hand, in Josephus' account of Salome Alexandra, which concludes *Ant* 13, we twice find the view that the people who let her reign have only themselves to blame (*Ant* 13 §§ 417, 430); in both passages Josephus characterizes her — alone among all figures in his works, just as she is virtually the only Jewish queen — as moved by "love of power" (φιλαρχία, φιλάρχων). Correspondingly, in the latter passage (his eulogy, as it were, for this queen), Josephus points out that her reign showed the stupidity (ἀσύνετον) of men who fail to maintain rule.[11] In other words, Salome Alexandra, as a woman, shouldn't have ruled, but no one can blame her for trying, just as — in the passage with which we began — the Herodians should not rule but Josephus did not blame them for trying. The people to blame are the legitimate rulers of the Jews, who failed to preserve that which was entrusted to them. It is a fact of life, apparently, that people who

---

[10] For the assimilation of Josephus' point of view by one of his closest students, see Schalit 1969: 481: "der Enderfolg darüber entscheidet, wer 'Recht' behält." Cf. D. R. Schwartz 1987: 10-13.

[11] This means, as is shown by the parallel at *Ant* 13 § 417 and by the explicit contrast here in § 430 between Salome being a woman and Josephus' complaint about men (ἀνδρῶν), that men are stupid if they let women rule. As Josephus explicitly opines in the next paragraph (§ 431), the things Salome wanted were unbecoming a woman. (Chamonard [1904: 201] notes that he doesn't know what the phrase in § 430 means and surmises that it is "sûrement altérée," and Marcus' LCL translation and explanation seem to miss the point.)

should not rule — such as women and Antipatrids — will try to; the people worthy of condemnation are the legitimate rulers who don't keep the illegitimates out. Similarly, just as in *Ant* 14 § 77 Josephus bemoans the loss of territory which had been taken by force from the Syrians, so too in *Ant* 13 § 431 he mourns the fact that the result of Alexandra's rule was the loss of Hasmonean sovereignty, which had been gained at the price of great danger and suffering. So the two striking points about Josephus' comments at *Ant* 14 §§ 77-78 are closely paralleled by his comments on Salome Alexandra, and the fact that they too are not paralleled in *War* bolsters our confidence that this is Josephus' own point of view.

As for the other bracket, it comes at the very end of *Ant* 14 (§§ 490-491), where, after the execution of Mattathias Antigonus, Josephus pauses to comment on the end of the Hasmonean line. Here he first emphasizes that the founders of the Hasmoneans accomplished much on behalf of the nation, but then goes on to explain that they — the Hasmoneans — threw away their rule by fighting amongst themselves (διὰ τὴν πρὸς ἀλλήλους στάσιν τὴν ἀρχὴν ἀπέβαλον) — just as at *Ant* 14 § 77 it was specifically the fraternal στάσις of Hyrcanus and Aristobulus which Josephus blamed for the beginning of the Hasmoneans' end. And here too, as there, Josephus complains that the result was the passage of the royal power from its prestigious priestly incumbents to a house of commoners (δημοτικῶν//οἰκίας . . . δημοτικῆς καὶ γένους ἰδιοτικοῦ). This passage also has no parallel in *War*, and its prominent position, at the end of the dynasty and the end of a book, confirms that here too we have Josephus' own opinion.

Josephus' stance, in *Antiquities*, is thus clearly that the Jews themselves were responsible for their fall. The leading citizens (οἱ δυνατοί — *Ant* 13 § 411) allowed a pushy woman to take power and had themselves to blame (§§ 417, 430), Hyrcanus allowed a troublemaker to push him into renewing the struggle against his brother (*Ant* 14 §§ 8ff), and when the leading Jews saw that Antipater and his sons were becoming real competition to Hyrcanus he failed to take notice of it (§§ 163ff); the result was that Herod eventually took over. Hyrcanus' end was that Herod killed him; although that was neither just nor fair (*Ant* 15 § 182), it was something reasonable people should have expected (*Ant* 15 § 20); after all, Alexandra too had given no consideration for deceny or justice (*Ant* 13 § 431). That's not something a *homo politicus* does.

In *Antiquities*, in other words, Josephus convicts Hyrcanus of having failed to do what politicians have to do but having still tried to play the game. His term of office falls into two periods, first 67-48 BCE, during which he competed with his brother Aristobulus, and then 48-40 BCE, which saw the conclusive rise of Antipater and his sons. Had Hyrcanus stayed out of politics in the first period, the Romans might not have had such an easy entrance into Judaea, or a reason to punish it by stripping it of its territories. Had he been a stronger figure in the second period, the Antipatrid takeover might have been prevented and a Hasmonean left at the head of the state. But he took neither course; he did compete but he couldn't rule, and the result was catastrophe.

Josephus makes this point in *Antiquities* in several passages. First, at the very beginning of Hyrcanus' specific line, we see his father and one of his uncles acting out the two proper options: at *Ant* 13 § 323, we read that Hyrcanus' father, Alexander Jannaeus, upon acceding to the throne, killed one of his brothers who had designs upon the crown, but held in honor another one [Absalom – cf. *Ant* 14 § 71] who preferred to live an unpolitical life (ἀπραγμόνως[12] ζῆν). These steps are then summarized (*Ant* 13 § 324) as Jannaeus having arranged his rule as it seemed advantageous to him (συμφέρειν αὐτῷ), following which he set off at war against the Greek cities of Palestine – no justification offered; συμφέρειν αὐτῷ was, apparently, enough. This is what kings do, "should do" if you wish. Neither the king's murder of his brother nor his war are condemned; they are, in context, steps just as reasonable as the respect the king allows those who stay out of his way.

Similarly, when Alexander died and was replaced by his widow, Salome Alexandra, Josephus' account makes the same values clear.[13] Namely, she had two sons, of whom Hyrcanus was said to have been unsuited for public office; but it was Hyrcanus whom she indeed appointed to public office, the high priesthood. Aristobulus, whose active character contrasted with that of Hyrcanus, she confined to private life. The parallel narratives in this case are worthy of closer

---

[12] For the term's Thucydidean background, see Nestle 1926 and Ehrenberg 1947. In Josephus, it appears only in *Antiquities*, including three times of Hyrcanus II (13 § 408; 14 §§ 6,13); cf. below, Part 3.

[13] It may be, as Marcus notes on *Ant* 13 § 321 (LCL), that Salome was already said to have followed the same policy upon the death of her first husband too; see also Sievers 1989: 135.

examination. According to *JW* 1 § 107, Alexandra easily won the affection of the populace. In § 108, however, we also read that she took firm hold of the government (ἐκράτησεν τῆς ἀρχῆς). Thereafter, in § 109, we read as follows:

> She had two sons from Alexander: the elder, Hyrcanus, due to his age she appointed high priest, as well as because he was too lethargic to give trouble about the whole, but the younger, Aristobulus, due to his hotheadedness she kept as a private person.

What Josephus seems to mean is that Salome appointed to the high priesthood the son who could be expected not to cause her any trouble about "the whole," i.e., the whole Hasmonean patrimony: high priesthood *plus kingship*.[14] She couldn't be high priest, but she did not want any trouble about remaining queen. From Aristobulus she feared such trouble, and she eventually got it (*Ant* 13 §§ 422ff).

In *JW* 1 § 107, referring to her piety and popularity, it is clear that Josephus was saying something positive about Salome. What of §§ 108-9? Steve Mason has recently claimed, in reference to this passage, that "Alexandra was commended for her judicious treatment of her sons. She gave the high priesthood to Hyrcanus because he was older and more subdued (νωθέστερον); Aristobulus, by contrast, was a 'hot-head' (θερμότητα, *JW* 1 §§ 109, 117) and would have been unsuitable for office" (Mason 1991: 251-52). However, νωθέστερον does not mean merely "subdued," which might only mean "disciplined" and so go well with "suitable for office," and the point of §§ 108-109 is not that Hyrcanus was suitable for the position he got but, rather, that he was so unenterprising that he could be depended upon not to seek more. Salome did what rulers do: they make sure to keep the competition under control. Salome had to appoint someone high priest, so she appointed the son who would pose no threat.

This point is made even more strongly, however, in the parallel at *Ant* 13 §§ 407-8. Here, Hyrcanus is first characterized by the clearly negative word ἀσθενής: he was too weak for government, while Aristobulus was "a man of action and of high spirit (δραστήριός τε ἦν καὶ θαρσαλέος)." Then, Josephus tells us that Alexandra appointed

---

[14] Thackeray apparently obscures some of Josephus' intent. Hyrcanus is said to have been νωθέστερον ἢ ὥστε ἐνοχλεῖν περὶ τῶν ὅλων, which Thackeray rendered "too lethargic to be troubled about public affairs" (*JW* 1 § 109 LCL). But ἐνοχλεῖν is in the active voice and περὶ τῶν ὅλων does not simply mean "about public affairs."

Hyrcanus to the high priesthood, due to his age "but however much more" (πολὺ μέντοι πλέον) due to his inaction (ἄπραγμον). That is, in comparison with *War*, in *Antiquities* Hyrcanus looks even less like a politician, while Aristobulus' energetic nature has improved, in comparison with *War*, from "hotheadedness" to being "a man of action and high spirit." Mason takes these changes to mean that Josephus no longer commends Salome; rather, "the implication is that Aristobulus ought to have been given the executive power" (Mason 1991: 252). In fact, however, these changes seem to mean just the opposite: they explain all the better why Salome appointed whom she appointed and feared whom she feared. Hyrcanus was really no threat; Aristobulus was real competition, and had to be dealt with as such.

Correspondingly, note that while in *War* Salome is said to have made Hyrcanus high priest due to his age and due to his harmless character, in *Antiquities* the first criterion, the one which makes Hyrcanus the rightful and legitimate candidate, is in the shadow of the other: "however much more" it was the matter of political expedience which moved Salome. This, indeed, was what was to be expected from the ruler whose reign Josephus would later summarize, as we have seen, as a strong lover of power (*Ant* 13 §§ 430-31).

Several more comparisons between *War* and *Antiquities* will show how thoroughgoing this distinction is.

At *JW* 1 § 117, we read that when Alexandra was taken ill, Aristobulus decided to seize the opportunity; with his numerous followers, he took possession of the fortresses and the money in them, used the latter to recruit mercenaries, and proclaimed himself king. That is, a self-serving putsch. In *Ant* 13 §§ 422-23, in contrast, he went to the fortresses where his father's friends were stationed, out of fear that — due to his brother's incapacity (ἀδύνατον) — the whole people (τὸ πᾶν γένος — so, not "family" as Marcus in LCL) might come under the control of the Pharisees. And it is not said that he proclaimed himself king. That is, Aristobulus is not said to have been a rebel, and he is said to have done what he assumed needed to be done for the good of the nation and the state, given his brother's weakness. And he did it in continuity with the dynasty: in contrast to *War*, we hear not of Aristobulus' followers and his mercenaries, but, rather, of his operating in concert with his father's friends.

Similarly, at *Ant* 14 § 44, defending himself before Pompey against the charge of usurpation, Aristobulus emphasizes that he had taken over power out of fear that due to his brother's being ineffective and hence contemptible, others might take over the realm; and he emphasized that his title was the same as that of his father. He had done what was necessary (ἐξ ἀνάγκης); Hyrcanus had not. The passage is unparalleled in *War*, and in Diodorus 40.2 (Stern 1974-84: no. 64), presumably based on a common source, where the scene before Pompey is described, Aristobulus' arguments are not given. Thus, they are Josephus' own contribution.

Again, when Aristobulus' son Antigonus appeared before Caesar, both of Josephus' accounts agree that he complained about the death of his father and the takeover of rule by Hyrcanus and Antipater (*JW* 1 §§ 195-96; *Ant* 14 § 140). But only the former version criticizes Antigonus for complaining against Hyrcanus and Antipater, saying that he ought to have confined himself to complaints against Caesar's enemies who had killed his father and brother; Antigonus, according to *War*, should not have mixed in "jealous pathos." In *Antiquities*, in contrast, there is no criticism of Antigonus for his complaint against Hyrcanus and Antipater, and, moreover, his complaint is made more political: whereas *War* has Antigonus complaining about having been banished together with his siblings from his native land (πατρίου γῆς), *Antiquities* has him complaining about his being thrown out of rule (τῆς ἀρχῆς ἐκβεβλημένου); nothing is said of his siblings. That is, in *War* Antigonus has a humanitarian plea and it is criticized, while in *Antiquities* he has a political plea and it is not criticized or characterized as being a result of jealousy. All politicians are supposed to seek office actively, and for the Josephus of *Antiquities*, it is good and praiseworthy for Hasmoneans to do so.

Apart from the vigorous politicians, *Ant* 14 also supplies us with examples of the other legitimate option: like Hyrcanus' uncle Absalom, one can choose not to participate in politics. There are four main examples. The first is supplied by Hyrcanus himself: according to *Ant* 14 § 6, Hyrcanus agreed to live unpolitically (ζῆν ἀπραγμόνως), just as Absalom once did (ἀπραγμόνως ζῆν – *Ant* 13 § 323). Had he kept to this agreement, Hyrcanus would have been just as praiseworthy. In the parallel at *JW* 1 § 122, in contrast, Hyrcanus is said to have been given a position of significance in the royal court: "the king's brother," along with all the honors pertaining thereto. While the truth of that statement may be debated (Laqueur 1920: 134-35; Schalit 1938-39), truth is of no significance here; what is important is that Josephus begins *Ant* 14 by showing how, in his mind, things could or should have been. From then on it is all downhill.

The next two cases of praiseworthy withdrawal from politics come during the siege of Jerusalem by Hyrcanus and Aretas. First, we read that when the siege began, it was the Passover season, so the most respectable Jews (οἱ δοκιμώτατοι τῶν Ἰουδαίων) left the country and fled to Egypt (*Ant* 14 § 21). Apparently, respectable Jews need take no share in the struggle.[15] Correspondingly, second, one especially pious Jew, Onias, hid himself when he saw the στάσις was continuing strongly (§ 22); apparently, he had been unwilling or unable to flee. When Hyrcanus' men caught him and asked him to curse Aristobulus and his fellow stasis-makers (συστασιαστῶν – § 22), his response was a prayer to God asking Him to help neither side. In other words, the Jewish religion – the realm of good and evil – has nothing to do with politics; and God indeed steps in only when some of Hyrcanus' men killed Onias (§ 25).[16]

The fourth case of respectable religionists who are not involved in affairs of state comes a few pages later, in the appeals made to Pompey. Here, alongside of Hyrcanus and Aristobulus who each appealed for the royal crown, a third group, termed "the nation" (ἔθνος – *Ant* 14 § 41), is said to have argued against both of them, claiming that the brothers were trying to change the native custom, which was government by priests, not by kings.

Thus, to summarize, *Antiquities* consistently teaches that politics is a nasty game, and one should either play it as it is to be played or leave it; Hyrcanus did neither. He was by nature unsuited to political life but did not leave it; the result was that during most of his career he engaged in στάσις against his brother, a στάσις which provided for the loss of the Hasmonean state and the Herodian takeover.

---

[15] When such people reappear in *Ant* 14 § 43 in support of Hyrcanus, the explanation is immediately given: they had been "procured" by Antipater. The true position of the Jewish people in that story is "a plague on both your houses;" see below.

[16] It is noteworthy that Josephus introduces here, via τούτῳ τῷ τρόπῳ, a story which explains the ensuing drought as punishment not – as per the introduction – for the murder of Onias, but, rather, for a desecration of the Temple cult. That story too, in turn, as the preceding story about Onias, has talmudic parallels; cf. Derenbourg 1867: 112-15; Cohen 1986: 13. Josephus' own interpretation is given in the introduction (*Ant* 14 § 25). As Marcus (LCL) points out, the fact that there are two separate references to the Passover festival (§§ 21, 25) is further indication of the source-splicing here.

To make this picture clear, Josephus not only repeatedly contrasts the active and effectual Aristobulus to the phlegmatic and ineffective Hyrcanus, but also shows us, time and again, a Hyrcanus who is a totally incompetent player in the arena he refuses to leave, a schlemiel. In *Ant* 14 §§ 4-7 he is completely deserted and flees alone to the citadel in Jerusalem, where he finds members of Aristobulus' family but fails to take them hostage, in the end completely capitulating to his brother (contrast *JW* 1 §§ 120-22, where he *and followers* take them hostage and trade them for a respectable compromise); at *Ant* 14 § 18 he promises to give Aretas territory and cities conquered by his father, something which, as we have seen, Josephus in *Ant* 13 § 431 and 14 § 77 regards as catastrophic (nothing like this in *JW* 1 § 126); at *Ant* 14 §§ 30-31 Hyrcanus can't even bribe and negotiate convincingly, but Aristobulus can (*JW* 1 § 128 has only Aristobulus bribing), just as *Ant* 14 §§ 34-36 has only Aristobulus bribing; at *Ant* 14 § 58 he has no party of supporters, only Aristobulus does (in *JW* 1 § 142 they both do);[17] at *Ant* 14 § 82 he is said to have been incapable of withstanding Alexander (unsaid in *JW* 1 § 160); at *Ant* 14 § 165 he is so unaware of his own interests that he ignores or is even pleased to learn that Antipater has given his gifts to Roman officials as if they were his own (*JW* 1 § 208 has him jealous and resentful of the growing popularity of Antipater and his sons); correspondingly, according to *Ant* 14 § 179 after Herod's aborted trial Hyrcanus still did nothing to stop Herod, due to his "cowardice and folly" (*JW* 1 § 212 has him stymied by real danger — ["the greater strength of the enemy"]); etc. Had such a person left politics, like Absalom or the religionists of *Ant* 14 §§ 21-24,41, he would have been praiseworthy; staying in, which resulted in στάσις and then in a Herodian takeover, bring upon him condemnation.

There are, then, apart from plain pro-Hasmoneanism, three elements which inform Josephus' understanding of Hyrcanus II in *Antiquities*; two are matters of principle and one is empirical. Josephus condemns στάσις assumes politics are divorced from religion, and condemns Hyrcanus for attempting to succeed in politics while being incapable of it. Where did he get these three points? The first is very Josephan (Bilde 1979: 190-91; Rajak 1983: 91-96). Beginning in the

---

[17] So too in Cassius Dio 37.15.2 (M. Stern 1974-84:no. 406). To point up the slant in *War*, it is interesting that in Dio's whole long account of Pompey's conquest of Jerusalem there is no mention of Antipater.

very preface of *War*, Josephus saw internal στάσις as the cause of the worst catastrophe ever to hit the Jews (*JW* 1 § 10). The theme reappears ceaselessly, including, specifically, as the explanation for the fall of the Hasmoneans (Pompey was drawn in by the διαστασιάσαντες of the last Hasmoneans – *JW* 1 § 19) and the institution of direct Roman rule (due to the people having κατεστασίασεν after Herod's death – § 20); in the *Life* too (§ 100) we find the notion that the Romans could expect the struggle of rival Jewish factions (πρὸς ἀλλήλους στάσεσιν) to bring about their destruction. So it was very natural for Josephus to apply this notion also to the particular catastrophe with which we are dealing here, viz., the end of the Hasmonean state and its replacement by Herod's kingdom. The second element too, namely, the separation of religion from state, is also a typically Josephan point in *Antiquities* (and his other works), as I have argued elsewhere (1983-84: 42-52; 1992: 29-56). The third element, however, the empirical point about Hyrcanus' constitution and capabilities, Josephus seems to have inherited from Nicolaus. But for Nicolaus the implication was very different. To this we must briefly turn.

3. *Nicolaus on Hyrcanus II*

In describing Hyrcanus, Nicolaus had to deal with a delicate problem. He had to describe him positively enough to be a worthy patron for Antipater and Herod, someone whose legitimacy would be transferred to the Antipatrids.[18] However, the reason for the transfer had to be made clear; the usurpation had to be justified. He accomplished these goals in three ways. First, of course, Nicolaus expended tremendous energy on exalting Antipater and his sons, including – as Motzo (1927) emphasized – transferring many of Hyrcanus' accomplishments to them. Second, while Nicolaus frequently notes Hyrcanus' non-political nature, he praises his character: right at the outset of *Ant* 14, Hyrcanus' tendency not to believe slander is characterized as a result of his decency and kindness (χρηστὸς ὢν...δι' ἐπιείκειαν); only undiscerning observers might conclude that he was ignoble and unmanly (ἀγεννῆ καὶ ἄνανδρον – *Ant* 14 § 13).[19]

---

[18] This happens implicitly throughout the story, explicitly at *JW* 1 § 244//*Ant* 14 §§ 325-26, where Hyrcanus recommends "Herod and his men" to Mark Antony.

[19] In further support of the assumption that this assessment derives from Nicolaus, recall that *Ant* 14 § 179 in fact attributes Hyrcanus' inability to move

Thus, for Nicolaus, Antipater and Herod were both active individuals (Antigonus: δραστήριος ἀνὴρ – JW 1 § 226; Herod: φύσει δραστήριος – JW 1 § 204), just as much as Aristobulus was; they contrast with
Hyrcanus, whose φύσις was different. But it is interesting that while
Antipater is once termed δραστήριος in War (1 § 226) and Herod –
twice (1 §§ 204,283), Aristobulus is never described this way. Rather,
the same quality is named by the negative term θερμότης (JW 1 § 109)
– "hot-headed." In Antiquities, in contrast, while all the War passages
are paralleled, Herod is never termed δραστήριος and the one time
Antipater is (14 § 8) the word is glossed by καὶ στασιαστής, giving it
a very negative valence, as we have seen. Rather, now it is Aristobulus
who is termed δραστήριος (13 § 407; 14 § 13) – no longer "hot-headed." This reversal is not just a fluke. What we see is two historians
sharing the same perception that the δραστήριος should rule; one unfit
for rule should not. For Josephus, the one who should have ruled was
Aristobulus; for Nicolaus, it was Antipater and Herod. But as for the
one unfit for rule, Josephus was freer to attack him; Nicolaus needed
Hyrcanus to legitimize Antipater. So it is only in Josephus' Antiquities,
as we have noted (n. 12), that the contrast becomes complete, only
there that Hyrcanus is portrayed as ἀπράγμων, opposite the δραστήριος.

For Nicolaus, then, Antipater and Herod justifiably stepped in, first
at Hyrcanus' side and then in his stead. They did what had to be done.
But for Josephus, an incapable Hasmonean should have been replaced
by the capable one, not by an Idumean. Note, for example, that
according to JW 1 § 124 Antipater encouraged and convinced Hyrcanus to seek the restoration of the kingdom which was duly his, whereas
according to Ant 14 §§ 8-14 Antipater was moved by jealousy and fear
for himself, and his main appeal to Hyrcanus was on the basis of the
false charge that Aristobulus was plotting to kill Hyrcanus. That is, in
War Nicolaus had Antipater doing what had to be done to protect the
legitimate ruler of the Hasmonean state; in Antiquities, Josephus has
Antipater looking out for himself.

---

against Herod to the former's ἀνανδρία and ἀνοία (unmanliness and folly). This
latter passage, however, is a Josephan composition, a result of his new use in
Antiquities of the tradition which had Herod summoned to the Sanhedrin (see
below). So Josephus himself viewed Hyrcanus as "unmanly," leaving the statement
at 14 § 13 to Nicolaus. As we have noted, in Part 2, Nicolaus himself explained
Hyrcanus' failure to move against Herod as a result of Herod's objective advantage (JW 1 § 212).

The same contrast reappears between *JW* 1 § 203 and *Ant* 14 §§ 157-58. In *War*, we find Antipater taking measures to organize the country, for he saw that Hyrcanus was too phlegmatic (νωθῆ) and without the energy needed for kingship (βασιλείας ἀτονώτερον). Note well: a statement has been made only about Hyrcanus' qualities as a king, and Antipater is doing what has to be done for the country. But in the parallel at *Ant* 14 §§ 157-58, we read only that when Antipater saw that Hyrcanus was dull and phlegmatic (βραδὺν καὶ νωθῆ) he appointed his own sons as governors. That is, a general statement condemning Hyrcanus (not just qua king) is followed by a report that Antipater took advantage of him. In *War*, presumably following Nicolaus, Antipater has responsibly stepped in to fill a power vacuum. In *Antiquities*, in contrast, Josephus has Antipater taking advantage of a weak sovereign.[20]

The latter two contrasts (*JW* 1 § 124//*Ant* 14 §§ 8-14; *JW* 1 § 203//*Ant* 14 §§ 157-58) are precisely the reverse of what we saw above regarding Aristobulus' putsch at the end of his mother's life. In that case, according to *War* Aristobulus self-seekingly took advantage of her weakness, while *Antiquities* has him looking out for the realm; here, with regard to Antipater, the caretaker of the state in *War* has been replaced by the self-seeking climber in *Antiquities*. The explanation, clearly, is that *War* is Nicolaus' version while *Antiquities* is Josephus'; for the Josephus of *Antiquities*, as we have seen, it is always good for a male Hasmonean to do what must be done to maintain office. This role reversal corresponds precisely to what we have seen above with regard to δραστήριος and θερμότης.

So far, then, we have seen that Nicolaus presented Antipater as Hyrcanus' faithful right-hand man and Hyrcanus as a good man who needed Antipater's help. That wouldn't do, however, for the relationship between Herod and Hyrcanus, for Herod eventually replaced and killed Hyrcanus. To cover this, Nicolaus provided an episode which supplied Herod with some justification: the episode of Herod's trial, one of the most confusing episodes in all of the parallel narratives of *JW* 1 and *Ant* 14 (Laqueur 1920: 171-86; Gilboa 1979-80; Efron 1987: 190-97). In *War* the story begins at 1 § 208: after reporting Herod's success in suppressing banditry in the Syrian borderlands, Josephus

---

[20] This difference between the two narratives is missed by Helm 1921: 509, who views *JW* 1 §§ 109,203 as simply agreeing with *Ant* 14 § 158.

comments that "In success (εὐπραγίαις) it is impossible to escape jealousy (φθόνον)." Then he goes on to report how Hyrcanus' jealousy and resentment was aroused by Herod's success, and fanned by malicious courtiers, until, after gradual inflammation, Hyrcanus' rage exploded and he summoned Herod to trial (1 § 210). This is very reminiscent of *JW* 1 § 67, where John Hyrcanus I's successes (εὐπρα-γίας), and those of his sons, aroused the envy (φθόνος) of the Jews, which grew until the smoldering flames burst out into open war. But that passage clearly derives from Nicolaus (as results not only from our general assumptions about *JW* 1 but also from specific local consider-ations[21]), and so we may safely assume that §§ 208-210 do too.

As the *War* story proceeds, we read that Herod went up to Jerusa-lem but escaped judgement due to the intervention of Sextus Caesar, the governor of Syria, who ordered Hyrcanus to release Herod. Herod assumed that his escape was contrary to Hyrcanus' wishes (*JW* 1 § 212), and – after Sextus Caesar appointed him governor of Coele-Syria and Samaria – planned to march upon Jerusalem and depose Hyrca-nus. From this, however, he was dissuaded by his father and brother,

---

[21] See D. R. Schwartz 1983: 158-59. I will respond briefly to two critiques. (1) Mason (1991: 222-227) has taken issue with my analysis of the parallel at *Ant* 13 § 288, claiming that Josephus authored it without help from Nicolaus. But at pp. 222-23 he apparently admits, in any case, that the statement in *JW* 1 § 67 is indeed to be traced to Nicolaus. Moreover, it is difficult to accept Mason's analysis of *Ant* 13 § 288-298, which concludes (p. 245) that Josephus could author the defamatory statement about the Pharisees at 13 § 288 because by oversight he failed to see that the traditional story he thereafter inserted had a pro-Pharisaic point of view. (2) In a lecture at the 1991 conference of the American Association for Jewish Studies, Professor David Williams argued that, judging from the use of a particle and two prepositions (γάρ, κατά and πρός) and its comparison to a data-base compiled from compositions by Nicolaus and Josephus, Josephus seems to have been the "final author" of *Ant* 13 § 288. Professor Williams kindly sent me a copy of the yet-unpublished paper, entitled "The Authorship of Anti-Phari-saic Material in *Antiquities*: A Stylometric Analysis." In response, we note that, even apart from the doubts one has about the appropriateness of statistical analysis for such a short text, the fact remains that, as Williams stipulates, "[Josephus] may have worked from source material when writing them." Thus, the point seems nugatory. In general, agreements, contradictions and changes in point-of-view, along with usage of striking vocabulary, appear to be better guides for source-analysis in ancient historiography; the methods which Williams applied were developed, as he indicates, not for the study of writers who used sources but, rather, for the identification of political essayists, each of whom has a well-identi-fied corpus of writings known with security to have been written independently. We have neither for Josephus nor Nicolaus.

arguing that he ought to spare the king under whom he had gained great power, and be grateful, for the present, for having escaped with his life. That is, Hyrcanus — moved by envy — had persecuted Herod, and Herod had exercised a noble forgiveness in sparing him for the present. When the time will come, Herod will be more justified in replacing the old man.[22]

Nicolaus' approach is made clear by the contrast with Josephus' version in *Antiquities*, which is influenced by a Jewish tradition of Herod's trial (cf. *b. Sanhedrin* 19a); there is no trial in the *War* version. Here, first of all, Herod poses a true threat, and it is the leading Jews (*Ant* 14 § 163) and the members of the Sanhedrin, not malicious courtiers, who initiate the move against him. In *Antiquities*, correspondingly, Hyrcanus — as noted above — is not jealous of Herod; the threat, as Laqueur emphasized so well (1920: 171-84), is to the state, not to Hyrcanus,[23] and Hyrcanus, who should have been responsible for the state, fails to recognize the threat. In fact, Hyrcanus secretly connives with Herod in managing the latter's escape (§ 177), thus eliminating the notion (*JW* 1 § 212) that Herod might think that Hyrcanus opposed his escape. Consequently, Herod's planned attack was not against Hyrcanus, as in *JW* 1 § 214, but, rather, against Jerusalem (*Ant* 14 § 181) — whose court had attempted to condemn him. (At this point [*Ant* 14 § 181], Josephus reverts to Nicolaus' version, where the enemy was Hyrcanus, not the Sanhedrin.)

Thus, the difference between Josephus and Nicolaus is, that while they both agree that Hyrcanus was ineffective when Antipater was at his side (Josephus condemning Hyrcanus for staying in the race and Nicolaus praising Antipater for serving his master well), when push came to shove and Hyrcanus, as ruler of the Hasmonean state, had to

---

[22] Unfortunately, it is not clear whether we have Nicolaus' account of Hyrcanus' death, for the account in *JW* 1 §§ 433-34 is so anti-Herodian that Stern (1991: 451) doubts it is Nicolaus'. Of the two accounts in *Ant* 15 §§ 165-78, one is attributed in § 174 to "Herod's memoirs," whatever that means, and the other is attributed to unnamed others who are hostile to Herod.

[23] Helm's complaint (1921: 510), that Laqueur's distinction is artificial since *Ant* 14 § 167 has the prominent Jews complaining not only that Herod did what only the Sanhedrin may do, but also that he executed his victims without Hyrcanus' permission, is hardly to the point. The point is that at the parallel at *JW* 1 § 209 there is no reference to the Sanhedrin, and that the new reference to it, in *Ant* 14 § 167, results in a self-contradiction — which points up the composite nature of the narrative there.

stand up against Herod, Josephus condemns him for failing to stand up. Nicolaus, in contrast, has Hyrcanus, motivated by jealousy and not by interests of state, initiate the persecution of Herod, thus exculpating Herod for later responding in kind.

4. *Conclusion*

In summary, we may say that in rewriting the history of this period for his *Antiquities*, Josephus imposed upon it the interpretational device of στάσις just as in his earlier work στάσις by those who failed to recognize the Roman facts of life had explained the final catastrophe of the Second Temple period, so too στάσις between those who failed to recognize the Roman and Antipatrid facts of life it is made to explain the fall of the Hasmoneans and the takeover by Rome and the Herodians. That στάσις was the struggle between the two sons of Salome Alexandra, and should have been avoided by the retirement from politics of Hyrcanus, who by nature was unfit to rule; had he stayed out of politics he would have been respected. He did not retire, however, and the struggle which ensued allowed for the Roman takeover. Moreover, after the Romans removed Aristobulus from the arena, Hyrcanus' incapacity prevented him from dealing with the new competition. Josephus turned the notion of Hyrcanus' incapacity, which Nicolaus had applied – invented? – in order to explain and justify the rise of the Antipatrids, not into a weapon to condemn the Antipatrids, as Laqueur thought, but into one to condemn Hyrcanus, and blame him for the fall of the Jewish national state.

JOSEPHUS' DESCRIPTION OF THE JERUSALEM TEMPLE: WAR, *ANTIQUITIES*, AND OTHER SOURCES

Lee I. Levine

Historians of antiquity often bemoan the fact that they are severely limited by the paucity of sources at their disposal. They wish for more but, alas, all are compelled to focus on the relatively small amount of sources available, analyzing and dissecting every piece of information to the fullest. Colleagues of the modern period are faced with the opposite problem; inundated with sources, they often have to make difficult decisions about what to *exclude*.

There is no simple solution to the quandary besetting the historian of antiquity, for even where there are sources available one always has to ask how representative these sources are, and how reflective they are of the society at large. At times, one may fall into the trap of assuming the historicity of an event or the accuracy of a depiction offered by a given source, and this is in large part due to the fact that it is nowhere contradicted or that there is no other means by which to measure its veracity. All too often credibility follows in the wake of availability.

On the other hand, the very existence of a number of different sources dealing with a specific topic does not assure an accurate reading of reality. Several sources dealing with the same subject may be contradictory and problematic, making it almost impossible to determine which, if any, of them is the more reliable. For example, the varying descriptions of the Jerusalem sanhedrin in Greek and Hebrew sources have led scholars over the generations to formulate a bewildering array of opinions on the subject (Mantel 1965: 54-101). An even more perplexing example of historical sources at seemingly cross purposes has to do with the Jerusalem Temple. The importance of the Temple and its centrality to Jewish society are well documented. Throughout the Second Temple period this institution served as the heart of Judean life, not only in terms of cult and ritual, but politically, socially, judicially, and culturally as well (Jeremias 1969: 27ff, 51ff, 73ff, 126ff). It is not surprising, therefore, that the Temple has been described in a variety of ways by Hellenistic and Roman authors such as Hecataeus (*AgAp* 1 § 197-99; Stern 1974-84: 1.39), Agatharchides (*AgAp* 1 § 209; Stern 1974-84: 1.107), Aristeas,[1] the writers of the Temple Scroll (Yadin 1977-83: 1.179-276; 2.129-200), and Tacitus (*Histories* 5.12.1; Stern 1974-84: 2.30, 57). The sources they have left us are at times cryptic, general, ambiguous or, alternatively, incredibly detailed; it is not always clear whether they were describing something real or painting an idealized portrait.[2]

Two literary sources – Josephus[3] and the Mishnah (*m. Mid.* 1-5. See Holtzmann 1913; Hollis 1934) – present a comprehensive picture of what appears to have been Herod's Temple of the first century CE. However, in examining these two sources we see that there is a minimal amount of agreement between them. Discrepancies are in evidence at every turn: the size of the Temple Mount, the number of outer gates, the size of the stones used in constructing the walls, the number of stairs leading up to the sacred precincts, the number and location of the inner gates, the plan and size of the inner gates, the height of the Temple and its doors, etc. Disagreement is apparent regarding specific details as well, for example, the location of the large Corinthian brass gate or of Nicanor's Gate (if indeed they are not one and the same[4]) and the size, shape and location of the Women's Court.

Upon further scrutiny our problem becomes even more complicated. It is one thing to try and reconcile diverse sources, it is quite another to reconcile contradicting information within a specific source. The discrepancies between Josephus' *War* and *Antiquities*, for example, are not insignificant. *JW* 5 § 192 reports that the area of the Temple

---

[1] *Ep. Arist.* 83-99. Cf. Bonfil 1972: 133; Vincent 1908-09.

[2] Some have opined that Josephus' description of the Temple courts of Solomon (*Ant* 8 §§ 95-98) in fact reflects those in the time of Herod. See Thackeray's comments in the LCL to *Ant* 5 §§ 622-23. See, however, the comments of Yadin 1977-83: 1.192-194. For other Second Temple descriptions of the pre-Herodian Temple, see Yadin 1977-83: 1.194-196. Convenient bibliographies relating to studies on the Temple may be found in Feldman 1984: 438-444; Purvis 1988: 1.178-192.

[3] *JW* 5 §§ 184-247; *Ant* 15 §§ 380-425. On Josephus' account of the Temple's construction, see Horbury 1991: 108-115.

[4] On this question, see now J. Schwartz 1991 and bibliography cited there.

Mount enclosed by Herod measured six stades, *Ant* 15 § 400 four stades; *Ant* 15 § 418 speaks of triple inner gates, *JW* 5 § 202 of double gates. According to *Ant* 15 § 391 the Temple was 120 cubits high, *War* fixes it at 90 or 100 cubits;[5] *Ant* 15 § 418 describes an undisclosed number of gates to the north and south of the Temple precincts and one to the east; *JW* 5 §§ 198-99 mentions eight to the north and south and four to the east and speaks of the separation of men and women upon entering the sacred precincts; *Ant* 15 §§ 418-19 instead speaks of men and women entering these precincts together.

The Mishnaic account of Tractate Middot also contains contradictory information. At various stages the Mishnah speaks of five, seven, and thirteen gates leading to the sacred courts.[6] Not only do the numbers vary but so do the names of some of these gates (cf. *m. Mid.* 1:5 and 2:6). On occasion, variant descriptions are offered within the Mishnaic or Rabbinic literature: how the Israelite court was separated from the priestly one: by mosaics, a wall, or differing heights (*m. Mid.* 2:6); whether Nicanor's Gate was flanked by two smaller gates or by two offices (cf. *m. Mid.* 1:4 and 2:6); which offices and gates stood to the north and south of the Temple building (cf. *m. Mid.* 5:3-4 and *b. Yoma* 19a).

There is no limit to the ingenuity of scholars in dealing with these baffling discrepancies. Only a few have opted for the priority of the Mishnah over Josephus for one or more of the following reasons: it is a halakhic document and therefore its details are precise; much evidence in it is attributed to R. Eliezer b. R. Jacob of the mid- to late first century and can therefore be presumed accurate, as the rabbis were keen to record a meticulous description of the Temple.[7]

More often, however, the primacy of Josephus' descriptions has been assumed owing to the fact that he was a priest living in Jerusalem during the last decades of the Second Temple period and was thus a first-hand witness; owing to his claims to accuracy as a professional

---

[5] *JW* 5 §§ 207, 209. Within *JW* there appears to be some confusion with the above two numbers cited. Moreover, in one place (§ 207) the back of the Temple building is described as narrower than the front; in other places, the same width (§§ 209, 215).

[6] See *m. Mid.* 1:1 (5 gates); 1:4 (7 gates); and 2:6 (13 gates; see also *m. Sheqalim* 6:2). For various attempts to explain this discrepancy, see *b. Tamid* 27a.

[7] Hildesheimer 1876-77; Klein 1939: 132-133; Kaufman 1977: 66. See also Hollis 1934: 18-20 and the comments of Luria 1968: 3-14.

historian; and, by default, owing to the rabbis' proclivity to idealize their descriptions with data taken from earlier (i.e., Biblical) periods.[8] Few historians have specified which of Josephus' depictions they prefer. Perhaps many were unaware of the scope and gravity of the internal contradictions and, as a result, they merely lumped together evidence from both *Antiquities* and *War*. Only on rare occasion has the issue of Josephus' contradictory evidence been raised. Recently, both Busink (1978-80: 2.36ff) and E. P. Sanders (1992: 59-60) have explicitly stated their preference for the description in *War*.

Another approach to this problem of reconciling the variant data has been to accept the reliability of both sources and then to try and resolve the differences between them. This approach claims that the Mishnah is to be relied upon for all descriptions of the Temple's *inner* sacred precincts, as it was this aspect of the Temple Mount complex that was of primary concern to the sages and, at the same time, accords credence to Josephus' descriptions regarding the surrounding Temple Mount (Avi-Yonah 1956: 396-397).

However, a second, more popular approach has been adopted, wherein the descriptions in Josephus and the Mishnah are assigned to different historical periods. Thus, it has been assumed that Josephus speaks of the first-century Temple while the Mishnah relates to a pre-Herodian structure of the Hasmonean era (Magen 1980: 47-53) or, according to some, to the Temple of Zerubbabel in the Persian period.[9] All of these attempts must also take into consideration the archeological finds, which, of course, present their own set of problems (see below).

Into this maze of opinion and speculation we tread cautiously and hesitantly, knowing full well that a myriad of conceivable positions has been suggested to date. In what follows we will attempt to delineate an overall strategy for dealing with this problem, suggest an approach to reconcile the various sources, point out several problems that will still remain unexplained, and, finally, examine the ramifications of our

---

[8] Vincent and Stève 1954-56: 2.517-25; Simons 1952: 404-8, esp. 407-8; Holtzmann 1913: 3; Thackeray, LCL to *JW* 5 § 197 (p. 259 note e); Feldman 1984: 440; Feldman in Feldman and Hata 1987: 42; see also Wacholder 1979.

[9] Luria 1968: 14; Brand 1960: 212, 216. Cf. Feldman in Feldman and Hata 1987: 42-43.

suggestion vis-à-vis several wider issues within Jewish society of the first century. We suggest commencing with the more certain and reliable data at hand and then following with what we consider to be the less certain and reliable information.

Beginning with the archeological material — the evidence revealed in excavations since the mid-19th century, and especially during the last twenty-five years, is definitive although, admittedly, quite limited in scope. The following are three of the more salient pieces of data to be garnered from excavations of the southern and western sectors of the Temple Mount:

(1) Herod expanded the Temple Mount area to the south, west, and north. The measurements of these areas at the time of the destruction of Jerusalem can be calculated rather precisely: the western wall was 488m long, the southern 280m, the northern 315m, and the eastern 460m, all together — some 1550m in circumference.[10]

(2) The number of gates in the western and southern walls of the Temple Mount has been determined with certainty, four on the west and two on the south.[11]

(3) These gates served a variety of purposes, and each one seems to have been designated for a specific function. The two southern gates offered access to the sacred Temple precincts, and the gate above Robinson's Arch near the southwestern corner of the Temple Mount gave entrance to the royal stoa, which spanned almost the entire southern part of the Temple Mount. There may have been a similar entrance from the southeast, thereby affording access from the two entrances at either end of the basilica to those approaching the Temple Mount from the south for non-cultic purposes. Barclay's Gate on the west may also have led to the basilica area, while two other western gates, further north, offered direct access to the Temple precincts: the gate associated with Wilson's Arch facilitated entry from the Upper City (for priests and other wealthy residents), and Warren's Gate gave entrance from the north and northwest of the Temple Mount (Ben-Dov 1982: 135-47).

In addition to the archeological material, we suggest assuming the intrinsic veracity of Josephus' descriptions of the Temple Mount — although given his propensity to exaggerate at times, and his inclination toward apologetics, his descriptions should always be taken with some degree of caution. The major difficulty in Josephus' accounts lies

---

[10] Vincent and Stève 1954-56: 2.528ff.; Simons 1952: 346; Busink 1978-80: 2.1005-1016; Ben-Dov 1982: 77.

[11] Vincent and Stève 1954-56: 2.539-53; Simons 1952: 357-69; Busink 1978-80: 2.951-79; Ben-Dov 1982: 135.

in the discrepancies between *War* and *Antiquities*, the most salient of which we have noted above. It would seem that the simplest and most reasonable explanation for these contradictions is that Josephus was, in fact, describing two different buildings, i.e., the Temple as it existed in two historical contexts. The *Antiquities* account reflects the Temple that Herod built ca. 20 BCE, while the *War* account reflects the Temple as known first-hand by Josephus and as viewed by Titus when he reached Jerusalem. In other words, it is the Temple described in *War* that was destroyed in 70.[12] The description of the Temple in the *Antiquities* account, at the end of Book 15, is set in the chronological context of Herod's reign; the *War* account in Book 5 describes the situation immediately following Titus' encampment by the walls of Jerusalem.

How, then, are we to explain the substantial differences between these two buildings? Here we have the good fortune of being aided by a variety of sources. While none clearly specifies what exactly was done during the eighty-year interim between the two periods described by Josephus, they do attest to the fact that the Temple building and the entire mount had undergone far-reaching renovations; ongoing repairs, alterations, and reconstruction appear to have been carried out during the course of the first century. References to these renovations are derived from independent sources and their combined impact is therefore all the more significant. In the gospel of John, the Jews responded to Jesus' claim, that were the Temple to be demolished he would rebuild it in three days, by saying: "It has taken forty-six years to build this Temple" (John 2:20)! It may thus be assumed that work on the Temple continued down to at least the mid-20s of the first century CE.

A second reference – from Rabbinic literature – alludes to construction work on the Temple Mount during the time of Rabban Gamaliel the Elder (fl. ca. 25-50 CE). While sitting on the monumental staircase south of the Temple (על גב המעלה בהר הבית) an Aramaic targum of Job was brought to him. Rabban Gamaliel ordered a construction worker to rebury it in one of the courses of the Temple wall.[13]

Finally, the best-known source regarding Temple repairs is Josephus himself, who speaks of the termination of work on the Temple Mount

---

[12] A point touched on by A. Büchler (1898: 678-682) but never developed.
[13] *t. Shabbat* 13.2 (Lieberman 57); Lieberman 1955-88: 3.204.

complex in 64 CE, which left no less than 18,000 workers unemployed.[14] Thus, on the basis of the above three sources, it appears reasonable to assume that extensive work was carried out on the Temple Mount complex during the 75-or-so years between the completion of the building (at least its first stage) by Herod and the termination of repair work in 64.[15]

In addition to the significant differences in the physical features of the Temple Mount attested by *War* in comparison with *Antiquities*, which we noted above (e.g., the doubling of the Temple Mount area and the design of the gates), the following changes may also be noted:[16]

(1) the number of inner gates increased significantly and they were modified from triple to double portals;

(2) the height of the Temple building was altered;

(3) the number of gates leading to the Temple's sacred precincts increased to twelve (Büchler 1898: 712-718);

(4) the so-called "Women's (or Outer) Court" became a walled-off area restricted now to women only;

(5) wealthy Diaspora Jews took a leading role in the lavish decoration of the Temple, as evidenced by Nicanor's Gate,[17] the gold-plating of the other gates by Alexander, an *alabarch* from Alexandria,[18] and the gifts of Helena and Monobaz (*m. Yoma* 3:10).

---

[14] *Ant* 20 § 219; Jeremias 1969: 22; Rhoads 1976: 82; Goodman 1987: 52-54; Rajak 1983: 124-125. Even after 64, there were plans to continue repairing and reconstructing the Temple. Agrippa II had timber brought from Lebanon to support the sanctuary and raise it another twenty cubits (*JW* 5 § 36).

[15] Cadoux 1937: 180-181 n. 6. On dating Herod's building itself, see Jeremias 1969: 21-22 n. 39; Schalit 1960: 194 and n. 744. Cf. Corbishley 1935: 26-27.

[16] See *JW* 5 §§ 192, 198-99, 202, 207, 209, 215; *Ant* 15 §§ 391, 400, 418-19 and n. 5 above.

[17] See *m. Yoma* 3:10; *t. Yoma* 2.4 (Lieberman 231); *y. Yoma* 3.41a; *b. Yoma* 38a; and J. Schwartz 1991. Some confusion exists over whether this gate's name derives from a donor (the usual assumption, but see Schwartz), and whether he was a Jerusalemite or an Alexandrian. Rabbinic literature claims the former (*b. Yoma* 38a) but Josephus and archeological evidence point to the latter, and this is undoubtedly correct. See *CIJ* 2.261-262 no. 1256; Kane 1978: 279-282. On Alexandrian artisans brought to Jerusalem, see *t. Yoma* 2.5 (Lieberman 231) and Lieberman 1955-88: 4.761.

[18] *JW* 5 § 206. Alexander was the father of Tiberius Alexander, praefect of Judea, and the brother of the Alexandrian Jewish philosopher Philo. Cf. *Ant* 18 § 259; on the lavish use of gold in the Temple, see Jeremias 1969: 24-25.

Given the basic credibility which we propose attaching to Josephus' descriptions of the Temple Mount, this material, in turn, may become a touchstone for evaluating other sources. Although we consider Mishnah Middot to be a less reliable historical source than Josephus regarding the Second Temple,[19] we find a not insignificant amount of material there in agreement with *War*. Both sources speak of a Women's Court, although many of the Mishnah's details are absent from *War*, and vice versa (*JW* 5 §§ 198-199; *m. Mid.* 2:5), each refers to a monumental eastern gate made of bronze,[20] a raven-chaser (*JW* 5 § 224; *m. Mid.* 4:6; see Lieberman 1950: 172-177), gold-plated doors (*JW* 5 §§ 201, 205, 207-208; *m. Mid.* 2:3), a series of steps leading from the Temple Mount to the sacred precincts and a ten-cubit wide terrace (חיל) at the top of the stairs (*JW* 5 §§ 196-197; *m. Mid.* 2:3), a chancel-screen around the sacred precincts (*JW* 5 § 193; *m. Mid.* 2:3), fifteen steps leading to the inner Israelite court and twelve from the priestly court to the Temple edifice (*JW* 5 §§ 206-207; *m. Mid.* 2:5; 3:6), identical measurements (100 x 100 cubits) for the Temple facade (*JW* 5 § 207; *m. Mid.* 4:6), the fact that the facade of the building was wider than the back parts,[21] the length of the sanctuary (היכל) and the Holy of Holies (40 and 20 cubits, respectively in *JW* 5 §§ 216, 219 and *m. Mid.* 4:7), three-storied chambers surrounding the Temple (*JW* 5 §§ 220-21; *m. Mid.* 4:3), a one-cubit high parapet separating the Israelite and priestly courts (at least according to one opinion in the Mishnah),[22] and an almost identical number of inner gates.[23] Thus, it would appear that much of what has been preserved in the Mishnah

---

[19] In addition to the relatively late final redaction of *m. Mid.* (5:4), its Biblical references (e.g., 2:1, 2:5, 3:1, 3:8, 4:1-2), and occasional internal disputes (2:5-6, 3:6, 4:6), it appears to have preserved material from the entire Second Temple period as the Temple went through periodic alterations. Yekonyâh's Gate (2:6) and the Shushan Gate (1:3) may well reflect the Persian period, references to Antiochus' persecutions the Hasmonean era (1:6, 2:3), and naming the Kiponos (Coponius?) Gate the early Roman period or the first century (1:3).

[20] Called a "Corinthian" gate in *JW* 5 §§ 201, 204 and Nicanor's Gate in *m. Mid.* 2:3.

[21] See *JW* 5 § 207; *m. Mid.* 4:7, although there is disagreement over how much this front part projected, 15 cubits on either side (*Middot*) or 20 (*JW*).

[22] *JW* 5 § 226; *m. Mid.* 2:6, following the opinion of R. Eliezer b. Jacob in the Mishnah.

[23] According to *JW* 5 §§ 198-199, there were twelve gates; according to Abba Yosi b. Hannan in *m. Mid.* 2:6, there were thirteen.

was indeed drawn from the immediate pre-70 reality.[24] Other material may reflect alternative traditions offering unsubstantiated filling-in of details or simply references to biblical sources (the disputes recorded in the Mishnah indicate how unclear some of these details were to later generations). It is also possible that some material may reflect either an earlier stage of reconstruction in the first century (cf. n. 19 above) or even a pre-Herodian structure.[25] For the present, however, such possibilities are only conjectural.

One of the most serious discrepancies we have been unable to account for relates to the area of the Temple Mount. Its perimeter, as reflected in archeological excavations (1550m), is far different from that spelled out in either *War* (ca. 1200m) or the Mishnah (1000m).[26] The difference between the actual site and Josephus' figure may be significantly reduced by assuming different measurements for the length of a stade (Josephus notes a circumference of 6 stades) or a generous margin of error. The Mishnah figure is surely influenced by Ezek 42:20.

---

[24] In numerous articles, Büchler has claimed that most Rabbinic traditions regarding the Temple reflect a time immediately preceding the outbreak of hostilities in 66 CE. See, for example, 1898; 1899: 61-62; and the chapters "On the History of the Temple Worship in Jerusalem" and "Family Purity and Family Impurity in Jerusalem before the Year 70 C.E." (1956: 24-98). A typical assertion of his is the following: "All these considerations should make it clear to us that the descriptions in the Mishnah of Tamid, Yoma, Pesahim, and Shekalim portray to us the newly organized divine service of the last decade before the destruction of the Temple" (1956: 63).

[25] For example, the number of stairs leading from the Temple Mount area to the sacred precincts, fourteen according to *JW* 5 §§ 197-198, and twelve according to *m. Mid.* 2:3; *JW* 5 § 197, 205 speaks of five additional stairs from the terrace (חיל) to the inner gates, an arrangement unknown to *m. Mid.*; *JW* 5 § 201 knows of doors plated in silver as well as gold, *m. Mid.* only of gold (2:3); *JW* 5 § 202 claims that the gates to the sacred area were 30 cubits high and 15 cubits wide), *m. Mid.* 2:3 speaks of 20 x 10; the door of the Temple porch (אולם) was 70 x 25 cubits according to *JW* 5 § 207, but only 40 x 20 cubits according to *m. Mid.* 3:7, although the height in Middot did not include five beams placed over the entrance; the door leading to the sanctuary (היכל) was 20 x 10 cubits (*m. Mid.* 4:1) or 55 x 16 cubits (*JW* 5 § 211); the size of the altar in *JW* is 50 x 50 cubits whereas that in *m. Mid.* is smaller, 32 x 32 cubits; the rules banning impure persons appear much stricter in *JW* than in *m. Mid.* (e.g. 5 § 227 and 2:5, respectively); *m. Mid.* 2:6 speaks of two entrances to the west of the Temple, *JW* knows of none (5 § 200); and, finally, the number of gates in the Women's Court -- one (*m. Mid.* 1:4, 2:6) or three (*JW* 5 §§ 198-199).

[26] Cf. above n. 10; *JW* 5 § 192; *m. Mid.* 2:1. See Simons 1952: 408ff.

The discrepancy regarding the number of gates leading to the Temple Mount likewise requires explanation. The one western gate mentioned in the Mishnah differs from the four offered by both archeological evidence and Josephus' accounts.[27] While many have opined that the Mishnah may reflect an earlier, pre-Herodian structure, the name Kiponos which it preserves (suggestively similar to the name of the Roman praefect Coponius of 6-9 CE) probably indicates a first-century setting.[28] Moreover, the discrepancy between the description of the Women's Court in the Mishnah (men and women together, a balcony erected during the Sukkot festival to separate the sexes, and four offices in each of the corners) and that in *War* (a separate walled-off section for women, with its own entrances) is also difficult to reconcile (*m. Mid.* 2:5; *JW* 5 §§ 198-199). Either the Mishnah portrays an imaginary reconstruction or it may represent an intermediate stage between the free mixing of men and women as described in *Antiquities* and the severe restrictions spelled out in *War*. If the latter be the case, the Mishnah would be referring to some intermediate stage in the first half of the first century CE. This possible reconstruction, however, may be logically sound but historically unrealistic.

Finally, let us turn to some of the implications of the above analysis on the wider issues facing Jewish society and Judaism of the first century. In the first place, it is eminently clear that throughout this period the Temple continued to retain its position as the central and focal institution of Jewish religious and political life. Partly as a result of the monumental archeological finds along the western and southern walls of the Temple Mount, there exists today a greater understanding and appreciation of the significant presence of the Temple in first-century Jewish life and its attraction and meaning for Jews in Jerusalem and Judea on the one hand, as well as for Diaspora Jewry on the other. During the pilgrimage festivals, tens if not hundreds of thousands of Jews from all over the world gathered at the Temple (Safrai 1965: 42-122). Temple-related matters such as priestly status, privileges and obligations, purity concerns, and details of the sacrificial cult had become more central to the Jewish religious agenda generally in late

---

[27] *m. Mid.* 1:3; *Ant* 15 § 410; and above n. 11.
[28] Klein 1939: 125; Holtzmann 1913: 50 (note); Hollis 1934: 245; Magen 1980: 45-47; Ben-Dov 1982: 140-141; Ben-Dov *et al.* 1983: 44-45.

Second-Temple Palestine. The various organized sects and other religious circles of the period often sought to define themselves in relationship to this central Jewish institution (S. J. D. Cohen 1984: 45-48; 1987: 106-7), and the concerns of the Temple helped define the agenda of many of these groups.

The dramatic increase in the number of Jews throughout the world — according to most estimates, ranging from about five to eight million, or one-tenth of the total population of the Empire — accorded the Temple an even greater degree of prominence. All Jews, whether in Israel or the Diaspora, whether Jews by birth or converts, viewed Jerusalem as their religious and ethnic center and as their mother city alongside their home cities.[29] The ongoing repairs and ornamentation of the Temple discussed above were a function of the growing and expanding populace which regarded this site as holy and of the enormous funds flowing into the city on a regular basis. The large numbers of people periodically flocking to Jerusalem also introduced substantial funds. As a result, the Temple grew in size and its embellishment from contributions, especially from Diaspora Jewry, continued unabated.

Moreover, the Temple continued to fulfill a wide range of religious needs, not only for the Jews at large but also for Nazirites, lepers, converts, and women after childbirth, thus reinforcing its primacy in Jewish consciousness.[30] Forces at work in and around the Temple, be they of Sadducean, aristocratic, Herodian or Pharisaic provenance, continued to make the necessary adjustments so that Temple ritual would remain accessible and focal in the lives of the people. It may not be coincidental that post-Herodian renovations of the building, as evidenced by the Mishnah and *War* descriptions, took many of these groups into consideration. The dramatic action taken by R. Simeon b. Gamaliel I with regard to the price of doves is a particularly illustrative case in point (*m. Ker.* 1:7; Büchler 1898: 702-4; E. P. Sanders 1992: 89). According to the Mishnah, prices had soared to such an extent that often women who could not afford to offer the prescribed sacrifices after miscarriages desisted from coming to the Temple. In the face of an explicit stipulation in the Torah to the contrary, R.

---

[29] *Sipre Deut* 354 (Finkelstein 416); Philo *Spec. Leg.* 1.12.68-70; *JW* 4 §§ 202-4.

[30] On Nazirites mentioned frequently in the first century, see *m. Nazir* 3:5, 6:11; *t. Nazir* 4.10 (Lieberman 140); cf. also *m. Nazir* 5:5; Acts 21:23-26; Büchler 1898: 697-702, and generally Sanders 1992: 70-92.

Simeon ruled that one dove would suffice for multiple miscarriages. As a result, the price of this commodity plummeted to 1/100 of its former rate and women were able to fulfill this obligation more readily.

On the other hand, this heightened degree of activity and the presence of increasing numbers of people, among them proselytes, semi-proselytes,[31] and perhaps even non-Jews, may have contributed to very different kinds of developments within the Temple precincts themselves. It would seem that one aspect of the religious ambience of first-century Jerusalem and its Temple was moving in the direction of exclusion and separatism.

A significant example in this regard is the public criticism by one Simeon of Agrippa I for entering the Temple precincts,[32] possibly owing to the king's problematic status as a descendant of converts.[33] Simeon's objections carried weight: succeeding to muster a considerable number of people in Jerusalem, he caused a stir and was immediately summoned to Caesarea for questioning by Agrippa. In the end, the king was placated — perhaps having been forced to capitulate — and not only released Simeon unpunished but even rewarded him with a gift! It has been suggested that this incident and others may reflect increased priestly dominance over both Temple affairs and Jerusalem religious life, possibly indicating a more severe and restrictive religious attitude and policy in general (D. R. Schwartz 1987a: 143).

The eighteen decrees enacted by Bet Shammai over the objections of Bet Hillel around the time of the outbreak of the rebellion in 66 also attest to the increasing xenophobia within certain Jewish circles. Most of these decrees were aimed at (or, at the very least, would have resulted in) the separation of Jew from non-Jew, as, for example, the one concerning the stipulation prohibiting the use of gentile oil (*y. Shabbat* 1.4.3c; Hoenig 1970: 63-75). The importance of purity issues in first-century Judaism has been emphasized by Büchler (1956: 64-98). While never absent from the Jewish agenda, and especially in the last centuries of the Second Temple period, these concerns may well have

---

[31] *Ant* 19 §§ 332-34. On the inclusion of proselytes in Temple precincts, see the clear-cut evidence of Rabbinic sources (e.g., *m. Bikkurim*. 1:4, *Mek. to Exod* 12.49 (Horowitz-Rabin 57) as well as comments by J. Baumgarten 1982: 215-25.

[32] See J. Baumgarten 1982; D. R. Schwartz 1987a: 137-143; cf. Feldman on *Ant* 19 §§ 332-34 (LCL pp. 370-71 note c).

[33] D. R. Schwartz 1987a: 130-143. Regarding the broader question on the inclusion vs. exclusion of various segments of the population in Temple ritual, see the suggestive remarks of Knohl 1991: 139-146.

reached an unprecedented pinnacle among certain groups during the decades prior to 70.[34]

The increasing restrictiveness within certain circles of first-century Judaism is reflected in a number of Temple alterations made in order to emphasize the distinction between Jew and non-Jew as well as between pure and impure. Later stages of the Temple building appear to have highlighted these distinctions more profoundly than Herod's edifice. For example, a greater number of steps separated the larger court, that was open to gentiles, from the sacred inner precincts, as had the chancel-screen — with its Greek and Latin inscriptions warning gentiles not to trespass — already in Herod's time. Jewish sensitivity to these issues in the first century is reflected in the near-stoning of gentiles who attempted to enter the holy precincts (Acts 21:27-36; Bruce 1970: 395; cf. Bickerman 1946-47).

Finally, the radically different descriptions in *Antiquities* and *War* regarding the place of women in the Temple clearly indicate an increasing division between the sexes (for purity and other reasons), resulting in a severe limitation in women's access to the inner Temple precincts and probably their participation in public ceremonies (Büchler 1898: 682-706). A women's section is never mentioned in connection with the temples of Solomon or Zerubbabel, nor indeed in *Antiquities*' description of Herod's edifice. As suggested above, the description in Rabbinic literature may be a kind of interim stage in the movement from the relatively open situation described in *Antiquities* to the apparently severe demarcation indicated in *War*. When and why this sharp division was introduced is difficult to say, but it was apparently of a short enough duration so as not to affect other frameworks of Jewish worship, such as the synagogue. Before and after 70, men and women appear to have jointly congregated at the synagogue, and there are no traces of separation within the synagogue confines throughout late antiquity and the early Middle Ages (S. Safrai 1963: 329-338; Z. Safrai 1989: 78-79; L. Levine 1991: 48-50).

Thus, it seems rather clear that the architectural developments and layout of the Jerusalem Temple in the decades prior to 70 were reflective of far-reaching social and religious changes. These physical

---

[34] Various theories have been proposed for dating gentile impurity. Büchler would date it to the early first century -- ca. 17-18 CE (1926-27: 7-15); Zeitlin to the year 65 and the time of the eighteen decrees (1947-48: 111 and literature cited there); Hoenig 1970; see, however Alon 1977: 146-189.

changes in the design and dimensions of the Jerusalem Temple ought not be divorced from deeper issues affecting contemporary Jewish society. Just as the Jerusalem Temple determined much of the Jewish religious agenda of the period, it likewise reflected some of the profound changes taking place among Jews of the first century CE. This is but another example of archeological material not only enhancing our knowledge of the past but relating to some of the basic institutional and religious issues of the day, offering, it would appear, new perspectives for consideration (Levine, forthcoming).

Finally, if our argument be granted, this Temple-related material affirms the basic integrity of Josephus as an historian of first-century Jerusalem. His descriptions are far from capricious, and apparent contradictions might often be explained by clarifying their historical circumstances and institutional contexts (cf. Z. Safrai 1989; B. Mazar 1989).

THE GEOGRAPHICAL EXCURSUSES IN JOSEPHUS

Per Bilde

1. *Introduction*

I have long wished to subject the geographical excursuses in Josephus to a closer examination because I believe that a proper description, analysis, understanding and interpretation of this material might lead to insights of general interest in the study of Josephus.[1]

Generally speaking, Josephus research during the past several decades has been marked by quite different interests. In particular, great efforts have been invested in the analysis of the personal position of Josephus, his attitude towards Rome and the Jewish people, and the characteristics of his politics, ideology and theology.[2] This trend was also reflected in the program for the *International Colloquium on Flavius Josephus in Memory of Professor Morton Smith* in November 1992. And indeed, it is both adequate and appropriate, because it is indispensable for any proper understanding and interpretation of Josephus' historiography.

However, these interests should not be allowed to dominate Josephus research completely. We need studies of specific texts and well-defined topics such as Pelletier 1962 on Josephus' adaptation of the *Letter of Aristeas*, Franxman 1979 on Josephus' treatment of Genesis, Feldman's numerous articles on "Hellenization" in Josephus, Egger 1986 on the Samaritans in Josephus, and Varneda 1986 on Josephus' historiographical methods.

In this contribution I intend to take up such a specific subject: the geographical excursuses in Josephus. My reason for this choice is the

---

[1] My interest in the geographical excursuses in Josephus was developed during the work on my dissertation and the following general monograph on Josephus, cf. Bilde 1983: 60, 130, 163, 174, 175; 1988: 98, 196, 203, and esp. 211-12.

[2] Cf. the recent examples, especially in Lindner 1972; Attridge 1976, 1984; van Unnik 1978; Cohen 1979; Bilde 1983, 1988; Schwartz 1990; Mason 1991. This interest is, however, much older and goes back to the works of Hölscher 1916 and Laqueur 1920, cf. the account on modern Josephus research in Bilde 1988: 123-71.

observation that it appears to be a characteristic feature in Josephus that he, in all parts of his work, has worked with excursuses on geographical and topographical as well as on a number of other specific phenomena. Accordingly, it is my intention to present briefly a description, an analysis, and, hopefully, an interpretation of a representative number of the geographical excursuses. I aim at exploring this phenomenon, and at discussing its significance for our understanding of Josephus as a historical writer. My method is simple: I begin by sketching the research history of our problem. I continue with a discussion of the category "geographical excursus," followed by a catalogue of the material I have judged adequate to present. The examination is rounded off by a brief analysis of this material with the aim of bringing out its characteristics and significance.

2. *Research History*

Strangely, the geographical excursuses have not been given much attention in Josephus research: To the best of my knowledge,[3] they have never been analysed as an independent topic.[4]

On the other hand, this material has in fact been taken up in connection with various other subjects such as the sources of the *Jewish War* or Josephus' historiographical methods:

In his work on Josephus and Vespasian (1921) Wilhelm Weber studied *some* of the geographical excursuses in the *Jewish War* with the result that they were assumed to reflect Roman military interests. And for that reason Weber concluded that these excursuses - almost *verbatim* - derived from Josephus' main source, Vespasian's military ὑπομνήματα/*commentarii* (cf. *Life* §§ 342, 358; *AgAp* 1 § 56).[5] Recent-

---

[3] In the bibliographies of Schreckenberg (1968; 1979) and Feldman (1984a, esp. pp. 735-36) I have been unable to find even one single study on the specific subject of the geographical, or even on any other of the numerous excursuses in Josephus.

[4] The same is the case in the geographical-topographical works of Boettger 1879; Smith 1894; Buhl 1896; Schlatter 1893; 1913; Abel 1933-38; Kopp 1959; Avi-Yonah 1966; Möller-Schmitt 1976 and Kasher 1990. The same result may be found in general representations of Jewish history in the Hellenistic and Roman periods such as Zeitlin 1962-78; Schürer 1973-87; Safrai-Stern 1974-76 and Smallwood 1976.

[5] Cf. Weber 1921: 79-80, 142-49. See esp. p. 149: "Sieht man auf das Ganze, dann ist der Eindruck der gleiche wie bei dem Exkurs über das Heerwesen: Josephus übernimmt die Tatsachen der Vorlage möglichst weitgehend. Nun hat

ly, this hypothesis has been accepted by Magen Broshi and Tessa Rajak.[6] In other words, one interpretation of the geographical excursuses in Josephus, which I have termed the *classical* (Bilde 1988: 126-28, 41), is that this material has not been provided by Josephus himself, but — more or less *verbatim* — has been borrowed from one of his sources.

Harold W. Attridge restricts himself to mentioning the fact, that Josephus' "historical account is interspersed with a number of excursuses providing background information on geographical and institutional matters." (1984: 194). Attridge continues by giving an extensive list of "the most important geographical sections," but there is not even a suggestion of an analysis of this phenomenon.[7]

A third position can be found in Varneda 1986. Pere Villalba i Varneda has provided the most extensive analysis of this material that I am aware of (1986: XIV, 121-24, 169-74). The author does not doubt that the geographical excursuses have been provided by Josephus himself (1986: 123, 173). In his discussion of the material he concentrates on a limited number of the more extensive excursuses: *JW* 3 §§ 419-22: the coast at Joppa; 3 §§ 506-21: Lake Gennesar; 4 §§ 2-10: Gamala; 4 §§ 452-75: Jericho; 4 §§ 607-15: Egypt and Alexandria.[8] It is his aim to inquire how this specific material has been used historio-

---

man wohl die Sicherheit, dass auch die Exkurse über das ganze Land und über den See Genezareth keineswegs freie Erfindungen des Josephus, sondern seiner Quelle entnommen sind."

[6] Cf. Broshi 1982: 381-82, and Rajak 1983: 216. Here Rajak refers to the works of Weber 1921 and Nicols 1978 (who has analysed Josephus' chronology only, and not his geographical excursuses). However, Rajak concludes this paragraph by voicing certain reservations towards this "classical" position. Also Feldman (1984b: 840) seems to accept Weber's hypothesis. This hypothesis is part and parcel of Weber's general theory of a comprehensive Roman source behind the *Jewish War*, a theory which, in another shape, was already presented in Schlatter 1893 (Josephus' source was Marcus Antonius Julianus, cf. also Schlatter 1923). For the general discussion of this theory, I refer to Bilde 1983: 28-30; 1988: 128. Finally, it should be mentioned that, according to Morr 1926, Josephus has drawn his geographical information in *JW* 4 §§ 451-85 from Poseidonius.

[7] The list in Attridge 1984: 194 is much more extensive than the material which, according to Weber 1921, belongs to this category.

[8] In this category Varneda also reckons *JW* 2 §§ 188-91: Ptolemais; 3 §§ 35-58: Galilee, Peraea, Samaria and Judaea; 5 §§ 136-247: Jerusalem and the Temple; 7 §§ 164-89: Machaerus, and 7 §§ 280-303: Masada. Accordingly, like Attridge 1984, Varneda defines the category of geographical excursuses much wider than Weber 1921.

graphically by Josephus. Therefore, he is not interested in the category as a whole, nor in what this material may else reveal on Josephus' historical interests.

Accordingly, it is evident that no consensus has yet been reached regarding this problem. Further, it seems to be obvious that even a clear attitude toward the geographical excursuses in Josephus has not yet crystallized in Josephus research. Therefore, it is a valid motivation to take up this problem in a more comprehensive manner than has hitherto been the case.

3. *Defining Our Task and Delineating the Material*

Once the reader has become aware of the issue of Josephus' excursuses on geographical and other sorts of specific data, such as cities, fortresses, harbours, agriculture, economics, military and political institutions and so forth, one seems to discover them everywhere.[9] So, it is our first task, out of this huge material, to select a limited collection, and to define what we, in this context, more precisely understand by *geographical* and by *excursus*:

First, *excursus* by which I here understand a relatively brief, rounded insertion in the general narrative, explaining a specific phenomenon in the main text, after which the author returns to his narrative thread.[10]

Accordingly, we have to leave out such pieces as Josephus' description of the places in Galilee and Gaulanitis he fortified during the winter 66-67 (*JW* 2 §§ 573-75; *Life* §§ 187-88), precisely because these lists do not interrupt the general account. The same applies to a number of other texts such as *JW* 1 § 417 and the parallel in *Ant* 16 § 142-43 (both on the fertile plain of Antipatris); *JW* 3 § 107 (where Josephus, in the context of his long description of the Roman army [*JW* 3 §§ 70-109], indicates the borders of the Roman Empire); *JW* 7 §§ 280-84, (see also § 303) (on the rock of Masada, where the account without interruption continues in a description of the fortress); *Ant* 2 § 18 (on the fertile soil in the region of Sikima/Shechem), and *Ant* 2 §§ 244-47 on Moses' ingenuous (θαυμαστός, cf. below) idea to control the dangerous snakes on his way to Ethiopia.

---

[9] Cf. Attridge 1984: 194; Varneda 1986: 121-24, 169-74.

[10] Varneda is not clear regarding the problem whether the excursuses are to be regarded as insertions, *id est* as interrupting the main text (cf. 1986: 123-24, 124, 170, 171).

Second, by *geographical* I understand descriptions, of a certain minimal extent (the length of which is of course open to discussion), of landscapes, rivers, lakes, mountains, valleys, caves, soil, fertility and other natural phenomena.

This means that we have to exclude a great amount of material having obviously the character of excursuses, but without referring to geographical phenomena in this sense.

Firstly, this is true of Josephus' extensive presentation of the Essenes (*JW* 2 §§ 120-61), of his brief explanations of the Roman tactics of the "tortoise" (*JW* 2 § 537) and of the Roman battering ram (*JW* 3 §§ 214-16). Similarly, this applies to Josephus' detailed descriptions of the location of the Roman legions (*JW* 2 §§ 365-87), appearing in the great speech of King Agrippa II (*JW* 2 §§ 345-404), of the Roman army itself (*JW* 3 §§ 65-69, 70-109, 115-26; 5 §§ 41-49), of the Roman siege wall against Jerusalem (*JW* 5 §§ 502-9), of the miraculous omens portending the fall of the Temple (*JW* 6 §§ 288-309), and of the Roman triumph (*JW* 7 §§ 123-62). Further, this holds true of Josephus' account of Moses' military campaign in Ethiopia (*Ant* 2 §§ 238-53), of his excursus-like account of Paulina in Rome (*Ant* 18 §§ 65-80), and of his descriptions of the high priestly vestments (*Ant* 18 §§ 90-94), the family of King Herod the Great (*Ant* 18 §§ 127-42), King Agrippa I (*Ant* 18 §§ 143-255), the particular politics of the Emperor Tiberius (*Ant* 18 §§ 169-78), the Jews in Babylon (*Ant* 18 §§ 310-79), the conjuration against the Emperor Gaius Caligula (*Ant* 19 §§ 17-273), the royal house of Adiabene (*Ant* 20 §§ 17-96), and the various ancient historiographers' interpretations of the Emperor Nero (*Ant* 20 §§ 154-57). Finally, this is true of Josephus' excursus on the historiographical work of his rival, Justus of Tiberias' (*Life* §§ 336-39).

Secondly, I intend to leave out a great amount of genuine geographical, inserted material simply because of its substantial length. The best known pieces of this sort are the following: The famous descriptions of the Jewish provinces in Palestine: Galilee, Peraea, Samaria and Judaea (*JW* 3 §§ 35-58), and of Jerusalem, the Temple and Antonia (*JW* 5 §§ 136-247); moreover, almost all the similar descriptions in the *Jewish War* and in the *Antiquities* of, in particular, the Herodian cities in Palestine and other countries, as well as the graphic presentations of the Hasmonean and Herodian fortresses;[11] and finally, all the so-called itineraries found in *JW* 1 §§ 277-81 (King Herod's journey to Rome); 1 §§ 608-13 (Antipater's journey from Rome to Caesarea); 2 §§ 66-72 (Varus' campaign from Antioch to Jerusalem); 2 §§ 499-516 (Cestius Gallus' campaign from Antioch to Judaea); 4 §§ 441-50 (Vespasian's campaign in the spring of the year 68); 4 §§ 659-63 (Titus' journey from Alexandria to Caesarea); 5 §§ 50-53 (Titus' campaign from Samaria to Judaea), and *Life* §§ 230-33 (The Jerusalem delegation's journey in Galilee).

Thirdly, I have decided to exclude excursuses of too modest an extent such as *JW* 1 § 134 (on Coreae as situated on the border between Decapolis, Judaea and Samaria); 3 § 34 (on Sepphoris as being the largest city of Galilee); 4 §§ 104-5 (on Cydasa between Tyrus and Galilee); 5 § 70 (and the related text in *Ant* 20 § 169, on the geographical situation of the Mount of Olives); *Ant* 1 § 244 (on the climate in Mesopotamia); 4 § 100 (on Jericho), and 9 § 7 (on En-Gedi and its products).

It follows that what I have in fact selected for closer scrutiny really has to be regarded as a modest selection from a huge amount of material, firstly, the great mass of excursuses in general, and secondly, a considerable amount of geographical descriptions from which I have only chosen a certain number. Further, it follows that the interpretation of the selected geographical excursuses has to be discussed in the broader context of all this material.

What is left are the relatively brief, but still substantial parenthetical explanations of geographic phenomena, often local peculiarities, which appear in the main text, and in which Josephus seems to give a short, inserted explanation before he continues his narrative.[12]

---

[11] Excepted from this rule are the purely geographical descriptions of the natural settings of a number of these sites: Jotapata, Gamala and Machaerus, but not Masada, for the reason mentioned above.

[12] I have found no clear-cut criterion on the basis of which an irreproachable definition of a *geographical excursus* could be established. Especially the category "brief" is difficult: A text like *JW* 4 §§ 104-5 might as well have been included in my catalogue, while pieces such as *JW* 1 § 138; 3 §§ 29, 413 and several of the samples from the *Antiquities* might have been excluded. Therefore, I admit that there is an element of fortuity in my estimate of what is a "relatively brief rounded 'geographical' insertion in the general narrative." It is, however, my hope that the definition I have given and the material I have chosen on this basis will appear to be representative.

4. *Catalogue*

JW 1 § 138: Jericho

A brief, obviously parenthetical description of the fertile soil of the region and its products of palms and balsam. There are no cross-references to *JW* 4 §§ 452-75 and *Ant* 4 § 100; 15 § 96 where Jericho is similarly described.

JW 1 §§ 405-6: Paneion

A supplementary, romantically exaggerated description of the scenery at Paneion with the towering mountain (Mount Hermon?), the mysterious cave with its enigmatic pool, and the springs (of the River Jordan?). The description is concluded by a reference to a later explanation of the problem of the sources of the River Jordan (cf. *JW* 3 §§ 509-15; *Ant* 15 § 364).

JW 1 § 409: The coast at Caesarea

A parenthetical description of the dangerous and harbour-less coast-line between Dora and Joppa which, in the context, serves to explain how useful Herod's construction of the port of Caesarea was. There are no cross-references to *JW* 3 §§ 419-21; *Ant* 15 § 333.

JW 2 §§ 188-91: Ptolemais

A broad, parenthetical description of Ptolemais and its geographical situation at the entrance to the Great Plain, with the surrounding mountains and the small river Beleus on the bank of which the tomb of Memnon may be seen. To this description is added a legendary account of the remarkable (θαυμαστός/θαυμασιώτερον) pit of vitreous sand nearby. Finally, the excursus is formally rounded off by an editorial remark.

JW 3 § 29: Antioch-on-the-Orontes

A brief, parenthetical description of the city of Antioch as being the third greatest in the Roman world.

JW 3 §§ 158-60: Jotapata

A parenthetical description of the characteristic geographical situation of Jotapata on a mountain top, being almost unassailable except from its northern side. The description is formally concluded by an editorial remark.

JW 3 § 413: The climate of Caesarea and Scythopolis

A brief, parenthetical description of these two cities' climate being mild during the winter and hot in the summer.

JW 3 §§ 419-21: The coast at Joppa

A parenthetical description of the rough and harbour-less coast at Joppa, though without any cross-references to *JW* 1 § 409; *Ant* 15 § 333.

JW 3 §§ 506-21: Lake Gennesar, the River Jordan and the plain of Gennesar

A broad, parenthetical, but interconnected account of these three sites: First, a description of the lake, its name, its measures, its wonderful waters with its excellent taste and pleasant temperature, and its fish (§§ 506-8); further, a description of the River Jordan, the strange story of its miraculous source in Lake Phiale, of Paneion, and of the course of the river through Lake Semechonitis into Lake Gennesar, and further through the desert valley into Lake Asphaltitis (§§ 509-15); finally, a flourishing description of the plain of Gennesar, its astonishing fertility, its remarkable climate, its numerous agricultural products, its almost miraculous productivity of walnuts, figs, olives and grapes, and its fertilizing spring at Capharnaum (§§ 516-21). This description is formally concluded, but there are no cross-references to the related descriptions of Paneion in *JW* 1 §§ 405-6; *Ant* 15 § 364.

JW 4 §§ 2-8: Gamala with Sogane, Seleucia, Lake Semechonitis and Daphne

A parenthetical, integrated description of the cities of Gaulanitis: First, the general geographical situation and political affiliation of Gamala, Sogane and Seleucia in Gaulanitis (§ 2), second, a brief description of Lake Semechonitis and Daphne (§ 3), and, third, a detailed description of the characteristic natural conditions of Gamala elinging to the camel-like mountain-top surrounded by inaccessible ravines except from the north-eastern side (§§ 4b-8).

JW 4 §§ 54-56: Itabyrion/Mount Tabor

A parenthetical description of Mount Tabor, its geographical situation, its height, its summit and its fortifications established by Josephus.

JW 4 §§ 452-75: Jericho

A broad, parenthetical description of Jericho, of its geographical situation in the Jordan Valley, of the mountains on both sides of the Valley (§§ 452-54); further, a description of the Jordan Valley itself — by Josephus also termed the "Great Plain" — with its extension and measures (§§ 455-56) and its climate (§§ 457-58); then follows a long, sub-excursus, inserted in the main excursus, on the legend of the miraculous spring which the prophet Elisha had once transformed from a damaging to a beneficial one (§§ 459-67); the narrative continues with a detailed description of the rich vegetation of date palms, balsam trees and other fruits (§§ 468-70), and with some reflections by the author on the beneficial climate of the area and the waters of the spring (§§ 471-73). The excursus is brought to an end by a brief general description of the area and the relations and surroundings of the city of Jericho (§ 474), and concluded by a formal editorial remark (§ 475). However, there are no cross-references to *JW* 1 § 138; *Ant* 4 § 100; 15 § 96.

JW 4 §§ (456), 476-85: Lake Asphaltitis

A broad description, which is partly connected with the foregoing one on Jericho and partly parenthetical, of the unique character of the waters of this lake, its bitterness, its buoyancy — which was tested by Vespasian — and its changing colours (§§ 476-78); further a description of the lake's production of bitumen, and of the use of this material in shipbuilding and medicine (§§ 479-81); this paragraph is followed by a description of the measures of the lake (§ 482) and of the adjacent land of Sodom, with references to the biblical tales of the miraculous destiny of that city the vestiges of which are still visible in some ruins and in the so-called Sodom-apples (§§ 482-84). The excursus is terminated by a formal editorial conclusion (§ 485).

JW 4 §§ (605), 607-15: Egypt and Alexandria

A broad, parenthetical description of the protective borders of Egypt (§§ 607-10a), of its measures (§ 610b), of the Nile (§ 611), and of Alexandria with its protected port, the lighthouse on the island of Pharos, and the rich trade of the harbour (§§ 612-15).

JW 7 §§ 164-70, (171-77), 178-89: Machaerus

A broad description of the geographical situation of this inaccessible mountain fortress at the eastern coast of Lake Asphaltitis (§§ 164-70);

the narrative continues with a description of the buildings constructed by King Alexander Jannnaeus and, in particular, by King Herod (§§ 171-77); this piece is followed by the legends of the miraculous rue plant, and of the dangerous and demon-deterrent Baaras root (§§ 178-85); further follows a description of the numerous hot and cold springs in the neighbourhood, some of which are highly remarkable (θαυμά-σειε, § 188), and are used for the most delightful baths, and some of which have medical properties (§§ 186-89a). The excursus is concluded by a brief remark about the chemical mines in this area.

Ant 2 §§ 249-50: Saba in Ethiopia
A parenthetical description of the natural protection and the constructed fortifications of the city of Saba. An addition to the Bible.

Ant 2 §§ 264-65: Mount Sinai
A parenthetical description of Mount Sinai, its height and its excellence for pasturage, elaborating on Exod 3:1.

Ant 3 §§ 1-2: The Sinai Desert
A brief, parenthetical description of the sandy desert near Mount Sinai, elaborating generally on Exod 15:22 (cf. Exod 16:1-2).

Ant 4 § 85: The River Arnon
A brief, parenthetical description (on the basis of Num 21:13) of the River Arnon, its source and course, and a brief remark on the rich region of the Amorites.

Ant 4 § 95: The country of the Amorites
A brief, parenthetical description of the country of the Amorites conquered by the Israelites: It is situated between the three rivers of Arnon, Jobak/Jabbok, and Jordan. An addition to the Bible.

Ant 5 § 77-78: The Land of Canaan
A parenthetical description, brief and general, of the nature of the Promised Land with its plains and mountains. Though this country is quite small, its fertility and its beauty exceeds those of all others (cf. *AgAp* 1 §§ 60-68).

Ant 14 §§ 422, (421-30): The caves (of Mount Arbela)
A brief, parenthetical description of the caves dug into the mountain half-way up the steep cliff. The description is inserted in the account of King Herod's war against the Galilean brigands.

Ant 15 § 96: Jericho

A brief, parenthetical description of the precious products of Jericho: the balsam and palm trees, though without cross-references to *JW* 1 § 138; 4 §§ 452-75; *Ant* 4 § 100.

Ant 15 § 333: The coast between Joppa and Dora

A brief, parenthetical description of the dangerous coast between Joppa and Dora, and of the poor harbours of these two cities. The description serves to illuminate the merits of King Herod in constructing the harbour of Caesarea. There are no cross-references to *JW* 1 § 409; 3 §§ 419-22.

Ant 15 § 364: Paneion

A brief, parenthetical description of the cave at Paneion, of the pool below and of the high mountain above the cave, but without cross-references to *JW* 1 §§ 405-6; 3 §§ 509-14.

Ant 18 § 249: Baiae

A brief, parenthetical description of the geographical situation of Baiae in Campania, its imperial buildings and its hot springs.

Ant 20 §§ 24-25: Carron

A brief, parenthetical description of the district of Carron (in Adiabene), its fertile soil, its products, and the remains of the ark of Noah (cf. *Ant* 1 § 92, though without explicit reference to this text).

5. *Analysis*

We turn to a brief examination of the material compiled in the catalogue: How can we describe and evaluate the literary form and the contents of the selected geographical excursuses? Does this material reflect certain common characteristics? How do they relate to Josephus' work in general? And, finally, does this material justify the Schlatter-Weber hypothesis?

If we look at the *literary form* of the collected material it is possible to make the following observations:

1) Our collection of geographical excursuses represents only a selection of a much larger amount of excursus-like accounts, as we saw in section three above (see also note 15 below): First, our catalogue represents only one part of a much more comprehensive mass of dif-

ferent types of geographical descriptions, whether digressive or not; second, this total amount of geographical descriptions represents only one part of Josephus' total number of excursus-like accounts of a great number of all kinds of "interesting" phenomena. Like Thucydides, Livy and other Graeco-Roman historians, Josephus seems to have had a predilection for adding this type of material to his historical narrative.[13] Therefore, what we have selected as geographical excursuses has to be interpreted in this context.

2) It seems to be a fact that the selected geographical excursuses have been inserted in every part of Josephus' two major historiographical works, although the insertions are much more numerous in the *Jewish War* than in the *Antiquities*. Even *Life* does not appear to be untouched by this phenomenon.

3) Quite a few of the excursuses in our catalogue are extensive, and thus closely related to the major part of Josephus' other digressions. However, most of them, especially those in the *Antiquities*, are rather brief and concentrated.

4) In some of the extensive cases we have observed that different units of texts have been literarily linked together: *JW* 3 §§ 506-21; 4 §§ 2-8; 4 §§ 452-75 (and §§ 476-85); 7 §§ 164-89. This phenomenon has been observed elsewhere in Josephus, e.g., in *Ant* 18 §§ 55-90.[14]

5) In the first eleven books of the *Antiquities* all the selected geographical excursuses appear as additions to the Bible, a fact pointing in the direction of their editorial character (cf. also Varneda 1986: 124, 174).

6) Some of the cases in the catalogue are rounded off by formal editorial remarks: *JW* 2 §§ 188-91; 3 §§ 158-60; 3 §§ 506-21; 4 §§ 452-75; 4 §§ 476-85. This phenomenon is well-known in Josephus and turns up everywhere in his works.[15]

---

[13] Cf. Bilde 1988: 203. Varneda has termed this general excursus phenomenon *ecphrasis* (1986: 169-80).

[14] This literary technique has been analysed in particular in Moehring 1959; Justus 1973.

[15] An instructive example appears in *JW* 2 § 161 where Josephus concludes his long digression on the Essenes with the words: "Such are the usages of this order" (τοιαῦτα μὲν ἔθη τοῦδε τοῦ τάγματος). Another related parallel is found in *JW* 3 § 58, where Josephus ends his description of the Jewish provinces in Palestine in the same manner. Similar editorial remarks emerge in *JW* 2 § 166 (editorial conclusion after the digression on the three Jewish religious schools), § 499 (editorial conclusion after the description of the tragedy of the Jews in Alexan-

7) Only in one case, *JW* 1 §§ 405-6, have we observed a formal cross-reference to related material elsewhere in Josephus' works. This is surprising because this phenomenon is one of the most common literary characteristics in the works of Josephus.[16]

Regarding the *contents* of the selected geographical excursuses I have made the following observations:

a) A great number of them are marked by concise, conspicuous and graphic descriptions of the natural phenomena in question. This is true especially in *JW* 1 § 138 (and its parallels), § 409 (and its parallels); 3 §§ 158-60; 4 §§ 4-8, 607-15; 7 §§ 164-70; *Ant* 2 §§ 249-50; 4 § 85, 95; 14 § 422; 15 § 364 and 18 § 249.[17]

b) A number of the excursuses are marked by an obvious interest in dramatic and romantic sceneries: *JW* 1 §§ 405-6, 409 (and its parallels); 3 §§ 158-60; 4 §§ 4-8; 7 §§ 164-70; *Ant* 14 § 422 and 15 § 364. This tendency is well-known as being most characteristic of Josephus' writings.[18]

c) Some of the geographical excursuses are marked by a typical tendency of Josephus to exaggerate in the description of natural phenomena and in the rendering of measures and numbers: *JW* 1 §§ 405-6; 3 §§ 506-21; 4 §§ 54-56; 7 §§ 164-89.[19]

---

dria), § 654 (editorial conclusion of the account of Simon Bar Giora); 3 § 98 (provisional editorial conclusion of the description of the Roman army); §§ 108-9 (final editorial remark after the digression on the Roman army (3 §§ 70-107); 3 § 442 (editorial conclusion of the description of the Jerusalemites' reaction to the news of the fall of Jotapata); 4 § 587; 6 § 192; *Ant* 3 §§ 158, 187, 257; 4 §§ 308, 331; 5 § 174; 6 § 350; 7 §§ 38, 394 etc.

[16] There are several hundreds of the kind, cf., e.g., *JW* 1 §§ 33, 118, 182, 344, 365, 406, 411, 418, 668; 2 §§ 114, 137, 222, 449 . . .; *Ant* 1 §§ 135, 137, 142 . . . ; *Life* §§ 10, 27, 41 . . . ; *AgAp* 1 §§ 1, 29, 47 . . . , cf. Bilde 1988: 128-29.

[17] The same qualities are found in a great number of descriptions elsewhere in Josephus such as the descriptions of Jerusalem, the Temple, the Hasmonean and Herodian cities and fortresses, the Jewish provinces in Palestine and the itineraries mentioned above in section three. In addition, it is possible to refer to the famous descriptions of the great battle scenes in Josephus' works, especially in the *Jewish War*.

[18] Josephus' taste for dramatic and emotional representation is evident especially in his description of individual destinies such as those of Joseph, Herod the Great, Agrippa I, Gaius Caligula and many others, cf. Bilde 1983:176; 1988: 48, 81, 95, 158, 192, 196, 204, 232; Varneda 1986: 235-41.

[19] Cf., e.g., Kopp 1959: 248; Avi-Yonah 1966: 211, 219; Cohen 1979: 33-34, 233; Broshi 1982: 383-84. In other cases, however, Josephus' rendering is realistic, as in, e.g., *JW* 2 § 188; 3 § 39; 4 §§ 452-75 etc., a fact which has often been noticed, cf. Broshi 1982: 379-81; Bilde 1983: 176 (with numerous references).

d) Other cases are marked by an obvious interest in unusual phenomena, often of enigmatic, legendary or miraculous character: *JW* 1 §§ 405-6; 2 §§ 188-91; 3 §§ 506-21; 4 §§ 452-75, 476-85 and 7 §§ 178-89.[20]

e) A few of our texts are marked by a characteristic interest in still visible "archaeological" remains: *JW* 2 §§ 188-91; 4 §§ 476-85 and *Ant* 20 § 25.[21]

f) A great number of our cases are clearly marked by an interest in natural phenomena such as soil and fertility: *JW* 1 § 138; 3 §§ 506-21; 4 §§ 452-75; *Ant* 2 §§ 264-65; 4 §§ 85, 95; 5 §§ 77-78; 15 § 96 and 20 § 25.[22]

g) The same feature reflects a specific interest in productivity and economy as well, an interest which is voiced especially in *JW* 2 §§ 188-91; 4 §§ 476-85, 607-15 and 7 §§ 178-89.[23]

h) Finally, I have noticed a curious interest in climatology: *JW* 3 § 413, 506-21; 4 §§ 452-75 and *Ant* 3 §§ 1-2.[24]

---

[20] This interest appears often in Josephus' works, cf. *JW* 1 §§ 286-87 (the miraculous rainfall on Masada); §§ 331-332 (King Herod's miraculous rescue in Jericho); 2 §§ 112-13 (King Archelaus' miraculous dream); 6 §§ 288-309 (the miraculous omens portending the fall of the Temple in Jerusalem); *Ant* 18 §§ 284-88 (the miraculous rainfall during the Gaius Caligula crisis in Palestine in the year 39-40); etc., cf. Bilde 1988: 201-2 (with other examples). In many of these texts we meet the characteristic word ϑαυμάσιος/ϑαυμαστός which appears to be a favourite of Josephus, cf. Rengstorf 1973-83 vol. 2, 1975: 317-18.

[21] The same interest turns up in *Ant* 1 § 92 (on the still existing relics of the ark of Noah); § 150 (on Abraham's tomb which is still visible); 10 §§ 264-65 (on Daniel's castle which is also visible at the time of Josephus).

[22] A similar interest in agriculture appears in a great number of Josephus texts such as *JW* 1 § 417; 2 §§ 200, 592; 3 §§ 42-44, 50; 4 § 84; *Ant* 2 § 18; 4 § 100; 8 § 174; 9 § 7; 15 §§ 299-316; 16 §§ 142-43, 271-73; 17 § 340; 18 §§ 31, 272-74, 283-84, 287; *Life* §§ 118-19; etc.

[23] Josephus' interest in economy emerges most conspicuously in his descriptions of the cities and agricultural colonies established by King Herod the Great: *JW* 1 § 403 and *Ant* 15 §§ 292-93 (Samaria); *JW* 1 §§ 408-15 and *Ant* 15 §§ 331-41 (Caesaraea); *JW* 1 § 417 and *Ant* 16 §§ 142-43 (Antipatris); *JW* 1 § 418 and *Ant* 16 § 145 (Phasaelis); etc. It appears, however, also in a number of other texts such as *JW* 2 § 427; 7 §§ 216-18; *Ant* 14 § 28; *AgAp* 1 §§ 60-68 (cf. below) etc.

[24] A similar interest appears in such texts as *JW* 3 § 312; *Ant* 1 § 244, cf. Varneda 1986: 123.

6. *Conclusions*

In section three we noticed that Josephus has a general predilection for digressions, and our material is most easily understood in this context. Furthermore, the geographical excursuses are marked by a number of characteristics which, for the most part, appear in many other parts of Josephus' works too. Finally, this material is found scattered all over Josephus' writings. Accordingly, we have to conclude that the geographical excursuses in Josephus are deeply integrated in to his works. On this background it is natural to assume that this material derives from the author himself.

This conclusion is perfectly in keeping with Josephus' editorial statement in the introduction to the *Jewish War* where he explicitly mentions geography as one of the phenomena he will be addressing in his work:

> In this connection I shall describe the admirable discipline of the Romans on active service and the training of the legions; the extent and nature of the two Galilees, the limits of Judaea, the special features of the country, its lakes and springs . . . .[25]

Further, this conclusion corresponds well with the interesting text in *AgAp* 1 §§ 60-68. Here Josephus is discussing some of the ethnic characteristics of the Jews, on the one hand, and of the non-Jews (Greeks, Egyptians, Phoenicians and others), on the other hand, in close connection with the basic geographical conditions of each ethnic group:

> Well, ours is not a maritime country; neither commerce nor the intercourse which it promotes with the outside world has any attraction for us. Our cities are built inland, remote from the sea; and we devote ourselves to the cultivation of the productive country with which we are blessed (§ 60) . . . .
> It was to their coming on their ships to traffic with the Greeks that the Phoenicians owed their own early notoriety; and through their agency the Egyptians became known and all whose merchandise the Phoenicians conveyed across great oceans to the Greeks (§ 63).
> As a general rule, all the nations with a sea-board, whether on the eastern or the western sea, were better known by authors desirous of writing history, while those who lived further inland remained for the most part unknown (§ 65). Surely, then, it should no longer excite surprise that our nation, so

---

[25] *JW* 1 § 22. The translation of this text as well as that from *AgAp* 1 §§ 60-68 are borrowed from LCL.

remote from the sea, and so deliberately living its own life, likewise remained unknown and offered no occasion to historians to mention it (§ 68).

In my view, therefore, the most important conclusion to be drawn
from the examination of the geographical excursuses in Josephus is the
insight that Josephus was deeply interested in geography, *id est*, in
matters of nature, landscape, climate, fertility, agriculture and, consequently, productivity and economy.[26]

From this conclusion follows that the Schlatter-Weber hypothesis -
that the geographical excursuses in Josephus (*id est* in the *Jewish War*),
in an almost unedited form, derive from the main source to that work,
either Antonius Julianus' work or Vespasian's military ὑπομνήματα /
commentarii - has to be at least radically modified. This hypothesis
overlooks a) that this material appears not only in the *Jewish War* but
also in the *Antiquities* and in the minor works as well, b) that the
extensive geographical excursuses seem to be closely related both to
the "small" ones and to the numerous other excursuses in Josephus as
well as to Josephus' works in general, and c) that the geographical
excursuses are not restricted to material of military interest.

Of course, it cannot be excluded that Josephus drew upon literary
and other sources, but it has to be acknowledged that if and when he
did so he generally reworked such sources and gave them his own
literary form and substantial character.[27]

---

[26] Similarly Varneda 1986: esp. 121-24, but in contrast to Franxman 1979: 13.
[27] Cf. Bilde 1988: 128-34, 195-96. Thus, my conclusion points in the same
direction as Lindner 1972.

PART V

VIEWS OF THE WAR

JOSEPHUS' ACTION IN GALILEE
DURING THE JEWISH WAR

Giorgio Jossa

The purpose of this paper is to discuss the reconstruction of events in Galilee at the beginning of the Jewish war which I proposed in the introduction of my recent translation of the *Life* by Flavius Josephus. For further details, therefore, I refer the reader to that introduction (Jossa 1992: 7-58).

This reconstruction, besides the analysis of some conclusive passages of the *War* and of the *Life*, is based on two interpretative presuppositions of Josephus' story. The first (Jossa 1992: 16-30) is that in the Palestine of those times and, more particularly, during the war against the Romans, two different trends were at work among the rebels: a moderate and a radical one. The first was typical of those *moderate* groups of Jews who fought for the strict observance of the law and for this reason asked for a change in the government's ways and more particularly, of those religious nationalists who fought for the return to the ancient tradition against the Herodian kings and the Hellenistic cities. The second trend, instead, was typical of those *radical* groups who fought for the liberation of the Jewish people and for the restoration of the kingdom of Israel. In other words, it involved those political rebels who dreamed of a social revolution against the Roman Empire and the Herodian dynasty. Josephus usually calls the exponents of the first trend "innovators" (νεωτερίζοντες) and those of the second "brigands" (λησταί). At the same time it appears that he considers νεωτερίζοντες the Zealots of the two Eleazars, sons of Ananias and of Simon respectively, who fought for the strict restoration of the tradition, for the purity of worship and of the Temple. On the other hand, he considers λησταί the Sicarii of Menahem and of Simon bar Gioras, who fought for the liberation of the Jewish nation, for the political independence of Israel.

Thus both the polemic overtones contained in those terms and the standpoint from which they are used become clear. By putting himself on the side of the Jewish religious authorities Josephus can charge those observant Jews fighting for a return to the tradition with being innovators and hence revolutionaries. Similarly, by putting himself on the side of the Roman political authorities he can charge those patriots fighting for the liberation of Israel with being brigands and hence "tyrants." It is also clear that the two terms do not have the same negative connotations. The first somehow betrays his difficulty in condemning both an attitude which stemmed from the strict observance of the traditions of Israel and some men who were part of the most observant groups of Jewish people. The second, instead, implies a final condemnation by Josephus, who, aristocrat as he is, cannot feel but horror for the supporters of a political and social revolution.

The second presupposition (Jossa 1992: 44-57) I spoke about at the beginning is that the famous "Galileans" of Josephus' *Life* are a group of Jews particularly attached to the law and to the tradition, who accept at least some of the ideological positions of the Shammaites and Zealots. Contrary to the opinion of Zeitlin, these Galileans' deepest motivations for their participation in the Jewish war are religious and national, not political and social, and their most hated adversaries are the Herodians and the Greeks, not the Romans. The Galilean protest expresses first of all an attachment to the religious tradition, a defence of national identity, and hence the Jewish population's hostility towards the Greeks and those Jews who are favourable to the Greeks, not the fighting for political freedom or the hopes for social emancipation and hence Jews' hatred against the Romans. They would, therefore, be in the terms (and in the conception) of Josephus, νεωτερίζοντες, or, as he says in the *Life*, νεωτερισταί, that is innovators on the plane of tradition and πάτρια ἔθη, not λησταί, that is rebels on a political and social level. Yet on this level the Galileans, though certainly hostile to the Roman rulers and to the notables of the city, are moderate, always troubled by the attacks of the λησταί and rather resigned to Roman rule. All this means that the Galileans of Josephus, contrary to the *communis opinio*, have nothing to do with Judas the Galilean, who is possibly a ληστής and is surely a rebel. From this it follows that the traditional image of Galilee as a land of political revolutionaries is largely to be revised.

Let us now pass to an analysis of what happened in Galilee. For a correct understanding of these developments, it is necessary first of all to weigh the nature of the appointment entrusted to Josephus by the government of Jerusalem. In fact, one of the crucial points of the story of the Jewish war against the Romans given by Josephus consists exactly in the mission of the then young priest and future Jewish historian in Galilee, in the autumn of 66 CE, on behalf of the popular government instituted in Jerusalem after the victory over Cestius Gallus. The nature of this mission depends obviously on the character of this government. It is also true nevertheless that on the nature of this mission depend in their turn, not only the judgement about the activities and personalities of the protagonists of the events in Galilee, but also the evaluation of the character of the government.

As it is known, Josephus gave us two versions of his mission in Galilee. According to that of *JW* 2 § 568 he was entrusted by those who had defeated Cestius Gallus with the task of leading the military operations against the Romans in Galilee.[1] The subsequent narrative of the *War* seems to confirm the military character of his mission. According to the version of *Life* §§ 28-29, on the contrary, he was sent by the authorities in Jerusalem with the goal of persuading the πονηροί to lay down their arms, in order to wait for the development of things.[2] In fact, the *Life* stresses continually Josephus' peaceful intentions in carrying out his mission. So scholars parted company in the

---

[1] After having said that "those who had pursued Cestius . . ., gathered in the Temple, appointed several commanders (στρατηγούς) for the war" (2 § 562), the text states in fact: "John son of Ananias was appointed commander (ἡγεμών) of Gophna and Acrabatene and Josephus, son of Matthias, of the two Galilees; to this last one's command (στρατηγίᾳ) Gamala too was added, the strongest city of the region" (2 § 568).

[2] "The Jerusalem leaders . . . sent me and two other priests, Joazar and Judas, respectable persons, to persuade the criminals (πονηρούς) to lay down their arms and to explain to them that it was better to reserve them for the nation's best men." A difference between the two accounts can be perceived not only as to the mission Josephus was charged with, but also as to the authority that entrusted him with it. In the *War*'s account those who appoint Josephus commander are the ones "who had pursued Cestius," gathered in the Temple with the pro-Romans who had joined them, i.e., a kind of revolutionary council, if not a popular assembly. *Instead,* in the *Life's* account those who send Josephus to Galilee, are "the leaders of Jerusalem," worried about falling in the brigands' and innovators' hands. They appear to be the aristocratic party's leaders, if not the Sanhedrin itself. But also in this case the difference between the two accounts depends on the different ways in which the historian wants to present the facts. There is no doubt, in fact, that Josephus was entrusted with his appointment by what in the *Life* he often defines "the community (the κοινόν) of Jerusalem," that is by the popular government constituted after the victory over Cestius Gallus (*JW* 5 §§ 65, 190, 341, 393).

interpretation of the two passages, and hence in the solution of the problem. R. Laqueur (1920: 103-8), for instance, who is never very gentle toward the Jewish historian, charged him with "lack of scruples." He concluded from the discrepancy that Josephus abused his appointment, assuming a military power that he had not been entrusted with, and building a tyrannical power in Galilee for himself by taking advantage of the situation. H. Drexler (1926: 299ff), on the contrary, was convinced that at the beginning of the revolt the aristocracy of Jerusalem, too weak and incapable to face the situation was half-heartedly involved in the war. Therefore he judged the *War* version more believable, because that of *Life* was openly affected by the polemic with Justus of Tiberias. In order to understand well the nature of Josephus' mission in Galilee, it is necessary to weigh both the character of the government of Jerusalem, as revealed mostly by the *War* story, and the political action pursued by Josephus in Galilee, as told mainly in the *Life*. This is my aim in these pages.

Josephus was entrusted with his appointment by the popular government constituted in Jerusalem after the victory over Cestius Gallus in October of 66 CE. There were several people responsible for this victory, according to the *War*. They were the Jews gathered in the holy city for the Feast of Tabernacles, who according to Josephus assailed the Romans when Cestius arrived (2 § 517). More exactly, a few days earlier, the followers of the captain of the Temple, Eleazar the son of the high priest Ananias, had defeated and driven the followers of Menahem, the grandson of Judas the Galilean, out of Jerusalem. Then the ones who assailed the Romans were clearly those "innovators," that is those religious nationalists, who gathered around Eleazar after he took the initiative of discontinuing the daily sacrifice on behalf of the Romans. They are the same who constituted the immediate precedent of the group of the Zealots, if not, more simply, Zealots themselves. They are, however, a group of observant Jews who fought for strict observance of law and tradition (Hengel 1961: 365ff; Jossa 1990: 69-77). But when this last group was repelled after a first victorious assault that had already cost Cestius more than five hundred men, Simon bar Gioras attacked the Romans from the rear while they were leaving Jerusalem (2 § 521). He was a young, strong and valiant man, destined to become one of the leaders, nay the chief leader, of the Jewish revolt; the one whom the Romans would pick out for the triumph ceremony and condemn to death as the true leader of the insurrection. Therefore he was Menahem's most legitimate successor, who likewise fought for a political and social revolution (Michel 1967-68: 402-8; Kreissig 1970: 143; Stern 1973: 146-47). Afterwards Cestius resumed the siege of Jerusalem (*JW* 2 § 527ff) and the assault of the Temple (2 § 535ff). When he suddenly resolved to retreat, he was surely assaulted both by the "innovators" of the Temple (2 §§ 529, 536) and by the "brigands" of the country (2 §§ 538, 541). But among them, one of the most important chiefs had to be Eleazar the son of Simon, if "the Roman spoils and the money taken from Cestius" (2 § 564) were in his charge. This Eleazar will have a role of the first rank during the siege of Jerusalem, as leader of that Zealot party, that will fight side by side with and against the men of John of Gischala and of Simon bar Gioras: the party of mainly priestly extraction that fights within the Temple enclosure for the purity of worship and tradition (Hengel 1961: 64ff, 373ff; Jossa 1980: 61-77; 92-94). There are at least three groups that helped in the Jews' victory over Cestius Gallus: the one of Eleazar son of Ananias, the one of Simon bar Gioras, and the one of Eleazar son of Simon. Therefore, the popular government that entrusted Josephus with the mission in Galilee should have been constituted mainly by these groups, if what the historian states is true: "those who had pursued Cestius, after going back to Jerusalem, attracted those who still supported the Romans to their side, some by force and others by persuasion and, gathered in the Temple, appointed several commanders for the war" (*JW* 2 § 562). It is on the basis of this passage that most scholars speak of the government of Jerusalem as a revolutionary one and regard Josephus' mission in Galilee as a military one.

But Josephus' account leaves out more things than it says. First of all, in the list of commanders (στρατηγοί) appointed by the government, Simon bar Gioras is missing. He is mentioned later on at 2 § 652, with the following statement: "in the toparchy of Acrabatene Simon, son of Gioras, after gathering many innovators, took to robberies, and not only ravaged the houses of the rich, but also abused their persons and since then it was clear that he started to act as a tyrant." On that same occasion it is added that "after an army was sent against him by Ananus and the authorities, he and his men took refuge with the brigands at Masada where he remained until Ananus and his other adversaries were killed, overrunning Idumaea" (2 § 653). Here Simon bar Gioras does not appear at all. It is also said that the

Acrabatene had John the son of Ananias as commanding officer (2 §
568). Therefore, the one who will be the main leader of the Jewish war
and who, after a probably moderate beginning,[3] will assume more and
more openly "brigandlike," that is, radical attitudes, not only has not
been entrusted with an appointment by the popular government, but
almost certainly departed or was sent away from Jerusalem because of
being at odds with government members. These differences became so
profound that Ananus and the other authorities felt compelled to send
an army against him. It appears clear that the popular government (at
least in its majority) does not share in any way Simon bar Gioras'
political and social attitudes, even though these will become openly
revolutionary only later on.

But Josephus' account contains another equally interesting piece of
information, when he says that "no appointment was in fact given to
Eleazar son of Simon, though the Roman spoils and the money taken
from Cestius, beyond many other things of the public treasure, were
in his charge, since he appeared to be tyrannic and the Zealots at his
dependance acted as bodyguards" (2 § 564). So even the man who will
be the leader of the Zealots and who had had such a relevant part in
the victory over Cestius Gallus that the expectations of having him
charged with the highest command would appear well founded,[4] did
not get any appointment from the government. According to Josephus
it will be the people themselves, the δῆμος, that later on will entrust
him with the highest powers (2 § 565). This might be the historian's
unintentional admission that the Zealots had deeper roots and a wider
consensus among the people than he would like us to believe. But as
a matter of fact the Zealots will have entrusted him more simply with
their own group leadership, since later on Eleazar will appear only as
the Zealots' chief (JW 5 § 5-8). Here, however, he does not get any

---

[3] Simon at the beginning is near to the groups of Eleazar son of Ananias and
Eleazar son of Simon and is not defined a "brigand", that is a radical. In the
Acrabatene he still lists mostly "innovators," that is moderate men, even though
"since then already . . . he started to act as a tyrant." Only after the coalition
with the brigands of Masada and Ananus' killing the radical character of Simon's
positions appears clearly. He first makes a number of "brigandlike raids in the
outskirts of Masada," then retreats in the mountains promising "freedom to the
slaves and rewards to the free men" (2 §§ 653-54; 4 §§ 503-8).

[4] Also the γάρ which editors usually do not translate points in this direction.
After having said that the city government was entrusted to Joseph son of Gorion
and to Ananus, Josephus uses it to introduce his remark about Eleazar.

appointment. So it appears clear that also the leader of the moderate group of Zealots does not enjoy enough esteem among the majority of the popular government.

A final piece of information is emphasized in Josephus' account. It refers to Eleazar son of the high priest Neus, who in the government allotment of appointments got Idumaea (*JW* 2 § 566). Since no source mentions a high priest called Neus, critics are inclined to identify this Eleazar with Eleazar son of Ananias, the one who had stopped daily sacrifices for the Roman emperor and afterwards had fought and killed Menahem the grandson of Judas. If this is true, it should be concluded that even a moderate of aristocratic descent, as surely this Eleazar was, who repelled the political and social revolution of the "brigand" Menahem (*JW* 2 §§ 443-48; Jossa 1980: 89-92), was considered too radical by the Jerusalem government to receive a particularly delicate appointment and that he was therefore sent to a peripheric region of Palestine which was less important for the war. If, on the contrary, it were untrue, we should conclude that no appointment was given by the government even to Eleazar son of Ananias, though he had been somehow the initiator of the revolt.

None of the three men most responsible for the victory over Cestius Gallus was therefore given relevant appointments by the new government. This says a great deal about the character of that government. Clearly they wanted to get out of the way the most prestigious and passionate persons as the most dangerous ones. But it is no less meaningful to see who is in fact appointed. Let us keep in mind, first of all, that Joseph son of Gorion and the high priest Ananus, both representatives of Jerusalem's aristocracy, were appointed "highest authorities of the city government" (2 § 563). We do not know anything about the former, neither before nor after this election, unless he is to be identified with Gorion son of Joseph mentioned at *JW* 4 §§ 159, 358, who first set himself against the Zealots and later was their victim.[5] Instead, we know rather a lot about the latter. He is the one, in fact, who will send an entire army against Simon bar Gioras "who started to act as a tyrant" (2 §§ 652-53), as we have already seen but also, according to Josephus, after doing his utmost in order to bring back

---

[5] As Drexler (1926: 299-300) suggests, recalling the similar exchange of names in the case of one of the messengers sent by Ananus against Josephus, in *JW* 2 § 628 and *Life* § 197.

to reason "those thoughtless of the so-called Zealots" (2 § 651),
having failed in his endeavour in this direction, will stir up all the
people to react against them (4 § 160). A man then not only a long
way from Simon bar Gioras' radical positions, but also clearly alien to
the Zealots' moderate ones. Obviously we can not disregard Josephus'
peculiar outlook, and his attempt to free Ananus from the responsibility for the war, while attributing it completely to "brigands" and
"innovators." Yet it is impossible to share those scholars' opinions who
want the Jewish aristocracy involved in the war against the Romans
together with the Zealots and victim only of their own weakness
(Drexler 1926: 208-81, 287ff; Ricciotti 1937: 1.5; 2.308-9). The tragic
end of Ananus too, who was killed by the Idumaeans who were
momentarily allied with the Zealots (4 § 316), is in reality a further
confirmation of his rather more ambiguous than weak attitude to the
war. His presence at the head of the government of Jerusalem means
therefore that the pro-Roman members still have, at this moment of
the revolt, the situation in their hands, having been successful in
keeping the popular government under their control.

This is confirmed, in my opinion, by all the appointments of the so-
called στρατηγοί, which we can pass judgment on. In fact, Jesus son
of Sapphas, perhaps another high priest, was placed in command of
Idumaea, together with Eleazar son of Neus, who supposedly is no one
else but Eleazar son of Ananias; whereas Niger, the Peraean, one of
those who made himself conspicuous by fighting against Cestius, was
enjoined to submit to their orders (2 § 566). The toparchy of Thamna,
with the cities of Lydda, Joppe, and Emmaus, was granted to John the
Essene, of whom we know absolutely nothing, but whose previous
participation in the renowned pacifist sect makes us suspect of his not
going into raptures about the war (2 § 567). Our historian Josephus,
son of Matthias, was sent to the two strategically very important
Galilees, since the Romans were certainly to come from the North (2
§ 568). Because of his aristocratic descent (*Life* §§ 1-6), because of the
influence of his friends (*Life* §§ 7-12, 204) and because of his recent
mission to Rome (*Life* §§ 13-16), Josephus may well be considered
pro-Roman at the time.

At this point it is difficult to believe that Josephus could have been
charged by the government of Jerusalem (or by its leaders) with a
different mission from that of skillfully restraining the most radical
elements of the countryside, as it is related in the *Life*, while waiting

for the Romans to arrive and try to save the situation somehow. As we shall see now, a careful analysis of his behaviour and of his relationships with the various Jewish groups in Galilee confirms expressly this hypothesis. Against it one cannot put forward the fact that Josephus in reality assumed the command of the military operations in Galilee, putting himself at the head of that "innovator" element of people, constituted by the so-called "Galileans." For this is only the outcome both of the development of the situation and of a choice made by Josephus, that can be singled out with relative accuracy (Jossa 1992: 44-57; cf. Laqueur 1920: 103ff, 245ff).

I have already said that at the moment of receiving the charge of going to Galilee, Josephus certainly does not have a hostile attitude towards the Romans. At the beginning of his mission his behaviour is essentially moderate and pro-Roman. According to the *Life* §§ 30-53, as soon as Josephus received the appointment, he went into the main cities of Galilee: Sepphoris, Tiberias, Gischala and Gamala. He finds ferment and turmoil everywhere. More exactly, in each city he finds two parties (στάσεις): one which intends to remain faithful to the Roman government, basically constituted by the ruling classes, whom Josephus calls simply the "Sepphorites," the "Tiberians" and so on; and another which shows signs of restlessness and longing for revolt, composed of, on the whole, a majority of the Galilean population, whom Josephus usually calls the "Galileans." Between these two parties, which we could also refer to as ῥωμαΐζοντες and νεωτερίζοντες, there is often a group of the undecided, as in Tiberias, where between the authorities' party, led by Julius Capellus, and that of the Galileans, headed by Jesus son of Sapphias, there is the party of the future historian and Josephus' adversary, Justus of Tiberias (*Life* §§ 32-36). In each of these cities Josephus gets in touch first with the local authorities (the βουλή, the πρῶτοι) and tries to convince the people to remain loyal to them. For instance, in the case of Sepphoris, Josephus finds the townsmen (but he is referring clearly to the authorities) worried about the Galileans' hostile attitude toward them. He strives to persuade them to keep their temper. The case of all the other cities of Galilee is clearly similar. Faced with the Galileans' most daring initiatives Josephus assumes an attitude of moderation and restraint. When, for instance, Jesus son of Sapphias and his followers destroy Herod Antipas' palace in Tiberias because of the unlawful images contained therein, he intervenes immediately to stop the pillage and to put the King's property in a safe place (*Life* § 68). When the Galileans in his service want to force two prominent subjects of King Agrippa, who have taken shelter with him, to have themselves circumcised, he denounces the attempt and succeeds, though laboriously, in preventing it (§§ 112-13). When some young men of the small town of Dabaritta assail the wife of Ptolemy, the procurator of the King, Josephus intervenes once more to prevent the theft and to put the woman's goods in a safe place (§§ 126-28). In all these events he acts therefore in full conformity with what appears to have been his mission: to try hard especially to prevent that the situation in the country precipitate but keeping open, instead, the possibility of an agreement with the Romans. Because of this attitude quite soon the Galileans begin to openly distrust his behaviour and to entertain well-founded suspicions of his covert actions in collusion with the enemy. These suspicions are vented in an unruly assembly in the Tarichaeae hippodrome, which functions almost as the headquarters of these Galileans. There Josephus is charged by Jesus son of Sapphias (*Life* §§ 132-35) and, if we may believe *JW* 2 § 599, by John of Gischala.

Following the *Life*'s account, therefore, in the first period of his mission, Josephus keeps an attitude of extreme caution as to the war against the Romans, sustaining the positions of the leading classes of the several cities of Galilee, who are faithful to the Romans, and restraining on the contrary the initiatives of the so-called Galileans, who are well-disposed toward the innovations. This confirms that the mission he has been charged with by the authorities of Jerusalem, is not that of leading a war in which neither he nor they trusted, but of keeping a peace that at that juncture appeared still possible.

Having said this, however, it is necessary to add right away two remarks: the first being that because of the complexity of the situation in which Josephus had to disarm the πονηροί without becoming estranged from the people, he was compelled from the beginning to make important concessions to the Galileans; the second is that the situation changed quickly, since both the development of events and his ambitions pushed him toward more advanced positions than he wished.

It stands to reason that Josephus' diplomatic mission was extremely difficult and his personal position very delicate. In fact, if he had limited himself to restraining the Galileans' more daring initiatives, backing the various cities' ruling classes, he would have had the great masses of Galileans quite soon against him, as the Tarichaeae assembly clearly proves. It was then necessary to pretend to yield, and sometimes to actually yield to their demands, even if it should displease the city authorities. This was done by Josephus from the beginning. When for instance Jesus son of Sapphias carried out the order of pulling down Herod's palace, he had no power or did not recognize the opportunity for preventing it, limiting himself to putting the King's property out of pillagers' reach and certainly alienating the Tiberias authorities (*Life* §§ 64-68). Besides, if the decision of pulling down the palace had come right from the government in Jerusalem, as Josephus explicitly affirms (§ 65), he did nothing but obey a government order, which evidently deemed it necessary to make some political concessions to the Galileans.

Furthermore, the return to Jerusalem of the two priests first sent on the mission with him (§ 77), whether spontaneously or urged by him we do not know, remarkably changed Josephus' position, leaving him essentially master of the field. Already then the fear of losing the Galileans' support and the wish of increasing his personal power, pushed Josephus to stake everything on daring. After neutralizing those more radical persons in the country whom he considers "brigands" in an extremely dangerous manner, namely by asking the city people to pay them a kind of protection money (§§ 77-78), he put himself resolutely at the head of the Galileans, clearly hoping to subdue them to his own will. It was a position that looked remarkably like the one taken by Ananus within the government of Jerusalem, and it had probably been agreed upon just with him. Ananus, taking the city's highest command, intended to bring back to reason "the thoughtless of the so-called Zealots." Similarly Josephus, taking the direct command of Galileans, evidently thought to succeed in better controlling these "innovators." But whether his personality was not as strong as Ananus' or his ambition eventually overturned his own purposes, Josephus ended up increasingly surrendering to the Galileans' pressures. He not only engaged thousands of Galileans, forming for himself a personal army of considerable proportions (*Life* §§ 99, 102, 107, 212, 242, 252, 268), he made the leaders of these Galileans, members of a private council of his own, to whom he entrusted the main decisions (§§ 79, 220, 228). He also helped with soldiers and workers those Galileans who had killed a relative of Agrippa's lieutenant and the brother of Justus of Tiberias in Gamala (§ 186). It is possible as well, of course, that by these methods he still thought he could be successfull in restraining the Galileans' rashness, as he maintains over and over again in the *Life*. But it is beyond doubt that he, in doing so, appeared as the leader of these "innovators," rather than the one who acted as a brake on them.[6] It is easily explained that in so doing he aroused suspicion and envy in John of Gischala, who, being certainly at this stage of the war still pro-Roman (Jossa 1992: 53-57), did not just invite the inhabitants of Tiberias, Sepphoris and Gabara to forsake Josephus (§§ 87, 123), but took the direct initiative of asking the authorities in Jerusalem to withdraw his command (§ 190). This episode is probably a turning-point in Josephus' life and also a clue for a better understanding of this period's events. If Ananus (not the government), Josephus' influential supporters in the aristocratic spheres notwithstanding, after hesitating for a while, made up his mind and sent a four-man deputation to Galilee, precisely charged with dismissing Josephus (§§ 191-198), this clearly means that in this phase of the war it was the still pro-Roman John of Gischala rather than the too ambiguous Josephus, who earned his trust. The latter's attitude toward the Galileans persuaded the Jewish aristocracy that in order to pursue the goal of the mission in Galilee, it was more suitable to rely upon John than Josephus.

This does not mean, though, that from the moment of the two priests' return to Jerusalem, Josephus thought of nothing else but creating in Galilee a personal power base for himself, and that he built this power on the direct support of "brigands," therefore putting himself openly at odds with the Jerusalem government and betraying completely the spirit of the mission that he had been entrusted with, as chiefly Laqueur (1920: 108) believed and Ricciotti (1937: 1.10) held too, though in more moderate terms. This thesis, in fact, stumbles over several objections. First of all, it is difficult to see in the two delegates' return to Jerusalem that radical turning-point in Josephus' behaviour, that Laqueur wants to see. Certainly, free of dealing without direct government control, Josephus could assume attitudes more openly favourable toward the Galileans. But he also continued to do his utmost in order not to let the situation deteriorate beyond repair, as the two just mentioned episodes of the request of circumcising

---

[6] This is what Kreissig (1970: 138) does not see, in my opinion. He believes that all of Josephus' actions aim at delivering Galilee to the Romans.

Agrippa's subjects and of the assault on the wife of the procurator Ptolemy clearly prove. In the second place, the fact that the government in Jerusalem will in any case eventually recognize Josephus' power, calling back the deputation sent by Ananus to take away his command, shows that this episode does not constitute a radical break in the previous situation. It is Laqueur's (1920: 115) opinion that the government made the best of a bad bargain, recognizing in lawful form the power Josephus had until then illegally exercised, depending on the agreement with the brigands. But would it have ever done such a thing if that power were completely unlawful and if it really relied upon the brigands? Last, but not least, this thesis is based on the identification of "innovators" and "brigands," two substantially different Jewish groups, as is clear already from *Life* § 28 (Jossa 1992: 16-30). It is also based on the non-identification of the "Galileans," who are a peculiar group of inhabitants of Galilee as attentive students of the *Life* well know (Jossa 1992: 44-57). As a matter of fact, Josephus did not rely upon the "brigands," as Laqueur and Ricciotti believe on grounds of a sole paragraph of the *Life* (§ 77), but upon the "Galileans," as is clear from the remainder of the *Life*. The Galileans are only "innovators": that is not "radical" elements who fight for a general revolt against the Roman government, but "moderate" elements who defend mostly the cultural and religious traditions of the country and live in constant fear of the "brigands" (§ 206).

Therefore it is not true that Josephus put himself at the head of the brigands, as Laqueur (1920: 108-16) writes, and that, having broken all relations with the government in Jerusalem, he became a thorough "rebel." He put himself, instead, at the leadership of the Galileans adopting the tactics of waiting and trying to still keep open the possibility of a mutual understanding with the Romans. Therefore, it is true that Ananus and his friends, sending the deputation to Galilee, show at last clearly that they do not trust Josephus anymore, but it is also true that the government in Jerusalem, confirming his power, shows that it shares the more open attitude toward the Galileans taken by Josephus and that it wants to back it up.

The situation then, as it is known, will change once more after Josephus' surrender at Jotapata and John's defence at Gischala. At that point it will be John who will become the surviving leader of the Galileans. It will be necessary only to inquire what would have changed the former pro-Roman man into an "innovator," whether it

was a definite inner evolution or just the pressure of the Galileans
(Rhoads 1976: 12-137; Rappaport 1982: 479-93). Certainly the Galileans who succeeded in escaping the Romans joined John's formation
and constituted his military support in Jerusalem. There is no reason
to think with Freyne (1980: 411) that the Galileans who, according to
Josephus, will support John in the further course of the war (*JW* 4 §§
558-59) should be understood now in an exclusively geographical sense,
though the word in the *War* has not yet the religious meaning it will
assume in the *Life*. On the contrary, the Galilean participation in the
Zealots' actions in the Temple area is the last corroboration of a
religious trend among them akin to the Zealots, a trend that was
present already in Galilee and that now involves John too. Josephus
is very harsh in his judgment on them (*JW* 4 §§ 560-63). This is
understandable since he strikes with a single blow at his former allies
and at his perpetual enemy: the Galileans and John of Gischala. Yet,
together with the Zealots they remain the expression of a more
moderate trend among the rebels in comparison with that of Simon
bar Gioras and of the Sicarii. This is the reason why in the triumph
celebrated in Rome at the end of the war, it will be Simon and not
John, who will be condemned to death as the leader of the rebellion.

WHERE WAS JOSEPHUS LYING –
IN HIS *LIFE* OR IN THE *WAR*?

Uriel Rappaport

One of the great obstacles in the research on the Jewish revolt against
Rome is the meagerness, if not the near absence of parallel sources
about it. With the exception of a few details, mentioned by historians
other than Josephus (Stern 1983:110-12; 1974-1984: *passim*), we
depend almost completely on his *War* as the only source. To arrive at
some meaningful historical understanding of the Jewish War, we are
forced to pass Josephus' evidence through the sieve of scientific
analysis and interpretation.

The most significant, though partial, parallel we do have concerning
the revolt is included within the Josephan corpus itself, that is the
events covered by both the *War* and the so-called *Life* of Josephus.
Obviously the cumulative value of these two sources is greatly dimin-
ished because both were written by the same author. Although we
have two sources, we have only one author, whose two reports are
marred by similar weaknesses – his involvement in the events he
describes; his personal, partisan, national and political interests; his
apologetics and his subservience to his Roman patrons.[1]

Nevertheless, we have no better opportunity to use comparative
methodology for research on the revolt than in the case of the events
described by both *War* and *Life*. The list of comparable events, though
not very long, is considerable, but we will not go into the details now.[2]

Besides the comparison of various events we must compare the
main theme concerning the revolt in each composition. This is unque-
stionably the role of Josephus in Galilee, as told in each one of them
(Cf. Cohen 1978: 8). This is a pivotal point, which reflects on other

---

[1] All these motives were discussed many times, and even additional motives
were ascribed to Josephus, such as his relations with Agrippa II, with the high
priesthood, with the Pharisees etc. See recently S. Schwartz 1990: *passim*.

[2] A comparison of both books can be found in Cohen (1978: 3-8; 261-63); Rajak
(1983: 154-66), and Bilde (1988: 39), who has mistakenly mentioned Justus in
referring to the *War*.

discrepancies in the two books, and may shed light on such problems as the leadership of the revolt and the policy of its government in general.

Josephus role in Galilee is sharply different in the *War* than in the *Life*. In the *War* he is a general and governor (στρατηγός) of Galilee,[3] appointed to lead the revolt against Rome in this region. He was expected to take care of all the necessary preparations to confront the Roman invasion, to overcome all kinds of disobedience toward the "revolutionary" government in Jerusalem and to reduce supporters of Rome and its allies.

In *Life* Josephus' role is considerably different. He reluctantly joined the rebels' side; he was sent to Galilee to minimize the rebellious tendencies; he was mainly absorbed in internal quarrels with people who are accused of being anti-Roman and fomenting revolt, an accusation which put him clearly on the Roman side (for more details see below).

Scholars differ about the veracity of the *War*'s account as compared to that of the *Life*, both on detail and on the general issue of Josephus' role in Galilee.[4] Those who prefer the *War* have seemingly a solid basis for their preference: the *War*'s account is far closer in time than *Life*'s to the events described; the *War*'s account is more concise and the events in Galilee are implanted within the general framework of the war. As compared to the *War*, *Life*'s account is treated with suspicion because it is primarily a defense against the attack of Justus of Tiberias, and as such is more prone to fabrication than the *War*.[5]

But what is the value of these criteria of time, framework and motivation? In my opinion they should be discarded. The closeness in time of a historian to his subject is of little importance in itself, in comparison to questions like the availability of sources, sound judge-

---

[3] Explicitly in *JW* 2 §§ 562-69. This word is avoided in *Life* § 29, a fact which accords with the spirit of the description there.

[4] Rajak (1983: 147) tries to bridge between the two accounts. Schürer (1973-87: 1. 53-4; 489-91) usually follows the *War*, appreciates *Life* very little and uses it only as a secondary source.

[5] Rajak (1973: 344-68); but cf. her more recent work (Rajak 1983: 152), where she departs from this opinion and suggests that in *Life* Josephus is replying to various authors, not only to Justus. Cf. also her article (1987) and Cohen (1979: 114). For a review of the changing positions concerning *War* and *Life* see Cohen (1979: 8-23). For recent works which give preference to *War* as against *Life* see Bilde (1988: 160-61; 174-75) and for the opposite position, *ibid.*, 175-76.

ment, relative objectivity etc. Since no great change is noticed in Josephus' approach to historiography (though his subject was changed) or in the availability of sources for his work on the Jewish revolt between the seventies and the nineties of the first century CE, the time elapsed between these decades is of little import for our discussion.[6]

The literary comparison between *War* and *Life* carries some weight, but mainly in relation to the more detailed report in *Life* versus *War*, not on Josephus' role in Galilee.[7]

The third and more important reason to prefer *War* to *Life* is *Life*'s tendentiousness, by reason of its being a response to Justus' accusa-

---

[6] Some historians think that in his *Life* Josephus used an earlier source than in the *War*, but whether right or wrong (we think the latter), it does not affect our argument. More important may be the change in Josephus' attitude, in these decades, towards Agrippa II and his relatives, the High Priesthood, the "upper" priesthood and the Pharisees/Rabbis, as suggested by S. Schwartz (1990). Yet even if such a change may explain Josephus' "new" attitude towards Agrippa or Simeon ben Gamaliel in *Life*, it does not affect the presentation of his own role in Galilee. Concerning Josephus' attitude towards the Pharisees see Mason (1991) and Feldman (1992h). A possible change in Josephus' position in Rome can be ascribed to Domitian's rule (81-96 CE) and to his policy towards Jews and Judaism. But should it be related to Josephus' description of his role in Galilee? Was he writing under the menace of reprisals because of his generalship in the rebellion (as presented in the *War*)? Were Justus' accusations aimed at condemning Josephus before Domitian? If so, did Josephus write *Life* to exculpate himself in Roman eyes? In fact, *Antiquities* was published in Domitian's days, and it shows less sympathy, not to say servility, to Rome, than *War*. One historian even suggested that in *Antiquities* one can find a certain warning to Domitian, in anticipation of inimical measures he may take against Jews (Case 1925: 10-20; Smallwood 1956: 10-11; Cohen 1978: 138). Josephus himself does not show that he had such considerations in *Life*. There he boasts about the favors that (even) Domitian conferred upon him (*Life* § 429). The publication of *Antiquities* under Domitian also testifies to Josephus' relative security at that time (93-94 CE; Cf. Thackeray, LCL vol 1: xi). So the major event in Josephus' literary career, between the publication of *War* and *Life*, was Justus' accusations, and in this light the differences between the two works should be seen. Furthermore, it can be argued that even if Josephus' position was less secure under Domitian, because of his unfriendly policy towards Judaism, and especially towards Judaizers (Smallwood 1976: 376-85), and if this attitude brought Josephus to change the description of his role in Galilee from στρατηγός to that of a pacifier of Galilee, it does not preclude the probability, that this was his real mission to Galilee, which he admitted only under the new circumstances of Domitian's later years.

[7] Cf. Rajak (1983: 154-66). We do not share her opinion that many of the discrepancies between the two works can be resolved because *War* and *Life* belong to different literary forms.

tions. Indeed in *Life* Josephus is compelled to respond to Justus' attack, and to defend his own behavior, so that he did not have historical truth in mind when he wrote *Life*, but rather his personal defense. So, it may be concluded, we should prefer the historical writing, with its Thucydidean pretence, than the personal apologetic piece of work which is *Life*.

But a few questions come to mind. Is the *War* a genuine "Thucydidean" work? As most scholars agree *War* is far from being Thucydidean and its veracity is often questionable. At least four kinds of considerations lead Josephus astray from the quest of truth: one is personal (his role in the war and his personal image); the second is political (that is partisan, defending his and his "party's" position in the war); the third is national (caring for his people's interests, as he understood them) and the fourth is the service he rendered to his Roman benefactors, the Flavians. Compared to *War*, *Life* with its defense of mainly personal interests, looks quite innocent.

Beyond this consideration we should ask whether a personal apologetic writing such as *Life*, is by definition untruthful. Such a statement is logically incorrect. The relation between accusation and defense is manifold. An accusation may be right and a defense wrong or *vice versa*, or both can be right or both can be wrong.

In *Life*'s case the situation is even more complicated, and various additional considerations interfere with our judgement. The foundation of Justus' accusations against Josephus can only be guessed (Cohen 1979: 114-20; Rajak 1983: 152-54), yet it looks as if Justus referred, at least partially, to *War* either for information against Josephus, or to strengthen some of his accusations. Even if this cannot be proved, Justus' claim that Josephus was a warmonger and incited Tiberias to revolt (Rajak 1983: 153, n. 21; 1987: 81-94) is confirmed in the *War*. So we may assume that his attack on Josephus on this point did not contradict *War* but was generally in line with it.

A few examples may show this changing of positions on Josephus' side. In *JW* 2 §§ 645-46 it is explicitly admitted that Tiberias wished, as did Sepphoris, to adhere to the Roman camp. It failed because of Josephus' military intervention. This fits well with what seem to be Justus' charges against Josephus, that he was responsible for Tiberias' misfortune (*Life* § 340).

The parallel section in *Life* §§ 381-89, mitigates considerably the above picture. According to it, Josephus rescued Tiberias from being sacked by the Galileans. This is contradictory to *JW* 2 § 646 (". . . he [Josephus] delivered it over to his soldiers [that is the above mentioned Galileans] to plunder").

Evidently Josephus could not stick to his story in the *War*, which substantiated Justus' accusations. He chose to admit, to some measure the truth, which suited his actual present interest, though it did not support his own self-image, which he cherished when he wrote *War* (Rappaport 1977: 91-97).

The hidden truth about his activity in Galilee in 66-67 is that in reality he did not possess much authority in Galilean affairs and that he sided with the moderates. This fact, which he preferred not to disclose in public in the seventies when he wrote the *War*, he admitted in *Life* § 175 because it served him better in the nineties than in the seventies.

In other words: writing in the seventies, Josephus depicted himself as a great and resourceful general. A general (στρατηγός) of Galilee, who despite his personal point of view, did all in his power to comply with his (supposed) task to fight the Romans. As such, he had to force Sepphoris and Tiberias, which inclined towards Rome and Agrippa II, to participate in the revolt.

In the nineties the situation was changed. He found himself attacked on various fronts including his responsibility for the misfortunes of Tiberias. This forced him to disclose that in reality he was not doing his job, contrary to what he declared in the *War*. Indeed he claimed that he tried to save both Sepphoris and Tiberias from Galilean reprisals. His support of the revolt was only a cover-up, so as not to raise the suspicions of the rebels (*Life* § 175).

Being attacked in this way, Josephus' defense must have been perforce different from the report on his activity in Galilee, as recounted in the *War*. Knowing *War* to be false and perceiving that it was being used against him directly or indirectly, by Justus, Josephus was forced in defending himself to deny some of his own allegations in the *War*. He was forced to replace them with new assertions which were hidden till then and which may represent the truth. In other words, Justus' accusations might have compelled Josephus to admit the truth about his role in Galilee and disclose various matters, which were inconvenient for him, and were not revealed in the *War*. If we are right, this reflects on various events and details recounted in the *War* as well as on the Jewish leadership in Jerusalem at that time. In our view Josephus' *Life* is a confession or an admission of his real role in Galilee, and not a deceitful denial. Justus' accusations based on, or at least in partial agreement with the *War* pushed Josephus into an impasse. Defending his *War* would have bound his hands in repelling Justus' attacks. So he wisely chose to give up his twisted report in the *War*, and to admit in *Life* some of the facts he was hiding in his *War*.[8]

Let us return now to the most important difference between *War* and *Life*, that is, as already mentioned, Josephus' role in Galilee (Rappaport 1983a: 36-47). In *JW* 2 § 563 he is one of the commanders appointed to prepare Judea against the Romans. Arriving in Galilee he tries to fulfill this assignment by recruiting a huge Jewish army (100.000 – *JW* 2 § 576; 60.000 + 350 horsemen + 4.500 "mercenaries" + 600 bodyguards – *JW* 2 § 583), organizing and drilling it in the Roman fashion. He declared himself to be faithful to this task, and to perform his duty till the bitter end. Only then, and only because of divine intervention, he went over to the Roman side.[9] When he is blamed of pro-Roman inclination he denies it forcefully (*JW* 2 § 594). The assumed role of commander (στρατηγός) of Galilee is also maintained in *JW* 2 § 647, as well as in battles against the Sepphoreans and Placidus (*JW* 3 §§ 59-63), as is his declaration of fidelity to the cause of the revolt.[10] Obviously the story of Jotapata crowns his Galilean command, although he refrained from discussing it in *Life* (see our discussion below). The policy as described by Josephus in the *War* is in line with the position of Hanan ben Hanan's government, which was discussed elsewhere (Rappaport 1983a: 34-36).

---

[8] See his own words in *Life* §§ 338-39: "being therefore, now compelled to defend myself against these false allegations, I shall allude to matters about which I have hitherto kept silent. My omission to make such a statement at an earlier date should not occasion surprise. For while veracity is incumbent upon a historian, he is nonetheless at liberty to refrain from harsh scrutiny of the misdeeds of individuals, not from any partiality for the offenders, but because of his own moderation." Cohen (1979: 114-15) comments that this statement is a commonplace, but even a commonplace is used to serve some aim, and in this case to exculpate Josephus from hiding relevant information from his readers.

[9] A detailed description with references to the *War* is to be found in Rajak (1983: 166-71).

[10] *JW* 3 § 137, a very suggestive passage indeed: "As for himself, although he might look for pardon from the Romans, he would have preferred to suffer a thousand deaths rather than betray his country and disgracefully abandon the command which had been entrusted to him, in order to seek his fortune among those whom he had been commissioned to fight."

In *Life* Josephus' role is different. Already in Jerusalem he is among those who wish to calm the tendencies toward revolt (*Life* §§ 17-19). He and others who shared the same conviction, because of the threat of death disguised their opinion and pretended to agree with the rebels (*Life* §§ 20-23, esp. 22-23, which refer to the time before Cestius' arrival). After the victory over Cestius Gallus, though the rebellion had gained wider support, the Jerusalem aristocracy sent Josephus with two other companions to still peaceful Galilee, in order to keep it that way, that is to curb the power, influence and activity of the rebels.[11] Josephus' role as peacemaker is revealed also through various incidents in his story. Sepphoris is initially pro-Roman and as such is helped by Josephus on his arrival in Galilee (*Life* §§ 30-31). In the *War* Sepphoris is described at the early stage of Josephus' activity in Galilee as cooperating with him on the anti-Roman side (*JW* 2 § 574). This is an example of Josephus' consistency in presenting his roles in both his reports (*War* and *Life*) by adjusting the secondary events to the general picture he wishes to present. This can also be seen in the Dabaritta incident, where though the story is the same in its general lines, in *Life* § 128 he openly admits his intention to give back the spoils to their owner.[12]

What is the truth then? Is there some hidden motive behind the differences, the additions and the omissions in *War* and *Life*? "Why did Josephus change his story from the first version (*War*) to the second (*Life*)?" (Cohen 1978: 1). It seems that, at least in part, they were dictated by Justus' accusations, which Josephus tried to refute.

What the exact contents of Justus' accusations against Josephus were, we can only guess. Whatever can be gleaned can only be arrived

---

[11] No clear description of them is given. They are mentioned as λησταί (*Life* §§ 77, 106, 145, 175, 206) or Galileans (*Life* § 30 et *passim*), never as Zealots or Sicarii. They may be identified by the name of their leader, as in the case of Jesus son of Sapphias. For John of Gischala see Rappaport 1983b: 46-57 (with bibliography in n. 2); 1982: 479-93; 1983c: 97-115 (Hebrew). For Galileans see Bilde 1988: 40-44, with references to further literature. For references to Josephus' text see Schalit 1968: 32. This role of Josephus as peacemaker is revealed also through various incidents in his story.

[12] In *War* the valuables were robbed from Agrippa's steward, Ptolemy, whereas in *Life* from Ptolemy's wife. I doubt if much can be concluded from this variance and I assume Josephus is simply adding a detail to his concise report in the *War*, with no hidden intention behind it. See *Life* § 126 and M. Stein, in his translation of *Life* (1959, note *ad loc.*, Hebrew).

at through Josephus' *Life*. It seems very probable that among other accusations, Justus blamed Josephus for Tiberias' entanglement in the revolt (*Life* §§ 338-341; 349). Although the city finally succeeded in extricating itself from its entanglement, nevertheless its position *vis-à-vis* Rome became vulnerable and its image besmirched, especially in comparison to Sepphoris, the city of peace (*Irenopolis*) and the favorite of Rome in Jewish Galilee (Seyrig 1950: 284-89; 1955: 157-59 and Meshorer 1979).

Evidently Josephus' personality and behavior were also denigrated by Justus. Josephus reciprocated by slandering and by boasting about his noble spirit and moral behavior. But this level of their polemics is historically much less important.

What really matters is the accusation that Josephus was responsible for Tiberias' misfortune, that is, its depiction as un-friendly to Rome, unlike its neighboring city, Sepphoris. If Josephus were indeed a sincerely devoted commander of this region and if he, supporting the rebellion's cause, successfully interfered with Tiberian affairs, then he must be guilty of the charge that because of him, Tiberias failed to come out of the war unsullied in Roman eyes.

But was Josephus the commander of Galilee in charge of leading it against the Romans? Or was he an envoy (with two others), sent to pacify Galilee? In *Life* he had only one motivation, if any, to distort the truth, and that was Justus' attack. In *War* he had various motivations, relating to his being a protégé of the Flavians, being implicated in the recent uproar in Judea, trying to depict his own person in a certain manner (Rappaport 1977; Cohen 1979: 91-97) and defending certain political and ideological positions. In *War* his role in Galilee was one component in the composite construction of Jewish leadership and society, which he built up, whereas in *Life* his role in Galilee is the central and only theme. In *War* the pressure on Josephus to distort the truth was much greater than in *Life*, and from this aspect as well *Life* is more credible than the *War*.

We think that the whole picture of the situation in Judea as described in the *War* is misleading.[13] Josephus, residing in Rome in the nineties as a writer favored by the establishment, was taken by

---

[13] See Rappaport (1983a: 34-36, 55-59; 1992). It is interesting to note that Salvador (1847: 2.44-53) understood the events in Galilee under Josephus' command, and by implication also the situation in Jerusalem, in a similar way, though his reading of the sources was rather naive.

surprise by Justus' attack. He was trapped by Justus not only because Justus disclosed unpleasant stories about him (whether they were true or false we cannot tell) and published a book purported to be a better and more trustworthy work than the *War*, but also because Justus could cite, and probably cited, Josephus' own work to prove his accusations, i.e., that Tiberias was unnecessarily damaged by Josephus and that Josephus fomented revolt in Galilee.

Josephus contends in many places, including *Life* §§ 339; 361-67, that his veracity is irreproachable. Nevertheless he gives up so easily the basic foundation of his *War*, that Hanan ben Hanan's government led the revolt in good faith as he himself was doing in Galilee. *War*'s veracity is broken to pieces by the new perspective he proposes in *Life*. Why then did he not try to uphold his *War*'s version faced with Justus' attack on him? Is it not because under Justus' attack it became indefensible? Justus had no interest in describing Josephus as a peace-maker, on the contrary, he wished to show him as a commander who failed in his task, caused mischief and brought disaster on those whose security was entrusted to him, and was an enemy of Rome. This picture can be drawn by partial and intentional use of the *War*. Josephus was forced to disclose the truth, to save his reputation, or even his neck, that neither his command of Galilee, nor Hanan's government, were ever intended to fight the Romans and so he cannot be responsible for Tiberias' entanglement in the war.

Probably it was even more difficult for Josephus to respond to Justus' accusations that he was lying about the siege of Jotapata (*Life* § 357). His only response is to point out that Justus was then far from the arena of war, and so deprived of αὐτοψία (seeing with his own eyes), while Josephus boasts (*AgAp* 1 § 55) αὐτοψία as his own virtue as a historian (Cohen 1979: 115, and n. 57 for bibliography). He also makes other irrelevant minor accusations.

Yet, a detailed review of his own participation in the war at Jota-pata could have been expected, as he had written concerning his activity in Tiberias and in Galilee. But Josephus terminated the story of his sojourn in Galilee with Vespasian's arrival there, and for the rest he refers the reader to the *War* (*Life* § 412). This cannot be taken as unintentional, since the end of *Life* should have, most naturally, been put at the real turning-point, when Josephus surrendered to the Romans and his career took a new start. In this way *Life* would really fully encompass the Galilean chapter in Josephus' career, whereas

Vespasian's invasion of Galilee did not influence his life in any meaningful way. Indeed, in *AgAp* 1 § 48 Josephus divides his career according to this line, that is before and after his Roman captivity.

How then can the conclusion of *Life*, as it stands, be explained? Josephus' explanation, that the concluding event at Jotapata was described in detail in the *War* (*Life* § 412) is not satisfactory,[14] and his grouping together the siege of Jotapata and his capture there with his conduct in the campaign and in the siege of Jerusalem, by referring to the *War*, is an exercise in misleading the reader (of which he was an expert). In any case it should be stressed, that Josephus did not refrain from dealing in *Life* with topics which were described by him in the *War*.

So the most probable explanation for the abrupt termination of *Life* is that Justus' accusations about his behavior in Jotapata (and probably also the means by which he managed to survive) and his description of his activity in Galilee, hit a very sensitive nerve and hurt Josephus deeply, both as a historian and as the person he tried so hard to depict through his false stories in the *War*.

Josephus chose not to respond in detail to Justus' accusations, that he was a liar and a coward (or a traitor to his own people). He preferred to cast doubt on Justus' veracity, on the basis of the general principle of αὐτοψία. Admitting the truth on this point would have been extremely harmful, as well as painful, to Josephus, and so he left Justus' accusations unanswered.

That Josephus is not indifferent to his prestige as a historian can be seen by his vehement defense of it in his *AgAp* 1 §§ 47-56, written, more or less, in the same decade as *Life*.[15] Evidently the understanding of the contradictions between *War* and *Life*, as proposed here, depends on some other assumptions too. We think that personal relations and local interests were more dominant in Galilean politics at that stage of the war than ideology, and that no major ideological issues then separated people like Josephus, Justus, John of Gischala,

---

[14] Rappaport 1983a. Rajak 1983: 154 and Cohen 1979: 116, n. 61; 121, n. 80, are aware of Josephus' silence about Jotapata in *Life*, but I do not find their explanations convincing.

[15] The themes of this passage resemble Josephus' prologue to the *War* (cf. Mason 1991: 76). He does not mention Justus, but other "despicable persons who malign his history." Justus may be one of them, but no argument with his specific criticism of *War* is taken up there by Josephus.

Simeon ben Gamaliel, Philippus ben Jakimos, Agrippa II, the Seppho-
rean leaders and the Tiberian aristocracy (Rappaport 1982: 481, 486,
488-9; 1983b: 53-54; 1983c: 99-100).

All of these people, as well as the aristocracy in Jerusalem and in
some of the major towns in the country, like Gadara in Peraea (*JW* 4
§ 414), aimed at some arrangement with Rome. Their double-faced
policy is veiled by Josephus in the *War*, but is unmasked in *Life*. This
we owe to Justus, who forced Josephus, as he himself admitted, to
disclose at least part of what he was hiding until then (see note 8
above).

JOSEPHUS IN GALILEE:
RURAL PATRONAGE AND SOCIAL BREAKDOWN

Seth Schwartz

There are those of us who have made a cottage industry of detecting Josephus' biases. But we have tended to neglect some of the most important ones, either because we share them or because we consider them too obvious to point out. One of these biases is Judaeocentrism: Josephus viewed his topic as consisting mostly of the history of the Judaeans. The Jewish war for Josephus was mostly the Judaean war; he said little about the Idumaean or Peraean wars, and, apart from his own activities, little even about the Galilean war. Likewise, the title of his second work can almost be translated "Judaean antiquities", and the religion Josephus defended in *Against Apion* is that of priests and scholars of the Torah, that is, essentially the Judaean religion and its urban diasporic offshoots, not the unknown and probably quite different religion of Galilee or Idumaea.

Another unremarked element in Josephus' *oeuvre* is his urban bias. This Josephus partly borrowed from his Greek models, for whom history meant the history of civilizations, and "civilizations" meant cities. But I think this bias also reflects his own experience. Josephus came from a landowning family (*Life* § 422) but seems to have grown up entirely in Jerusalem (*Life* §§ 7-9). Since his father survived at least until the time of Josephus' surrender (*JW* 5 § 533), it is probable that the son never had to worry much about the family farm. And from 71 on Josephus apparently lived in the city of Rome, though he continued to own land in Judaea (*Life* §§ 422, 425, 429).

For us as historians, these presumably unconscious biases are far more damaging than those commonly noted because they shaped his narrative in more profound ways. When for example Josephus says the Pharisees were powerful, we can observe that they play little role in his account of the history of the later second temple period and so correct his misrepresentation. But what can we do when confronted with his silence about the countryside, and areas outside Judaea? But of course his silence is not complete. Josephus spent a few miserable months among the country people of Galilee. He probably didn't understand them very well, and certainly had plenty of reasons to lie about details of his visit. Nevertheless, this Galilean episode is important because Josephus' reports of it mark his only major departures from his urban and Judaean biases — at least one can say that here their influence on his account is more subtle than usual.

This rare information allows us to consider some frequently contested issues: How should we imagine rural social relations in Palestine — as a system in which wealthy and poor were generally bound to each other by ties of reciprocal obligation — i.e., patronage, as in a "normal" Mediterranean society or, as Goodman (1987) has suggested for Judaea, as one in which relations between rich and poor were purely contractual and patronage was therefore insignificant? Was the great revolt caused and/or accompanied by socio-economic collapse?

I will argue that Galilee, at least, was a patronal society; that the partial urbanization of the district by Antipas and the drainage of wealth from it due to the imposition of direct Roman rule brought about the formation of a class of absentee landlords, and the impoverishment of the poorer farmers; these developments in turn brought about a partial collapse of the patronal system, resulting in the rise of brigandage and the growth in power of some country landlords. While these changes cannot explain the outbreak of revolt, they form an essential part of its background.

1. *Patrons and Clients in Galilee*

Martin Goodman (1987: 51-75), in his fundamental discussion of social conditions in first-century Judaea , has argued that Judaea was not a patronal society in any significant way. The point seems overstated and many of his arguments are of questionable validity;[1] nevertheless

---

[1] E.g., Goodman argues that Judaean peasants were normally bound to landowners only by contract. The peasants knew that the "divinely ordained ideal" required each man to *own* his own plot, and so, as tenants, felt resentment towards the owners: ties of reciprocal obligation were not sanctioned by custom and did not develop. Similarly, the wealthy were obliged in bad times to provide help to the poor; the poor were not obliged to be grateful. For these reasons, Judaea never became in any significant way a patronal society. But the Judaean peasants' awareness of various "divinely ordained ideals" (i.e., biblical passages) is questionable, and contractual relationships, in themselves, between tenant and landlord would not have (and in many societies have in fact not) precluded the

Goodman may be partly right: patronage was somewhat less important in Judaea than in many other rural districts of the eastern Mediterranean. Can we extrapolate from Judaea to the rest of Palestine? Did the baneful economic influence of the Temple and city of Jerusalem interfere with normal social relations in other parts of the country as well? Revolutionary Lower Galilee will have to serve as a test case.

Needless to say, Josephus never comes out and says that patronage was important in the part of Galilee he knew; his account merely assumes it was. While in Galilee, Josephus, by his own account, behaved in ways which can best be understood as indicating that he wished to be thought of, either by his readers in the 80s and 90s or by his victims in the 60s, as a patron of the local landowners and city elites. This explains his (alleged) attempts to protect the pro-Roman Sepphorites from brigands and hostile country people (*Life* § 31),[2] his claim to have protected the country landowners from brigands by establishing himself as the latters' employer (behavior typical of rural nobility),[3] his treatment of the leading landlords as φίλοι and συνεκδή-μοι (*Life* § 79), the latters' attendance on Josephus at dinners and on other occasions,[4] and his insistence that the πλῆθος of the Galileans were motivated in their actions mainly by εὔνοια and πίστις towards him (*Life* § 84). Josephus' pretensions of patronage also *partly* explain his insistence that he performed all these services without taking money in return, even those monies due him as a priest (*Life* §§ 80-1). We know Josephus well enough to have had doubts about all this in any case; what is remarkable, though, is how transparent Josephus allows his pretense to be: he admits that he permitted his brigands to plunder the farms of his Galilean protégés if they failed to provide

---

development of extra-contractual ties based on an ideology of reciprocal benefit. Nor would the legal obligation of charity have done so – gratitude to benefactors being a common human impulse neither ordained nor forbidden by biblical law – unless we suppose that the collection and distribution of it was administered by the state, as in modern welfare systems. But such a system in 1st century Judaea is as poorly attested as a fully developed patronal system and perhaps less plausible.

[2] Though Josephus represents this as an example of his peaceable behavior in Galilee. Nevertheless, it is not impossible that Josephus tried to win the support of the Sepphorites by controlling the brigands and peasants who were molesting them. If this were his purpose, he failed to attain it: his later relations with the city were hostile (*Life* §§ 104-11).

[3] Hopwood 1989: 171-85; cf. Jossa in this volume.

[4] *Life* §§ 79, 144, 220, 228, 305-6, 368.

protection money (*Life* § 78); that his "φίλοι" were in fact hostages (*Life* § 79); that the Galilean πλῆθος was actually motivated more by fear than by good-will (*Life* § 207); and that he often treated his "clients" with incredible brutality (the severing of hands is practically a *leitmotif* of the *Life*).[5] But this very transparency probably indicates that Josephus was not trying to impress the readers of his book and suggests in fact that he *did* pretend to behave as a patron while in Galilee. Josephus presumably believed his behavior would be correctly understood by the Galileans and therefore effective. As far as Josephus knew in the 60s, then, rural Lower Galilee was striated vertically by a network of patronage[6] at the top of which he tried to set himself.

Was Josephus' evaluation of local conditions correct? To answer this question, I will begin with a brief survey of what we know about land-tenure in Galilee. Such a survey is in order because it will permit us to evaluate, on the basis of our understanding of patronal systems elsewhere in the rural ancient Mediterranean world, the likelihood of widespread patronage in Galilee. This is so because it is usually supposed that there is a rough correlation between landholding patterns and patronage.[7] Districts in which there are many small farms and several larger ones are generally considered fertile territory for the growth of a patronal system, whereas in a district carved into vast slave-worked plantations patronage will obviously be insignificant.

Unfortunately we know little about land tenure in first-century Galilee. Josephus' reports on the matter are well known: members of the Herodian family, e.g. Queen Berenice, owned land (κόμαι) in lower Galilee, in the vicinity of Beth Shearim (*Life* § 119), and this was presumably farmed by tenants. At least some of the city aristocrats of Tiberias and Sepphoris were landowners and some of their holdings may have been large: Josephus mentions a certain Crispus, one of the εὐσχήμονες of Tiberias, who sat out the revolt in his κτήσεις, located, interestingly enough, across the Jordan (*Life* § 33). Josephus' hostages

[5] *Life* §§ 147; 153 (cf. 113): Josephus tactfully fails to mention that he stole arms and money from the Trachonite refugees whom he "helped escape" from his own men; §§ 171-3; cf. 177: the Galileans had cut off the hands of Justus' brother. See below for an attempt to explain this.
[6] And not horizontally into social classes or, presumably, classes based on religious criteria as perhaps in Judaea: Goodman 1987: 66-7. For a discussion of patronage as social system, see Johnson and Dandeker 1989: 223-8.
[7] For a useful discussion, see Garnsey and Woolf 1989: 153-70.

were apparently prosperous landowners, though their farms were not
necessarily massively larger than the average and may have been
worked not by tenants but by family members, day-laborers and/or
small numbers of slaves. Finally, Josephus mentions figures like John
of Gischala, and a certain Jesus (possibly the same as the leader of the
poor faction at Tiberias) who owned a castle in Gabara (*Life* § 246;
see below). Such men, about whom I will say more later, were obviously significant landlords who seem to have owned, or in some other way
controlled, their villages. I would suggest the following pattern: the
flatter, richer land on the boundary between Lower Galilee and the
Jezreel Valley was typically carved into large estates owned by absen-
tees and farmed by tenants; in the hillier areas there was a mixture of
large and small holdings worked for the most part by their owners.
Such a supposition conforms with the evidence of Josephus and also
with patterns of land tenure in other pre-modern rural societies – in
which in a given district the better land will tend to be concentrated
in the hands of fewer owners. Conversely, there is not the slightest
evidence for slave-worked *latifundia*, and no reason in the absence of
evidence to posit their existence on a large scale. Nor do Josephus or
the Gospels provide any reason to suppose that extended kinship
groups,[8] or local communities, or the state, could provide consistent
support to poorer farmers in the inevitable and frequent case of crop-
failure. There is no hint before the Mishnah of the sort of institution
which was later to be characteristic of all Jewish communities: the
גבאי־צדקה ("charity wardens"), the תמחוי ("soup kitchen"), the free-
loan society:[9] "charity" was apparently for the most part still a personal matter and therefore presumably a significant factor in the establishment of networks of relations between classes. In other words, in most

---

[8] On the decline of the extended family, see Goodman 1987: 68-9.

[9] Even such institutions can be exploited by wealthy individuals to establish
control over or reciprocal ties with poorer farmers. גבית צדקה ("collection of
charity") and similar positions were often in medieval and early modern Europe
sinecures for local bigshots, and it may have been so in late antique Palestine too
(on the oligarchic and evergetistic [the word is mine] structure of the European
Jewish communities – increasingly so as time went on – see Baron 1948: 34-51).
For an excellent example of a landlord's exploitation of his presidency of a
charitable society, see Hinton 1966: 30-31; for the coexistence of patronage and
the ideology of obligatory charity, see J. Pitt-Rivers, quoted by Scott 1977: 27. It
should be superfluous to point out, by the way, that biblical law requires charity,
but says nothing about the mechanisms for its collection and distribution.

parts of Galilee the preconditions for a patronal society existed: poor and rich lived in close proximity.[10]

The picture of Galilee painted by Josephus entirely conforms with these suppositions. With important exceptions, to be discussed later, the significant divisions in Galilean society were not horizontal and class-based, but vertical, according to lines of patronage. The *War* and the *Life* seem to be in agreement about this. Let me first return to an incident already mentioned, which occurred soon after Josephus' arrival: according to the *Life* (§§ 77-9), Josephus, unable to disarm the local brigands, "persuaded" the πλῆθος to pay them off and then had the brigands swear to keep away from the countryside unless they were summoned or had not been paid. Under the circumstances, Josephus obviously needed somehow to secure the loyalty of the Galilean country people, and this he did by taking as hostages οἱ ἐν τέλει τῶν Γαλιλαίων — i.e., obviously, the leading landowners of lower Galilee. What he takes for granted is that these Galileans somehow controlled the poorer people. This is made explicit in the story as told in the *War*, which is otherwise much sanitized.[11] In the end the plan failed, but not because of weakness in the ties between the δυνατοί and the πλῆθος.[12] Indeed, the Galilean δυνατοί are consistently represented as influential among the peasants. When Josephus announced to the Galilean leaders his desire to give up his command, they sent messengers into the countryside who assembled throngs of Galileans to protest Josephus' departure. The story may be true: Josephus reveals that the peasants had no love for him (§ 207) — rather, they feared his brigands. In any case, what is important is the peasants' responsiveness to the δυνατοί. Josephus reports other cases as well.[13]

---

[10] In such circumstances, common in the pre-modern Mediterranean world, patronage is often thought to have been nearly universal. The precise legal aspect of the relationship between rich and poor is probably irrelevant. See Garnsey-Woolf 1989: 158-61.

[11] *JW* 2 § 570: συνιδὼν δ᾽ὅτι τοὺς μὲν δυνατοὺς οἰκειώσεται μεταδιδοὺς τῆς ἐξουσίας αὐτοῖς, τὸ δὲ πᾶν πλῆθος, εἰ δι᾽ἐπιχωρίων καὶ συνήθων τὰ πολλὰ προστάσσοι κ.τ.λ.

[12] The prevalence of brigandage of course demonstrates that the patronal networks often failed; I leave this aside for the moment but will return to it below. Josephus does provide one possible example, from Upper Galilee, of local landlords' loss of control over a section of the population — *Life* §§ 185-8. But this is at Gamala, a place with a tangled history (see Cohen 1979: 160-9; Price 1991: 75-94). The landlord was perhaps the king and the πρῶτοι his agents.

[13] e.g., §§ 305-6. In some cases, though, when Josephus speaks of Galilean πρῶτοι, he *may* be referring to brigand-chiefs.

John of Gischala may be another example of successful rural patronage. The capsule biography of John in Book 2 of the *War*, in which Josephus claims that his enemy had been a poor man and attained wealth and power through deceit and brigandage, is of interest mostly as a sample of stock denunciation (2 §§ 585-7), though even here Josephus admits that John was surrounded by friends (whom John had duped) and behaved charitably (though his φιλαν-θρωπία was false).[14] The *Life*, which portrays John as the leading man of Gischala and by implication as a prosperous landowner,[15] is almost certainly closer to the truth. John's influence over the local peasants, and apparently also over the local brigands,[16] was considerable and extended also to the Jewish inhabitants of some villages in the nearby Tyrian territory, who viewed him as protector. Furthermore, this mutual relationship continued long after it had ceased to serve the interests of the peasants: many of them followed John to Jerusalem (*JW* 4 § 106).

To sum up, in social terms, Lower Galilee (and perhaps also Upper Galilee — though John may not have been typical) was a more or less normal rural district of the eastern Mediterranean: most of the inhabitants were small farmers (whether tenants or owners); there was a smaller number of wealthier farmers. In many cases, members of these groups were bound to each other by, among other things, bonds of reciprocal, extra-legal, obligation — i.e., of patronage. We know this because interestingly enough these bonds generally withstood the outbreak of the Revolt, so that Josephus witnessed and reported their effects: John of Gischala and many other Galilean landlords retained the loyalty of their clients. It was to a large extent at a higher level that the system was shaken: Agrippa II lost his hold on some (but not all) of his Jewish subjects, and among those who lived under Roman rule, at least some landowners were willing to entertain the idea of

---

[14] Yet Josephus' claim in the *War* may have some basis in fact: possibly John had become increasingly wealthy and powerful shortly before the Revolt. See below for reasons this may have happened.

[15] In *Life* § 74, Josephus implies that the large quantity of oil John sent to Caesarea Philippi actually belonged to John; in the *War*, he buys up other people's oil.

[16] Josephus says he was restrained from protesting against John's profiteering schemes by his fear of the local "πλῆθος" (*Life* § 76). This is transparently apologetic, but the relationship it assumes between John and his village may be real and is in any case consistent with Josephus' other reports of John's activities.

revolt. It seems unlikely, then, that the Galilean revolt was either caused or accompanied by major social collapse. Still, the collapse of relations between many of the Galilean landlords and their patrons requires explanation — in order to provide it we must return to social and economic conditions: these may not completely explain the revolt, but they are certainly part of its background. I begin with brigandage.

2. *Brigands and Social Breakdown*

The presence of brigandage in Galilee was an important precondition for the outbreak of war because it made available to would-be rebel leaders a body of men experienced at violence; its prevalence is probably also the strongest indication of social trouble in the district before the war. Why was it so common? The economy of Galilee was necessarily always fragile, notwithstanding Josephus' idealized musings about the district's fertility (*JW* 3 §§ 41-3). In fact, though Lower Galilee was the richest district in Palestine, it was relatively poor, even by Mediterranean standards. In view of this, Josephus' startling claim (another indication of his urban bias?) that even the most indolent were attracted to a life of farming (3 § 42) may mean, if it means anything at all, only that peasants were chronically under-employed, as they often are in subsistence economies, and in especially good years could scrape by on relatively little work. But most years were not especially good and many were positively bad.[17] Hence, patronage or none, whoever the ruler, and whatever the normal land tenure patterns, a small proportion of the rural population was always liable to fall through the cracks — to go from ownership to long term indebtedness to tenancy to enslavement, and finally, in the worst case, to starvation. Those who escaped starvation still had options: emigration cost money and was risky but may still have been common — at any rate, this may partly explain the size and extent of the Jewish diaspora; others will have moved to Tiberias, Sepphoris, Caesarea, Ptolemais, Tyre or Jerusalem in hope of finding work there: in many cases they would have ended up beggars; still others will have become brigands.[18] In short, brigandage was probably nearly universal in pre-

---

[17] On the frequency of crop failure in *rainier* parts of the Mediterranean basin, see Garnsey 1988: 8-16.

[18] See Goodman 1987: 60-66. B. Isaac's comments on brigandage in Judaea (1984, esp. 176-83; and compare 1992: 78-83) must be considered purely preliminary; the many works on the topic by R. Horsley (1979; 1981) are marred by the

modern rural economies, including in Galilee, just as street crime is in
modern cities, and for many of the same reasons. It is attested in
Galilee at all periods for which there is evidence. Furthermore, if it is
true that Jews refrained from exposing excess children, then economic
pressures were necessarily more severe in Jewish Palestine than
elsewhere in the eastern Mediterranean, so that even in otherwise
calm periods brigandage was perhaps more common.[19]

Yet the number and size of the brigand groups mentioned by
Josephus show that the period preceding the revolt was one of
heightened distress, if not by any means absolute collapse. At the very
beginning of the war, Cestius Gallus' deputy Caesennius Gallus is said
to have pursued τὸ δὲ στασιῶδες καὶ ληστρικὸν πᾶν in the vicinity of
Sepphoris into the hill country and there slain 2,000 of them (*JW* 2 §§
510-2); if this was the same group who soon after pillaged Sepphoris
because of its submission to Cestius, then Caesennius did them
relatively little damage (*Life* §§ 30-1).[20] Josephus' number, if it were
accurate, would imply a vast troop of brigands; obviously, though, it
cannot be assumed to be so. The next information comes from the
story, already mentioned, of Josephus' "pacification" of the local
brigand chiefs. The *Life* generally seems more dependable than the
War about numbers, but gives none here. *JW* 2 §§ 583-4, however,
mentions that 4,500 μισθοφόροι were in his service in Galilee; presumably these are identical with *Life*'s brigands. But this figure is unfortunately no more credible than that of 60,000 (still less than 100,000) for
Josephus' civilian forces. Probably better are the figures Josephus
provides in *Life* for the size of his forces (presumably for the most part
consisting of his bully-boys) in separate actions: he went from Cana to
Tiberias with 200 men to meet John (*Life* §§ 90-2); the "bold youths"

---

author's naive (or ideologically motivated) over-use of the "social bandit" model,
derived from E. Hobsbawm (1959; 1969); see Blok 1972. The fundamental general
study of ancient brigandage is now Shaw 1984.

[19] Possibly the tax burden was heavier too, due to the priestly gifts and temple
tax. But Josephus' account of his and his associates' activities in Galilee (especially
Life § 63) seems to show that the priestly gifts were not regularly given, at least
not in Galilee; see the discussion in Sanders 1992: 145-69. But, though Sanders
assumes that all farmers always paid the priestly gifts, his evaluation of economic
conditions in Palestine is implausibly optimistic.

[20] But Josephus does not suggest this and specifically does not call the belea-
guerers of Sepphoris "brigands"; rather, they are οἱ Γαλιλαῖοι and τὰ πλήθη. But
this does not exclude the possibility that some were brigands. The group mentioned in the *War* consists of both brigands and revolutionaries.

of Dabaritta who robbed the wife of King Agrippa's steward (*Life* §
126) were most likely Josephus' brigands – at any rate, when Josephus
failed to give them their cut 600 of them (now explicitly called λησταί)
marched on him (*Life* § 145). The only thing certain about what
happened next is that it bore little resemblance to Josephus' account
of it in *Life*, but the figure of 600 may be worth taking seriously. Later,
around the time of the Jerusalem delegation, Josephus says he had
3,000 "hoplites" in his service, and raised an additional 5,000 from the
Galilean peasantry (*Life* § 213). These numbers are too round and
perhaps also too large, and it is impossible to tell what percentage of
the 3,000 were brigands (cf. also the 500 hoplites Josephus sent to
escort the Jerusalem delegation home – *Life* § 332). Yet the numbers
are not absurdly large and the percentage of brigands among Josephus'
"regular" forces, to the extent that he had them, was probably high
(Cohen 1979: 211-13). I would suggest that the size of the Lower
Galilean brigand population on whom Josephus could reasonably
expect to draw for support was 2,000+/-1,000.

There were, in addition, brigand bands which did not cooperate with
Josephus, or at least retained their integrity even if they were willing
to make deals. When Josephus arrived at Sepphoris, the inhabitants
hired a bandit from the Galilee-Ptolemais frontier called Jesus, with
800 men, to protect them from Josephus. Josephus obscures what
happened next, but apparently some sort of bargain between the
competing bosses was struck. Soon after, a Galilean brigand chief, also
named Jesus, the leader of 600 men, turned up at Jerusalem; there he
was hired by Ananus and his faction to accompany the delegates sent
to remove Josephus. There is no way to determine whether or not the
two Jesuses are identical (Schalit 1968; Feldman, LCL 9, *index: sub
voce*; Goodman 1987: 224). After the failure of the Jerusalem delegation, Josephus says he brought about the defection of 4,000 (so *Life* §
371; in *JW* 2 § 625, 3,000) members of John's faction (Cohen 1979:
225-6) plausibly supposed that these constituted John's faction in
Lower Galilee. Some of these were certainly brigands, but not all: in
both *JW* 2 § 624 and *Life* § 370 Josephus says he had threatened to
seize the *property* of John's partisans, a commodity brigands are
generally supposed to have lacked.

In sum, we cannot calculate the number of brigands in lower Galilee
in 66, nor their exact proportion in the population. We can, however,
with a minimum of trust in *Life*'s statistics, speak of orders of magni-
tude. Let us suppose that Palestine as a whole could support a

maximum of one million people, and so posit a maximum of c.200,000 for Galilee.[21] Lower Galilee was more intensively farmed and less mountainous, and so more populous than the north: let us assume for it a population of 120,000. Josephus' evidence suggests a number of between 1,500 and (let's say) 8,000 for the brigands — between slightly over 1% and about 7% of the entire population — or between c.5% and 20% of men between 16 and 60. Now, brigandage was an option available only to healthy young men, and was notoriously dangerous, so brigands must have constituted a relatively small percentage of those — even of those men of military age — who failed to find "normal" means of subsistence. All this is both crude and speculative but does, I hope, suffice to establish that even Galilee, which was richer and less bellicose than Judaea, was experiencing unusually severe social and economic problems in the 60s. Why?

The factors which contributed to an increase in economic pressure in first-century Palestine in general are well-known. Under Herod and, for that matter, under the Hasmoneans, the tax burden in Palestine was no doubt heavy, but some of the revenues were pumped back into the local economy — especially in the form of soldiers' pay under the Hasmoneans and construction workers' salaries under Herod (Gabba 1990: 165-68). Herod's descendants continued to keep troops and fund building projects but — since their tax bases were smaller — on a smaller scale than their ancestors, apart from the disappearance of income from plunder, which had been significant under some of the Hasmonean rulers. Furthermore, under Roman rule, the tax burden remained heavy, but revenues were generally not reinvested in the Palestinian economy; rather, they were lost to corrupt local administrators and to the Imperial treasury at Rome. This was no trivial matter: jobs created by the Hasmoneans' and Herod's local reinvestment of wealth had provided a significant safety net for the "excess" population of Palestine.

What of Galilee? Galilee had avoided this drainage of wealth far longer than the other Jewish areas of the country, since it had remained under royal rule until the death of Agrippa I in 44.[22] On how

---

[21] For the maximum population of Palestine see Hamel 1990: 137-40, substantially agreeing with Broshi 1979. The estimates for Galilee are my own guesses. Needless to say, the margin of error in all cases is considerable.

[22] Whether the Romans collected regular tribute from "client kings" is perhaps unanswerable; see Braund 1984: 63-7, and D.R. Schwartz 1990: 132 n.102. If they did, then a general decline will have set in under Herod. Still, there is no question

large a scale did Antipas and his nephew reinvest in Galilee? In Agrippa's case we cannot answer. Josephus typically says practically nothing of his treatment of Galilee, concentrating instead on the favors he bestowed on Jerusalem and on Greek cities (*Ant* 19 §§ 293-96; 331; 335-37; 343-45). Inscriptions from the pagan semitic areas of his kingdom warn us of the incompleteness of Josephus' narrative (Schürer 1973-87: 1.445 n. 19 and 452 nn. 41-42). In Antipas' case, though, Josephus does not leave us entirely ignorant. Antipas founded Tiberias and also raised Sepphoris to something approaching city status.[23] Antipas no doubt believed that these initiatives would be beneficial — first of all to himself, because the cities were, because of their names Tiberias and Autokratoris (*Ant* 18 § 27), an indisputable expression of his loyalty to his patron, the Roman emperor, and because by founding the cities he created (or rewarded) a class of mostly Jewish aristocrats loyal to himself.[24] But presumably he also believed that the founding of cities would confer a variety of benefits on the district, e.g., providing for some of the locals construction jobs, and, when the cities were built, the amenities, and prestige, of city life, convenient markets for surplus agricultural production, and so on.

But the cities were a mixed blessing for the following reasons. It is a truism that ancient cities were generally exploitative of the country-side, but Tiberias and Sepphoris were small places with tiny territories; the creation of Tiberias, presumably by synoecism of villages in the area (this must be the factual basis of Josephus' polemical account)[25] was necessarily disruptive, but only in a small area; Sepphoris was simply a big village with altered status. So the cities' effects on Galilee

---

that Herod and his descendants oversaw significant redistributions of wealth, whatever its source (in the case of Agrippa I, some of it was borrowed from highly placed Roman friends; one should resist a nationalist interpretation of this). No Roman administrator is known to have behaved likewise, though Pilate had tried to fund the construction of an aqueduct (make-work for his garrison troops, or a building project for the local unemployed?) from the temple treasury.

[23] On Tiberias and Sepphoris, see Schürer 1973-1979: 2.172-82. Antipas built a wall around Sepphoris and renamed the town Autokratoris — *Ant* 18 § 27.

[24] As is well known, the Tiberian aristocrats of Josephus' day, who probably were the grandsons of the city's founders, had in many cases Herodian names (see *Life* §§ 32-33; 96) and mainly remained loyal to their Herodian overlord despite being harrassed by Josephus and other rebel-chiefs (see note 27 below).

[25] Josephus (*Ant* 18 §§ 37-8) claims Antipas forced Galilean peasants to leave their land and settle in Tiberias, but lured to the town poor outsiders by offers of housing and land. This slight absurdity reminds us of Josephus' hostility to the city and warns us to take his account of its foundation with a grain of salt.

as a whole cannot have been nearly as drastic as those, described by
Goodman (1987), of Jerusalem on Judaea in the wake of the Hasmonean expansion and Herod's massive construction. Still, the foundation
of the cities cannot have been entirely inconsequential: a striking, and
probably basically true feature of Josephus' accounts of Galilee, is his
reports of the deep hatred and resentment the Galilean country
people felt for the Sepphorites and Tiberians (cf. *Life* § 384, and
evidence adduced by Cohen 1979: 207 and *passim*). Reportedly, the
Galileans hated the Sepphorites for their loyalty to Rome (*Life* § 30).
There may be some truth to this but it is surely not the whole story,
for there is (and can be) no similar explanation for their hatred of
Tiberias. Josephus may provide a hint in a frustratingly vague piece of
polemic against Justus of Tiberias. Josephus claims that at the start of
the war, Justus had hoped to take command of Galilee. But his hope
was disappointed: "for the Galileans were hostile to the Tiberians due
to their rage at what they had suffered at his (Justus'; or, "their")²⁶
hands before the war" (*Life* § 392). This may be connected to *Life* §
177, where Josephus claims that before the war, "the Galileans" had
cut off the hands of Justus' brother on the charge of having forged
γράμματα. Amputation of hands, despite its frequent appearance in
Life, is not attested as a penalty in any of the legal systems – Greek,
Roman, or Jewish (but see Deut 25:11-12) – likely to have been in
force in Palestine. It is at most a type of rough, extra-legal "justice".
What sort of writing was Justus' brother alleged to have forged?
Presumably documents which had somehow prejudiced the interests of
the country people (which is what Γαλιλαῖοι normally means in *Life*)
in such a way as to make them extremely angry – deeds, or tenancy or
loan contracts. Once again Josephus is frustratingly vague. At any rate,
at both *Life* §§ 177 and 392 Josephus may be inventing, or he may
have been aware of specific cases of or a general tendency towards
mistreatment of the country people by some well-to-do Tiberians.

I would like to take up these hints and suggest that one of the more
damaging effects which the foundation of the cities had in Galilee was
the creation of a large class of absentee landlords. As I pointed out
earlier, absenteeism had not been entirely unknown in the district even
before the first century, especially in the more accessible (and fertile)
parts of Lower Galilee, near the Plain. Ptolemaic and Seleucid

---

²⁶ For the suggestion that the correct reading is ὑπ'αὐτῶν, see Cohen 1979: 136
n. 124 and 207 n. 50. The suggestion is questionable.

monarchs and courtiers had owned land in and near the region,[27] and perhaps some of this much later turns up in the possession of members of the Herodian family: I have already mentioned the estate of Queen Berenice, centered on Beth Shearim, on the border of Galilee and the Jezreel Valley (*Life* § 119). It is reasonable to suppose that tenants working on such estates were especially liable to exploitation by distant landlords (whose power bases lay elsewhere) mainly interested in collecting rents, and local agents who had nothing to gain and a great deal to lose by being nice. However, the *normal* situation in Lower Galilee before the first century, and in Upper Galilee even during it (as also in Judaea and Idumaea at earlier periods) was rather different. Josephus' account suggests, as I have indicated, that the most conspicuous figure in Galilee was the country landlord.[28] There were many such people and their behavior necessarily varied widely, but the cases we know of suggest that many of them had strong ties to their villages and in the surrounding countryside and could depend, if the need arose, on the support of the farmers who worked their land or owned small plots nearby (and vice versa). The wealthier members of this group generally also had ties of friendship to their social equals, often in the cities: thus John had acquaintances in Tiberias, Gabara and Jerusalem. Powerful country landlords of this sort had once been common throughout Palestine, and the most ambitious of them had repeatedly used their patronal and other relations to exert a destabilizing influence on the country, exploiting any weakness in the central government for their own advancement. The Tobiads, the Hasmoneans, and the Herodians had all come from this class, and the latter two families had recognized its importance and responded by intimidation, cooptation, bribery and slaughter. It was the considerable achievement of the later Hasmoneans and Herod to have maintained the allegiance of the country landlords of Galilee, so that the district,

---

[27] On private ownership of land outside city territories in the Hellenistic east see Kreissig 1977: 19-20. For the area around Galilee, see Landau 1966: 54-70; 2 Macc 12:27, with commentary of Abel; Isaac and Roll 1982: 104-6.

[28] The importance of this type in Hellenistic and Roman Palestine was noted by Tcherikover 1937: 48-51, and Rostovtzeff 1957: 1.270. (Rostovtzeff believed these people were also large-scale capitalists, a view extrapolated from Josephus' tales of John of Gischala's profiteering schemes, and corresponding to a view of ancient commerce now generally discredited.) I have found occasional acceptance of this view (e.g., Applebaum 1989: 244), but little subsequent discussion. For a suggestion that the Hasmoneans and Herodians had started as members of this class, see S. Schwartz 1993.

despite its remoteness and populousness, generally remained at peace. But this peace was disturbed by the foundation of the cities: some of the new elites may have been recruited from among the old landlords, but others may have been loyal courtiers owed a favor.[29] In the latter case they will have been rewarded with gifts of land in Galilee and nearby areas, and/or invested whatever wealth they made in the cities in such land. The rise of this class, whose treatment of the country people was likely to have been, or to have been thought, exploitative, was not only a blow to the prestige of the country landlords but also increased, perhaps significantly, the numbers of peasants left outside any functioning patronal network (for the effects of absenteeism on Patronage, see Garnsey and Woolf 1989: 158-61; Silverman 1977: 8). Such peasants had the option of seeking the support of the country landlords, and the wealthier and more ambitious of the latter will have welcomed their advances: hence the importance of figures like John of Gischala. But in general the country landlords were increasingly overburdened by taxes and could do little to help: hence the rise of brigandage and the importance of the brigand chiefs with their huge bands of followers.

I will now conclude by returning briefly to the questions I raised at the beginning of this paper: first-century Galilean society was characterized by the pervasiveness of patronage. In this respect it was, despite its Jewishness, an absolutely normal pre-modern agrarian society of the Mediterranean basin. The Herodian temple, whose powerful influence on the Judaean countryside rendered Judaea socially and economically fairly unusual, had little socio-economic

---

[29] Josephus says that some of the settlers in Tiberias were prominent Galileans (*Ant* 18 § 37). Jesus ben Sapphias may be an example: when Jonathan and his 2,000 back-up troops at Gabara heard that Josephus was marching on them, they withdrew into the castle of a certain Jesus (*Life* § 246). Jesus' identity is uncertain: Schalit 1968, "Iesous" no. 2, and Feldman, LCL index, suggest that he is b. Sapphias; Cohen 1979: 215 n. 66 suggests that "Jesus" is a mistake for "Simon", previously mentioned as leading man of Gabara (*Life* § 124). If Schalit and Feldman are right, then perhaps b. Sapphias' family had been prominent country landowners who were recruited into the Tiberian aristocracy; or perhaps Jesus himself had settled in Tiberias; or Jesus' ancestor had been given a Galilean country estate upon recruitment. Jesus was unusual among the Tiberian aristocracy in having some support in the countryside (this is apparently the implication of *Life* § 66: see Cohen 1979: 218). However, Antipas may have preferred to settle his own courtiers in the town, to serve as a counterbalance to the old landlords (see Jones 1971: 275). It may be no accident that Herodian names occur among the city elites (and among military personel), not among country people.

influence in Galilee. Furthermore, communally or governmentally administered organs of redistribution of wealth, which would surely have influenced the structure of the society had they existed, seem to have been as yet insignificant there.

Josephus' account suggests that by the middle of the first century this patronal system, though it had not collapsed, was under increasing stress — in part for reasons which affected Palestine generally (and which affected Galilee somewhat less than the other districts), but in part due to urbanization. The main consequences of the foundations of Tiberias and Sepphoris in the early first century were the creation of a class of absentee landlords based in the cities, a decline in the position of the country landlords (and so a breakdown in relations between them and *their* Herodian and Roman patrons), and the impoverishment of small farmers. These processes in turn produced a partial breakdown of the patronal system, the most conspicuous manifestations of which were the development of a number of large bands of brigands; the violent hostility between the urban upper classes and the country people which is such an important theme of Josephus' account; and finally the adherence of expanded groups of clients to the wealthier and more ambitious country landlords. In short, social and economic changes in first-century Galilee produced conditions *in part* favorable to revolt. But conditions were less dire in Galilee than elsewhere in the country, and the Galilean social system was still partly functioning; the number of Galileans devoted to the revolt was not finally very large. The Galilean rebels were mostly either enslaved on the spot by Vespasian, or fled with their patrons who, following the ancient pattern, endeavored to exploit the breakdown of order and seize control at Jerusalem. There they met the same fate as the Judaean rebels. Galilee emerged from the revolt relatively little damaged — which is not to say unchanged. In the years following the revolt, the Romans "normalized" the new province of Judaea — expanding their military presence there, and in conjunction with this, building roads.[30] The remoteness of the Galilean hills had

---

[30] For road and city construction in the province of Syria and the Nabataean kingdom after the Revolt, see Bowersock 1973: 133-40; in Judaea in the early and middle 2nd century, see Isaac 1992: 107-11; on the integration of Syria (in the broad sense) into the Roman provincial system in the 1st century, see Rey-Coquais 1978: 48-53. (The articles of Bowersock and Rey-Coquais illustrate, incidentally, that Josephus wasn't the only historian with an urban bias.) Roads in Galilee before 70 had generally been little more than rocky paths; vehicles had to pass

always been one of the preconditions for the strength of the country
landlords (as also of the brigand chiefs), and the creeping normaliza-
tion of the province (not to mention urbanization and the war) must
have greatly reduced their influence.[31] The domesticated Galilee of
the third and fourth centuries which we encounter in the Talmud
Yerushalmi was a very different place from the Galilee which in the
first century was the scene of Josephus' downfall.

---

either south or north of the district: see Josephus' description of the road between
Jotapata and Gabara – JW 3 § 141; Isaac and Roll 1982: 8-10.

[31] Some passages in Rabbinic literature suppose the post-destruction rise of
מציקין (oppressors, tax-collectors?). The meaning of the word and the significance
of the change, if any, remain uncertain. See Klein 1967: 55ff.; Alon 1980: 59-64.

PART VI

ASPECTS OF JOSEPHUS' BIOGRAPHY

IMAGINING SOME DARK PERIODS IN JOSEPHUS' LIFE

Gohei Hata

No Josephan scholar has ever discussed what sorts of transactions Josephus might have made with Nero when he visited Rome in 64 CE to petition the Emperor for the release of "certain priests of his acquaintance" (*Life* § 13). After their release, Josephus seems to have departed from Rome immediately, but no scholar has ever discussed where Josephus went and what he was doing for two years before his final return to Jerusalem in the early summer of 66 CE. Failure to fill in the intervening two years has resulted in a lacuna in the study of Josephus' life. If we could use our imagination to fill in this period, we would have a different approach to the accounts of his *Life* and of the *War*.

This paper is special in nature in that we may go to extremes in our imagination, even at the risk of falling into the category of historical *fiction* on our part in places where Josephus keeps silent, or when we doubt the truthfulness of some of his reports and judge them as *fictitious*. Thus, we do not claim that we have reconstructed some of the dark periods in the life of Josephus, but our paper will suggest, we hope, that Josephus failed to report something very important, namely his transactions with the Emperor Nero and his military training in Alexandria on his way back to Jerusalem and that without these two important postulates in mind, it would be hard for us to understand the selection of Josephus as commander in the districts of Galilee, his precarious position throughout the war, and his survival in the war.

In this paper, we will trace his life from beginning to end, except the period of his military activities in Galilee, mainly on the basis of his accounts in *Life* and *War*, and try to speculate about what he was hiding and fill in some of the lacunae in his accounts.[1]

---

[1] On some serious problems related to Josephus' life, see the relevant section in Feldman 1984: 75-98. Basic scholarly discussions on the life of Josephus are: Niese 1914; Thackeray 1929; Rajak 1983; Bilde 1988; Hadas-Lebel 1989.

I

In the beginning of *Life* (§§ 1-5), Josephus tells of his genealogy, of which he proudly declares that his family is "not undistinguished," tracing its descent back to the Hasmonean priestly and royal ances-tors.[2] According to *Life*, Josephus' father was born in the tenth year of the reign of Archelaus in Judaea, and Josephus was born in the year when Gaius Caligula became emperor in Rome. We learn from this that his father was born in 6 CE and that Josephus was born in 37 or 38 CE when his father was at the age of thirty-one. Josephus seems to have been the second son because the name of his father, "Matthias," was given to his brother (*Life* § 8). The first son was usually named after his father at that time.[3] Since Josephus himself says that his ancestors were not only priests but that they also belonged to "the first of the twenty-four courses" (*Life* § 2) of the priestly division and that "the high priests and the leading men of the city" (*Life* § 9) frequent-ed his house, we would imagine that Josephus' father was a Sadducee and that his ancestors had traditionally been Sadducees. From this we would further imagine that Josephus was brought up in the Sadducean tradition.[4]

Josephus tells us in *Life* §§ 10-12 what he was doing for three years from the age of about sixteen. According to this: (1) Josephus submit-ted himself to the hard training of three religious sects of his day, that is, the Pharisees, the Sadducees, and the Essenes; (2) he lived with Bannus, a hermit in the wilderness, for three years; and (3) at age

---

[2] On the genealogy of Josephus, see the useful discussions of Schürer 1973-87: 1.45-46,46 n.3; Rajak 1983: 14-21; Bilde 1988: 28-29; Hadas-Lebel 1989: 17-23; Mason 1992: 36-8. Mason (38) states: "As for the genealogy itself, it is easiest to believe that Josephus was unclear about the details of his parentage beyond two or three generations, but that he was forced by rhetorical convention to provide an impressive pedigree. He knew very well that his Roman readers had no access to (and probably no interest in) the public archives of Jerusalem." Mason's understanding may eventually be shared by those scholars who attempt to go into Josephus' genealogy.

[3] If the custom of giving a grandfather's name to the first son were popular, Josephus might have been the first son, but we call attention to the fact that Josephus does not boast of his being the first son in his *Life*.

[4] Mason (1991: 342-56) convincingly argues that Josephus never claimed to be a Pharisee, though he does not suggest that Josephus was brought up in the Sadducean tradition. In his review of the Pharisees of *Jewish Antiquities*, Neusner (1987: 281) points out that "nothing in his account suggests he was a Pharisee, as he later claimed in his autobiography."

nineteen, he "began to engage in public affairs, following the Pharisaic school."[5]

Aside from the question of time, namely, that Josephus somehow managed, between the ages of sixteen and nineteen, *not only* to study *in depth* three religious sects, but also to spend three years in the wilderness, we would doubt the truthfulness of his report in other ways as well. First, we would wonder how Josephus at age sixteen could study the tenets and practices of the Pharisees and the Essenes besides those of the Sadducees of which his family must have been very proud. If he did it, it would have been a serious rebellion against his family tradition. Second, if Josephus had become a "devoted disciple" (ζηλωτής) of Bannus (*Life* § 11), the logical selection of his way of life at age nineteen would have been that of the Essenes or of another sect of that kind, away from mainstream Judaism.[6] However, according to Josephus, he chose the Pharisaic way of life, which would have been a rejection of the two strong "influences" of his life, that of Bannus

---

[5] Most scholars, though they are puzzled Josephus' account, seem to accept a revised version of it. Thus, they speculate that Josephus studied the three religious sects for a brief period (two or three months) and thereafter lived with Bannus for three years. Rajak (1983: 34-39) is not an exception, but her attempt to understand Josephus' account is worth reading.

[6] It may be worth pointing out several similarities not only in Greek expressions but also in biblical themes between the account in *Life* and Josephus' paraphrase of the account of Daniel in *Ant* 10 §§ 186-276. The expressions "after a thorough investigation (εἰ πάσας καταμάθοιμι) in *Life* § 10 and "I submitted myself to hard training" (σκληραγωγήσας ἐμαυτὸν) in *Life* § 11 correspond to "they [the youth at court] . . . mastered all the learning (πᾶσαν . . . ἐξέμαθον παιδείαν) in *Ant* 10 § 194 and "to live austerely" (σκληραγωγεῖν ἑαυτὸν) in *Ant* 10 § 190 respectively. The "three years" with Bannus correspond to the "three years" in Dan 1:5 during which Nebuchadnezzar is said to have trained some of the people of Israel to make them of service to him. Besides these similarities, the Greek expressions "I made great progress in my education . . . for my love of letters" (εἰς μεγάλην παιδείας προύκοπτον ἐπίδοσιν...διὰ τὸ φιλογράμματον) in *Life* §§ 8 and 9 and the reference to Josephus' excellent "memory and understanding" in *Life* § 8 seem to correspond in form and content to "(And these youths, because of . . . their zeal in learning letters and their wisdom, made great progress" (δι᾽ . . . σπουδῆς τῆς περὶ τὴν παίδευσιν τῶν γραμμάτων καὶ σοφίας ἐν προκοπῇ γενομένους) in *Ant* 10 § 189 and to the reference to the youth's innate "knowledge and understanding" Dan 1:4 respectively. Josephus' emphasis on his distinguished background and his relationship to a royal family in *Life* §§ 1-6 and *Ant* 10 § 185 (Dan 1:3) is the same. These similarities would indicate that Josephus, by projecting himself into Daniel, might have expected his readers to see in him a Danielic figure.

and of the Sadducean background of his family. Josephus evidently makes a false report of his inclination to the Pharisees, the reason for which we shall later speculate upon. If the report of his life from sixteen to nineteen is fictitious, then what was he doing during this period? No one knows, but here we would go to the extreme of imagining that he was in the Roman auxiliary camp of Caesarea as a mercenary because this could certainly be a matter he had to hide throughout his life. He tried to hide it by inventing a story of his living with Bannus for three years in the wilderness, a story which could not be proven false easily. As we have already noted, Josephus says that at age nineteen he "returned to the city (of Jerusalem) and began to engage in public affairs, following the Pharisaic school" (*Life* § 12).[7] According to our imagination, Josephus returned to Jerusalem not from the wilderness but from Caesarea and "began to engage in public affairs" as a Sadducee, just as his father did.

II

At about the age of twenty-seven, Josephus made a trip to Rome for the release of "certain priests" of his acquaintance (*Life* § 13). This was certainly one of his "public affairs" and the time was perhaps the early spring of 64 CE. According to Josephus, "I reached Rome after being in great jeopardy at sea. For our ship foundered in the midst of the sea of Adria, and our company of some six hundred souls had to swim all that night. About daybreak, through God's providence, we sighted a ship of Cyrene, and I and certain others, about eighty in all, outstripped the others and were taken on board" (*Life* § 15).[8] We wonder if the shipwreck story Josephus tells here to his readers is factual.[9] We could doubt the truthfulness of this report for the following two reasons. First, no matter how good a swimmer Josephus was (we wonder where he learned to swim — did he learn in the sea off Caesarea?), it would have been extremely difficult for him to keep

---

[7] On the translation of this passage, see Mason 1991: 342-56, where he discusses Josephus' religious quest.

[8] Hadas-Lebel (1988: 64-67) discusses in detail a possible route of Josephus' voyage.

[9] While Rajak (1983: 43-44) points out that the shipwreck motif is commonplace in ancient writings and that Josephus' shipwreck story shows his tendency to "pick out traditional themes and happenings," she is cautious enough to doubt the truthfulness of the story.

swimming "all night" until a ship of Cyrene took him and some other survivors on board. Second, if one had such an intense life-threatening experience, psychologically, one would either recount it in minute details (as in the shipwreck story in Acts 27:13-44) or keep totally silent about it. Josephus' report here is colorless and vague, with no personal feeling in it at all. Our question is then: Why did Josephus invent this story? Any story of shipwreck catches the attention of those who listen to it. In addition, by inventing a story that only eighty of some six hundred people were saved, Josephus believed he could impress upon his readers that he was under the special care of "God's providence" from the very beginning of his appearance on the stage of history. Like τύχη, εἱμαρμένη, δαίμων, χρεών etc., the expression "God's providence" (πρόνοια θεοῦ), which Josephus uses not only in this report but also in other accounts, is an attractive and convenient term for any story-teller.[10] It requires no logical, rational, or circumstantial explanations. Josephus, a skillful story-teller, knew its effective use, and employed it not only to presage his appearance on the stage of history, but also to keep the interest of his readers after plowing through the twenty books of *Jewish Antiquities* to which his *Life* was attached.

III

From the shipwreck, Josephus continues, "Landing safely at Dicaearchia, which the Italians call Puteoli, I formed a friendship with Aliturus, an actor[11] of Jewish origin who was a special favorite of Nero. Through him I was introduced to Poppaea, Caesar's consort, and took the earliest opportunity of soliciting her aid to secure the liberation of the priests. Having, besides this favor, received large gifts from Poppaea, I returned to my own country" (*Life* § 16).

Josephus does not tell us how he came to know the actor. That is not important for our purpose, but here we could imagine that Josephus, through the agency of the actor, met not only Poppaea

---

[10] Josephus was certainly a story-teller with his Greco-Roman readers in mind. Regarding his use of these terms to introduce novelistic and entertaining elements see Rengstorf 1973-83.

[11] The Greek word μιμολόγος for actor would suggest that Aliturus was one of the pantomime actors who, like musicians or poets, entertained the guests at the dinner table. Cf. Tryphon in *Ant* 12 § 212 and Suetonius, *Tiberius* 61.

Sabina but also her husband Nero for the release of "certain priests" of his acquaintance. Nero was the same age as Josephus.

Josephus' information given about the "certain priests" is insufficient. According to *Life* § 13, they were sent to Rome "on account of a minor and trifling charge,"[12] by Felix, the procurator of Judaea (52-59 CE), and detained there. This means that they had been detained in Rome for at least five years and for as long as twelve years. Although the trial and punishment of those sent to Rome from the provinces often hinged upon the emperor of the time,[13] the detention of prisoners for such a long period "on account of a minor and trifling charge" seems to be unusual. Their charges might have been some serious political offenses or they might have had Roman citizenship.[14]

We would imagine that the gifts which Josephus brought from Jerusalem are now at the bottom of the Adriatic Sea. Yet, we learn

---

[12] The translation of this passage is from S. J. D. Cohen 1979: 61.

[13] According to Suetonius, *Augustus* 32-34, Augustus was speedy in holding a hearing, and according to *Ant* 18 §§ 170-78, Tiberius was indifferent to prolonging the ordeal of the prisoner.

[14] Roman procurators often detained people "on account of a minor and trifling charge" and then released them in exchange for money. According to *Ant* 20 § 215, when Albinus, procurator of Judaea (62-64 CE), heard that Gessius Florus was coming to Judaea as his successor, he released those who had been imprisoned "on account of a minor and trifling charge" (the same expression), after accepting money. If the priests of Josephus' acquaintance were brought in under this charge, Felix could have released them in exchange for money. The fact that the procurator could not take that measure seems to suggest that: (1) they had Roman citizenship and demanded a hearing before Caesar; or (2) they were arrested because they were engaged in some anti-Roman activities in or out of Jerusalem. S. J. D. Cohen (1979: 60-62) discusses the difference in nuance of Josephus' use of the phrase "on account of a minor and trifling charge" between *Life* and *Ant*. According to him, the phrase in *Life* § 13 is the one which "Josephus would use to cover revolutionary activities." With Cohen, we would imagine that they were engaged in some political activities against Rome in the time of Felix. We would further imagine that: (1) because of their strong influence and popularity even after they were sent to Rome, the so-called revolutionaries kept demanding of the Jerusalem authorities to have direct negotiations with the Roman emperor for their release; (2) the Jerusalem authorities, at the prospect of the coming war, came to think that the anti-Roman sentiments of those priests in Rome had undergone some change because of the passage of time and their observance of Roman power; (3) the Jerusalem authorities could thus expect that if the priests returned to Jerusalem, they could exercise their influence to avoid a direct confrontation with Rome; and (4) they decided to dispatch Josephus to Rome for the negotiation of their release. According to our speculation, Josephus' mission was highly political, not private, from the beginning.

that Josephus received "large gifts" from Poppaea (*Life* § 16). This seems to be complete nonsense and makes us wonder if Josephus was hiding something important, for example, some secret transaction he had had with Nero.[15] We would also wonder here what sort of conversation Josephus had with Nero. We would imagine that when Josephus met Nero, the Emperor first inquired about the political situation in Palestine and was surprised to hear of the maladministration of the Roman procurators there and of the impending Jewish revolt against Rome. Then Nero proposed to Josephus that he perform some clandestine activities in Palestine in exchange for the release of the "certain priests." We expect that Josephus accepted Nero's proposal because there was no alternative way for him to obtain their release and because he could convince himself that he was being loyal to the Roman cause, after observing the might of the Roman empire on his way to Italy. At that point, Nero released the priests and gave Josephus the "large gifts." Having had an audience with Nero and having received the gifts from him could be the facts Josephus had to hide, especially because the war against Rome started in the twelfth year of Nero's reign (*JW* 1 § 20; 2 § 284). Josephus seems to have tried to hide these facts by introducing Poppaea Sabina instead of Nero to the scene and signaling already in *Ant* 20 § 195 that she was a Jewish sympathizer.

What were the undercover activities proposed by Nero to Josephus? These were to maintain order in Palestine by muzzling the anti-Roman political and religious fanatics in Jerusalem and other cities of Palestine. They also included providing smooth passage for the Roman forces in case they should invade Palestine. Josephus was given the "large gifts" to use as operating funds with which to execute the mission assigned to him, evidently the "mission impossible." If our imagination is on track, we would further imagine that on his way back to Jerusalem, Josephus was ordered to see the regular Roman forces

---

[15] Feldman (*ABD* 1992: 982) says: "The fact that the emperor gave some gifts to Josephus (whereas we would have expected Josephus to bring gifts to the emperor) could be explained most readily if we assume that Nero hoped thereby to persuade Josephus to use his influence to defuse the impending Jewish revolt against Rome. We do not know whether Josephus attempted such a mission, but in any case, the revolt did break out two years later." According to our hypothesis (see n. 14), the Jerusalem authorities seem to have tried to use the influence of the priests detained in Rome, and Nero also seems to have tried to use the priests' influence as well as that of Josephus.

(the fifteenth legion) in Alexandria and, if necessary, to have some
military training. If the released priests had been engaged in some
anti-Roman activities in Palestine,[16] they could be brainwashed in the
Roman military camp of Alexandria. During his stay in Alexandria
which lasted for more than one year, Josephus seems to have had an
opportunity to visit some places in Egypt. His interest in and repeated
references to the Temple of Onias both in the *War*[17] and in the
Antiquities,[18] and his collection of the stories of Moses and the Exodus
in the Egyptian versions in the *Antiquities*[19] and especially in *Against
Apion* would suggest that he had sufficient time in Alexandria to visit
Leontopolis, where the Temple of Onias stood, and other places in the
same nome of Heliopolis.[20]

IV

In June of 66 CE, the priests of the Temple in Jerusalem ceased to
offer sacrifices for the welfare of the Romans. Though Josephus says
in a rather circuitous way that this cessation "laid the foundation of
the war with the Romans" (*JW* 2 § 409. Cf. 2 §§ 411-17), this was
evidently tantamount to a declaration of war to the Romans.

Josephus and the priests returned to Jerusalem in the early summer
of that year. According to *Life* § 17, Josephus (and the priests) urged
the various factions not to revolt against Rome by emphasizing that
they were "inferior to the Romans, not only in military skill, but in

---

[16] See our discussion in n.14.

[17] It is interesting to note that in the very beginning of his narrative (*JW* 1 § 33)
Josephus refers to the temple of Onias and promises his readers to return to this
matter "in due course," about which he talks in detail in *JW* 7 §§ 421ff. Josephus
seems to have had a clear picture of the temple of Onias when he was composing
the *War* in Greek (see the contribution by Parente above).

[18] See Josephus' favorable description of the Temple of Onias in *Ant* 13 §§ 63ff.
and his repeated references to the Temple in *Ant* 12 § 388; 13 § 285; 20 §§ 236-37.

[19] For example, information about Moses' expedition to Ethiopia as told in *Ant*
2 § 238 seems to have been collected by Josephus while he was in Egypt.

[20] If Josephus had a chance to visit local areas of Egypt when he accompanied
Vespasian and Titus in 69 CE or if he had a chance to visit Alexandria after 70
CE, he could have developed his interest in the Temple of Onias, and the stories
of Moses or the Egyptian versions of the Exodus, which later led him to purchase
in Rome the written sources on Moses (sources mentioned in *Against Apion*), but
it is hard for us to imagine that such an opportunity was given to Josephus in 69
CE or after 70 CE. Therefore, we would imagine that Josephus' stay in Alexandria
around 65 CE was the only occasion for him to see some parts of Egypt.

good fortune." Josephus' experience with the regular Roman forces in Alexandria might have induced him to his efforts of persuasion.

Persuasion is not an easy matter, especially when people are bent on revolt or war. As Josephus himself says in *Life* § 20, his "incessant reiteration of warning" brought him into "odium and the suspicion of siding with the enemy," and as a result he had to "seek asylum in the inner court of the Temple." Why did Josephus give warning to the Jerusalemites so incessantly as to risk his own life? If his statement is true, we would suppose that giving warnings was one of the tasks assigned to him by Nero. Of course, the same task would have been expected of the released priests, both by Nero and by the Jerusalem authorities.[21]

Often with the beginnings of a war, the initial victory causes morale to climb and makes people blind. They refuse to believe that the victory was brought about by some fortuity rather than by their own power, and believe that the state of victory would continue to the very end of the war. The Jerusalemites were no exception, as their reactions show after they had defeated the Roman force of Cestius in the autumn of that year (*Life* §§ 24-5, *JW* 3 § 9, Cf. *JW* 2 §§ 499ff.).[22]

According to *JW* 2 §§ 562-68, after the defeat of Cestius, the "wartime council" or the "provisional government" (τὸ κοινόν) was convened in Jerusalem for selecting commanders to conduct the war with Rome. Although the nature of this council and its relationship with the Sanhedrin at this time is not clear at all, Josephus was appointed commander of Upper and Lower Galilee and of Gamala. Regarding strategy, these districts were the most important for the defense of Jerusalem. Why then was Josephus appointed commander of such important districts? This appointment is certainly puzzling to us especially because the council members could easily foresee that Nero would instruct his general to muster in Antioch the regular Roman forces of the East, invade Galilee first, and then proceed to Jerusalem. Since Josephus (and the released priests) failed to achieve their assigned task in Jerusalem, he would have desperately sought

---

[21] See our discussion in n.14.

[22] In *Ant* 7 §§ 74-5, Josephus seems to have projected the victory of the Jews over Cestius' army into that of the Hebrews and the defeat of an army of Philistines. Not only in this place but also in other places of his *Antiquities*, Josephus seems to have projected his personal experiences or what he witnessed into his paraphrase of the stories.

some districts outside of Jerusalem to execute Nero's mission. If
Josephus could foresee, as the council members supposedly did, where
the Roman forces would be mustered and which areas of Palestine
they would invade, he would have tried to obtain the position of
commander of Galilee. He did, in fact, obtain it.[23]

According to *Life* § 29, Josephus was sent to Galilee together with
two priests, Joazar and Judas, "to induce the disaffected to lay down
their arms."[24] Who were these two priests? On the basis of the fact
that the same Greek adjective καλὸς κἀγαθὸς to denote the characters of the "certain priests" in *Life* § 13 is employed for the description of the characters of both Joazar and Judas in *Life* § 29, we would
suppose that both Joazar and Judas were the "certain priests" of
Josephus' acquaintance who had been detained in Rome.[25]

According to *JW* 2 § 576, Josephus "levied in Galilee an army of
upwards of a hundred thousand young men, all of whom he equipped
with old arms collected for the purpose," and trained them in the

---

[23] As to the appointment of Josephus as commander, Rajak (1983: 21) states:
"Whatever Josephus' talents, it is improbable that he would have been appointed,
especially before he had proved his ability, unless he was of equal social standing
with these men (i.e., men of high priestly rank who were likewise appointed
commanders in other districts)." For our argument, Rajak's reference to Josephus'
ability or his "equal social standing with these men" seems to be not necessarily
a persuasive reason. We would speculate about the reason why Josephus, who
seems not to have been very familiar with the districts of Galilee and of Gamala,
was appointed commander of these areas.

[24] According to our hypothesis in n.14, Josephus went to Galilee for the purpose
mentioned in *Life* § 17, although the "war-time council" in Jerusalem did send
him and other commanders for the purpose mentioned in *JW* 2 § 563, that is, "to
conduct the war" with the Romans.

[25] The proximity of the two occurrences in *Life* § 13 and 29 would support our
hypothesis that both Joazar and Judas were the released priests. The reason for
Josephan scholars' failure to identify them as such was probably due to Thackeray's English translation in LCL. He translated the καλοὺς κἀγαθοὺς in *Life* § 13
as "very excellent men" and the same expression in *Life* § 29 as "men of excellent
character," thus obscuring the repetition of this descriptive phrase and hindering
our identification of the two men. If a further usage in *Life* § 256 also indicates
these same released priests, then their number might have been three, because
that passage says: "Had my case against John been tried and had I produced some
two or three men of excellent character as witnesses to my behavior . . ." Were
these released priests really "very excellent men"? No one can tell their characters, but there is a great possibility that Josephus thought of the use of this
adjective when he was reading of his account of Daniel in *Ant* 10 § 204 where the
same expression appears. See our discussions of Josephus' use of the story of
Daniel in nn. 6, 30, 45, 48 (cf. the contribution by Mason above).

Roman fashion. Although the figure in this passage is a gross exaggeration,[26] Josephus' report on levying a large number of young people in Galilee, providing them with old arms, and training them in the style of the Roman army (*JW* 2 §§ 577-82) seems to strengthen our hypothesis that Josephus was indeed given operating funds by Nero and that he had some intensive military training in Alexandria.[27]

In the winter of 66-67 CE, Nero, who was then staying in Achaia (Greece),[28] instructed Vespasian to lead the Roman army in the war against the Jews in Palestine (*JW* 3 § 7). On this occasion, we would imagine, Nero revealed to Vespasian that he had already arranged for a Jew named Josephus to do some clandestine activities for the Roman cause. After sending his son Titus to Alexandria to muster the fifteenth legion, Vespasian himself proceeded by land to Syria, "where he concentrated the Roman forces and numerous auxiliary contingents furnished by the kings of the neighboring districts" (*JW* 3 § 8). Titus joined his father at Ptolemais of Syria. Thus, the "united army" of Vespasian's fifth and tenth legions and Titus' fifteenth legion, together

---

[26] We could see the same gross exaggeration in "one million, one hundred thousand" (*JW* 6 § 420) as a total figure of Jewish victims of the war or in "two million seven hundred thousand" (*JW* 6 § 425) as a total figure of those assembled in Jerusalem at the time of Passover before the war, and in other figures of casualties throughout the *War* and *Life*. Although Josephus says that "the victims thus outnumbered those of any previous visitation, human or divine"(*JW* 6 § 429), the exaggeration in casualties would have served Josephus to give his readers an impression that "the war of the Jews against the Romans, the greatest not only of the wars of our own time, but, so far as accounts have reached us, well nigh of all that ever broke out between cities or nations" (*JW* 1 § 1), and as a result his readers would have concluded that both Vespasian and Titus were great generals. Although we cannot speculate whether Vespasian and/or Titus instructed Josephus to exaggerate the figures of Jewish casualties, we should bear in mind that any officially announced war-time figures are almost always inaccurate not only in ancient wars but also in modern ones. Both sides exaggerate the number of the casualties of the other and minimize the number of their own casualties. The only exception in modern wars is Hiroshima whose casualties America, the victor, minimized extremely for fear of the international reactions to the use of an atomic bomb.

[27] Josephus describes in detail the military training of the Roman forces in *JW* 3 §§ 70-109. This section seems to have been written partly on the basis of his own experience in Alexandria and, we would suppose that when it was censored by the Roman officers in the Roman camp of Titus after the war, it became an integral part of the pamphlet of warning to be sent to his co-religionists beyond Euphrates or in Adiabene. We will later discuss this pamphlet again.

[28] Suetonius, *Nero* 19, mentions Nero's trip to Achaia.

with a considerable force of auxiliaries (*JW* 3 §§ 65-9), was now ready for the invasion of Palestine. The Romans invaded Galilee in May, 67 CE (JW 3 § 142).

Since various and insightful analyses of Josephus' activity in Galilee according to the versions of the *War* and *Life* have already been made by many scholars, including a thorough study by Shaye J. D. Cohen, we will not go into the contradictions and discrepancies between the two versions.[29]

The town of Jotapata in Galilee fell in July, 67 CE (*JW* 3 § 339). According to Josephus, when the town was on the point of being taken, he succeeded in plunging into a deep pit, in which "forty persons of distinction" were already hiding. On the third day, this hiding place was betrayed to the Roman camp by a woman. Two Roman tribunes rushed to the place and urged Josephus to surrender. Here we would like to call attention to the fact that there does exist a deep pit in Jotapata into which Josephus claimed to have jumped.[30]

---

[29] As a translator of S. J. D. Cohen's work (1979) into Japanese (Japanese title: *Iosefusu – Sono Hito to Jidai (Josephus – The Man and His Age)* [Tokyo: Yamamoto Shoten Publishing House, 1991]), I have become a little skeptical of western scholars' approach to the life of Josephus. The premise in their approach is that Josephus was a historian. Certainly Josephus considers himself as such (see his criticism of contemporary or Greek historians in the preface to the *War*), but we would wonder if Josephus is telling a story as a historian in the modern sense of the word. As long as there are many entertaining elements, digressions, exaggerations, and imaginative inventions both in *Life* and in the *War*, which are indispensable to any story-telling, and as long as Josephus always had in mind a Greco-Roman audience who looked for entertainment, it seems appropriate that we should approach Josephus not as a historian but as a story-teller. From this approach, our attitude toward those sources would also change. In Japanese culture, there is a story-telling genre called "Kodan," in which feats of some historical figures are told to an audience, using entertaining elements. The audience knows from the beginning that although there are some historical kernels in the story, it has been highly embellished by these entertainment elements. So, on the basis of this analogy, we wonder how much exactness the Greco-Roman audience expected from Josephus in his telling of the war in Palestine through his account in the *War*.

[30] Josephus' experience in the pit might have led him to think of himself as a Danielic figure who was thrown into a lion's den. Indeed, the townspeople in the pit might have been like lions to Josephus. We visited Jotapata three times, and during our third visit (March 27, 1987) we believe we finally found the pit in which Josephus jumped. Mrs. Motoko Kitajima who accompanied us in our trip wrote about the day of our discovery in her *Tabi to Ongaku* (Trips and Music) (Tokyo: Hoiku Shiryosha Publishing House, 1991), pp. 277-78.

Ancient Jotapata is now called Jodephat in Israel. There is a Moshav in its neighborhood and on the opposite side of the hill which we could see from the Moshav, there is a pit which fits exactly Josephus' description. The opening of the pit is spacious enough for only one person at a time to lower himself and gives "access on one side to a broad cavern, invisible to those above," as Josephus claims in *JW* 3 § 341. If packed, the cavern is large enough for housing "about forty people" (*JW* 3 § 342). Thus, there is no reason for us not to believe that Josephus plunged into the deep pit and found a certain number of the townspeople hiding there.

According to *JW* 3 §§ 353-4, Josephus offered up a silent prayer to God before his surrender to the Roman army. This prayer has been analyzed by many Josephan scholars. Since we have assumed that Josephus accepted Nero's mission, we could understand this prayer on the basis of this assumption. We would contend that this prayer was a reconfirmation of the Roman cause due to the shift in fortune, assisted by God, which Josephus had first glimpsed on his trip to Rome, where he was impressed by Nero's strength. When Josephus was to surrender, the townspeople around him in the pit "pointed their swords at him and threatened to kill him"[31] if he surrendered to the Romans (*JW* 3 § 360), and they proposed to end their lives in mass suicide. Josephus then harangued them on the crime of such an act, but in vain. In the end, they killed each other according to the order made by the lots they threw, but Josephus escaped death (*JW* 3 §§ 362-91). We would wonder how Josephus could harangue in the pit where "forty townspeople" are supposed to have been tightly crowded and we would also wonder how they could commit suicide in a place like that. Even those scholars who believe in Josephus' account have wondered if there were some tricks left unmentioned.[32] We will not go into this problem, but we would suggest that all those in the pit, including Josephus, might have made a mass surrender to Vespasian or that Josephus alone might have surrendered, leaving behind the

---

[31] This expression of swords and threatened death is one of Josephus' literary *topoi*. S. J. D. Cohen (1979: 219 n.75) cites *JW* 2 § 619. We would add *JW* 4 § 603 where a hesitant Vespasian was threatened into accepting imperial honors. Josephus says: "But on his declining, the officers pressed him more insistently and the soldiers, flocking round with drawn swords, threatened him with death, if he refused to live with dignity."

[32] For example, Rajak (1983: 171) refers to one of the possible tricks. See also Thackeray 1929: 14.

townspeople in the pit for destruction. In any event, Josephus' performance in the pit described in his account is theatrical and therefore quite dubious. It could stimulate the curiosity of his audience, but it would invite the doubts of skeptics.

Josephus was brought before Vespasian and Titus, to whom he was an enemy commander. Thus Vespasian could have put him to death on the spot "by right of war" (νόμῳ πολέμου).[33] What Vespasian did, however, was merely to put him in custody (*JW* 3 § 398, *Life* §§ 413-4). Not only that, Vespasian also provided him with "raiment and other precious things" (*JW* 3 § 408),[34] and allowed him to marry a Caesarean woman (*Life* § 414). A series of these favors which, as Josephus himself proudly says, were a definite sign of "a respect beyond the common lot of a prisoner" (*JW* 3 § 438), would again suggest that Vespasian received some instruction from Nero about Josephus' mission. Only our hypothesis would explain "every care"(*Life* § 414) Josephus received in the Roman camp.[35]

Josephus predicted before Vespasian and Titus that they would become Roman emperors (*JW* 3 §§ 400-402). This is indeed one climax of his theatrical play. However, he seems to have made such a prediction because if he were to be sent to Nero, he would be put to death not only as an enemy commander but also as a traitor to the Roman cause. According to Josephus, when his "prophecy" (literally "what he said before" in Greek) was fulfilled, Vespasian had one of his men sever his chain with an axe (*JW* 4 § 629. Cf. *AgAp* 1 § 48). This is definitely Josephus' invention because his marriage to a Caesarean Jewess in the Roman camp and above all his disclosure of her virginity in *Life* § 414 indicate that he was already released and active in the Roman camp prior to the fulfillment of his prediction.[36]

---

[33] In his paraphrase of Elisha's reply to King Joram, Josephus seems to have projected his experience. Elisha said: "that it was right to kill those who were captured by the law (right) of war, but that these men had done no harm to his country, and without knowing it, had come to them by the power of God" (*Ant* 9 § 58).

[34] The Greek word for "precious things" ("precious gifts" in Thackeray, LCL) is κειμήλιοι in plural form, which means "gem, jewel, something precious, treasure; valuable objects, article of value." See Rengstorf 1973-83: 2.485. Were these precious things booty and were they given to Josephus as gifts for his marriage with a Caesarean Jewess?

[35] What is important for our argument is why such special favors, including marriage, were given to Josephus. Rajak (1983) does not ask such a question.

[36] Rajak (1983: 187) discusses the possibility of Josephus' earlier release in the Roman camp and suggests that severing Josephus' chain with an axe might have been "ceremonial." We would rather like to see the invention of this account in

Nero committed suicide on June 9, 68 CE. After the short reigns of Galba and Otho, Vitellius was hailed as emperor on January, 69 CE. When this news reached Caesarea, Vespasian was proclaimed emperor first by the officers of his army (*JW* 4 §§ 601-4), and then by the Roman forces in Alexandria (*JW* 4 §§ 617-19).[37] Vitellius was assassinated in Rome in December, 69 CE.

Vespasian and Titus went to Alexandria accompanied by Josephus. There they heard the news of Vitellius' assassination (*JW* 4 § 656). Vespasian sailed for Rome to become emperor. Josephus' Caesarean wife left him around this time (*Life* § 415), he then married an Alexandrian woman (*Life* § 415). He returned to Caesarea with Titus and Tiberius Alexander, the former Jewish prefect of Egypt who was familiar with Jerusalem (*JW* 2 § 220).

The siege of Jerusalem began around the Passover of 70 CE. The twelfth legion also joined the three forces of Titus. Josephus demonstrated his usefulness as one of the spokesmen for the Roman camp. He addressed the so-called revolutionaries within the wall and asked them to surrender to the Roman army (*JW* 5 §§ 360-419, 541; 6 §§ 94-117, 129, 365).[38] This was dangerous work. Words of hatred, scorn and ridicule as well as stones and rocks were hurled against him from within the wall (*JW* 5 § 541).[39] As a result of his repeated addresses and warnings, some did desert to the Roman camp (*JW* 5 §§ 538, 548; 6 § 113, 117). This created another job for him to do in the Roman

---

light of the account of *Ant* 18 §§ 195-204, where Josephus describes in detail the prison life of Agrippa I in Rome. According to it, a German co-prisoner prophesies to Agrippa I that he will soon be released from his chains and "be advanced to the highest point of honor and of power." The conversation between these two prisoners ends with a remark: "The German who made these prophecies was as ridiculous in Agrippa's eyes then as he later turned out to be deserving of admiration." It seems possible to imagine that Josephus had his source for *Ant* 18 §§ 195-204 in mind when he described himself in chains. By describing himself in the same state of condition as Agrippa I, Josephus could expect the sympathy of his readers.

[37] On the allegiance of the Roman forces under Tiberius Alexander, see also Suetonius, *Vespasian* 6.

[38] The content of any call to surrender seems to be very simple: If you willingly surrender, your life is guaranteed, otherwise not. In Josephus' paraphrase of Rapsakes' call in *Ant* 10 §§ 9-10, his own call might actually be reflected. See also the descriptions in *Ant* 3 §§ 19-21; 4 § 190; 6 § 20; 8 §§ 127-9, 296-7.

[39] See Josephus' descriptions of Moses who was stoned by his fellow Jews (*Ant* 3 § 12; 4 §§ 11, 22) and of David who was stoned by the relatives of Saul (*Ant* 7 § 207).

camp. It was "the least glamorous, but probably the most important, of his functions, interrogation of prisoners and deserters" (Seth Schwartz 1990: 8). Thanks to his efforts, Titus and Tiberius Alexander could have gathered information about the Jewish forces within the wall, the kinds and amount of the arms they were concealing, the locations of the underground passages (Cf. *JW* 6 §§ 430-33), the number and living conditions of the citizens within the wall, including their remaining food and water supplies, etc.

In *Life* § 418, Josephus refers to his "personal misfortunes" (ἐμαυτοῦ συμφορῶν), without explaining what they are. These plural misfortunes seem to indicate the fate of his parents who were captured by Simon (*JW* 5 §§ 418, 533, 544). The account of *JW* 6 § 432 suggests that when the Roman army broke through the wall, they evacuated "those who had been captured by the tyrants." If Josephus' parents had been evacuated at that time, he would have mentioned it in *Life* § 419, in which he says that when given permission by Titus after the war, he secured the liberation of first his countrymen, second his brother and fifty friends, and third, all friends and acquaintances whom he recognized. Failure to mention the rescue of his parents would suggest that they were executed, perhaps soon after Josephus began to address the revolutionaries or just before the fall of the Temple and the City.[40]

The Temple was burned down on August 30, 70 CE (*JW* 6 § 250) and the city of Jerusalem fell on September 26/27, 70 CE (*JW* 6 §§ 407, 435).

After the war, Titus visited cities in and outside of Palestine to give rest to his soldiers and to express his thanks to those kings who provided him and his father with auxiliary forces (*JW* 7 §§ 20, 23, 36-9, 96, 105-16). Josephus would have been with Titus all the way through. If so, we would wonder what he was doing during these several months in the camp of Titus. According to Josephus, he wrote the war narrative in his "vernacular tongue," i.e, in Aramaic and sent it to his fellow Jews beyond the Euphrates or in Adiabene (*JW* 1 §§ 3, 6). We have already suggested elsewhere that the present Greek version of the *War*

---

[40] In his description of the fate of John Hyrcanus' mother (and his brothers) in *Ant* 13 §§ 231-33, Josephus might have projected the fate of his own mother or thought of her fate. Hyrcanus' mother was brought upon a wall by Ptolemy and maltreated in the sight of all. Ptolemy threatened to hurl her down headlong if Hyrcanus did not give up the siege.

is not a translation of the first version which Josephus claims to have written and that the first version would have been much shorter.[41] If Josephus' account of the war in Aramaic were a shorter one, writing it could be done within a short period of time in any place other than Rome, though many Josephan scholars have taken it for granted that Josephus wrote it in Rome (e.g Seth Schwartz 1990: 10). Partly because the so-called revolutionaries had already sent emissaries to the co-religionists beyond the Euphrates to foster revolt (*JW* 6 § 343; cf. *JW* 1 § 5 and 3 § 108), and perhaps mainly because among those captives to be sent to Rome were the members of the royal family of Adiabene (*JW* 6 § 357) who fought against the Romans during the war (*JW* 2 § 520; cf. § 388; 5 § 474), we would suggest that writing a pamphlet or a booklet with the nature of a warning (*JW* 3 § 108) seems to have been a matter of urgency. This urgency seems to suggest that Josephus composed it under the surveillance of the Roman officers in the Roman camp of Titus. As a result, this pamphlet seems to have given Josephus another chance for demonstrating his renewed loyalty to the Roman cause and willingness to be of service to Titus and thus could further ensure his chances of survival in Rome.

Josephus accompanied Titus to Alexandria, and then sailed for Rome with him after the winter of 71 CE (*JW* 7 § 117). According to *Life* § 422, some time before his departure for Alexandria, Josephus' lands in Jerusalem were confiscated for the Roman garrisons and replaced with other land on the plain. The temporary owner of this new land was perhaps Josephus' brother Matthias, the sole survivor of his nearest kinsmen.

V

In Rome, the joint triumphal ceremonies of Vespasian and Titus were held. Josephus depicts the celebrations in detail (*JW* 7 §§ 121-162), but curiously enough, he does not mention exactly when they were held. Not only that, we cannot find in the descriptions any personal feelings

---

[41] See Hata 1975. Cf. criticism by Rajak 1983: 176; Feldman 1984: 811 (no. 3212e), 833-34 (no. 3298a); Seth Schwartz 1990: 30. To our regret, there are still some scholars who believe that the Greek version of the *War* is a translation from the first version.

of Josephus at the sight of the ceremonies.[42] This might indicate that Josephus himself did not witness the ceremonies or that he wrote Book 7 of the *War* in the time of Domitian (81-96 CE) when, thanks to the passage of time,[43] he could report them as if he had been an eye-witness.

In Rome, Josephus transformed himself from a commander to a story-teller[44] of the past war (*War*); a story-teller, apologist and defender of the past history of his nation (*Antiquities*); an apologist of his own past behavior in the war (*Life*); and a staunch defender and polemist for his people against defamation of the antiquity of Jewish history (*Against Apion*).

According to *Life* §§ 423-24, Josephus was given "a lodging in the house which he (i.e. Vespasian) had occupied before he became Emperor," "the privilege of Roman citizenship" and "a pension." Vespasian also presented him with "a considerable tract of land in Judaea" (*Life* § 425). Of course, as Josephus himself writes, these privileges "excited envy and thereby exposed (him) to danger."[45] Feldman (1984: 92) comments on the purpose of Vespasian's favors that "one cannot avoid conjecturing that Josephus had done something to earn such magnificent treatment." We would wonder if Vespasian thanked Josephus for his continuing dedication to the Roman cause from the time of Nero, including his writing a pamphlet of warning. In Rome, perhaps within two years after his arrival, he divorced his Alexandrian wife and married a Cretan Jewess (*Life* §§ 5, 427), perhaps his third or fourth wife.[46]

What does a "lodging" mean? The Greek word would suggest that Josephus' stay in the house of Vespasian was temporary until he found a permanent place to live outside of Vespasian's palace. His confession

---

[42] According to Suetonius, *Domitian* 2, in the ceremonies Domitian was riding on a white horse behind his father and Titus. If true, the sight should have been quite impressive to any attentive onlooker. Cassius Dio 65.12 also refers to him riding on a military horse. The lack of Josephus's reference to the kind of horse (see *JW* 7 § 152) could argue against Josephus' presence in the ceremonies.

[43] For the date of composition of *War* 7, see Cohen 1979: 84ff.

[44] We hesitate to label Josephus a historian. See n. 29 above.

[45] In his attempt to exonerate himself from various accusations, Josephus evidently projects himself into Daniel in *Ant* 10 §§ 250-252. See also David's words to Saul in *Ant* 6 §§ 285-89.

[46] Who is the woman whom Josephus refers to as his wife detained by the revolutionaries in *JW* 5 § 419? Is she a rhetorical invention?

of failure to attain "precision in the pronunciation" of Greek because of the "habitual use of his native tongue" (*Ant* 20 § 263) and the incessant indictments by his fellow Jews, including those of Jonathan (*Life* § 424; *JW* 7 §§ 437-53) and Justus of Tiberias (*Life* §§ 336ff),[47] would indicate that he resided in a Jewish section of Rome. Of course, he would have frequented the Flavian court from there to obtain some important information for writing the semi-official account of the war in Greek, for making a report of the progress of his writing, or for making a self-defense before the Emperor against various accusations from his fellow Jews. His special interest in court stories, as told in the *Antiquities*, might also suggest his frequent visits to the Flavian court.

Why was the "privilege of Roman citizenship" given to Josephus? According to Suetonius, *Claudius* 25, Roman citizenship was a prerequisite for those foreigners who wanted to have a Roman name. Thus, it might have been given to Josephus as a lawful procedure for granting him the Flavian name.[48]

According to *Life* § 429, Domitian gave Josephus the privilege of tax exemption on his land in Palestine.[49] The granting of this privilege, called ἀτέλεια in Greek, would indicate that Josephus had by then expressed his strong desire to return to Palestine to the Emperor. Here we recall Josephus' report of his selection of the Pharisaic way of life in *Life* § 12 and his favorable descriptions of the Pharisees in the *Antiquities*. Though perhaps his wish was not realized, he seems to have begun to prepare himself for returning to Palestine by painting on canvas some (not all) favorable pictures of the Pharisees in Palestine because, with the disappearance of both the Sadducees and the Essenes in Palestine after the war, the Pharisees became the sole ruling class. How convenient that Josephus had the wisdom and foresight at the age of nineteen to choose that way of life after "years"

---

[47] Concerning the indictments made by Justus of Tiberias and Josephus' response, see S. J. D. Cohen 1979: 114ff.

[48] When given the Flavian name, Josephus might have thought of Daniel who was given the name of Belteshazzar. It is interesting to note that Josephus in *Ant* 10 § 188 changes from the chief eunuch in Scripture to the king, who changed the names of the youths, including Daniel, and ordered them to use their new names. (See also the contribution by M. Goodman below).

[49] According to *JW* 1 § 194, Julius Caesar conferred on Antipater, the father of Herod, the privilege of Roman citizenship with exemption of taxes and thus made him an enviable man. In *Ant* 14 § 137, the exemption of taxes is also coupled with the privilege of Roman citizenship.

of intense study and consideration! Perhaps, if a different sect had emerged as the ruling class, Josephus' religious conclusions at that early age would have presaged that turn of events. It was perhaps when he was composing the latter parts of the *Antiquities* and the *Life* that he felt a longing for his homeland. No wonder, as more than fifteen years had already passed in Rome by then.[50]

What was the nature of his "pension" (σύνταξις χρημάτων)? Was it given to Josephus out of Vespasian's personal estate or from military funds? Was it temporary or for life? We know nothing, and we leave speculation on this matter to other scholars.

VI

Using a formula which he often employs in concluding his description of some miraculous event in the first ten books of the *Antiquities*,[51] Josephus concludes his narrative in *Life* by saying that "such are the events of my whole life: from them let others judge as they will of my character" (*Life* § 430).

So we conclude our attempts to fill in some of the dark periods in the life of Josephus: let our readers judge as they will our imaginative attempts. However, in closing, we would like to emphasize once again that it is very important for any Josephan biographer to fill in the intervening two years from 64 CE to 66 CE because it was the events during these two years that constituted a turning point in the life of Josephus. If he had not accepted Nero's mission, he would not have been torn between his loyalty to the Jewish people and his loyalty to the Roman cause.

---

[50] Josephus' desire to return to Palestine may well be expressed in his paraphrase of Ezra's prayer in *Ant* 10 § 143.

[51] See *Ant* 1 § 108; 3 §§ 81, 268, 323; 4 § 158; 8 § 262; 10 § 281.

JOSEPHUS AS ROMAN CITIZEN

Martin Goodman

"In spite of his efforts, Josephus must have been a very lonely man in his old age." This judgement by Zvi Yavetz (1975:432), a distinguished historian of the Roman empire, seems to me to be unduly pessimistic, and I shall explore in this paper some reasons for believing that the truth may lie elsewhere. It is true that, on the one hand, by the end of his life Josephus had probably lost his favoured place in the imperial court, and on the other, that after his death his writings seem to have been totally ignored in the rabbinic Jewish tradition. But there were other inhabitants of Rome apart from the imperial family, and rabbinic texts emanated only from a very restricted region of the Jewish world. I shall consider here the possibility that Josephus might have found other, more congenial, company in Rome, especially among the Jews of the city.

Jews had lived in Rome since the mid first century BCE, if not earlier (Leon 1960: 4-5). Jewish captives had been sold on the slave markets by Pompeius after the capture of Jerusalem in 63 BCE and by Sosius after his capture of Jerusalem in 37 BCE. The descendants of such slaves formed the nucleus of the eleven or so synagogues attested in the city in the high empire (Schürer 1973-87: 3. 95-8). For most of the Julio-Claudian period, the Jews of Rome had lived peacefully as part of the heterogeneous population of the sprawling capital city. Expulsions under Tiberius and Claudius can only have been temporary or partial (Schürer 1973-87: 3. 75-8), since Jews still formed a sizable community in the time of Nero (cf. Acts 28:17-29).

How "Roman" did these Jews feel themselves to be? None of their writings are known to survive, apart from inscriptions on stone which are not always easy to date, so only surmise is possible. What can be said with some certainty, however, is that nothing in the evidence precludes the possibility that the Jews were well integrated into Roman society, even if the temporary expulsions may have left behind a residue of tension and prejudice. It may indeed be significant in itself that Jews chose to continue to live in Rome in large numbers, a choice which they presumably made quite freely, and there are some indications in the extant evidence that Jews might identify themselves at least to some extent with the surrounding Roman culture.

Thus, although the Jewish inscriptions of Rome are mostly in Greek rather than in Latin, this was not an absolute rule (Leon 1960: 76-7), and in any case use of Greek was not unusual among those of the Roman plebs whose origins lay in the east. The names adopted by some of the Jewish communities recorded in the epigraphic record may be indicative of integration. The names Ἀυγουστήσιοι and Ἀγριππήσιοι may suggest either that Augustus and his friend Marcus Agrippa had been their patrons or that the original membership of these communities consisted in their slaves and freedmen. Other synagogue names may show local attachment to particular areas of the city, such as the Καμπήσιοι (named after the Campus Martius) and the Σιβουρήσιοι (named after the Subura). The name of the synagogue of the Βερνακλήσιοι or Βερνακλώσιοι may have distinguished the indigenous Jews (vernaculi) from immigrants (Schürer 1973-87: 3. 95-8).

The literary evidence about Roman Jews is sparse but also points towards some degree of integration into the life of the city. Jews on occasion took a prominent part in Roman public life, to the chagrin of Cicero when he spoke in defense of Flaccus (Flac. 28 [66]). The throng of Jews who lamented the murdered Julius Caesar in 44 BCE was noted by Suetonius (Iul. 84.5).

The main explanation of such Jewish integration as occurred is simple. Most of the Jews of Rome were Roman citizens. In Roman law, all slaves who had been owned by a Roman citizen and formally granted their liberty in front of a magistrate received citizenship and could hand it on to their descendants in perpetuity.

But although these Jews might view themselves as fully part of Roman society, for most of the Julio-Claudian period there was no reason for their Roman loyalty to affect their maintenance of a deep interest in Jerusalem. According to Josephus, more than eight thousand Roman Jews tried to influence Augustus' decision about the disposition of Herod's kingdom when embassies came from Judaea in 4 BCE (JW 2 §§ 80-83; Ant 17 §§ 300-301). The expulsion of some Jews in 19 CE was a punishment, according to Josephus (Ant 18 §§ 81-4), for the dishonesty of Jewish miscreants who had swindled a convert out of a large sum of money on the pretext that they were sending it to the Temple in Jerusalem.

Such Jews might quite justifiably see themselves, in effect, as Romans of the Jewish faith, whose dual loyalties cohabited without problem. They might be encouraged in such a belief by the well-attested popularity of Jewish customs among some of their gentile neighbours (cf. Schürer 1973-87: 3. 160-5). Jews had long held the notion that outsiders of all kinds could, as proselytes, become Jewish if they adopted Jewish practices and identified themselves as Jews (cf., e.g., Cohen 1983, 1989). Since Roman Jews experienced no difficulty in accepting the logical possibility of such gentile Romans becoming Jewish while remaining Roman, they should have found it equally easy to see themselves as fully part of Roman society even when they also wished to stress their Jewish identity.

If Jews in Rome in the mid-first-century CE did indeed feel comfortable with their dual identity, the change in their status in Rome after the failure of the Jewish Revolt must have come as an awful shock.

It is worth trying to empathise with the likely reactions of Roman Jews to the events of 66-70 CE. In the preceding four years the Jews in distant Judaea had fought and lost a great war. The Jews in Rome might have been expected to grieve, heartbroken by this attack upon the sanctuary which they held dear. But they could also argue that these tragic events had not been in any way their fault. So far as is known, they had taken no part whatsoever in the war: it may be significant that Josephus chose not even to mention their *reactions* at any stage in the conflict, even though when he was writing he was actually living in Rome, and even though he was quite forthcoming about the eruption of violence elsewhere in the Jewish diaspora (*JW* 2 §§ 477-98).

But Jews in Rome were not to escape the results of the war. Imagine the horror of Roman Jews at the triumphal procession of Vespasian and Titus, with the parade through Roman streets of sacred vessels from the Temple (*JW* 7 §§ 148-52). Roman Jews will have watched with deep gloom the erection of the victory arches with their depressing reliefs (cf. Dessau 1892-1916: nos. 264-5). Every day when they used cash for petty transactions, they were reminded of the disaster by the issue of thousands of imperial coins of different types celebrating the Jewish defeat as the main justification for the seizure of power by the Flavian dynasty (Mattingly and Carson 1923-75: 2. 115-18). The symbolism of the *fiscus Judaicus*, harrowing for all Jews, must have been particularly galling for those in Rome who could see before their own eyes the rebuilding of the idolatrous temple of Jupiter out of the taxes they were compelled to pay (Cassius Dio 66.7.2; cf. *JW* 7 § 218).

It would be unsurprising if some of the Roman Jews who felt most integrated into Roman society reacted to this trauma by rejecting Judaism in order to be accepted as proper Romans. A fine example of the integration of apostates into Roman society was particularly prominent in this period to lead them in this way. Tiberius Julius Alexander, nephew of the Jewish philosopher Philo, was described by Tacitus as an *inlustris eques Romanus* (*Ann.* 15. 28. 3). If I interpret Suetonius (*Dom.* 12. 2) correctly (Goodman 1989), it was such apostates whose plight came to light when Domitian tightened up on the collection of the *fiscus Judaicus*, compelling even an old man of ninety, who had presumably denied his Jewish origins, to be stripped before an open court to see whether he was circumcised. The significance of such ex-Jews among the Roman plebs may be gauged both from the apparent sympathy with which Suetonius narrated his story, in contrast to his denigration of Jewish cult as superstition at *Tib.* 36, and from the prominence accorded in 96 CE by Nerva to his policy of "removing the *calumnia* of the *fiscus Judaicus*", which was widely advertised on coins issued by the mint of the city of Rome (*RIC* 1926: 2. 227-8, nos. 58, 82).

But what of the Jews holding Roman citizenship who decided, despite the disaster, to insist on the validity of their long-held dual loyalty? It seems reasonable to assume that at least some remained to fill the synagogues: gentile authors writing in the city, such as Juvenal (*Satires* 3.13-14; 6.542-7), still assumed that there was a Jewish community in their midst after the destruction of the Temple. If this is correct, one and perhaps the preferred, spokesman of such Jews will surely have been Josephus.

On a very crude level, of course, Jews in Rome must have seen Josephus as a highly desirable patron. He was an important person in Roman society. Titus and Agrippa II took him seriously enough to give their approval to his work (cf. *Life* §§ 362-67). According to Eusebius (*Hist. eccl.* 3.9.2), he won sufficient prestige to be honoured with a statue in the city and for his work to be placed into public libraries. It is undoubtedly right to insist that he was never as close to the centre of imperial power as he liked to suggest he was. Perhaps he belonged in the same category in the imperial court as doctors and magicians, philosophers and buffoons (Yavetz 1975: 432). But his court connections were substantially greater than most Jews could ever dream to achieve, and the practice of second-order patronage, which gave prestige to those believed to have influence higher up the social ladder, was an established part of life in the Roman empire (Saller 1982). It is worth recording the usefulness to Josephus himself, when he visited Rome before the revolt, of the Jewish actor Alityrus, who had a foothold in the court of Nero (*Life* § 16). What mattered to the Jews of Rome was not so much Josephus' personal religious stance — Agrippa I had been enthusiastically accepted by Jews as their champion despite the dubious nature of his Judaism as a friend and companion of Caligula (c.f. *Ant* 18 §§ 166-8) — as his willingness to be identified as a Jew even when he was sited so close to the heart of Roman power. One may doubt whether he had much social contact with Jews among the Roman plebs, let alone whether he mingled in sabbath services in the slums of Trastevere (although it is a plausible conjecture that he attended a synagogue somewhere in the city), but it is perhaps not so impossible that such Jews might have joined the morning *salutatio* at his house to ask for his help and *amicitia*.

That Josephus portrayed himself to the world as a pious Jew is not in doubt. The purpose of writing the *Antiquities* and *Against Apion* was to defend and extol Judaism. But did Josephus, as perhaps other Jews who lived in the city, also think of himself as a Roman?

Josephus certainly *could* have stressed his Roman identity, if he so wished. It is true that, unlike many of the existing Jewish inhabitants of the city of Rome, he did not inherit his Roman citizenship but was granted it by Vespasian (*Life* § 423) while in his thirties. But a man in his early thirties is young enough to adopt a new persona and new values, particularly when it is expedient.

Furthermore, Josephus knew quite well that it was possible for outsiders like him to identify entirely with the Roman state once they had been given Roman citizenship. In his attack on Apion, who had expressed astonishment that Jews could be called Alexandrians, he responded: "Have not the Romans in their generosity given a share of their name to nearly all men, not just to individuals but to whole nations? For those who were once Iberians and Tyrrhenians and Sabines are now called Romans" (*AgAp* 2 § 40). The phenomenon was correctly observed. A few examples of such assimilation of provincials into Roman society will suffice to illustrate the point. Already by Josephus' time, many rich provincials from Spain or Gaul had come to see themselves as *Roman* aristocrats. In the early third century, Cassius Dio, who was Greek and composed his history in Greek but who was also a second-generation Roman senator and eventually twice consul, seems to have seen the history of Rome as the story of his own society. By the mid-third century the emperor Philip "the Arab" led the Romans in the celebrations of the city's millennium in 247-8 CE despite his own origins near the Syrian Leja'.

Thus Josephus *could* have identified himself with Roman society. Much of his writing was aimed at convincing both Jews and Romans that the practice of Judaism was not incompatible with living in a Roman society, and it would have been entirely logical for him to present himself as a "Roman of the Jewish faith".

But did he do so? The best evidence for such an attitude is to be found in *Against Apion*. I shall argue that one purpose of this treatise, which was explicitly aimed at non-Jewish readers, was implicitly to recommend the Jewish way of life as compatible with Roman *mores* (see also Goodman forthcoming, 1994).

Against Apion is more usually interpreted either as an example of an allegedly common genre of Jewish-Greek apologetic (e.g. Schürer 1973-87: 3. 609-16), or associated with the struggle between Jews and Greeks in first-century Alexandria which had provoked the original treatise by Apion to which Josephus replied (e.g. S. Schwartz 1990: 21, 23). However, there is little evidence that other writings existed in antiquity which might have belonged to the genre of Jewish apologetic into which *Against Apion* allegedly might have fitted, and the attack on Apion, which occupies only a section of the two books, may have been just a literary device for a more general assault on Greek culture, and a means to select those aspects of Judaism most easily defended to a gentile readership. There is much in favour of viewing the work as a product of the time and place when it was written, probably in the city of Rome either in the last days of Domitian or in the principate of Nerva or Trajan (Keeble 1991).

In that context, it is striking that, in his attack on the Greeks, Josephus chose not so much to describe Judaism as *compatible* with, or even related to Greek culture, as previous Jewish writers had done, as to claim that the Jewish way of life was demonstrably *superior* to Hellenism. And what is most relevant to the present argument, the qualities in Judaism which he picked out to make his point were strikingly similar to those aspects of Roman *mos* that Latin authors trumpeted when they too wanted to compare themselves favourably to Greeks.

Thus, according to Josephus, Jews oppose innovation (*AgAp* 2 §§ 182-3) and encourage sobriety (2 §§ 204). They stress the value of the community above the individual (§ 196), oppose homosexuality (§ 199), keep their women submissive (§ 201), and honour their parents (§ 206). They take seriously their duties towards their friends (§ 207). They love justice, welcome hard work, avoid extravagance and show courage in defensive war (§§ 291-2). They occupy themselves in crafts or agriculture (§ 294). Their wisdom is practical as well as theoretical (§§ 173-4), and they have a serious attitude to life, as they demonstrate by their willingness to die for the sake of their laws (§§ 271-2). Some of this platitudinous moralising might also be found in any non-Jewish Greek author, but what I want to stress here is that such qualities are the reverse of those espoused by fickle Greeks in Rome as described by Latin writers in the city during the late Republic and the early empire (cf. Petrochilos 1974: 35-62).

More positively, Josephus did not include Rome in the list of nations whose customs compared so poorly with the excellence of Judaism according to *AgAp* 2 §§ 237-86. This may have been not just out of tact but from a desire to show, by careful selection in his description of the Jewish way of life, that in many important aspects Jews and Romans shared the same ideals.

Thus Josephus might well have seen himself as in some sense Roman as well as Jewish while he was writing his histories and apologetic works. If so, did his Roman identity affect the way in which he wrote about the past?

Perhaps, at least sometimes. The Roman rather than Jewish perspective of the title of the *Jewish War* has long been noted by scholars (Stern 1987a: 47; cf. Bilde 1988: 71-3). Josephus himself wrote that his history was περὶ τοῦ Ἰουδαϊκοῦ πολέμου (*Life* § 27). It has also long been remarked that Josephus extolled the Roman state throughout his writings. God was on the Roman side (*JW* 5 §§ 367-8, 412), hence they held the whole world in thrall (*JW* 5 §§ 366). The gloating description of Titus' triumph in *JW* 7 §§ 123-57, uncomfortable material for modern readers, may perhaps be best understood as expression of this ambivalence. It was the divine will that the Temple's treasures should be brought to Rome. Thus, in identifying with the victor, Josephus could claim that he was being a good Jew. In any case, in the conquest of Jerusalem he was proud to have been on the Roman side. At least one other Jewish participant in the war may have shared his viewpoint — Agrippa II, another Jew who had once been pious enough to act as guardian of the Temple, but who was also a Roman citizen and a companion of Titus when the Temple was destroyed.

But Josephus' identification with Rome went only a certain way, for, in his own estimation, Josephus was irremediably ἀλλόφυλος when he wrote for Greeks and Romans (*JW* 1 § 16). He wrote in the introduction to the *Antiquities* that the *Jewish War* had been an account of the war fought "by us Jews against the Romans" (*Ant* 1 § 4); he contrasted the sale of his books to "many Romans" on the one hand to his sale of books to "many of our people" on the other (*AgAp* 1 § 51). Jews, like Egyptians, were slaves to the Romans (*AgAp* 2 § 125). Josephus praised Romans for not compelling *subiecti* to break their ancestral laws (*AgAp* 2 § 73), implying that Jews are subjects of Rome; it was an odd virtue to praise when Rome had destroyed the Temple where alone, as Josephus recognised, Jews were permitted to worship with sacrifices (*AgAp* 2 § 193).

It seems that, despite his Roman status, Josephus did not talk about himself as Roman and did not in the final analysis interpret the past as a native Roman would. In his self-description at the beginning of the *Life* (§§ 1-12), he did not even mention his Roman name or citizenship. To Agrippa, who wrote to him in Greek, he was simply "dearest Josephus" (*Life* §§ 365-6), without title. The earliest extant use of the name "Flavius Josephus" seems to be in the manuscripts of the *Jewish War*, where it is found in the title of the work in Codex Parisinus 1425 (Schürer 1973-87: 1. 47, note 4). It is unlikely that the title in the manuscripts originated with Josephus.

Thus Rome in Josephus' histories is always a distant Italian power, an alien state with which Jews, like other provincials, must do business, rather than an empire to which its inhabitants can feel proud to belong (cf. Stern 1987a: 50; 1987b: 76). The word ῥομαιστί in *Ant* 14 § 191, where it occurs within the text of a decree sent by Julius Caesar to the people of Sidon, means writing in Latin, specifically contrasted to writing ἑλληνιστί, even though most imperial business in Judaea will have been conducted in Greek. The expression ῥωμαΐζειν (*JW* 2 § 562) is a political term which means "to favour the Roman side" during the conflict in A.D. 66, rather than "to act like a Roman" on the analogy of ἰουδαΐσειν (which at least at *JW* 2 § 454 probably means "to act as a Jew") and ἑλληνίζειν. The only passage in which Jews are described as acting in Roman fashion concerns the organization of the rebel army in Galilee: at *JW* 2 § 577, Josephus claims that he divided his army ῥωμαϊκώτερον, "more along Roman lines". But the whole point of even this passage is that Romans are the other side, the enemy, whom it might be prudent to imitate, but into whose ranks it was presumed inconceivable that Jews might enter. The blockage which prevented a Jew like Josephus imagining himself as ever being fully part of Roman society lay as much in his mentality as in any prejudice or institutional hindrance within the Roman system.

For such reticence about his Roman identity one might perhaps suggest some personal reasons. Josephus wrote a little about his four wives, one from Jerusalem, one from Caesarea, one from Alexandria and one from Crete, and he gave the names of his sons by the last two wives. The names are standard Jewish names of the period: by his first wife, Hyrcanus; by his Cretan wife, Justus and a Simonides Agrippa (*Life* §§ 5, 426-7). There is no indication that the wives were Roman citizens, and indeed such a status would be rather implausible for a Jewish woman from Crete, even if she may have originated from Judaea and even if she was of distinguished parentage, as Josephus claimed (*Life* § 427). In that case, Josephus' *family* would not have enjoyed Roman citizenship, even though he did, for the status could only have been passed on if both parents were citizens or if Josephus had been granted not just citizenship but also *conubium*, with foreign wives, a notable privilege of which, if he had it, he might have been expected to boast (cf. Sherwin-White 1973: 268). Perhaps Josephus treated his citizenship as simply an extra honour from the emperor, on a par with the grant of land near Jerusalem, which is the context in which he referred to it in the *Life* (§§ 422-3).

But one may further add possible, more structural, reasons why Josephus was a Jewish more than a Roman author. The essence of Flavian propaganda after 70 CE was not just to revel in the Judaean victory as justification for Vespasian's seizure of the purple, but to claim precisely that Judaism and Roman power were not compatible; since Josephus' main line of argument in the *Jewish War* was the precise opposite, the view, common in past generations, that what he wrote was Flavian propaganda is thus rather bizarre. The parade of the most sacred relics of a conquered nation was not normal in a Roman triumph. There is no parallel, as far as I know, to the *fiscus Judaicus* as a symbolic payment to a Roman cult by the devotees of a discredited foreign superstition. Roman Jews who continued to follow Jewish practices after 70 CE could well be seen by non-Jewish Romans as outside the pale of acceptable Roman society. Prejudice attached even to the most eminent. Agrippa II and his sister Berenice were, as descendants of Herod, from the fifth generation of their family to hold Roman citizenship. Their political sympathies with Rome were blatant throughout their careers: Agrippa had been on Titus' staff when Jerusalem was sacked, and he held the *ornamenta praetoria* (Cassius Dio 66. 15. 4) But to Juvenal (*Satires* 6. 158), he was a *barbarus*, and when rumour had it that Titus wanted to marry Berenice, popular Roman feeling compelled him to send her away (Cassius Dio, *ibid*; Suet. *Tit.* 7. 1-2).

What I am suggesting is that Josephus should be given credit for extraordinary bravery in standing up for the right of Roman Jews to continue to practise their religion even in a deeply hostile environment. In all the discussions of Josephus' tortuous attempts to justify his past tortuous career, modern scholars too infrequently recall that he did not have to write anything at all. Unlike modern academics, Josephus , with his estate in Judaea kindly granted by Vespasian (*Life* § 425), was under no compulsion to publish. He did so, voluminously, not primarily to protect his social status by winning the patronage of rich Romans — one may doubt how useful an ally Epaphroditus was in Roman society — nor to defend his own reputation — the autobiographical parts of his output comprise only a small fraction of the total — but to defend Judaism at a time when it was under exceptional pressure. The sheer length and thoroughness of the *Antiquities* are testimony to the seriousness with which he undertook his chosen role. If the Jews of Rome were as grateful for his efforts as they should have been, Josephus in his old age will not have been a lonely man.

BIBLIOGRAPHY

AB   Anchor Bible. New York: Doubleday.
ABD
  1992   *Anchor Bible Dictionary*. New York: Doubleday.
Abel, F.-M.
  1933-38 *Géographie de la Palestine*. 2 vols. Paris: Lecoffre-Gabalda.
  1946   Simon de la tribu de Bilga. Pp. 52-58 in *Miscellanea Giovanni Mercati*.
         Testi e studi 121. Città del Vaticano.
  1949   *Les Livres des Maccabées*. Paris: Gabalda.
Abel, F.-M. and Starcky, J.
  1961   *Les Livres des Maccabées*, 3rd ed. Paris: Cerf.
Adam, A.
  1972   *Antike Berichte über die Essener*. Kleine Texte für Vorlesungen und
         Übungen 182. 2nd edition. Berlin: de Gruyter.
Albert, K.
  1902   *Strabo als Quelle des Josephus*. Diss. Würzburg. Aschaffenburg: Schnip-
         perschen.
Alon, G.
  1977   *Jews and Judaism in the Classical World*. Jerusalem: Magnes.
  1980   *The Jews in Their Land in the Talmudic Age*. Jerusalem: Magnes.
Applebaum, S.
  1980   A Fragment of a New Hellenistic Inscription from the Old City of
         Jerusalem. Pp. 47-60 (Hebrew and Greek; English summary p. III) in
         *Jerusalem in the Second Temple Period: Abraham Schalit Memorial
         Volume*, ed. A. Oppenheimer, U. Rappaport, and M. Stern. Jerusalem:
         Yad Izhak Ben-Zvi.
  1989   Josephus and the Economic Causes of the Jewish War. Pp. 237-64 in
         Feldman and Hata 1989.
Ariel, D. T.
  1990   *Excavations at the City of David 1978-1985 Directed by Yigal Shiloh*. Vol.
         2: *Imported Stamped Amphora Handles, Coins, Worked Bone and Ivory
         and Glass*. Qedem 30. Jerusalem: The Institute of Archaeology of the
         Hebrew University.
Attridge, H. W.
  1976   *The Interpretation of Biblical History in the Antiquitates Judaicae of
         Flavius Josephus*. Missoula MO: Scholars.
  1984   Josephus and his Works. Pp. 185-232 in *Jewish Writings of the Second
         Temple Period*, ed. M. Stone. Assen and Philadelphia: Van Gorcum and
         Fortress.

Avi-Yonah, M.
1956   The Second Temple. *Sepher Yerushalayim*, ed. M. Avi-Yonah. Jerusa-
        lem: Bialik (Hebrew).
1966   *The Holy Land from the Persian to the Arab Conquests (536 B.C. to A.D.
        640). A Historical Geography.* (Hebr. 1951, 3rd Eng. ed.) Grand Rapids
        MI: Baker Book House.

Axelsson L. E.
1987   *The Lord Rose up from Seir. Studies in the History and Tradition of the
        Negev and Southern Judah.* Coniectanea Biblica. Old Testament Series
        25. Stockholm: Almquist & Wiksell.

Baethgen, F.
1886-87 Siebzehn makkabaeische Psalmen nach Theodor von Mopsuestia.
        Zeitschrift für die alttestamentliche Wissenschaft 6: 261-88; 7: 1-60.

Bardtke, H.
1973   *Zusätze zu Esther*, in *Jüdische Schriften aus Hellenistisch-römischer Zeit*
        I/1. Gütersloh: Mohn.

Bar-Kochva, B.
1973   The Status and Origin of the Garrison at the Akra on the Eve of the
        Religious Persecutions. *Zion* 38: 32-47 (Hebrew).
1989   *Judas Maccabaeus: The Jewish Struggle Against the Seleucids.* Cambridge:
        Cambridge Univ.

Baron, S.
1948   *The Jewish Community.* Vol.2. Philadelphia: JPS.

Barthélemy, D. and Milik, J.T.
1955   *Qumran Cave I.* DJD I. Oxford: Clarendon.

Bartlett J. R.
1982   Edom and the Fall of Jerusalem, 587 B.C. *Palestine Exploration
        Quarterly* 114: 13-24.
1989   *Edom and the Edomites.* Journal for the Study of the Old Testament
        Supplement Series 77. Sheffield: Sheffield Academic.

Baruq, A.
1957   Léontopolis. Pp. 359-372 in *Dictionnaire de la Bible Suppl.* 5.

Bauer, W.
1924   Essener. Pp. 386-430 in *RE* Supplement 4.

Bauer, W.
1958   *Wörterbuch zum Neuen Testament*, 5th ed. Berlin: Töpelmann.

Baumgarten, J.
1982   Exclusions from the Temple: Proselytes and Agrippa I. *Journal of
        Jewish Studies* 33: 215-25.

Beale, G. K.
1980   The Danielic Background for Revelation 13:18 and 17:9. *Tyndale
        Bulletin* 31: 163-70.
1984   *The Use of Daniel in Jewish Apocalyptic Literature and in the Revelation
        of St. John.* Lanham MD: University Press of America.

Beall, T. S.
1988   *Josephus' Description of the Essenes Illustrated by the Dead Sea Scrolls.*
        Society for New Testament Studies Monograph Series 58. Cambridge:
        Cambridge University.

Beckwith, R. T.
1979-81 Daniel 9 and the Date of Messiah's Coming in Essene, Hellenistic,
        Pharisaic, Zealot and Early Christian Computation. *Revue de Qumran*
        10: 167-202.

Beek, M. A.
1943   Relations entre Jérusalem et la Diaspora égyptienne au IIe siècle av.
        J.C. *Oudtest.Studiën* 2: 119-143.

Beit-Arieh I.
1989   New Dates on the Relationship Between Judah and Edom toward the
        End of the Iron Age, Pp. 125-32 in: S. Gitin et al. (eds.), *Recent
        Excavations in Israel*, Winona Lake: Eisenbrauns.

Ben-Dov, M.
1980   The Seleucid Akra - South of the Temple. *Cathedra* 18: 22-35 (He-
        brew).
1982   *In the Shadow of the Temple.* Jerusalem: Keter.

Ben-Dov, M., *et al.*
1983   *The Western Wall.* Jerusalem: Ministry of Defence.

Bengtson, H.
1937-52 *Die Strategie in der hellenistischen Zeit: Ein Beitrag zum antiken Staats-
        recht* (Münchener Beiträge zur Papyrusforschung und antiken Rechts-
        geschichte 27, 32, 36). 3 vols.

Benzinger
1901   Daphne (3). *RE* 4.2136-2138.

Bertholdt L.
1806-8 *Daniel aus dem Hebräisch-Aramäischen neu übersetzt und erklärt.*
        Erlangen: Palm.

Bevan, A. A.
1892   *A Short Commentary on the Book of Daniel.* Cambridge: University.

Beyer, K.
1984   *Die aramäischen Texte vom Toten Meer.* Göttingen: Vandenhoeck and
        Ruprecht.

Bi(c)kerman(n), E. (J.)
1933   Ein jüdischer Festbrief vom Jahre 124 v.Chr. (2 Makk 1:1-9). *Zeitschrift
        für die neutestamentliche Wissenschaft* 32: 233-54 = 1980: 136-58.
1934   Leontopolis. *Encyclopaedia Judaica* 5.796-97.
1935   La charte séleucide de Jérusalem. *Revue des Etudes Juives* 100: 4-35 =
        1980: 44-85.
1937   *Der Gott der Makkabäer.* Berlin: Schocken.
1938   *Institutions des Séleucides.* Paris: Geuthner.
1939-44 Héliodore au Temple de Jérusalem. *Annuaire de l'Istitut de Philologie
        et d'Histoire Orientales et Slaves* 7: 5-40 = 1980: 159-91.

1946   The Edict of Cyrus in Ezra 1. *Journal of Biblical Literature* 65: 249-75
          = 1976: 72-108.
1946-47   The Warning Inscription of Herod's Temple. *Jewish Quarterly Review*
          37: 387-405 = 1980: 210-24.
1958   The Altars of Gentiles. A Note on the Jewish "Ius sacrum." *Revue
          internationale des droits de l'antiquité* 3/5: 137-64 = 1980: 324-46.
1976   *Studies in Jewish and Christian History*. Part 1. Leiden: Brill.
1980   *Studies im Jewish and Christian History*. Part 2. Leiden: Brill.

Bienkowski P.
1992   *Early Edom and Moab. The Beginning of the Iron Age in Southern
          Jordan*. Sheffield: Sheffield Academic.

Bilde, P.
1979   The Causes of the Jewish War According to Josephus. *Journal for the
          Study of Judaism* 10: 179-202.
1983   *Josefus som historieskriver. En undersøgelse af Josefus' fremstilling af
          Gaius Caligulas konflikt med jøderne i Palæstina (Bell 2, 184-203 og Ant
          18, 261-309) med særligt henblik på forfatterens tendens og historiske
          pålidelighed*. København: Gad.
1988   *Flavius Josephus between Jerusalem and Rome: His Life, his Works, and
          their Importance*. Sheffield: JSOT.

Blenkinsopp, J.
1974   Prophecy and Priesthood in Josephus. *Journal of Jewish Studies* 25:
          239-62.

Bloch, H.
1879   *Die Quellen des Flavius Josephus in seiner Archäologie*. Leipzig:
          Teubner.

Blok, A.
1972   The Peasant and the Brigand: Social Banditry Reconsidered. *Compara-
          tive Studies in Society and History* 14: 494-503.

Boecker, H. J.
1964   *Redeformen des Rechtslebens im Alten Testament*. Wiss. Monographien
          zum AT 14. Neukirchen-Vluyn: Neukirchener.

Boettger, G.
1879   *Topografisch-historisches Lexikon zu den Schriften des Flavius Josephus*.
          Leipzig (rp. Amsterdam: Hakkert 1966).

Bonfil, R.
1972   Judah and Jerusalem in the Letter of Aristeas. *Bet Mikra* 17: 131-42
          (Hebrew).

Boschi B. G.
1067   Tradizioni del Pentateuco su Edom. *Rivista Biblica* 15: 369-383.

Bouché-Leclercq, A.
1903-7   *Histoire des Lagides* 1-4. Paris: Leroux.
1913-14   *Histoire des Séleucides 323-64 (avant J.C.)*. Paris: Leroux.

Bousset, W.
1903   *Die Religion des Judentums im neutestamentlichen Zeitalter*. Berlin:
          Reuther & Reichard.

1926   *Die Religion des Judentums im späthellenistischen Zeitalter.* rev. Hugo
        Gressman. 3rd ed. Tübingen: Mohr.

Bowersock, G.
1973   Syria under Vespasian. *Journal of Roman Studies* 63: 133-40.

Brand, J.
1960   Concerning an Article on the Second Temple. *Tarbiz* 29: 210-214
        (Hebrew).

Braund, D.
1984   *Rome and the Friendly King.* London: Croom Helm.

Briant, P.
1982   *Rois, tributs et paysans: Etudes sur les formations tributaires du Moyen
        Orient ancien.* Annales litteraires de l'Université de Besançon 269;
        Centre de Recherches d'Histoire Ancienne vol. 43. Paris: Les Belles
        Lettres.

Broshi, M.
1979   The Population of Western Palestine in the Roman-Byzantine Period.
        Bulletin of the American Schools of Oriental Research 236: 1-10.
1982   The Credibility of Josephus. *Journal of Jewish Studies* 33: 379-84.

Brown, C. A.
1992   *No Longer be Silent: First Century Jewish Portraits of Biblical Women.
        Studies in Pseudo-Philo's "Biblical Antiquities" and Josephus's "Jewish
        Antiquities".* Gender and the Biblical Tradition. Louisville, KY:
        Westminster/John Knox.

Bruce, F. F.
1951   *The Acts of the Apostles.* London. 3rd rev. ed. Grand Rapids: Eerdmans,
        1990.
1959   The Interpretation of Daniel. Pp. 59-65 in his *Biblical Exegesis in the
        Qumran Texts.* Grand Rapids: Eerdmans.
1965   Josephus and Daniel. *Annual of the Swedish Theological Institute* 4:
        148-62.
1969   The Book of Daniel and the Qumran Community. Pp. 221-235 in *Neo-
        testamentica et Semitica,* ed. E. E. Ellis and M. Wilcox. Edinburgh:
        Clark.

Brunet de Presle, W.
1865   *Notice et textes des papyrus grecs du Musée du Louvre et de la Biblio-
        thèque Impériale.* Vol. 18 of *Notices et extraits des Manuscrits de la
        Bibliothèque Impériale.* Paris: Imprimerie impériale.

Bruyne, D. De
1932   *Les anciennes traductions latines des Machabées.* Anecdota Maredsolana
        4. Abbaye de Maredsous.

Büchler, A.
1896-97 Les sources de Flavius Josèphe dans le Antiquités (XII,5–XIII,1). *Revue
        des Etudes Juives* 32: 176-199; 34: 69-93.
1897a   The sources of Josephus for the History of Syria (In "Antiquitates"
        XII,3–XIII,14). *Jewish Quarterly Review* 9: 311-349.

1898   The Fore-court of Women and the Brass Gate in the Temple of Jerusalem. *Jewish Quarterly Review* 10: 678-718.
1899   The Nicanor Gate and the Brass Gate. *Jewish Quarterly Review* 11: 46-63.
1899a   *Die Tobiaden und Oniaden im II. Makkabäerbuch und in der verwandten jüdisch-hellenistischen Literatur.* Wien: Holder.
1926-27   The Levitical Impurity of the Gentile in Palestine before the Year 70. *Jewish Quarterly Review* 17: 7-15.
1956   *Studies in Jewish History.* London: Oxford University.

Buhl, D. F.
1896   *Geographie des alten Palästina.* Freiburg i. B. und Leipzig: Mohr.

Burchard, C.
1977   Die Essener bei Hippolyt. *Journal for the Study of Judaism* 8: 1-41.

Busink, T.
1978-80   *Der Tempel von Jerusalem: von Salomo bis Herodes.* 2 vols. Leiden: Brill.

Cadbury, H. J.
1927   *The Making of Luke-Acts.* New York: Macmillan.

Cadoux, C. J.
1937   A Tentative Synthetic Chronology of the Apostolic Age. *Journal of Biblical Literature* 56: 177-91.

Calder III, William M.
1992   Morton Smith. *Gnomon* 64: 382-384.

Calmet, A.
1726   *Commentaire litteral sur tous le Livres de l'Ancien et du Nouveau Testament.* Tome sixième. Paris: Emery-Sangrain-Martin.

Carmignac J., and Guilbert P.
1961   *Les textes de Qumran*, vol. I. Paris: Letouzet & Ané.

Case, S. J.
1925   Josephus' Anticipation of a Domitianic Persecution, *Journal of Biblical Literature* 44: 10-20.

Chamonard, J.
1904   see Reinach 1900-1932

Charles, R. H.
1929   *A Critical and Exegetical Commentary on the Book of Daniel with Introduction.* Oxford: University.

Charlesworth J. H.
1983   *The Old Testament Pseudepigrapha*, vol 1, Garden City/New York: Doubleday & Co.

CIJ
1936-52   *Corpus Inscriptionum Iudaicarum,* ed. J.-B. Frey. 2 vols. Rome: Pontificio Istituto di Archeologia Cristiana.

Cohen, G. M.
1978   *The Seleucid Colonies: Studies in Founding, Administration and Organization.* Historia Einzelschriften 30. Wiesbaden: Steiner.

Cohen, S. J. D.
1979   *Josephus in Galilee and Rome: His Vita and Development as a Historian.*
        Columbia Studies in the Classical Tradition 8. Leiden: Brill.
1983   Conversion to Judaism in historical perspective: from biblical Israel to
        post-biblical Judaism. *Conservative Judaism* 36.4: 31-45.
1984   The Significance of Yavneh: Pharisees, Rabbis and the End of Jewish
        Sectarianism. *Hebrew Union College Annual* 55: 27-53.
1986   Parallel Historical Tradition in Josephus and Rabbinic Literature. Pp.
        7-14 in *Proceedings of the Ninth World Congress of Jewish Studies*, Vol.
        B/1. Jerusalem: World Union of Jewish Studies.
1987   *From the Maccabees to the Mishnah.* Philadelphia: Westminster.
1989   Crossing the boundary and becoming a Jew. *Harvard Theological Review*
        82: 13-33.
1990   Religion, Ethnicity, and 'Hellenism' in the Emergence of Jewish
        Identity in Maccabean Palestine. Pp. 204-223 in *Religion and Religious
        Practice in the Seleucid Kingdom*, ed. Per Bilde et al. Aarhus: Aarhus
        University.

Collins, J. J.
1974   *The Sibylline Oracles of Egyptian Judaism.* Society of Biblical Literature
        Dissertation Series 93. Missoula.
1977   *The Apocalyptic Vision of the Book of Daniel.* Missoula: Scholars.

Corbishley, T.
1935   The Chronology of the Reign of Herod the Great. *Journal of Theologi-
        cal Studies* 36: 22-32.

CPJ
1957-64 *Corpus Papyrorum Judaicarum*, eds. V. A. Tcherikover, A. Fuks, and M.
        Stern. 3 vols. Cambridge MA: Harvard University; Jerusalem: Magnes.

Cresson B. C.
1972   The Condemnation of Edom in Post-Exilic Judaism. Pp. 125-148 in *The
        Use of the Old Testament in the New and Other Essays. Studies in honor
        of W. F. Stinespring*, ed. J. M. Efird. Durham: Duke University.

Cuq, E.
1927   La condition juridique de la Coéle-Syrie au temps de Ptolémée V
        Epiphane. *Syria* 8: 143-62.

Dancy, J. C.
1954   *A Commentary on I Maccabees.* Oxford: Blackwell.

Daube D.
1977   *Typologie im Werk des Flavius Josephus.* Sitzungsberichte der Bayeri-
        schen Akademie der Wissenschaften, Phil.-hist.Klasse 1977, Heft 6.
        München.

1977a   Three Legal Notes on Josephus after His Surrender. *Law Quarterly
        Review* 93: 191-94.

Decoster, K.
1989   Flavius Josephus and the Seleucid Acra in Jerusalem. *Zeitschrift des
        Deutschen Palästina-Vereins* 105: 70-84.

Del Medico, H. E.
1952   Les Esséniens dans l'oeuvre de Flavius Josèphe. *Byzantinoslavica* 13: 1-45; 189-226.

Delcor, M.
1968   Le Temple d'Onias en Egypte. Reéxamen d'un vieux problème. *Revue Biblique* 75: 188-203.

Delia, D.
1991   *Alexandrian Citizenship During the Roman Principate.* American Classical Studies 23. Atlanta: Scholars.

Dequeker, L.
1985   The City of David and the Seleucid Acra in Jerusalem. Pp. 193-210 in *The Land of Israel: Cross-Roads of Civilizations*, ed. E. Lipinsky. Orientalia Lovaniensia Analecta 19. Leuven: Peeters.

Derenbourg, J.
1867   *Essai su l'histoire et la géographie de la Palestine d'après les Thalmuds et les autres sources rabbiniques.* Première partie *Histoire de la Palestine depuis Cyrus jusqu'à Adrien.* Paris: Imprimerie Impériale.

Dessau, H.
1892-1916 *Inscriptiones Latinae Selectae.* 3 vols. Berlin: Weidmann.

Destinon, J. von
1882   *Die Quellen des Flavius Josephus. I Die Quellen der Archäologie Buch XII-XVII; Jüd.Krieg B. I.* Kiel: Lipsius & Tischer.

Dhorme, P.
1926   *Le livre de Job.* Deuxième ed. Paris: Gabalda.

Dicou, B.
1990   *Jakob en Esau, Israël en Edom.* Voorburg: Publivorm.

Diebner, B., and Schult, H.
1975   Edom in alttestamentlichen Texten der Makkabäerzeit, *Dielheimer Blätter zum Alten Testament* 8: 11-17.

Dillman, A.
1853   *Das Buch Henoch übersetzt und erklärt.* Leipzig: Vogel.

Dimant, D., and Rappaport, U. (eds.)
1992   *The Dead Sea Scrolls: Forty Years of Research.* Leiden: Brill; Jerusalem: Magnes.

Dittenberger, W.
1903   *Orientis Graeci Inscriptionie Selectae* I. Leipzig: Hirzel = *OGIS*.

Doran, R.
1990   Jason's Gymnasium. Pp. 99-109 in *Of Scribes and Scrolls: FS John Strugnell*, ed H. Attridge et al. Lanham, NY: University Press of America.

Drexler, M.
1925   Untersuchungen zu Josephus und zur Geschichte des jüdischen Aufstandes 66-70, *Klio* 19 : 277-312.

Driver, R. S.
1900   *The Book of Daniel with Introduction and Notes.* Cambridge: Cambridge University.

Drüner, H.
1896   *Untersuchungen über Josephus.* Ph.D. Dissertation, Marburg.

Dupont-Sommer, A.
1960   *The Essene Writings from Qumran.* 2nd edition. Trans. G. Vermes. Oxford: Blackwell.

Efron, J.
1987   *Studies on the Hasmonean Period.* St. in Judaism in Late Antiquity 39. Leiden: Brill.

Egger, R.
1986   *Josephus Flavius und die Samaritaner: Eine terminologische Untersuchung zur Identitätsklärung der Samaritaner.* Novum Testamentum et Orbis Antiquus 4. Freiburg (Switzerland) and Göttingen: Universitätsverlag and Vandenhoeck & Ruprecht.

Epstein, J.
1964   *Introduction to the Text of the Mishna.* 2d ed. 2 vols. Jerusalem: Magnes (Hebrew).

Ehrenberg, V.
1947   Polypragmosyne: A Study in Greek Politics. *Journal of Hellenic Studies* 67: 46-67.

Ettelson, H. W.
1925   The Integrity of I Maccabaees. *Transactions of the Connecticut Academy of Arts and Sciences* 27: 249-384.

Ewald, C. H. A.
1864   *Geschichte des Volkes Israel. Vierter Band. Geschichte Ezra's und der Heiligherrschaft in Israel bis Christus.* 3rd ed. Göttingen: Dieterich.
1868   *Die Propheten des Alten Bundes. Dritter Band. Die jüngsten Propheten des Alten Bundes mit den Büchern Barukh und Daniel.* 2nd ed. Göttingen: Vandenhoek & Ruprecht.

Farmer, W. R.
1956   *Maccabees, Zealots, and Josephus: An Inquiry into Jewish Nationalism in the Greco-Roman Period.* New York: Columbia University.

Farris, M. H.
1990   The Formative Interpretations of the Seventy Weeks of Daniel. Dissertation: University of Toronto.

Feldman, L. H.
1962   The Sources of Josephus' *Antiquities* 19. *Latomus* 21: 320-333.
1965   see Thackeray *et al. 1926-65 (LCL).*
1968a   Abraham the Greek Philosopher in Josephus. *Transactions of the American Philological Association* 99: 143-56.
1968b   Hellenizations in Josephus' Account of Man's Decline. Pp. 336-53 in *Religions in Antiquity: Essays in Memory of Erwin Ramsdell Goodenough,* ed. J. Neusner. Studies in the History of Religions 14. Leiden: Brill.

1970   Hellenizations in Josephus' Version of Esther. *Transactions of the American Philological Association* 101: 143-70.

1976   Josephus as an Apologist to the Greco-Roman World: His Portrait of Solomon. Pp. 69-98 in *Aspects of Religious Propaganda in Judaism and Early Christianity*, ed. E. S. Fiorenza. Notre Dame: University of Notre Dame.

1982   Josephus' Portrait of Saul. *Hebrew Union College Annual* 53: 45-99.

1984   *Josephus and Modern Scholarship (1937-1980)*. Berlin; New York: de Gruyter.

1984a   Abraham the General in Josephus. Pp. 43-49 in *Nourished with Peace: Studies in Hellenistic Judaism in Memory of Samuel Sandmel*, eds. F. E. Greenspahn, E. Hilgert, and B. L. Mack. Chico: Scholars.

1984b   Flavius Josephus Revisited: The Man, his Writings, and his Significance. Pp. 763-862 in *Aufstieg und Niedergang der römischen Welt II.21.2.* Berlin/New York: de Gruyter.

1984-85 Josephus as a Biblical Interpreter: the *'Aqedah*. *Jewish Quarterly Review* 75: 212-52.

1986   Josephus' Portrait of Deborah. Pp. 115-28 in *Hellenica et Judaica: Hommage à Valentin Nikiprowetzky*, eds. A. Caquot, M. Hadas-Lebel, and J. Riaud. Leuven-Paris: Éditions Peeters.

1987-88 Pro-Jewish Intimations in Anti-Jewish Remarks Cited in Josephus' Against Apion. *Jewish Quarterly Review* 78: 187-251.

1988a   Josephus' Portrait of Noah and Its Parallels in Philo, Pseudo- Philo's *Biblical Antiquities*, and Rabbinic Midrashim. *Proceedings of the American Academy for Jewish Research* 55: 31- 57.

1988b   Josephus' Version of Samson. *Journal for the Study of Judaism* 19: 171-214.

1988c   Use, Authority, and Exegesis of Mikra in the Writings of Josephus. Pp. 455-518 in *Mikra: Text, Translation, Reading and Interpretation of the Hebrew Bible in Ancient Judaism and Early Christianity*, eds. M. J. Mulder and H. Sysling. Compendia Rerum Iudaicarum ad Novum Testamentum, sect. 2, vol. 1. Assen: Van Gorcum.

1988-89 Josephus' Portrait of Jacob. *Jewish Quarterly Review* 79: 101-51.

1989a   Josephus' Portrait of David. *Hebrew Union College Annual* 60: 129-74.

1989b   Josephus' Portrait of Joshua. *Harvard Theological Review* 82: 351-76.

1990   Prophets and Prophecy in Josephus. *Journal of Theological Studies* 41: 400-407.

1991-92 Josephus' Portrait of Moses. *Jewish Quarterly Review* 82: 285- 328.

1992a   Josephus' Interpretation of Jonah. *Association for Jewish Studies Review* 17: 1-29.

1992b   Josephus' Portrait of Ahab. *Ephemerides Theologicae Lovanienses* 68: 368-84.

1992c   Josephus' Portrait of Daniel. *Henoch* 14: 37-96.

1992d   Josephus' Portrait of Hezekiah. *Journal of Biblical Literature* 111: 597-610.

1992e   Josephus' Portrait of Joseph. *Revue Biblique* 99: 379-417, 504- 28.

1992f   Josephus' Portrait of Nehemiah. *Journal of Jewish Studies* 43: 187-202.

1992g   Josephus' Portrait of Samuel. *Abr-Nahrain* 30: 103-45.

1992h   Review of Mason 1991 *Journal for the Study of Judaism* 23:122-5.

1993 *Jew and Gentile in the Ancient World: Attitudes and Interactions from Alexander to Justinian*. Princeton: Princeton University.

Feldman, L. H., and Hata, G. (eds.)
1987 *Josephus, Judaism and Christianity*. Leiden: Brill.
1989 *Josephus, the Bible and History*. Detroit: Wayne State University.

Field, Fr.
1875 *Origenis Exaplorum quae supersunt* 2. Oxford: Clarendon.

Finkelstein, I.
1992 Edom in Iron Age I. *Eretz Israel* 23: 216-23.

Fischer, T.
1975 Zum jüdischen Verfassungsstreit von Pompeius (Diodor 40,2). *Zeitschrift des deutschen Palästina-Vereins* 91: 46-49.
1980 *Seleukiden und Makkabäer*. Bochum: Brockmeyer.

Flusser, D.
1972 The Four Empires in the Fourth Sibyl and the Book of Daniel. *Israel Oriental Studies* 2: 148-75.

Fraidl, F.
1883 *Die Exegese der Siebzig Wochen Daniels in der Alten und Mittleren Zeit*. Graz: Von Leuschner & Lubensky.

Frankel, Z.
1852 Einiges zur Forschung über den Oniastempel. *Monatsschrift für Geschichte und Wissenschaft des Judentums* 1: 273-277.

Franxman, T. W.
1979 *Genesis and the "Jewish Antiquities" of Flavius Josephus*. Biblica et Orientalia 35. Rome: Biblical Institute.

Frey, J. B. see *CIJ*

Freyne, S.
1980 The Galileans in the Light of Josephus' *Vita*. *New Testament Studies* 26: 397-413.

Fuks, G.
1990 Josephus and the Hasmoneans. *Journal of Jewish Studies* 41:166-176.

Gabba, E.
1958 *Iscrizioni greche e latine per lo studio della Bibbia*. Torino: Marietti.
1990 The Finances of King Herod. In *Greece and Rome in Eretz Israel*, ed. A. Kasher et al. Jerusalem: Yad Ben-Zvi.

Gafni, I. M.
1980 On the Use of I Maccabees by Josephus Flavius [in Hebrew]. *Zion* 45: 81-95. Rev. English trans. 1989.
1989 Josephus and 1 Maccabees. Pp. 116-31 in Feldman and Hata 1989.

Garnsey, P.
1988 *Famine and Food Supply in the Graeco-Roman World*. Cambridge: Cambridge University.

Garnsey, P. and Woolf, G.
1989 Patronage of the Rural Poor in the Roman World. In Wallace-Hadrill 1989.

Gaston, Lloyd
1970   *No Stone on Another: Studies in the Significance of the Fall of Jerusalem in the Synoptic Gospels.* Novum Testamentum Suppl. 23. Leiden: Brill.

Geffcken, J.
1902   *Komposition und Entstehungzeit der Oracula Sibyllina.* Texte und Untersuchungen, ed. A. von Harnack NF 8. Leipzig: Hinrichs.

Gens, C. H. J. de
1978/80 Idumaea. *Jaarberichten van het Vooraziatisch-Egyptisch genootschap.* Ex Oriente Lux 26: 53-74.

Gilboa, A.
1979-80 The Intervention of Sextus Julius Caesar, Governor of Syria, in the Affair of Herod's Trial. *Scripta Classica Israelica* 5: 185-194.

Gladigow, B.
1989   Aetas, aevum und saeclorum ordo: Zur Struktur zeitlicher Deutungssysteme. Pp. 255-271 in Hellholm 1989.

Goldingay, J. E.
1989   *Daniel.* Word Biblical Commentary. Dallas: Word Books.

Goldstein, J. A.
1976   *I Maccabees.* AB 41.
1983   *II Maccabees.* AB 41A.
1989   The Hasmonean Revolt and the Hasmonean Dynasty. Pp. 292-351 in vol. 2 of *The Cambridge History of Judaism,* eds. W. D. Davies and L. Finkelstein. Cambridge: Cambridge University.

Goodman, M. (D.)
1987   *The Ruling Class of Judaea: The Origins of the Jewish Revolt against Rome A.D. 66-70.* Cambridge: Cambridge University.
1989   Nerva, the *Fiscus Judaicus* and Jewish identity. *Journal of Roman Studies* 79: 40-44.
1992   Jewish Proselytizing in the First Century. Pp. 53-78 in *The Jews Among Pagans and Christians in the Roman Empire,* eds. J. Lieu, J. North, and T. Rajak, London-New York: Routledge.
Forth-   The Roman identity of Roman Jews. In *Menahem Stern Memorial Vo-*
coming *lume,* eds. I. M. Gafni, A. Oppenheimer and D. R. Schwartz. Jerusalem: Z. Shazar Center.

Grainger, J.
1990   *The Cities of Seleukid Syria.* Oxford: Clarendon.

Gray, R.
1993   *Prophetic Figures in Late Second Temple Jewish Palestine: the Evidence from Josephus.* Oxford: Oxford University.

Griffiths, J. G.
1989   Apocalyptic in the Hellenistic Era. Pp. 273-293 in Hellholm 1989.

Grimm, C. L. W.
1853   *Das erste Buch der Maccabäer.* Dritte Lieferung of *Kurzgefasstes exegetisches Handbuch zu den Apokryphen des AT.* Leipzig: Hirzel.

Habicht, C.
1976   2. *Makkabäerbuch*. Jüd. Schriften aus hell.-röm. Zeit I/3. Gütersloh: Mohn.

Hadas-Lebel, M.
1986   Rome "Quatrième empire" et le symbole du porc, Pp. 297-312 in: *Hellenica et Judaica. Hommage à V. Nikiprowetzky*, ed. A. Caquot *et al.* Paris/Leuven: Peeters.
1987   L'évolution de l'image de Rome auprès des juifs en deux siècles de relations judéo-romains -164 à +70. Pp. 715-856 in vol 2.20.2 of *Aufstieg und Niedergang der römischen Welt*. Berlin: De Gruyter.
1989   *Flavius Josèphe*. Paris: Fayard.
1991   *Jérusalem contre Rome*, Paris: Cerf.

Hamel, G.
1990   *Poverty and Charity in Roman Palestine*. Berkeley: Univ. of California.

Hanhart, R.
1964   Zur Zeitrechnung des I. Makkabäerbuches. Pp. 49-96 in A. Jepsen and R. Hanhart, *Untersuchungen zur jüdischen Chronologie*. Beihefte zur Zeitschrift für die alttestamentliche Wissenschaft 88. Berlin: Töpelmann.

Hardouin, J.
1699   *Chronologia Veteris Testamenti ad Vulgatam editionem exacta et nummis antiquis illustrata*. Paris: J. Boudot.
1709   *De LXX. Hebdomadibus Danielis, pro R. P. Joanne Harduino... adversus R. P. Bernardum Lamy... defensio*. Pp. 881-903 in *J. Harduini ... opera selecta, tum quae jam pridem Parisiis edita nunc emendatiora et multo auctiora prodeunt, tum quae nunc primum edita*. Amsterdam: J.L. De Lorme.

Hartberger, B.
1986   *"An den Wassern von Babylon...". Ps 137 auf dem Hintergrund von Jer 51, der biblischen Edom-Traditionen und babylonischer Originalquellen*. Bonner Biblische Beiträge 63. Frankfurt/M.: P. Lang.

Hartman, L. F., and Di Lella, A. A.
1978   *The Book of Daniel*. AB 23.

Hasel, G.F.
1984   כרת. *Theologisches Wörterbuch zum Alten Testament* 4.355-67.

Hata, G.
1975   Is the Greek Version of Josephus' Jewish War a Translation or Rewriting of the First Version? *Jewish Quarterly Review* 66: 89-108.
see also Feldman, L. H., and Hata, G. (eds.)

Hatch, E., and Redpath, H. A.
1897-1906 *A Concordance to the Septuagint*. 3 vols. Oxford: Clarendon.

Hayard, R.
1982   The Jewish Temple at Leontopolis. A Reconsideration. *Journal of Jewish Studies* 33: 425-443.

Hellholm, D. (ed.)
1989   *Apocalypticism in the Mediterranean World and the Near East: Proceedings of the International Colloquium on Apocalypticism, Uppsala, August 12-17, 1979.* 2nd ed. Tübingen: Mohr (1st ed. 1983).

Helm, R.
1921   Review of Laqueur 1920. *Philologische Wochenschrift* 41: cols. 481-493, 505-516.

Hengel, M.
1961   *Die Zeloten. Untersuchungen zur jüdischen Freiheitsbewegung in der Zeit von Herodes I bis 70 n.Chr.* Leiden: Brill (rev. Engl. transl. 1989).
1966   Die Synagogeninschrift von Stobi. *Zeitschrift für die alttestamentliche Wissenschaft* 57: 145-83.
1969   *Judentum und Hellenismus: Studien zu ihrer Begegnung unter besonderer Berücksichtigung Palästinas bis zur Mitte des 2. Jh.s v.Chr.* Wissensch. Unters. z. NT 10. Tübingen: Mohr.
1974   *Judaism and Hellenism: Studies in their Encounter in Palestine during the Early Hellenistic Period.* 2nd ed. Trans. J. Bowden. London: SCM (trans. of 1969).
1989   *The Zealots: Investigations into the Jewish Freedom Movement in the Period from Herod I until 70 A.D.* Trans. D. Smith (cf. 1961 above) Edinburgh: Clark.

Herzfeld, L.
1863   *Geschichte des Volkes Jisrael von Vollendung des zweiten Tempels bis zur Einsetzung des Mackabäers Schimon zum Hohen Priester und Fürsten.* 2nd ed. vol. 2. Leipzig: Wilfferodt.

Hildesheimer, I.
1876-77 Die Beschreibung des herodianischen Tempels im Tractate Middoth und bei Flavius Josephus. Pp. 1-32 in *Jahresbericht des Rabbiner-Seminars für das orthodoxe Judenthum.* Berlin.

Hinton, W.
1966   *Fanshen: A Documentary of Revolution in a Chinese Village.* New York: Monthly Review Press.

Hirsch, S. A.
1906   The Temple of Onias. Pp. 39-80 in *Jews' College Jubilee Volume.* London: Luzac.

Hitzig, F.
1838   *Das Buch Daniel erklärt.* Kurzgefasstes exegetisches Handbuch zum Alten Testament. Leipzig: Weidmann (2nd ed. 1850).

Hobsbawm, E.
1959   *Primitive Rebels.* Manchester: Manchester University.
1969   *Bandits.* London: Weidenfeld and Nicolson.

Hoenig, S.
1970   Oil and Pagan Defilement. *Jewish Quarterly Review* 61: 63-75.

Hofmann, J. C. K.
1836   *Die siebenzig Jahre des Jeremias und die siebenzig Jahrwochen des Daniels.* Nürnberg: Otto.

Holleaux, M.
1899   Sur un passage de Flavius Josèphe (Ant.Jud. XII 4 § 155). *Revue des Etudes Juïves* 39: 161-174.

Hölscher, G.
1904   *Die Quellen des Josephus für die Zeit vom Exil bis zum jüdischen Kriege.* Leipzig: Teubner.
1916   Josephus. *RE* 9.1934-2000.

Hollis, F. J.
1934   *The Archaeology of Herod's Temple.* London: Dent.

Holtzmann, O.
1913   *Middot: Von den Massen des Tempels.* Text, Übersetzung u. Erklärung. *Die Mischna,* eds. G. Beer and O. Holtzmann, vol. 5.10. Giessen: Töpelmann.

Hopwood, K.
1989   Bandits, Elites and Rural Order. Pp. 171-85 in Wallace-Hadrill 1989.

Horbury, W.
1991   Herod's Temple and 'Herod's Days'. Pp. 108-115 in *Templum Amicitiae: Essays on the Second Temple Presented to Ernst Bammel,* ed. W. Horbury. Sheffield: JSOT.

Horsley, R.
1979   Josephus and the Bandits. *Journal for the Study of Judaism* 10: 37-63.
1981   Ancient Jewish Banditry and the Revolt Against Rome. *Catholic Biblical Quarterly* 43: 409-32.

Horst, P. W. van der
1984   *Chaeremon: Egyptian Priest and Stoic Philosopher. The Fragments collected and trans. with explanatory notes.* Etudes préliminaires aux religions orientales dans l'Empire Romain 101. Leiden: Brill.

Isaac, B.
1984   Bandits in Judaea and Arabia. *Harvard Studies in Classical Philology* 88:171-203.
1992   *The Limits of Empire: The Roman Army in the East.* Rev. ed. Oxford: Oxford Univ.

Isaac, B., and Roll, I.
1982   *Roman Roads in Judaea I: The Legio-Scythopolis Road.* B.A.R. International Series 141. Oxford: B.A.R.

Jastrow, M.
1872   Einiges über den Hohenpriester Onias IV. in Aegypten und die Gründung des Tempels zu Heliopolis. *Monatsschrift für Geschichte und Wissenschaft des Judentums* 21: 150-55.

Jeremias, J.
1962   *Jerusalem zur Zeit Jesu. Kulturgeschichtliche Untersuchung zur neutestamentlichen Zeitgeschichte,* 3rd ed. Göttingen: Vandenhoeck & Ruprecht (rev. Engl. ed. 1969)
1969   *Jerusalem in the Time of Jesus.* London: SCM (rev. trans. of 1962).

Johnson, T., and Dandeker, C.
1989   Patronage: Relation and System. In Wallace-Hadrill 1989.

Jones, A. H. M.
1971   *Cities of the Eastern Roman Provinces*. 2nd ed. rev. by M. Avi- Yonah
        et al. Oxford: Clarendon (1st ed. 1937).

Jonge, M. de
1978   *The Testaments of the Twelve Patriarchs. A Critical Edition of the Greek
        Text*. Leiden: Brill.

Jossa, G.
1980   *Gesù e i movimenti di liberazione della Palestina.* Brescia: Paideia.
1992   *Flavio Giuseppe, Autobiografia.* Studi sul giudaismo e sul cristianesimo
        antico 3. Napoli: D'Auria.

JPS   The Jewish Publication Society of America

Juster, J.
1914   *Les Juifs dans l'empire romain. Leur condition juridique, économique et
        sociale.* 2 vols. Paris: Geuthner.

Justus, B.
1973   Zur Erzählkunst des Flavius Josephus. *Theokratia* 2: 107-36.

Kane, J. P.
1978   Ossuary Inscriptions of Jerusalem. *Journal of Semitic Studies* 23: 268-82.

Kasher, A.
1985   *The Jews in Hellenistic and Roman Egypt.The Struggle for Equal Rights*,
        Tübingen: Mohr.
1988   *Jews, Idumaeans, and Ancient Arabs. Relations of the Jews in Eretz-Israel
        with the Nations of the Frontier and the Desert during the Hellenistic and
        Roman Era (332 B.C.E. - 70 C.E.).* Texte und Studien zum antiken
        Judentum 18. Tübingen: Mohr.
1990   *Jews in Hellenistic Cities in Eretz-Israel: Relations of the Jews in Eretz-
        Israel with the Hellenistic Cities during the Second Temple Period (332
        BCE - 70 CE).* Tübingen: Mohr.

Kaufman, A. S.
1977   New Light upon Zion: The Plan and Precise Location of the Second
        Temple. *Ariel* 43:

Kaufmann, Y.
1977   *History of the Religion of Israel*, vol. 4. *From the Babylonian Captivity to
        the End of Prophecy*. New York: Ktav (trans. from Hebrew).

Keeble, K.
1991   A critical study of Josephus, *Contra Apionem*. Unpublished M.Phil.
        Dissertation, University of Oxford.

Klein, S.
1939   *Land of Judea*. Tel-Aviv: Dvir (Hebrew).
1967   *Land of Galilee*. Jerusalem: Mosad Harav Kook (Hebrew).

Klostermann, E. (ed.)
1904   *Das Onomastikon der biblischen Ortsnamen. Eusebius Werke*. Vol. 3.
        Griechische christliche Schriftsteller. Leipzig: Hinrichs (Rp. Hildes-
        heim: Olms, 1966).

Knohl, I.
1991   Participation of the People in the Temple Worship - Second Temple
        Sectarian Conflict and the Biblical Tradition. *Tarbiz* 60: 139-46 (He-
        brew).

Koehler, L.; Baumgartner, W.; *et al.*
1967-90 *Hebräisches und Aramäisches Lexikon zum Alten Testament.* Leiden:
        Brill.

Kooij, A. van der
1986   A Case of Reinterpretation in the Old Greek of Daniel 11. Pp. 72-80
        in *Tradition and Re-interpretation in Jewish and Early Christian Litera-
        ture.* Festschrift for J. C. H. Lebram, ed. J. W. van Henten *et al.* SPB
        36. Leiden: Brill.

Kopp, C.
1959   *Die heiligen Stätten der Evangelien.* Regensburg: Pustet.

Kottek, S. S.
1994   *Medicine and Hygiene in the Works of Flavius Josephus.* Studies in
        Ancient Medicine 9. Leiden: Brill.

Kraemer, R. S.
1989   On the Meaning of the Term 'Jew' in Greco-Roman Inscriptions.
        Harvard Theological Review 82: 35-53.

Kraft, H.
1981   Eusebius von Caesarea, *Kirchengeschichte.* 2nd ed. Darmstadt:
        Wissensch. Buchgesellschaft.

Kreissig, H.
1970   *Die sozialen Zusammenhänge des judäischen Krieges.* Berlin: Akademie
        Verlag.
1977   Landed Property in the "Hellenistic" Orient. *Eirene* 15: 5-26.

Kuhn, P.
1989   *Offenbarungsstimmen im Antiken Judentum. Untersuchungen zur BatQol
        und verwandten Himmelsstimmen.* Tübingen: Mohr.

Lagrange, M.-J.
1892   Topographie de Jérusalem. *Revue Biblique* 1: 17-38.

Lamy, B.
1699   *Apparatus chronologicus et geographicus ad commentarium in Harmo-
        niam sive concordiam quatuor Evangelistarum.* Paris: Anisson.

Landau, Y. H.
1966   A Greek Inscription Found Near Hefzibah. *Israel Exploration Journal*
        16: 54-70.

Laqueur, R.
1920   *Der jüdische Historiker Flavius Josephus: Ein biographischer Versuch auf
        neuer quellenkritischer Grundlage.* Giessen 1920 (rp. Darmstadt:
        Wissensch. Buchgesellschaft, 1970).

Launey, M.
1949-50 *Recherches sur les armées hellénistiques,* Bibliothèque des Ecoles
        Françaises d'Athènes et de Rome 169. 2 vols. Paris: Boccard.

LCL　　　Loeb Classical Library

Lebram, J.
1974　　Der Idealstaat der Juden. Pp.233-253 in *Josephus-Studien*. Festschrift
　　　　für Otto Michel, ed. O. Betz. Göttingen: Vandenhoeck u. Ruprecht.
1989　　The Piety of the Jewish Apocalypticists. Pp. 171-210 in Hellholm 1989.

Le Glaz, M.
1991　　in M. Le Glaz, J. L. Voisin, and Y. Le Bohec *Roman History*, Paris,
　　　　PUF.

Lengerke, C. von
1835　　*Das Buch Daniel. Verdeutscht und ausgelegt*. Königsberg: Bornträger.

Leon, H. J.
1960　　*The Jews of Ancient Rome*. Philadelphia: JPS.

Levenson, E. R.
1966　　*New Tendentious Motifs in Antiquities: A Study of Development in
　　　　Josephus' Historical Thought*. Unpublished M.A. Dissertation, Columbia
　　　　University.

Levine, L. I.
1991　　From Community Center to 'Lesser Sanctuary': The Furnishings and
　　　　Interior of the Ancient Synagogue. *Cathedra* 60: 36-84 (Hebrew).
Forth-　Archeology and the Religious Ethos of Pre-70 Palestine. In *Hillel and
coming　Jesus*, ed. J. Charlesworth. Minneapolis: Fortress.

Levy, J.
1939　　The Feast of the 14th day of Adar. *Hebrew Union College Annual* 14:
　　　　127-151.

Lieberman, S.
1950　　Hellenism in Jewish Palestine. Texts and Studies. New York: JTS.
1955-88 *Tosefta Ki-Fshutah*. 10 vols. New York: Jewish Theological Seminary.

Lindner, H.
1972　　*Die Geschichtsauffassung des Flavius Josephus im Bellum Judaicum.
　　　　Gleichzeitig ein Beitrag zur Quellenfrage*. Leiden: Brill.

Lowe, M.
1976　　Who were the Ἰουδαῖοι? *Novum Testamentum* 18: 101-130.
1981　　Ἰουδαῖοι of the Apocrypha. *Novum Testamentum* 23: 56-90.

Lucas, E. C.
1989　　The Origin of Daniel's Four Empires Scheme Reexamined. *Tyndale
　　　　Bulletin* 40: 185-202.

Luria, B. Z.
1968　　The Temple Mount Precincts. *Beth Mikra* 13: 3-15 (Hebrew).
1981　　The Location of the *Akra* at the Northern Part of the Temple Mount.
　　　　Cathedra 21: 31-40 (Hebrew).

Magen, Y.
1980　　The Gates of the Temple Mount according to Josephus and the
　　　　Mishnah. *Cathedra* 14: 47-53 (Hebrew).
1986　　A Fortified Town of the Hellenistic Period on Mount Garizim.
　　　　Qadmoniot 19: 91-101.

Maier, J.
1990   *Zwischen den Testamenten: Geschichte und Religion in der Zeit des Zweiten Tempels.* Die neue Echter Bibel, Ergänzungsbd.3. Würzburg: Echter.
1993   Israel und "Edom" in den Ausdeutungen zu Deut 2,1-8. Pp. 135-84 in *Judentum: Aus-blicke und Einsichten. Festgabe zum 70. Geburtstag von Kurt Schubert,* eds. C. Thoma, G. Stemberger, and J. Maier, Judentum und Umwelt 43. Frankfurt a. M.: P. Lang.

Mantel, H.
1965   *Studies on the History of the Sanhedrin.* Cambridge, MA: Harvard.

Marcus, R. see Thackeray *et al.* 1926-65

Marsham, J.
1682   *Chronicus Canon Aegyptiacus, Hebraicus, Graecus et Disquisitiones.* London: Roycroft.

Marti, K.
1901   *Das Buch Daniel erklärt.* Kurzer Hand-Commentar zum Alten Testament 18. Tübingen Mohr.

Marti, K., and Beer, G.
1927   *'Abôt: Väter. Text, Übers. und Erklärung. Die Mischna.* Vol. 4.9. Giessen: Töpelmann.

Mason, S.
1991   *Flavius Josephus on the Pharisees: A Composition-Critical Study.* Studia Post-Biblica 39. Leiden: Brill.
1992   *Josephus and the New Testament.* Peabody, MA: Hendrickson.

Mattingly, H., and Carson, R. A. G.
1923-75 *Coins of the Roman Empire in the British Museum.* 9 vols. London: British Museum.

Mayer, G.
1974   *Index Philoneus,* Berlin-New York: De Gruyter.

Mazar, B.
1989   Josephus Flavius and the Archaeological Excavations in Jerusalem. Pp. 325-329 in Feldman and Hata 1989.

Melamed, E. Z.
1951   Josephus and Maccabees I: A Comparison (Hebrew). *Erez-Israel* 1: 122-30.

Mertens, A.
1971   *Das Buch Daniel im Lichte der Texte vom Toten Meer.* Stuttgarter Biblische Monographien 12. Würzburg: Echter Verlag.

Meshorer, Y.
1979   Sepphoris and Rome. Pp. 159-71 in *Greek Numismatic and Archaeology: Essays in Honor of M. Thompson,* eds. O. Mørkholm and N. M. Waggoner. Wettern:

Mesnil du Buisson, R. Du
1935   Le Temple d'Onias et le camp Hyksôs à Tell el Yahoudiye. *Bulletin de l'Institut française d'archéologie orientale* 35: 59-71.

Michel, O.
1967-68 Studien zu Josephus. Simon bar Giora, *New Testament Studies* 14: 402-8.

Moehring, H. R.
1957 Novelistic Elements in the Writings of Flavius Josephus. Diss.: Univ. of Chicago.
1959 The Persecution of the Jews and the Adherents of the Isis Cult at Rome A.D. 19. *Novum Testamentum* 3: 293-304.

Möller, C., and Schmitt, G.
1976 *Siedlungen Palästinas nach Flavius Josephus.* Wiesbaden: Reichert.

Momigliano, A. D.
1930 *Primee Linee di Storia della Tradizione Maccabaica.* Roma: Società editrice del Foro Italico (rp. Amsterdam: Hakkert, 1968).
1975 *Alien Wisdom: the Limits of Hellenization.* Cambridge: Cambridge University.
1980 Ciò che Flavio Giuseppe non vide. Introduction to Italian trans., *Il buon uso del tradimento,* of P. Vidal Naquet, *Flavius Josèphe ou du bon usage de la trahison.* Rome: Editori Riuniti = Pp. 305-17 in *Settimo contributo alla storia degli studi classici e del mondo antico.* 1984. Rome.
1987 What Josephus did not see. Pp. 108-119 in *On Pagans, Jews and Christians.* Middletown, CT: Wesleyan University. = trans. of Momigliano 1980 by J. Weinberg.

Mommsen, T.
1870 Cornelius Tacitus and Cluvius Rufus. *Hermes* 4: 320-22 = *Ges. Schr.* 7, 1909: 248.

Montgomery, J. A.
1927 *A Critical and Exegetical Commentary to the Book of Daniel.* International Critical Commentary. New York: Schribner's Sons.

Moore, G. F.
1927 Simon the Righteous. Pp. 348-364 in *Jewish Studies in Memory of Israel Abrahams.* New York: Jewish Institute of Religion.
1929 Fate and Free Will in the Jewish Philosophies According to Josephus. *Harvard Theological Review* 22: 371-389.

Mørkholm, O.
1960 A posthumous issue of Antiochus IV of Syria. *Numismatic Chronicle* 50: 25-30.
1961 Eulaios and Lenaios. *Classica et Mediaevalia* 22: 32-43.
1963 Studies in the Coinage of Antiochus IV of Syria. Hist.-filos. Medd. Kgl. Dan. Vid. Selsk. 40 no. 3.
1964 The Accession of Antiochus IV of Syria. *The American Numismatic Society Museum Notes* 11: 63-76.
1966 *Antiochus of Syria.* Classica et medievalia. Copenhagen: Gyldendal.

Morr, J.
1926 Die Landeskunde von Palästina bei Strabon und Josephus *Philologus* 81: 256-79.

Motzo, R. B.
1924   Una fonte sacerdotale antisamaritana in Giuseppe. Pp. 180-206 of *Saggi di storia e letteratura giudaico-ellenistica*. Firenze: Le Monnier.
1924a   Giuseppe e il I Maccabei. Pp. 207-214 of *Saggi di storia e letteratura giudaico-ellenistica*. Firenze: Le Monnier.
1927   Ircano II nella tradizione storica. *Saggi cagliaritani di storia e filologia* 1: 1-18. Rp. with original pagination shown, in *idem, Ricerche sulla letteratura e la storia giudaico-ellenistica*, ed. F. Parente. Roma: Centro Editoriale Internazionale, 1977: 719-36.

Moulton, J. H., and Milligan, G.
1930   *The Vocabulary of the Greek Testament. Illustrated from the Papyri and the Other Non-Literary Sources*. London.

Nadel, B.
1966   Józef Flawiusz a terminologia rzymskiej inwektywy politycze] [in Polish]: Josephus Flavius and the Terminology of Roman Political Invective]. *Eos* 56: 256-72.

Naville, E.
1890   *The Mound of the Jews and the City of Onias*. Memories of the Egyptian Exploration Fund 7. London: K. Paul, Trench, Trübner.
1891   *Bubastis (1887-1889)*. Eighth Memoir of the Egyptian Exploration Fund. 2nd ed. London: K. Paul, Trench, Trübner.

Nestle, E.
1884   Zu Daniel. 1) Dan 9,26. *Zeitschrift für die alttestamentliche Wissenschaft* 4: 247.

Nestle, W.
1926   *Apragmosyne* (Zu Thukydides II 63.). *Philologus* 81: 129-140.

Neusner, J.
1972   Josephus' Pharisees. Pp. 224-44 in *Ex Orbe Religionum: Studia Geo Widengren Oblata*, eds. C. J. Bleeker, S. G. F. Brandon, and M. Simon. Supplements to Numen = Studies in the History of Religions 21-2. Leiden: Brill.
1987   Josephus' Pharisees: A Complete Repertoire. Pp. 274-92 in Feldman and Hata 1987.

Nicols, J.
1978   *Vespasian and the Partes Flavianae*. Wiesbaden: Steiner.

Niese, B.
1903   *Geschichte der griechischen und makedonischen Staaten seit der Schlacht von Chaeronea III. Von 188 bis 120 v.Chr*. Gotha: Perthes.
1914   Josephus. Pp. 569-79 in vol. 7 of *Encyclopaedia of Religion and Ethics*, ed. J. Hastings. Edinburgh: Clark.

Nöldeke T.
1864   *Über die Amalekiter und einige andre Nachbarvölker der Israeliten*, Göttingen: Vandenhoeck & Ruprecht.

NRSV   *New Revised Standard Version*

Obst, E.
1924   Johannes Hyrkan II. Cols. 788-791 in *RE Suppl.* 4.

Oepke, A.
1967   ὄναρ. *Theological Dictionary of the New Testament* 5.220-38.
OGIS   *see Dittenberger, W.*

Paganoni, M.
1986   *Dimenticare Amalek.* Firenze: Giuntina.

Parente, F.
1994   Τοὺς ἐν Ἱεροσολύμοις Ἀντιοχεῖς ἀναγράψαι (*II Macc* IV,9): Gerusa-
        lemme è mai stata una πόλις? *Rivista di Storia e Letteratura Religiosa*
        30: 3-38.

Paret, H.
1856   Über den Pharisäismus des Josephus. *Theologische Studien und Kritiken*
        29: 836-37.

Parker S. T. (ed.)
1987   *The Roman Frontier in Central Jordan: Interim Report on the Limes
        Arabicus Project, 1980-1985,* vol. 1-2. BAR International Series 340.
        Oxford: B.A.R.

Paul, A.
1992   Flavius Josèphe et les Esséniens. Pp. 126-38 in Dimant and Rappaport
        1992.

Pelletier, A.
1962   *Flavius Josèphe, adaptateur de la Lettre d'Aristée. Une réaction atticisante
        contre la koiné.* Études et Commentaires 45. Paris: Klincksieck.

Perles, F.
1921   Notes sur les Apocryphes et Pseudépigraphes. *Revue des Études* juives
        73: 179.

Petit, M.
1992   Les Esséens de Philon d'Alexandrie et les Esséniens. Pp. 139-55 in
        Dimant and Rappaport 1992.

Petrie, W. M. F.
1906   *Hyksos and the Israelite Cities.* British School of Archaeology in Egypt.
        London.

Petrochilos, N. K.
1974   *Roman Attitudes to the Greeks.* Athens.

Price, J.
1991   The Enigma of Philip ben Jakimos. *Historia* 40: 75-94.
1992   *Jerusalem under Siege.* Leiden: Brill.

Purvis, J. D.
1988   *Jerusalem, The Holy City - A Bibliography.* Metuchen, NJ: Scarecrow.

Pusey, E. B.
1876   The prophecy of the 70 Weeks and of the Death of the Messiah, and
        the Attempts to Make the 70 Weeks End with Antiochus Epiphanes.
        Pp. 164-233 of E.B. Pusey, *Daniel the Prophet: Nine Lectures Delivered
        in the Divinity School of the University of Oxford.* 3rd ed. London: Parker
        (1st ed. 1864).

Rabello, A.M.
1980   The Legal Condition of the Jews in the Roman Empire. Pp. 662-762 in vol. 2.13 of *Aufstieg und Niedergang der römischen Welt.*

Rajak, T.
1973   Justus of Tiberias, *Classical Quarterly* 23:345-368.
1978   Moses in Ethiopia: Legend and Literature. *Journal of Jewish Studies* 29: 111-22.
1983   *Josephus: The Historian and His Society.* London: Duckworth.
1987   Josephus and Justus of Tiberias. Pp. 81-94 in Feldman and Hata 1987.

Ranovich, A. B.
1950   *Ellenizm i ego istoricheskii rol'.* Moscow: Izdatelstvo Akademija Nauk. Trans. into German by K. Diesing and O. Roth, *Der Hellenismus und seine geschichtliche Rolle.* Berlin: Akademie-Verlag, 1958.

Rappaport, U.
1969   Les Iduméens en Egypt. *Revue de Philologie* 43: 73-82.
1972   Leontopolis. *Encyclopaedia Judaica* 11: 31.
1977   Josephus Flavius: Notes on his Personality and his Work. *HaUmma* 15:89-95 (Hebrew).
1982   John of Gischala: From Galilee to Jerusalem. *Journal of Jewish Studies* 33: 479-93.
1983a   *Judea and Rome: The Jewish Revolts.* The World History of the Jewish People 11. Jerusalem (Hebrew).
1983b   John of Gischala in Galilee. *The Jerusalem Cathedra* 3: 46-57.
1983c   John of Gischala in Jerusalem. Pp. 97-115 in *The People and Its History*, ed. M. Stern (Hebrew).
1992   The Jewish Leadership in Jerusalem in the First Half of the Great Revolt. Pp. 133-42 in *Leaders and Leadership*, eds. I. Makkin and Z. Tzahor. Jerusalem: Z. Shazar Center. (Hebrew).

RE   A. Pauly, G. Wissowa, and W. Kroll, *Realencyclopädie der klassischen Altertumswissenschaft. 1893-1978.*

Reinach, T.
1900   Un préfet juif il y a deux mille ans. *Revue des Etudes Juives* 40: 50-54.
1930   *Flavius Josèphe. Contra Apionem. Texte établi et annoté.* Paris. Collection G. Budé.

Reinach, T., Chamonard, J. *et al.*
1900-32 *Oeuvres complètes de Flavius Josèphe.* 7 vols. Paris: Leroux.

Rengstorf, K. H.
1964   Die Stadt der Mörder (Mt. 22.7). Pp. 106-29 in *Judentum, Urchristentum, Kirche: Festschrift für Joachim Jeremias*, ed. W. Eltester. Beihefte zur Zeitschrift für die neutestamentliche Wissenschaft 26. 2nd ed., Berlin: Töpelmann.
1967   λῃστής. *Theological Dictionary of the New Testament* 4.257-62.

Rengstorf, K. H. *et al.*
1973-83 *A Complete Concordance to Flavius Josephus.* 4 vols. Leiden: Brill.

Rey-Coquais, J.-P.
   1978   Syrie romaine de Pompée à Diocletien. *Journal of Roman Studies* 68:
            44-77.

Rhoads, D. M.
   1976   *Israel in Revolution: 6-74 C.E. A Political History based on the Writings
            of Josephus.* Philadelphia: Fortress.

RIC II
   1926   *The Roman Imperial Coinage II*, ed. H. Mattingly *et al.* London: Spink.

Ricciotti, G.
   1937   *Flavio Giuseppe, La guerra giudaica.* 3 vols. Torino: SEI.

Robert, J. and L.
   1968   *Bulletin epigraphique. Revue des Etudes Grecques.* 81: 478-79 no. 325.
   1970   *Bulletin epigraphique. Revue des Etudes Grecques.* 83: 469-73 no. 627.
   1974   *Bulletin epigraphique. Revue des Etudes Grecques.* 87: 279 no. 500.
   1977   *Bulletin epigraphique. Revue des Etudes Grecques.* 90: 403 no. 434.

Robert, L.
   1927   Sur le traité d'isopolitie entre Pergame et Temnos. *Revue des Etudes
            Grecques* 40: 214-19 = 1969.
   1964   *Nouvelles Inscriptions de Sardes.* Paris: Maisonneuve.
   1969   Sur le traité d'isopolitie entre Pergame et Temnos. Pp. 214-23 of *Opera
            Minora Selecta*, vol. 1. Amsterdam: Hakkert = 1927.

Rösch, M.
   1834   Die 70 Wochen des Buches Daniel genau chronologisch nachgewiesen.
            Theologische Studien und Kritiken 7: 276-303.

Rostovtzeff, M. I.
   1957   *Social and Economic History of the Roman Empire.* 2nd ed. Oxford:
            Clarendon.

Rowley, H. H.
   1959   *Darius the Mede and the Four World Empires in the Book of Daniel: A
            Historical Study of Contemporary Theories.* Cardiff: University of Wales.

Safrai, S.
   1963   Was There a Women's Gallery in the Ancient Synagogue? *Tarbiz* 32:
            329-38 (Hebrew).
   1965   *Pilgrimage at the Time of the Second Temple.* Tel-Aviv: Am Hasefer
            (Hebrew).

Safrai, S.; Stern M.; *et al.* (eds.)
   1974-76 *The Jewish People in the First Century.* Vol. 1-2. Assen/Amsterdam: Van
            Gorcum.

Safrai, Z.
   1989   Dukhan, Aron and Teva: How Was the Ancient Synagogue Furnished?
            Pp. 69-84 in *Ancient Synagogues in Israel: Third-Seventh Century C.E.*,
            ed. R. Hachlili. BAR International Series 499. Oxford: B.A.R.
   1989a   The Description of the Land of Israel in Josephus' Works. Pp. 295-324
            in Feldman and Hata 1989.

Saller, R. P.
1982   *Personal Patronage under the Early Empire*. Cambridge: Cambridge University.

Salvador, J.
1847   *Histoire de la domination romaine en Judee*. 2 vols. Paris: Guyot et Scribe.

Sanders, E. P.
1992   *Judaism: Practice and Belief 63 BCE - 66 CE*. London: SCM; Philadelphia: Trinity.

Sartre, M.
1991   *L'Orient romain. Provinces et societés provinciales en Mediterranée orientale d' Auguste aux Severes*. Paris: Seuil.

Satran, D.
1980   Daniel: Seer, Prophet, Holy Man. Pp. 33-48 in *Ideal Figures in Ancient Judaism: Profiles and Paradigms*, eds. J. J. Collins and G. W. E. Nickelsburg. Chico: Scholars.

Saulnier, C.
Forth-   La cité hellénistique de Jerusalem à l'époque du grand prêtre Jason.
coming *Transeuphratène* 6-7.

Sawyer J. F. A. - Clines D. J. A. (eds.)
1987   *Midian, Moab and Edom. The History and Archaeology of Late Bronze and Iron Age Jordan and North-west Arabia*. Journal for the Study of the Old Testament Supplement Series 24. Sheffield: Sheffield Academic.

Schäfer, P.
1977   The Hellenistic and Maccabaean Periods. Pp.539-604 in *Israelite and Judaean History*, eds. J. H. Hayes and J. M. Miller. Philadelphia: Westminster.
1991   Der vorrabbinische Pharisäismus. Pp.125-175 in *Paulus und das antike Judentum*, eds. M. Hengel and U. Heckel. Tübingen: Mohr.

Schalit, A.
1938-39 Has Hyrcanus been appointed "Brother of the King?". *Bulletin of the Jewish Palestine Exploration Society* 6: 145-48 (Hebrew).
1960   *King Herod*. Jerusalem: Bialik (Hebrew; rev. German ed. 1969).
1962   Die frühchristliche Überlieferung über die Herkunft der Familie des Herodes. Ein Beitrag zur Geschichte der politischen Invektive in Judäa. *Annals of the Swedish Theological Institute* 1: 109-160.
1968   *Namenwörterbuch zu Flavius Josephus*. A Complete Concordance to Josephus Flavius, Supp. 1, ed. K. H. Rengstorf. Leiden: Brill.
1969   *König Herodes: Der Mann und sein Werk*. Studia Judaica 4. Berlin: de Gruyter (rev. German ed. of 1960).

Schlatter, A.
1893   *Zur Topographie und Geschichte Palästinas*. Stuttgart: Vereinsbuchh.
1913   Die hebräischen Namen bei Josephus. *Beiträge zur Förderung christlicher Theologie* 17. Gütersloh: Bertelsmann (rp. 1970: 143-263).
1923   Der Bericht über das Ende Jerusalems: Ein Dialog mit Wilhelm Weber. *Beiträge zur Förderung christlicher Theologie* 28. Gütersloh: Bertelsmann (rp. 1970: 1-68).

1970   *Kleinere Schriften zu Flavius Josephus*, ed. K. H. Rengstorf. Darmstadt: Wissensch. Buchgesellschaft.

Schreckenberg, H.
1968   *Bibliographie zu Flavius Josephus*. Leiden: Brill.
1979   *Bibliographie zu Flavius Josephus. Supplementband mit Gesamtregister.* Leiden: Brill.

Schreiner S.
1979   Mischehen - Ehebruch - Ehescheidung. Betrachtungen zu Mal 2,10-16. *Zeitschrift für die alttestamentliche Wissenschaft* 91: 207-28.

Schürer, E.
1901-11 *Geschichte des jüdischen Volkes im Zeitalter Jesu Christi.* 3rd and 4th ed. vol. 1-4. Leipzig: Hinrichs.
1973-87 *The History of the Jewish People in the Age of Jesus Christ (175 B.C. - A.D. 135)*, rev. and ed. G. Vermes *et al.* 3 vols. in 4. Edinburgh: Clark.

Schwabe, M., and Melamed, E.
1928   Zum Text der Seronepisode in I Macc. und bei Josephus. *Monatsschrift für Geschichte und Wissenschaft des Judentums* 72: 202-4.

Schwartz, D. R.
1981   Priesthood and Priestly Descent: Josephus, *Antiquities* 10.80. *Journal of Theological Studies* 32: 129-35.
1983   Josephus and Nicolaus on the Pharisees. *Journal for the Study of Judaism* 14:157-171.
1983-84 Josephus on the Jewish Constitutions and Community. *Scripta Classica Israelica* 7: 30-52.
1987   Wilderness and Temple: on Religion and State in Judaea in the Second Temple Period. Pp. 61-78 in *Priesthood and Kingship*. Jerusalem: Zalman Shazar Center (Hebrew).
1987a   *Agrippa I, The Last King of Judaea*. Jerusalem: Zalman Shazar Center (Hebrew; English trans. 1990).
1987b   On Abraham Schalit, Herod, Josephus, the Holocaust, Horst R. Moehring, and the Study of Ancient Jewish History. *Jewish History* 2/2:9-28.
1989-90 On Drama and Authenticity in Philo and Josephus. *Scripta Classica Israelica* 10: 113-129.
1990   *Agrippa I: The Last King of Judaea*. Tübingen: Mohr (= rev. Engl. trans. of 1987a).
1992   *Studies in the Jewish Background of Christianity*. Wissenschaftliche Untersuchungen zum Neuen Testament 60. Tübingen: Mohr (Siebeck).

Schwartz, J.
1985   Be'er Ha-Qar, Bôr Heqer and the Seleucid Akra. *Cathedra* 37: 3-16 (Hebrew).
1991   Once More on the Nicanor Gate. *Hebrew Union College Annual* 62: 245-283.

Schwartz, S.
1990   *Josephus and Judaean Politics*. Leiden: Brill.
1993   A Note on the Social Type and Political Ideology of the Hasmonean Family. *Journal of Biblical Literature* 112: 305-9.

Scott, J.
1977   Patronage or Exploitation. In *Patrons and Clients in Mediterranean Societies*, ed. E. Gellner and J. Waterbury. London: Duckworth.

Seeligmann, I. L.
1948   *The Septuagint Version of Isaiah. A Discussion of its Problems*. Mededelingen en Verhandelingen n. 9 van het Vooraziatisch-egyptisch genootschap "Ex Oriente Lux". Leiden: Brill.

SEG   *Supplementum Epigraphicum Graecum*

Seyrig, H.
1950   Irenopolis - Neronias - Sepphoris. *Numismatic Chronicle* 10: 284-89 rp. in his *Scripta Numismatica*, Paris 1986, 461-66).
1955   Irenopolis - Neronias - Sepphoris: An Additional Note. *Numismatic Chronicle* 15: 157-59 (rp. in his *Scripta Numismatica*, Paris 1986, 467-69).

Shaw, B.
1984   Bandits in the Roman Empire. *Past and Present* 105: 3-52.

Sherwin-White, A. N.
1973   *The Roman Citizenship*. 2nd ed. (1st edn., 1939). Oxford: Clarendon.

Shutt, R. J.
1961   *Studies in Josephus*. London: SPCK.

Sievers, J.
1989   The Role of Women in the Hasmonean Dynasty. Pp. 132-46 in Feldman and Hata 1989.
1990   *The Hasmoneans and Their Supporters: From Mattathias to the Death of John Hyrcanus I*. USF Studies in the History of Judaism 6. Atlanta: Scholars.

Silverman, S.
1977   Patronage as Myth. In *Patrons and Clients in Mediterranean Societies*, ed. E. Gellner and J. Waterbury. London: Duckworth.

Simons, J.
1952   *Jerusalem in the Old Testament*. Leiden: Brill.
1959   *The Geographical and Topographical Texts of the Old Testament*. Leiden: Brill.

Sixtus Senensis
1566   *Bibliotheca Sancta*. Venice: Gryphius.

Smallwood, E. M.
1956   Domitian's Attitude Toward the Jews and Judaism. *Classical Philology* 51: 1-13.
1970   *Philonis Alexandrini Legatio ad Gaium*, Leiden: Brill.
1976   *The Jews under Roman Rule from Pompey to Diocletian*. Leiden: Brill (corr. rp. 1981).

Smith, G. A.
1894   *The Historical Geography of the Holy Land*. London: Hodder & Stoughton (rp. London and Glasgow: Collins 1973).

Smith, J. Z.
1985   What a Difference a Difference Makes. Pp. 3-48 in *"To See Ourselves as Others See Us": Christians, Jews, "Others" in Late Antiquity*, eds. J. Neusner and E. S. Frerichs. Scholars Press Studies in the Humanities. Chico, CA: Scholars.

Smith, Morton
1951a   *Tannaitic Parallels to the Gospels*. Philadelphia: Society of Biblical Literature.

1951b   The So-called Biography of David in the books of Samuel and Kings. *Harvard Theological Review* 44: 167-69.

1952   The Common Theology of the Ancient Near East. *Journal of Biblical Literature* 71: 135-147.

1954   The Manuscript Tradition of Isidore of Pelusium. *Harvard Theological Review* 47: 205-210.

1956   Palestinian Judaism in the First Century. Pp. 67-81 in *Israel: Its Role in Civilization*, ed. Moshe Davis. New York: Jewish Theological Seminary/Harper.

1958a   An Unpublished Life of St. Isidore of Pelusium, edited from manuscripts in Athens and Mt. Athos. *Eucharisterion: Timetikos Tomos Hamilka S. Alivizatou*. ed. G. Kondiares. 429-38. Athens.

1958b   The Image of God: Notes on the Hellenization of Judaism. *Bulletin of the John Rylands Library*. 40: 473-512.

1958c   The Description of the Essenes in Josephus and the Philosophoumena. *Hebrew Union College Annual* 29: 273-313.

1960-61   The Dead Sea Sect in Relation to Ancient Judaism. *New Testament Studies* 7: 347-60.

1965   *Heroes and Gods* (with Moses Hadas). New York: Harper & Row.

1967   Goodenough's *Jewish Symbols* in Retrospect. *Journal of Biblical Literature* 88: 53-66.

1968   Historical Method in the Study of Religion. *History and Theory*. Beiheft 8: 8-16.

1971a   *Palestinian Parties and Politics that Shaped the Old Testament*. New York: Columbia Unversity.

1971b   Prolegomena to a Discussion of Aretalogies, Divine Men, the Gospels, and Jesus. *Journal of Biblical Literature*. 90: 174-99.

1971c   Zealots and Sicarii: Their Origins and Relations. *Harvard Theological Review* 64: 1-19.

1975   On th Wine God in Palestine. Pp. 815-29 in *Salo Baron Jubilee Volume*, ed. S. Lieberman. New York/Jerusalem: American Academy for Jewish Research.

1977   Messiahs: Robbers, Jurists, Prophets, and Magicians. *Proceedings of the American Academy for Jewish Research* 44: 185-195.

1978a   *Jesus the Magician*. San Francisco: Harper & Row.

1978b   On the History of the 'Divine Man.' Pp. 335-45 in *Paganisme, Judaisme, Christianisme: Mélanges offerts à Marcel Simon*. Paris: De Boccard.

1980   Pauline Worship as Seen by Pagans. *Harvard Theological Review* 73: 241-250.

1981   The History of the Term 'Gnostikos.' Pp. 796-807 in vol. 2 of *The Rediscovery of Gnosticism*, ed. B. Layton. Leiden: Brill.

1982   Helios in Palestine. *Eretz Israel* 16: 199-214 (English section).
1983a   On the History of *ΑΠΟΚΑΛΥΠΤΩ* and *ΑΠΟΚΑΛΥΨΙΣ*. Pp. 9-20 in Hellholm 1989.
1983b   Terminological Boobytraps and Real Problems in Second Temple Judaeo-Christian Studies. Pp. 295-306 in *Proceedings of the Fourteenth Congress of the International Association for the History of Religions.*
1984   Jewish Religious Life in the Persian Period. Pp.219-78 in *Cambridge History of Judaism. vol 1: The Persian Period*, ed. W. D. Davies. Cambridge: Cambridge University.
1987   A Note on Some Jewish Assimilationists: the Angels. *Journal of the Ancient Near East Society* 16-17: 207-212.
Forthcoming: The Gentiles in Judaism. *Cambridge History of Judaism*. Vol. 3.

Solin, H.
1983   Juden und Syrer im westlichen Teil der römischen Welt. Pp. 587-789 in vol. 2.29.2 of *Aufstieg und Niedergang der römischen Welt.*

Sparks, H. F. D.
1984   *The Apocryphal Old Testament*. Oxford: Clarendon.

Strack, L. M.
1902-3   Inschriften aus der Ptolemäerzeit II. *Archiv für Papyrusforschung* 1: 537-561.

Steckholl, S. H.
1967   The Qumran Sect in Relation to the Temple of Leontopolis. *Revue de Qumran* 21: 55-69.

Stegemann, H.
1989   Die Bedeutung der Qumranfunde für die Erforschung der Apokalyptic. Pp. 495-530 Hellholm 1989.

Stein, M.
1959   Josephus Flavius, *Life* (translated into Hebrew), Tel-Aviv.

Sterling, G. E.
1992   *Historiography and Self-Definition: Josephos, Luke-Acts and Apologetic Historiography*. Novum Testamentum Suppl. 64. Leiden: Brill.

Stern, M.
1960   The Death of Onias III (2 Macc 4.30-38). *Zion* 25: 1-16 (Hebrew).
1965   The Books of Maccabees and 'Jewish Antiquities' as Sources for the Hasmonean Revolt and the Hasmonean State (Hebrew). Pp. 7-11 in his *The Documents on the History of the Hasmonean Revolt*. Tel- Aviv: Hakibbutz Hameuhad. Rp. as pp. 37-48 in *The Seleucid Period in Eretz Israel: Studies on the Persecutions of Antiochus Epiphanes and the Hasmonean Revolt*, ed. B. Bar-Kochva. Tel-Aviv: Hakibbutz Hameuhad, 1980.
1973   Zealots. *Encyclopaedia Judaica*, Year Book 1973: 135-52.
1974-84 *Greek and Latin Authors on Jews and Judaism*. 3 vols. Jerusalem: Israel Academy of Sciences and Humanities.
1983   The Sources for the Great Revolt. Pp. 89-112 in Rappaport 1983a.
1987   Josephus and the Roman Empire as Reflected in "The Jewish War." Pp. 71-80 in Feldman and Hata 1987.

1987a   Josephus the Historian of the *Jewish War*. Pp. 41-57 in *Studies in Historiography,*, ed. J. Salmon, M. Stern, and M. Zimmermann. Jerusalem: Zalman Shazar Center for Jewish History (Hebrew).
1991   *Studies in Jewish History: The Second Temple Period*, eds. M. Amit, I. Gafni, and M. D. Herr. Jerusalem: Yad Izhak Ben-Zvi (Hebrew).
1992   *The Kingdom of Herod*. Tel-Aviv: Ministry of Defence (Hebrew).
1992a   'Antioch in Jerusalem': The Gymnasium, the Polis and the Rise of Menelaus. *Zion* 57: 233-46 (Hebrew).

Stillwell, R. (ed.)
1938   *Antioch on-the-Orontes II. The Excavations 1933-1936.* Princeton: Princeton Univ.

Strange, J.
1991   Jerusalems topografi i hasmonæisk tid. Akra-problemet. *Dansk Teologisk Tidsskrift* 54: 81-94.

Strauss, H.
1960   The Fate and Form of the Menorah of the Maccabees. *Eretz-Israel* 6: 122-29 (Hebrew).

Swain, J.
1940   The Theory of the Four Monarchies: opposition history under the Roman Empire. *Classical Philology* 35: 1-21.

Taylor, J. E.
1980   *Seleucid Rule in Palestine* (Duke Univ. diss., 1979). Ann Arbor: Univ. Microfilms.

Tcherikover, V.
1937   Palestine under the Ptolemies. *Mizraim* 4/5: 7-90.
1959   *Hellenistic Civilization and the Jews*. Trans. from Hebrew by S. Applebaum. Philadelphia: JPS.

Tcherikover V. A.; Fuks, A.; Stern, M. *see CPJ*

Tchernowitz, H.
1946   The Pairs and the House of Onias. Pp. 232-47 in *Louis Ginzberg Jubilee Volume*. New York: Am. Acad. for Jewish Research (Hebrew).

Thackeray, H. St. J.
1904   Josephus. Pp. 461-473 in *A Dictionary of the Bible*, ed. J. Hastings. Extra Volume (5). Edinburgh: Clark.
1929   *Josephus: The Man and the Historian*. N.Y.: JIR (Rp. New York: Ktav 1967).

Thackeray, H. St. J.; Marcus, R.; Wikgren. A.; and Feldman, L. H.
1926-65 *Josephus with an English Translation* in 9 (10) vols; LCL. London–Cambridge, MA: Heinemann - Harvard University.

Thomas, J.
1895   Amalec, Amalécite. Cols. 426-32 in *Dictionnaire de la Bible*. Vol. 1, Paris: Letouzey.

Tomson, P. J.
1986   The Names Israel and Jew in Ancient Judaism. *Bijdragen: Tijdschrift voor filosofie en theologie* 47: 120-40.

Trebilco, P.
1991   *Jewish Communities in Asia Minor.* Society for New Testament Studies, Monograph Series 69. Cambridge: Cambridge University.

Trever, J. C.
1985   The Book of Daniel and the Origin of the Qumran Community. *Biblical Archaeologist* 48: 89-102.

Trüdinger, K.
1918   *Studien zur Geschichte der griechisch-römischen Ethnographie.* Diss. Basel.

Truman, H. S.
1960   *Mr. Citizen.* New York: Random House.

Tsafrir, Y.
1975   The Location of the Seleucid Akra in Jerusalem. *Revue Biblique* 82: 501-21.
1980   The Site of the Seleucid Akra in Jerusalem. *Cathedra* 14: 17-40 (Hebrew).

Unnik, W. C. van
1978   *Flavius Josephus als historischer Schriftsteller.* Heidelberg: Schneider.

Varneda   *see* Villalba i Varneda, P.

Vatable, F.
1745   *Biblia Sacra cum universis Franc. Vatabli, et variorum interpretum annotationibus.* Editio postrema. Paris.

Vaux, R. de
1936   *Binjamin-Minjamin. Revue Biblique* 45: 400-402.

Vermes, G.
1981   The Essenes and History. *Journal of Jewish Studies* 32,1: 18-31.
1982   *The Dead Sea Scrolls: Qumran in Perspective.* Revised edition. London: Collins.
1987   *The Dead Sea Scrolls in English.* 3rd ed. Sheffield: Sheffield Academic.

Vermes, G., and Goodman, M. D., eds.
1989   *The Essenes according to the Classical Sources.* Oxford Centre Textbooks 1. Sheffield: JSOT.

Vermes, G. and Millar, F. *et al.* (eds.) *see* Schürer 1973-87.

Villalba i Varneda, P.
1986   *The Historical Method of Flavius Josephus.* Leiden: Brill.

Vincent, A.
1937   *La religion des judéo-araméens d'Eléphantine.* Paris: Geuthner.

Vincent, L. H.
1908-09 Jérusalem d'apres la lettre d'Aristee. *Revue Biblique* 17: 520-532; 18: 555-575.

Vincent, L. H., and Stève, M. A.
1954-56 *Jérusalem de l'Ancien Testament.* 2 vols. Paris: Gabalda.

Wacholder, B. Z.
1979   *Messianism and Mishnah: Time and Place in the Early Halakhah.* Cincinnati: Hebrew Union College.

Wacholder B. Z., and Abegg M. G.
1992   *A Preliminary Edition of the Unpublished Dead Sea Scrolls. The Hebrew and Aramaic Texts from Cave Four.* Fascicle 2. Washington: Biblical Archaeology Society.

Wächter, L.
1969   Die unterschiedliche Haltung der Pharisäer, Sadduzäer und Essener zur Heimarmene nach dem Bericht des Josephus. *Zeitschrift für Religions- und Geistesgeschichte* 21: 97-114.

Wallace-Hadrill, A.
1989   *Patronage in Ancient Society.* London-New York: Routledge.

Weber, W.
1921   *Josephus und Vespasian: Untersuchungen zu dem Jüdischen Krieg des Flavius Josephus.* Berlin: Kohlhammer (rp. Hildesheim: Olms 1973).

Weippert, M.
1982   Edom und Israel. *Theologische Realenzyklopädie* 9: 291-99.

Weiss, H.-F.
1979   Pharisäismus und Hellenismus: zur Darstellung des Judentums im Geschichtswerk des jüdischen Historikers Flavius Josephus. *Orientalistische Literaturzeitung* 74: 421–433.

Wellhausen, J.
1905   Ueber den geschichtlichen Wert des zweiten Makkabäerbuchs im Verhältnis zum ersten. *Nachrichten von der königlichen Gesellschaft der Wisssenschaften zu Göttingen.* Philol.-hist. Klasse 117-63.

Whiston, W.
1987   *The Works of Josephus: Complete and Unabridged. New Updated Edition.* Peabody MA: Hendrickson Publishers [Original ed. 1737].

Whittaker, M.
1984   *Jews and Christians: Graeco-Roman Views.* Cambridge: Cambridge University.

Wieseler, C.
1839   *Die 70 Wochen und die 63 Jahrwochen des Propheten Daniel erörtert und erläutert.* Göttingen: Vandenhoek & Ruprecht.

Wightman, G. J.
1989-90 Temple Fortresses in Jerusalem, Part I: The Ptolemaic and Seleucid Akras. *Bulletin of the Anglo-Israel Archaeological Society* 9: 29-40.

Wilcken, U.
1927   *Urkunden der Ptolemäerzeit (Ältere Funde). Erster Band. Papyri aus Unterägypten.* Berlin-Leipzig:

Will, E., and Larché, F.
1991   *Iraq el Amir. Le château du Tobiade Hyrcan.* Institut Français d'Archéologie et du Proche Orient. Beirut-Damascus-Amman.

Williams, M. H.
1990   Domitian, the Jews, and the 'Judaizers'. *Historia* 39: 196-211.

Willrich, H.
1895   *Juden und Griechen vor der Makkabäischen Erhebung.* Göttingen: Vandenhoek & Ruprecht.
1901   Der Chelkiasstein. Ein Beitrag zur Geschichte der Juden in Aegypten. *Archiv für Papyrusforschung* 1: 48-56.

Wills, L. M.
1990   *The Jew in the Court of the Foreign King: Ancient Jewish Court Legends.* Minneapolis: Fortress.

Yadin, Y.
1977-83 *The Temple Scroll.* 3 vols. Jerusalem: Israel Exploration Society.

Yavetz, Z.
1975   Reflections on Titus and Josephus. *Greek, Roman and Byzantine Studies* 16: 411-32.

Zeitlin, S.
1947-48 The Warning Inscriptions of the Temple. *Jewish Quarterly Review* 38: 111-16.
1950   Introduction. *The First Book of Maccabees.* New York: Harper.
1962-78 *The Rise and Fall of the Judean State: A Political, Social and Religious History of the Second Commonwealth.* Vol. 1-3. Philadelphia: JPS.

Zimmerli, W.
1954   Die Eigenart der prophetischen Rede des Ezechiel: Ein Beitrag zum Problem an Hand von Ez. 14,1-11. *Zeitschrift für die alttestamentliche Wisssenschaft* 66: 1-26.

Zorell, F.
1911   *Novi Testamenti Lexicon Graecum.* Paris.

INDEX OF ANCIENT SOURCES

2. BIBLICAL LITERATURE

3. QUMRAN AND PSEUDEPIGRAPHA

INDEX OF SUBJECTS

INDEX OF GREEK WORDS

STUDIA POST-BIBLICA

1. KOSMALA, H. *Hebräer – Essener – Christen*. Studien zur Vorgeschichte der frühchristlichen Verkündigung. 1959. ISBN 90 04 02135 3
3. WEISE, M. *Kultzeiten und kultischer Bundesschluß in der 'Ordensregel' vom Toten Meer*. 1961. ISBN 90 04 02136 1
4. VERMES, G. *Scripture and Tradition in Judaism*. Haggadic Studies. Reprint. 1983. ISBN 90 04 07096 6
5. CLARKE, E.G. *The Selected Questions of Isho bar Nūn on the Pentateuch*. Edited and Translated from Ms Cambridge Add. 2017. With a Study of the Relationship of Isho'dādh of Merv, Theodore bar Konī and Isho bar Nūn on Genesis. 1962. ISBN 90 04 03141 3
6. NEUSNER, J. *A Life of Joḥanan ben Zakkai (ca. 1-80 C.E.)*. 2nd rev. ed. 1970. ISBN 90 04 02138 8
7. WEIL, G.E. *Élie Lévita, humaniste et massorète (1469-1549)*. 1963. ISBN 90 04 02139 6
8. BOWMAN, J. *The Gospel of Mark*. The New Christian Jewish Passover Haggadah. 1965. ISBN 90 04 03142 1
11. NEUSNER, J. *A History of the Jews in Babylonia*. Part 2. The Early Sasanian Period. ISBN 90 04 02143 4
12. NEUSNER, J. Part 3. From Shahpur I to Shahpur II. 1968. ISBN 90 04 02144 2
14. NEUSNER, J. Part 4. The Age of Shahpur II. 1969. ISBN 90 04 02146 9
15. NEUSNER, J. Part 5. Later Sasanian Times. 1970. ISBN 90 04 02147 7
16. NEUSNER, J. *Development of a Legend*. Studies on the Traditions Concerning Joḥanan ben Zakkai. 1970. ISBN 90 04 02148 5
17. NEUSNER, J. (ed.). *The Formation of the Babylonian Talmud*. Studies in the Achievements of the Late Nineteenth and Twentieth Century Historical and Literary-Critical Research. 1970. ISBN 90 04 02149 3
18. CATCHPOLE, D.R. *The Trial of Jesus*. A Study in the Gospels and Jewish Historiography from 1770 to the Present Day. 1971. ISBN 90 04 02599 5
19. NEUSNER, J. *Aphrahat and Judaism*. The Christian-Jewish Argument in Fourth-Century Iran. 1971. ISBN 90 04 02150 7
20. DAVENPORT, G.L. *The Eschatology of the Book of Jubilees*. 1971. ISBN 90 04 02600 2
21. FISCHEL, H.A. *Rabbinic Literature and Greco-Roman Philosophy*. A Study of Epicurea and Rhetorica in Early Midrashic Writings. 1973. ISBN 90 04 03720 9
22. TOWNER, W.S. *The Rabbinic 'Enumeration of Scriptural Examples'*. A Study of a Rabbinic Pattern of Discourse with Special Reference to *Mekhilta d'Rabbi Ishmael*. 1973. ISBN 90 04 03744 6
23. NEUSNER, J. (ed.). *The Modern Study of the Mishna*. 1973. ISBN 90 04 03669 5
24. ASMUSSEN, J.P. *Studies in Judeo-Persian Literature*. [Tr. from the Danish]. (Homages et Opera Minora, 12). 1973. ISBN 90 04 03827 2
25. BARZILAY, I. *Yoseph Shlomo Delmedigo (Yashar of Candia)*. His Life, Works and Times. 1974. ISBN 90 04 03972 4

26. PSEUDO-JEROME. *Quaestiones on the Book of Samuel*. Edited with an Introduction by A. Saltman. 1975. ISBN 90 04 04195 8
27. BERGER, K. *Die griechische Daniel-Exegese*. Eine altkirchliche Apokalypse. Text, Übersetzung und Kommentar. 1976. ISBN 90 04 04756 5
28. LOWY, S. *The Principles of Samaritan Bible Exegesis*. 1977. ISBN 90 04 04925 8
29. DEXINGER, F. *Henochs Zehnwochenapokalypse und offene Probleme der Apokalyptik-forschung*. 1977. ISBN 90 04 05428 6
30. COHEN, J.M. *A Samaritan Chronicle*. A Source-Critical Analysis of the Life and Times of the Great Samaritan Reformer, Baba Rabbah. 1981. ISBN 90 04 06215 7
31. BROADIE, A. *A Samaritan Philosophy*. A Study of the Hellenistic Cultural Ethos of the Memar Marqah. 1981. ISBN 90 04 06312 9
32. HEIDE, A. VAN DER. *The Yemenite Tradition of the Targum of Lamentations*. Critical Text and Analysis of the Variant Readings. 1981. ISBN 90 04 06560 1
33. ROKEAH, D. *Jews, Pagans and Christians in Conflict*. 1982. ISBN 90 04 07025 7
35. EISENMAN, R.H. *James the Just in the Habakkuk* Pesher. 1986. ISBN 90 04 07587 9
36. HENTEN, J.W. VAN, H.J. DE JONGE, P.T. VAN ROODEN & J.W. WEESELIUS (eds.). *Tradition and Re-Interpretation in Jewish and Early Christian Literature*. Essays in Honour of Jürgen C.H. Lebram. 1986. ISBN 90 04 07752 9
37. PRITZ, R.A. *Nazarene Jewish Christianity*. From the End of the New Testament Period until its Disappearance in the Fourth Century. 1988. ISBN 90 04 08108 9
38. HENTEN, J.W. VAN, B.A.G.M. DEHANDSCHUTTER & H.W. VAN DER KLAAUW. *Die Entstehung der jüdischen Martyrologie*. 1989. ISBN 90 04 08978 0
39. MASON, S. *Flavius Josephus on the Pharisees*. A Composition-Critical Study. 1991. ISBN 90 04 09181 5
40. OHRENSTEIN, R.A. & B. GORDON. *Economic Analysis in Talmudic Literature*. Rabbinic Thought in the Light of Modern Economics. 1992. ISBN 90 04 09540 3
41. PARENTE, F. & J. SIEVERS (eds.). *Josephus and the History of the Greco-Roman Period*. Essays in Memory of Morton Smith. 1994. ISBN 90 04 10114 4
42. ATTRIDGE, H.W. & G. HATA (eds.). *Eusebius, Christianity, and Judaism*. 1992. ISBN 90 04 09688 4
43. TOAFF, A. *The Jews in Umbria*. Vol. I: 1245-1435. 1993. ISBN 90 04 09695 7
44. TOAFF, A. *The Jews in Umbria*. Vol. II: 1435-1484. 1994. ISBN 90 04 09979 4
45. TOAFF, A. *The Jews in Umbria*. Vol. III: 1484-1736. 1994. ISBN 90 04 10165 9

DATE DUE

			Printed in USA